Not Just Another Cold War

T0397645

Not Just Another Cold War

The Global Implications of the US-China Rivalry

BÅRD NIKOLAS VIK STEEN

OXFORD
UNIVERSITY PRESS

OXFORD
UNIVERSITY PRESS

Oxford University Press is a department of the University of Oxford.
It furthers the University's objective of excellence in research, scholarship,
and education by publishing worldwide. Oxford is a registered trade mark of
Oxford University Press in the UK and in certain other countries.

Published in the United States of America by Oxford University Press
198 Madison Avenue, New York, NY 10016, United States of America.

© Oxford University Press 2025

All rights reserved. No part of this publication may be reproduced, stored in a retrieval system,
transmitted, used for text and data mining, or used for training artificial intelligence, in any form or
by any means, without the prior permission in writing of Oxford University Press, or as expressly
permitted by law, by licence or under terms agreed with the appropriate reprographics rights
organization. Inquiries concerning reproduction outside the scope of the above should be sent
to the Rights Department, Oxford University Press, at the address above.

You must not circulate this work in any other form
and you must impose this same condition on any acquirer.

Library of Congress Cataloging-in-Publication Data

Names: Steen, Bård (Nikolas Vik), editor.
Title: Not just another cold war : the global implications of the
U.S.-China rivalry / edited by Bård Nikolas Vik Steen.
Description: New York : Oxford University Press, 2025. | Includes index.
Identifiers: LCCN 2024039672 (print) | LCCN 2024039673 (ebook) |
ISBN 9780197799895 (hardback) | ISBN 9780197799901 (paperback) |
ISBN 9780197799925 (epub) | ISBN 9780197799932
Subjects: LCSH: United States–Foreign relations—China. | China—Foreign
relations—United States. | Strategic rivalries (World politics) |
World politics—21st century—Forecasting.
Classification: LCC E183.8.C5 N69 2025 (print) |
LCC E183.8.C5 (ebook) |
DDC 320.9/05—dc23/eng/20241228
LC record available at https://lccn.loc.gov/2024039672
LC ebook record available at https://lccn.loc.gov/2024039673

DOI: 10.1093/9780197799932.001.0001

Paperback printed by Integrated Books International, United States of America
Hardback printed by Bridgeport National Bindery, Inc., United States of America

This book is dedicated to David Dollar, who passed away before it could be published.

We miss him.

Contents

Acknowledgments

This book is the result of the 185th Nobel Symposium. It was made possible with the support of the Nobel Foundation and the Norwegian Institute for Defence Studies. Special thanks to Tyler Barrot, Lucas Burns, Øystein Tunsjø, and Henrik Hiim. Their support for this project has been invaluable. Without Aurora Thori Lima, nothing would be possible.

List of Contributors

Jo Inge Bekkevold is Senior Advisor at the Norwegian Institute for Defence Studies (IFS). From 2011 to 2017, he was Head of the Centre for Asian Security Studies at IFS. Bekkevold is a former career diplomat, with several postings to East Asia, including eight years with the Norwegian embassy in Beijing. Since joining IFS in 2011, Bekkevold has written extensively on Chinese foreign policy and Asian security. His recent publications include *India's Great Power Politics: Managing China's Rise*, *Sino-Russian Relations in the 21st Century*, and *China in the Era of Xi Jinping: Domestic and Foreign Policy Challenges*.

Thomas J. Christensen is the James T. Shotwell Professor of International Relations and Director of the China and the World Program at Columbia University. He arrived from Princeton University, where he was William P. Boswell Professor of World Politics of Peace and War, Director of the Princeton-Harvard China and the World Program, and faculty director of the Master of Public Policy Program. From 2006 to 2008 he served as Deputy Assistant Secretary of State for East Asian and Pacific Affairs with responsibility for China, Taiwan, and Mongolia. His most recent book, *The China Challenge: Shaping the Choices of a Rising Power*, was an editors' choice in the New York Times Book Review. All opinions expressed in this chapter are Christensen's own and do not necessarily reflect those of the US government.

David Dollar was a Senior Fellow in the China Center at the Brookings Institution and host of the trade podcast, *Dollar and Sense*. Previously, Dollar worked for twenty years for the World Bank, including as China Country Director. He also represented the US Treasury in Beijing from 2009 to 2013. His other World Bank assignments focused on Asian economies, including South Korea, Vietnam, Cambodia, Thailand, Bangladesh, and India. Dollar also worked in the World Bank's research department. Dollar's publications focus on reform in China, economic growth, and poverty reduction. He has a PhD in economics from New York University and a BA in Asian Studies from Dartmouth College.

Alice Ekman has overseen the Asia portfolio at the European Union Institute for Security Studies since September 2019. Ekman also manages regular "Track 1.5" dialogues with the EU's partners in Asia and coordinates the EU member committee of the Council for Security Cooperation in the Asia-Pacific. Ekman was formerly Head of China Research at the French Institute of International Relations in Paris. She has also been Visiting Scholar at Tsinghua University, the National Taiwan Normal University, and the Asan Institute for Policy Studies, in South Korea. Ekman is proficient in Mandarin.

M. Taylor Fravel is the Arthur and Ruth Sloan Professor of Political Science and Director of the Security Studies Program at the Massachusetts Institute of Technology. Fravel studies international relations, with a focus on international security, China, and East Asia. His books include *Strong Borders, Secure Nation: Cooperation and Conflict in China's Territorial Disputes* and *Active Defense: China's Military Strategy since 1949*. Fravel received his PhD from Stanford University. In 2016, he was named an Andrew Carnegie Fellow by the Carnegie Corporation.

François Heisbourg is senior advisor for Europe at the International Institute for Strategic Studies (IISS) and special advisor of France's Fondation pour la Recherche Stratégique (FRS). He has served as international security advisor to the Defence Minister of France, professor at Sciences-Po Paris, and director of the FRS. He contributed to the French government's white paper on terrorism and defense, served on the International Commission on Nuclear Non-Proliferation and Disarmament, and was a coauthor of the Finnish government's report on "The Effects of Finland's Possible NATO Membership." His latest book is *Leçons d'une guerre* (Odile Jacob, 2023).

Henrik Stålhane Hiim is a professor at the Norwegian Institute for Defence Studies at the Norwegian Defence University College. His main research interests are nuclear strategy and Chinese foreign and security policy. His recently published book, *Strategic Assistance: China and International Nuclear Weapons Proliferation*, explores China's approach to the nuclear programs of Pakistan, Iran, and North Korea. His work has appeared in publications such as *International Security*, *International Affairs*, *Journal of Contemporary China*, *Survival*, and *War on the Rocks*.

Scott L. Kastner is a Professor in the Department of Government and Politics at the University of Maryland, College Park. He is author of *War and Peace in the Taiwan Strait*; *China's Strategic Multilateralism: Investing in Global Governance*, with Margaret Pearson and Chad Rector; and *Political Conflict and Economic Interdependence across the Taiwan Strait and Beyond*. His research has also appeared in journals such as *International Security*, *International Studies Quarterly*, *Journal of Conflict Resolution*, *Comparative Political Studies*, and *Security Studies*.

Arthur R. Kroeber is a founding partner and head of research at Gavekal Dragonomics, a China-focused economic research service with offices in Beijing and Hong Kong. Before establishing Dragonomics, he spent fifteen years as a financial journalist in China and South Asia. He is adjunct professor of economics at New York University Stern School of Business and a member of the Council on Foreign Relations and the National Committee on US-China Relations. His book, *China's Economy: What Everyone Needs to Know* (2nd ed., 2020), is published by Oxford University Press.

Robert S. Ross is Professor of Political Science at Boston College and Associate at the John King Fairbank Center for Chinese Studies, Harvard University. Ross's research focuses on Chinese security policy and defense policy, East Asian security, and US-China relations. He has taught at Columbia University and at the University of Washington and in 1989 was a Guest Scholar at the Brookings Institution. His recent publications include *Chinese Security Policy: Structure, Power, andPolitics*; *China's Ascent: Power, Security, and theFuture of International Politics*; and *New Directions in the Study of Chinese Foreign Policy*.

Bård Nikolas Vik Steen is a geopolitical analyst and security policy advisor. He was a member of the secretariat to the Norwegian Defence Commission of 2021, which delivered the most comprehensive review of the Norwegian Armed Forces since the Cold War. Steen previously served as the Programme Manager of the Research Department at the Norwegian Nobel Institute. His latest book, *Nuclear Disarmament: A Critical Assessment*, was published by Routledge in 2019. All opinions expressed in this book are Steen's own and do not necessarily reflect those of the Norwegian Ministry of Defence or any other agency of the Norwegian government.

Bruno Tertrais is the Deputy Director of the Fondation pour la Recherche Stratégique (FRS), a leading French think tank on international security issues, and a Non-Resident Fellow at Institut Montaigne. After working at NATO's Parliamentary Assembly, Tertrais worked for the Ministry of Defence and the RAND Corporation. He joined FRS in 2001. He was a member of the committees in charge of the white papers on defense and national security in 2007–2008 as well as in 2012–2013. His latest book is *La Guerre des mondes. Le retour de la géopolitique et le choc des empires* (2023).

Øystein Tunsjø is Professor and Head of the Security in Asia Program at the Norwegian Institute for Defence Studies at the Norwegian Defence University College. Tunsjø is author of *The Return of Bipolarity in World Politics: China, the United States and Geostructural Realism*; *Security and Profits in China's Energy Policy: Hedging against Risk*; and *US Taiwan Policy: Constructing the Triangle*. Tunsjø has published articles in *Survival, International Relations, Cooperation and Conflict*, and the *National Interest*. Tunsjø holds a PhD in International Relations from the University of Wales, Aberystwyth.

Stephen M. Walt is the Robert and Renée Belfer Professor of International Affairs at Harvard's Kennedy School of Government. He is a columnist at *Foreign Policy* magazine and a board member of the Quincy Institute for Responsible Statecraft. Walt is a Fellow of the American Academy of Arts and Sciences and received the International Studies Association's Distinguished Senior Scholar award in 2014. His latest book is *The Hell of Good Intentions: America's Foreign Policy Elite and the Decline of U.S. Primacy*.

Odd Arne Westad is the Elihu Professor of History and Professor of Global Affairs at Yale University. He is a scholar of modern international affairs, with a specialization in the history of eastern Asia since the eighteenth century. Westad has also worked on the history of the Cold War, China-Russia relations, and the Chinese Communist Party. Among his best-known books are *The Global Cold War*, *Restless Empire*, and *The Cold War: A World History*. Westad joined the faculty at Yale after serving as School Professor of International History at the London School of Economics and as the S. T. Lee Professor of US-Asia Relations at Harvard University. He is a fellow of the British Academy.

Elizabeth Wishnick is Senior Research Scientist in the China and Indo-Pacific Security Affairs Division, Center for Naval Analyses. Wishnick is also a Senior Research Scholar at the Weatherhead East Asian Institute, Columbia University. She is an expert on Chinese and Russian foreign policy. Wishnick is the author of *Mending Fences: The Evolution of Moscow's China Policy from Brezhnev to Yeltsin*, and of *China's Risk: Energy, Water, Food and Regional Security*, which will be published by Columbia University Press. Wishnick is proficient in Mandarin and Russian.

Introduction

Bård Nikolas Vik Steen

In the spring of 2024, the US government let it be known that China provides support that have allowed Russia to sustain its war of aggression in Ukraine and resurrect significant parts of the Soviet-legacy military-industrial complex. US and North Atlantic Treaty Organization (NATO) officials also pointed out how China's unparalleled industrial capacity has allowed Russia to withstand sanctions. The response to this news was predictable. As Western leaders piled on the criticism, comparisons with the Cold War became frequent. The realization that China and the West are backing opposing sides of a large-scale war in Europe made the feeling of Cold War déjà vu too strong to resist.

It was another reason why the rivalry between China and the United States has become known as the "new cold war." Some still use the term to refer to the relationship between Russia and the West,[1] whereas others use it to describe great power relations between the United States, China, and Russia.[2] Increasingly, however, it refers to the defining relationship of twenty-first-century international politics: the rivalry between China and the United States, the world's only superpowers, and their competition for security and influence.[3]

In the past decade, the "new cold war" has become the topic of newspaper headlines, books, podcasts, and a growing pile of special issues.[4] Scholars and diplomats warn that Cold War II might still be avoided, and advocacy groups use the catchphrase for all it is worth in their arguments for rearmament or disarmament.[5] The contest is being compared to the *Lord of the Rings*.[6] And in the ultimate act of pop-cultural approval, even Wikipedia has an entry for the "Second Cold War." The term has taken root and resistance might well be futile.

Objectives

However, that must not stop us from judging the new superpower rivalry on its own merits. Whatever its sobriquet, this superpower rivalry is very

Bård Nikolas Vik Steen, *Introduction*. In: *Not Just Another Cold War*. Edited by: Bård Nikolas Vik Steen, Oxford University Press. © Oxford University Press (2025). DOI: 10.1093/9780197799932.003.0001 different from the forty-five-year contest between the Soviet Union and the United States—so different that many of the lessons from that titanic struggle may be ineffectual or even dangerous if applied to the present context. At the same time, we must not forget the lessons learned from successfully navigating the nuclear standoff of the last century. Some of them are as useful and important today as they were during the Cold War. With stakes this high, it is critical to identify what this superpower rivalry is and what it is not.

While some might dread the idea of another academic discussion about the dangers of historical analogy, that is not the purpose here. We are not pointing fingers at humanity's preference for analogy or misconceptions about history repeating itself. Instead, we use the parallels that people relate to in order to showcase and highlight the characteristics of this new momentous struggle. That is the purpose of this book. By comparing it to the Cold War, we show what differentiates the rivalry between China and the United States. Bringing its features and sensitivities into the light, we attempt to trace its likely trajectory. Perhaps most importantly, we try to explain what this tells us about how to approach a moment in history that looks to be at least as dangerous and as difficult as the Cold War. We demonstrate that this conflict differs significantly from the Cold War and show why that matters, while also filling a significant gap in the literature.

The parallels are plain to see: two superpowers going head to head, one democratic, the other authoritarian, both economic and industrial giants that dominate the global economy; two military forces locked in an arms race, held back only by the destructive power of the other; two superpowers competing in every area of life and engaged in an increasingly tense security dilemma. Like the Cold War, it is a rivalry that is having a profound impact on our politics, our economics, and our culture. And, at least for now, it shares the key distinguishing characteristic that it has not turned "hot."

At the same time, the rivalry between China and the United States could not be more different from the Cold War. Where Europe was the epicentre of the Cold War, this military contest plays out across the Pacific. Where the Cold War pitted the most sophisticated free market in history against what turned out to be a failed economic experiment, this is a conflict between economic peers with deep economic ties. Where the Cold War was defined by the ideological struggle for dominance between communist and capitalist economic systems, it is the turn toward free market capitalism that has supercharged China's bid for power and influence. Where the Cold War was characterized by a nuclear arms race, the rivalry between China and the United States may also be shaped by a race for computing power. And, most banal but important of all, where the Cold War was fought between Russia and the United States, this is a contest between China and the United States.

However, these contrasts and similarities also help make many of the most important aspects of the new superpower rivalry visible. Instead of repeating never-ending debates about the value or dangers of historical comparison, this book embraces it as a fresh and relatable approach to the most consequential relationship in the twenty-first century. Such a comparison provides us with a powerful lens through which we can tease out what lessons to take from the last heavyweight competition, what is different and what is new.

To increase our understanding of the rivalry, we depend on accurate descriptions of its characteristics and their implications. But we are also in need of descriptions that are easily understood and that play to the human preference for comparison and contrast. By reflecting on the characteristics of the rivalry between China and the United States, while drawing parallels to the Cold War we all know and understand, this volume captures the nature of a conflict that will define international politics in our time. It does so in a way that not only highlights aspects that have not previously been considered but also ties its findings to historical analogies that make them understood, remembered, and easier to apply. And it identifies points of difference where the present rivalry might have to be handled differently-in order to avoid the mistakes of the past or walk unknowingly into greater peril.

Overarching Themes

In the following pages, sixteen leading strategic thinkers consider eight different aspects of the superpower rivalry between China and the United States. The authors provide a unique view of its trajectory and its consequences by analysing its historical, economic, military, technological, geopolitical, and diplomatic ramifications. Their findings offer important insights not only for what they imply but also for their clear and concise presentation. The relationship between China and the United States is important to us all. We have therefore attempted to write a book that makes cutting-edge research available not just to academics or policy makers, but to any interested reader.

What we find is a rivalry that may be even more consequential and dangerous than the Cold War. China's economic strength means that its military power potential is significantly greater than the Soviet Union's ever was. And while nuclear deterrence still plays an important and pacifying role, the risk of war between superpowers may be greater than ever. The level of economic integration between the United States, China, and the rest of the world is also much more profound than during the Cold War. That has important deterrent effects. But deep economic ties could also increase the damage caused by conflict. The deepening economic and technological rivalry that is underway may disrupt global supply chains and cause significant harm to the global economy.

Since the invasion of Ukraine, China and Russia's "limitless" partnership and its impact on international relations has also become increasingly apparent. While we are not yet seeing the formation of the Cold War's distinct Eastern and Western "blocs," China, Iran, and North Korea's support for Russia's economy and military-industrial complex certainly gives off a familiar aroma. Seeing the West as intent on putting a stop to their rising influence, Beijing and Moscow are becoming increasingly vocal about their efforts to shape an international system that is safe for autocracies. And with China supporting a Russian military machine that presents a serious threat to European security, Western states are growing increasingly sceptical of the risks that come with their Eastern dependencies.

Exactly how this will turn out is difficult to predict, but many of the outcomes discussed in this volume suggest that we are in for a period of instability. The world might continue toward an ever-deepening global rift between democracies and autocracies. We might face a rudderless and chaotic system where only some alliances persist. Or we might see a situation where the United States and China go toe to toe over the Pacific but large parts of the world are left to their own devices, each taking what they can and the weak suffering what they must in the absence of a higher authority. Of course, some unforeseen turn of events that leads us back to the unipolar world we used to inhabit cannot be ruled out, but the contributors to this book do not consider that particularly likely.

This great drama of the twenty-first century is also taking place at the same time as what appears to be one of the great technological revolutions in history. Developments in artificial intelligence (AI) alone have now reached a stage where they appear certain to change human civilization forever. And AI is only the first among several emerging technologies with the potential to do so. While the exact implications this technological revolution is likely to have on the Sino-American rivalry remain uncertain, this book finds that it could intensify security dilemmas and increase the risk of nuclear escalation. This is especially disconcerting when combined with its finding that the dispute over Taiwan has the potential to imply that the rivalry between China and the United States may not be remembered as a "cold" war at all.

Indeed, this is a book that deals with the big questions. Across eight thematic sections, it contributes to and critiques several of the central debates of contemporary international relations, geopolitics, and international history. Perhaps unsurprisingly, most chapters consider the issue of "power transition" in one way or another. Referring to Thucydides's two-thousand-year-old observation that war tends to result when one power rises to match the power of the reigning hegemon, it is among the most enduring theoretical debates in the social sciences.[7]

This book offers new insights into how power transition may play out in the Sino-American instance. Explicit and implicit comments on hegemonic war theory, long cycle theory, power transition theory, and the rise and fall of great powers are a theme running through every section.[8] The chapters in this book study the economic foundations of China's hegemonic challenge, how the transition from US hegemony to bipolar competition over Pacific Asia could lead to power vacuums in other parts of the world, and how change affects the international system and the risk of war. We discuss whether a different geographical context might lead to more or less instability, contemplate whether ideological and technological trends might lead to Cold War–like behaviour, and consider why and how power transition between China and the United States may not have to end with war.

A closely related issue is the debate over whether the present international system should be considered bipolar or multipolar. Most of the contributors to this book agree that its bipolar nature is one of its key characteristics, as well as an obvious parallel to the Cold War. Much like the Cold War, they argue, China and the United States are by far the two most powerful states in the international system, constituting two dominant poles with far greater influence over world affairs than other states. As the opening chapter reminds us, however, opinions still differ on this point.

A final overarching topic is China and Russia's challenge to the existing international order and the US response to it. Since Xi Jinping came to power and brushed aside any lingering ideas that China would play the part of "responsible stakeholder," China and the United States have been locked in an increasingly outspoken competition to shape the international order. Whereas the United States and its allies work to preserve the status quo, China has taken on the revisionist role, openly stating its preference for a system that gives greater leeway to China and likeminded states. Exactly what world order China prefers is less clear, even though there is no lack of initiatives coming out of Beijing. Whether Chinese revisionism can be reconciled with the United States' vigorous defence of the status quo remains to be seen. One thing seems certain, however: If this power struggle is ideologically motivated, it is very different from the ideological motivations behind the Cold War.

Structure and Key Findings

Odd Arne Westad opens the proceedings with a reflection on humanity's need for comparison and analogy before he teases out the lessons that may be gleaned by comparing the Cold War and the US-China rivalry. Reminding us that historical comparison is of value to policy makers because it provides the metaphors on which many leaders base their decisions, Westad notes several to keep in mind. Westad argues that there are significant differences between the Cold War and the US-China rivalry. Perhaps most significant among them is that he still considers the international system to be multipolar and defined by several centres of power, as opposed to the bipolar system that defined the Cold War. While acknowledging that China and the United States are the most powerful actors in the system, Westad argues that, unlike the Cold War, other major powers remain relatively unrestrained by them. While Westad argues this makes for significant differences, he nevertheless thinks the Cold War offers important lessons on crisis management and the importance of maintaining cordial relations when the stakes are high.

In Chapter 2 Øystein Tunsjø disagrees with Westad's analysis of the international system. In his view, China and the United States' undisputed position at the top of the international power hierarchy means that bipolarity is the essential parallel between the international system of today and that of the Cold War. Instead, Tunsjø argues that the key differences between the two rivalries are to be found in their geopolitical and economic context and that this makes for a very different rivalry than the Cold War. In his view, the level of interconnectedness between the United States and China is likely to create a new dynamic where the mix of strategic rivalry and economic interdependence will lead to a state of "conflictual coexistence." While Tunsjø believes many of the ties between China and the United States will hold, he argues that this international system could prove more unstable than that of the Cold War. Tunsjø also believes there are likely to be fewer proxy wars and contends that in a world of "conflictual coexistence," there is less pressure on secondary states to choose sides. Under the new superpower rivalry, secondary states can maintain equidistance and promote greater autonomy than during the Cold War.

The primary reason for the US-China rivalry is the spectacular growth of China's economy over the last thirty years. It already presents a greater economic challenge to the United States than the Soviet Union, and the future of the U.S.-China rivalry will depend heavily on China's economic prospects. Consequently, David Dollar begins Part II by examining the strengths and weaknesses of China's economy. In Dollar's view, how well China does in the next thirty years will largely be determined by its response to four big challenges: an ageing population and corresponding labour force decline, an inefficient allocation of capital that overinvests in property and infrastructure while underfinancing the dynamic private sector, a looming water crisis that will worsen with climate change, and China's energy use. An effective response to these challenges will require more market-oriented policies than the Chinese Communist Party has demonstrated in recent years. Nevertheless, Dollar concludes that it would be very surprising if China did not become the largest economy in the world by 2035. In his view, the catch-up potential latent in China's huge population is simply too great.

Arthur Kroeber is less bullish on China's behalf. He argues that China's growth strategy relies too heavily on investment in technology-intensive industries and does not place sufficient emphasis on improving inefficiencies. This "state venture capitalism" could in Kroeber's view lead China to succeed in fostering some globally competitive technology industries but may not be enough to sustain the growth necessary to fully catch up with the United States. However, Kroeber admits that China's technological capabilities are likely to improve considerably under both scenarios, probably ensuring that the US-China rivalry endures and intensifies. Whether or not China realizes its full economic potential and barring some unforeseen political collapse, Kroeber argues that Beijing and Washington are likely to be going toe to toe for the foreseeable future.

Part III takes on the increasingly tenuous military balance and considers how it shapes the prospects for a new Cold War. Robert Ross argues that the geostrategic context of US-China competition means that this will not be Cold War II. He points out that this rivalry takes place in the maritime theatre of East Asia and that this comes with a set of important geopolitical preconditions that have distinct implications for the character of the US-China competition. Ross argues that China's naval capabilities and global presence will continue to grow but that US containment efforts will make Beijing less likely to become a global maritime power. Instead, Ross contends that the United States and China are likely to reach a point of naval parity and that this will require both parties to concentrate their naval forces in East Asia. In Ross's estimation, the emergence of China and the United States as rival maritime powers, competing for regional dominance over East Asia, probably means that there will no longer be a global maritime hegemon. While this makes it likely that the US-China rivalry will continue and intensify, it will probably take a very different form from that of the Cold War.

Thomas Christensen notes that the Russian invasion of Ukraine has made him more uncertain of whether military competition in Asia will morph into a cold war. Christensen points out that the invasion may have unleashed forces that override the dynamics that could have kept the US-China rivalry from reaching Cold War levels of enmity. In Christensen's view, the intensifying decoupling of the United States and China and an emerging authoritarian axis between China and Russia may have reduced the cost of a global ideological struggle. This is particularly concerning in light of rising tensions over Taiwan, and Christensen reminds us that "cold wars do not necessarily stay cold."

Part IV looks at the impact of technology on the new superpower rivalry. Taylor Fravel provides an instructive overview of the US-China "tech war" and the US effort to restrict China's access to critical technologies. Fravel notes how competition for technological advantages will be a central feature of the competition between the United States and China in ways not seen during the Cold War. Advancing at rates never seen before, technology has become the ultimate "force multiplier," conferring immense advantages not only for the military but also for economic development. Fravel concludes that the rivalry creates strong incentives to limit access to one another's technology. Combined with the close links between US and Chinese markets, this is already making export controls one of the rivalry's key battlegrounds.

Henrik Hiim considers how the rapid advance of technology in a period of superpower competition affects the security dilemma. Hiim highlights two particularly concerning developments. One is the proliferation of advanced precision-strike technology, which he finds to undermine nuclear stability and contribute to China's nuclear expansion. The other is the deployment of capabilities that generate significant first-strike incentives, such as counterspace weapons. Hiim argues that the US-China security dilemma will be very hard to mitigate in a period of rapid technological advancement. In an ominous conclusion, Hiim warns that while arms racing and security competition are virtually guaranteed, armed conflict between superpowers is also becoming increasingly likely.

Part V assesses the impact of the increasingly close relationship between China and Russia following the war in Ukraine and its effect on security dynamics between China and the United States. Elizabeth Wishnick examines the benefits Chinese officials derive from the Sino-Russian partnership as well as their limitations in a globalized world. According to Wishnick, this is not the Cold War alliance of the 1950s. Rather, China seeks a Russian partnership to change the rules of global governance from within and buttress its global economic and security positions. Despite evidence of misgivings in some advisory circles, Wishnick concludes that Xi is unlikely to change course. In her view, it will take some unforeseen, fundamental divergence of interests for Russia to not support Beijing's political goals.

Alice Ekman agrees that the partnership between Russia and China has come to stay. While it may be very different from the Sino-Soviet relationship of the Cold War, the Ukraine war shows that the Russia-China partnership could be a defining feature of the superpower rivalry between China and the United States. Ekman analyses the opportunities and challenges of the Sino-Russian relationship over the next five years and considers the central role Russia occupies within China's coalition-building strategy. While some limits persist due to the risks of close association with an ostracized Russia Ekman believes the partnership is likely to consolidate rapidly in years to come. In Ekman's view, Russia and China's shared resentment of the West and their ambition to restructure global governance are likely to fuse them together rather than split them apart.

Part VI considers how the geographical context of the US-China rivalry sets it apart from the Cold War and how this may impact global stability. Jo Inge Bekkevold points out how the shared bipolar distribution of power makes the Cold War a natural point of reference for the US-China rivalry. Nevertheless, geography and the different contextual origins of the two systems set them squarely apart. Examining the two rivalries through a geopolitical lens, Bekkevold explains how geography informs the United States' and China's distinct strategies. He also concludes that the US-China rivalry could result in an increasingly peripheral role for Europe and that China creates an economic order where polarization is likely to come about more slowly than during the Cold War.

Bård Nikolas Vik Steen considers how China's rise is shifting global geostrategic power away from the Euro-Atlantic theatre and argues that this is likely to result in increased global instability. Having demonstrated how China's massive military buildup forces the United States to move an increasing share of its military resources to the Pacific, Steen argues that Europe is unlikely to fill the gap that the U.S. leaves behind. While the European response to Russia's invasion of Ukraine suggests that NATO should be able to adjust to a new reality, nonaligned regions that have traditionally relied on the US security umbrella may face greater turbulence in the years to come. If the United States becomes preoccupied in Asia and Europe is unable to pick up the slack, Steen argues that the Middle East, North Africa, and nonaligned parts of Europe and the Caucasus is likely to experience increased instability. With the United States increasingly preoccupied with China, the world must prepare for a more perilous future.

Part VII considers whether NATO can survive a new superpower rivalry centred on the Pacific rather than the Euro-Atlantic region the alliance was created to protect. Francois Heisbourg suggests that the Russian invasion of Ukraine and the cross-strait tension between China and Taiwan may have provided a preliminary answer to this question. The ongoing war has brought NATO's role to the fore while transforming the transatlantic operating system. The invasion has also led to strategic interaction between the Euro-Atlantic and Indo-Pacific areas in a practical manner, entailing coordination, or even a degree of integration between strategies and policies in both theatres. While Heisbourg acknowledges that this is a provisional conclusion, he argues that the arrangement may well develop into a durable modus operandi.

Stephen Walt sees little reason to believe that Europe will balance China. Walt notes that states are most likely to balance when powerful states are located nearby, when they possess significant power projection capabilities, and when they display revisionist intentions. European states are therefore unlikely to balance China in Walt's estimation. China is simply too far away to pose a direct threat to Europe's security. Walt also points out that Europe lacks the military capacity to affect the balance of power in Asia, and Russia's invasion of Ukraine will focus future rearmament efforts closer to home, which could open up a rift between NATO's European and American members. To preserve transatlantic harmony and protect shared values, Walt concludes that NATO's European members should gradually take over primary responsibility for the defence of Europe as the United States shifts its main military effort to Asia.

Part VIII looks at Taiwan and the increasing risk that the US-China rivalry may turn "hot." Scott Kastner considers the increasing risk of war in the Taiwan Strait, arguing that the underlying sovereignty dispute is intractable and highly salient in both Beijing and Taipei. Prospects for a peaceful solution are also worsened by several structural and domestic political factors that make it difficult for either side to make credible long-term promises relating to the dispute. In turn, the Taiwan Strait will remain a potential flashpoint for conflict, and Kastner sees several very concerning signs that war may be on the horizon. He nevertheless concludes that war is not inevitable. Leaders in Washington, Taipei, and Beijing can still take several actions that foster stability without having to walk away from their key interests.

Bruno Tertrais provides the concluding chapter and considers how a hot war over Taiwan may play out. Tertrais considers the context and probability of such a calamity before he walks us through each stage of escalation, showing how such a war would present a significant challenge to the US military. Tertrais concludes that this is a conflict that will not just determine the future of the People's Republic of China or the United States and its allies; the serious risk of nuclear escalation means that it could decide much, much more.

This book offers an early take on the defining relationship of international politics in the twenty-first century. It offers unique insights into the key questions policy makers, academics, and the general public will have to come to terms with in navigating a new geopolitical era. To that end, we have attempted to write a volume that is both accessible and engaging to anyone interested. Hopefully, that will help in navigating what promises to be another great challenge for humanity—even if it is not just another cold war.

Notes

1. Edwards Lucas, *The New Cold War: Putin's Threat to Russia and the West* (Bloomsbury, 2014).
2. See Gilbert Achcar, *The New Cold War: The US, Russia and China—From Kosovo to Ukraine* (Westbourne Press, 2023); David E. Sanger, *New Cold Wars: China's Rise, Russia's Invasion and America's Struggle to Defend the West* (Penguin Random House, 2024); George S. Takach, *Cold War 2.0: Artificial Intelligence in the New Battle between China, Russia, and America* (Pegasus Books, 2024).
3. See Dmitri Alperovitch, *World on the Brink: How America Can Beat China in the Race for the Twenty-First Century* (PublicAffairs, 2024); Robin Niblett, *The New Cold War: How the Contest between the US and China Will Shape Our Century* (Atlantic Books, 2024).
4. See, for example, "A New Kind of Cold War: How to Manage the Growing Rivalry between America and a Rising China," *The Economist*, May 16, 2019, https://www.economist.com/leaders/2019/05/16/a-new-kind-of-cold-war; Michael Hirsh, "No, This Is Not a Cold War-Yet," *Foreign Policy*, May 7, 2024, https://foreignpolicy.com/2024/05/07/cold-war-peace-united-states-china-xi-decoupling-trade/; Timothy Garton Ash, "A New Cold War? World War Three? How Do We Navigate This Age of Confusion?," *The Guardian*, May 3, 2024, https://www.theguardian.com/commentisfree/article/2024/may/03/cold-war-world-history-future; Dmitri Alperovitch, "How the U.S. Can Win the New Cold War," *Time*, May 1, 2024, https://time.com/6971329/us-china-new-cold-war/; Evan Osnos, "Sliding toward a New Cold War," *The New Yorker*, February 26, 2023, https://www.newyorker.com/magazine/2023/03/06/sliding-toward-a-new-cold-war; Ryan Hass et al., "Should the US Pursue a New Cold War with China?," Brookings, January 31, 2024, https://www.brookings.edu/articles/should-the-us-pursue-a-new-cold-war-with-china/; Ronald U. Mendoza, "Navigating the Political Economy of Cold War 2.0," *The Diplomat*, February 12, 2024, https://thediplomat.com/2024/02/navigating-the-political-economy-of-cold-war-2-0/; Andrew Harding, "The New Cold War: China Takes on Europe," Heritage Foundation, March 5, 2024, https://www.heritage.org/europe/commentary/the-new-cold-war-china-takes-europe.
5. Wang Jisi, "America and China Are Not Yet in a Cold War: But They Must Not Wind Up in Something Even Worse," Foreign Affairs, November 23, 2023, https://www.foreignaffairs.com/united-states/america-and-china-are-not-yet-cold-war.
6. Niall Ferguson, "The Second Cold War Is Escalating Faster Than the First," Bloomberg, April 21, 2024, https://www.bloomberg.com/opinion/articles/2024-04-21/china-russia-iran-axis-is-bad-news-for-trump-and-gop-isolationists.
7. See Thucydides, *The History of the Peloponnesian War* (Duke University Press, 2012). See also Graham Allison's repopularization of the theory and its theoretical siblings: G. Allison, *Destined for War: Can America and China Escape Thucydides's Trap?* (Houghton Mifflin Harcourt, 2017).
8. See R. Gilpin, *War and Change in World Politics* (Cambridge University Press, 1981); J. J. Mearsheimer, *The Tragedy of Great Power Politics*, updated ed. (W. W. Norton, 2014); A. Organski, *World Politics* (Alfred A. Knopf, 1958); A. Organski and J. Kugler, *The War Ledger* (University of Chicago Press, 1980); G. Modelski and W. R. Thompson, "The Long Cycle of World Leadership," in *Seapower in Global Politics, 1494–1993* (Palgrave Macmillan, 1988); W. R. Thompson, "Polarity, the Long Cycle, and Global Power Warfare," *Journal of Conflict Resolution* 30, no. 4 (1986): 587–615; George Modelski, *Exploring Long Cycles* (Lynne Rienner Publishers, 1987).

I

THIS IS NOT COLD WAR II

1

The Cold War and Our Own Times

Differences, Similarities, and Lessons

Odd Arne Westad

Throughout human history, we have tended to compare the future with the immediate past. The valuable principle of drawing on human experience in making our decisions predisposes us to do so. But also, we have a propensity for regarding our own personal experience as more valuable than that of others, including our ancestors, simply because we have experienced it ourselves. This is a more doubtful proposition, as historians, psychologists, and investment managers have frequently pointed out. It is more based on the assumption that there is conceptual safety in presumed repetition than on any falsifiable study of the past.[1]

This is of course not saying that assumed repetition is always untrue. Sometimes it is made true, since those who make decisions critical for all of us often think in terms of the past. My late Harvard Kennedy School colleague and former US secretary of defense Ashton Carter always insisted that history is the only discipline that has any value to policy makers simply because it provides the metaphors through which leaders think.[2] This need for understanding history in terms of causality and metaphor is hard to argue with. It is less certain that we can learn from history in terms of finding repetitions or cycles. This chapter will look at differences and similarities between the Cold War international system and the pattern of international affairs that seems to come together in the 2020s and, in conclusion, discuss whether there are significant lessons from the Cold War that leaders ought to draw on today.

Before we move to comparisons and lessons, let us briefly consider the debate about historical recurrences and its near relative, path dependency, in history and the social sciences. The idea that human history tends to repeat itself is not only very old but also very significant in many worldviews. In

Odd Arne Westad, *The Cold War and Our Own Times*. In: *Not Just Another Cold War*. Edited by: Bård Nikolas Vik Steen, Oxford University Press. © Oxford University Press (2025). DOI: 10.1093/9780197799932.003.0002

China the historical and political search for patterns that repeat go back to the pre-Han era (before 200 BCE) and became part of the orthodoxy for Chinese historians and political leaders at least after the Three Kingdoms era five hundred years later. Often referred to, with a gross oversimplification, as "the mandate of Heaven," some of this thinking sets out a cyclical pattern of the rise and fall of empires and the international systems that they create.[3] In the West, both Plato and Aristotle assumed (in very different ways) that human history was cyclical in nature. More so than their Chinese counterparts, they were skeptical of the idea that humans could learn from the past, except through the accumulation of knowledge, since each cycle was significantly different in natural as well as God- and man-made conditions from those of the past.[4]

As we get closer to our own time, the idea of repetitive patterns within historical cycles does not go away. In some ways it grows stronger, since political thinkers from Machiavelli to Marx and twentieth-century economists and modernization theorists used it within teleological concepts or ideas about progress. In many of these cases, enemies who had to be defeated for history to resume its natural course always had much in common; they repeated traits from the last round of battles. In the American political imagination, Communists inherited many of the traits that Nazis and fascists had stood for. In denigrating Napoleon III, Marx insisted that "Hegel remarks somewhere that all facts and personages of great importance in world history occur, as it were, twice. He forgot to add: the first time as tragedy, the second time as farce." Marx was inaccurate about Hegel, and possibly also about Louis-Napoléon Bonaparte, but he did reflect patterns that later became an integral part of Marxist historicism.[5]

Our thinking about comparing the Cold War era and today's world should be understood within these frameworks of thought. Even though I am profoundly skeptical of the idea of repetitions, I do not deny that they, almost by necessity, play a significant role in how people reflect on the past and the present. This opening chapter is first and foremost an argument for taking comparisons more seriously, by considering differences and similarities between the past and the present. It is strongly influenced by the concept of "applied history," as developed by Graham Allison and Niall Ferguson at Harvard, even if I am less sanguine than Professors Allison and Ferguson about the promise of meaningfully "applying" lessons of history on our contemporary challenges.

Differences

As America's failed invasions in the Middle East and Russia's failed invasion of Ukraine have made clear, we now live in a posthegemonic, postconquest world. Great powers can still attempt to invade and occupy foreign territory, but their chances of success are limited and the costs are extremely high. There are several reasons for this turn. One is the diffusion of technology, including military technology, which severely limits the advantages that great powers have over smaller and weaker states. Another is the decline in the ideological, or world-ordering, benefits that great powers have over others. The willingness of other countries, or even political movements, to comply with ideological calls for conformity from imperial centers has been in steep decline since the Cold War ended. Economic power is also much more diffuse, with a massive shift from the Atlantic world toward Asia.

Let us look at these differences between the Cold War and today more closely. But before doing so, it is worth noting that these general trends, although coming to the fore in the post–Cold War era, have been underway for quite some time. The breakdown of Western empires in the middle part of the twentieth century should be seen as one starting point. Imperial collapses led to a dramatic expansion in the number of individual states claiming territorial sovereignty. As a rule, postimperial states have been very successful in defending their sovereignty, though not always in expanding it beyond territorial control to monetary or commercial issues. And superpower wars against postcolonial states were rarely successful during the Cold War, as the United States experienced in Korea and Vietnam, and the Soviet Union in Afghanistan.[6]

The three big differences between the Cold War era and our own time are the lack of bipolarity, the global expansion of capitalism, and the reduction in ideological drivers in international affairs. Taken together, these differences are significant enough that it does not make sense to call today's international system a cold war. Doing so is not just a sign of intellectual laziness; it is also inaccurate enough to be dangerous in policy-making terms. In addition to the problems with regard to repetition and cycles that we have already discussed, there is of course the use of simile in terms of explaining the motives of enemies and rivals. Hitler's aims for Germany were very different from the Kaiser's, irrespective of what many of Germany's adversaries thought in the 1930s. British imperialism in the 1890s was vastly different from that of the 1840s and '50s, in spite of what most opponents of imperial expansion believed. These differences matter significantly in policy-making terms.[7]

The Cold War was a strongly bipolar international system. The United States and the Soviet Union dominated international affairs through their military strength and their ideological universalisms. There was no major international issue in which the two powers were not involved in one form or another, most often through supporting opposing parties and proclaiming opposite viewpoints. This opposition was not just a presentational consideration. It derived, often directly, from their ideological understanding of how the world worked and which challenges they would encounter from the other power, then and in the future. The political thinking on either side made no room for gray zones; other countries were either with one superpower or with the other. A country's foreign policy orientation determined how superpower elites viewed its domestic politics. Americans regarded India as being in the Soviet camp, irrespective of its (mostly) democratic politics; Soviets believed that China broke with the USSR in order to ally with the West, without regard to the Chinese Communist Party's (CCP's) increasingly radical Communist regime under Mao.

Bipolarity did not mean of course that the two sides were equally powerful. In economic terms, and probably also in military and strategic terms—at least before nuclear parity was reached in the 1970s—one superpower was, as it were, much more "super" than the other. The United States could deliver a standard of living to many of its own citizens that was unheard of in the Soviet Union. The Americans also had a much wider international presence than did the Soviets; by the time the Cold War ended, the United States had close to eight hundred military bases abroad. The Soviets had a little more than a tenth of that number. But power equality is not necessary for bipolarity. Both England versus Spain in the late sixteenth and early seventeenth century and the Song versus the Liao states in the eleventh century were very unequal contests but could still be said to represent bipolar international systems.[8]

Cold War bipolarity was reinforced by the division of Europe, then the most important continent, into two military alliance systems, one dependent on the United States and the other on the Soviet Union. The North Atlantic Treaty Organization (NATO) had sixteen members, mainly in Western Europe. The Warsaw Pact had half that number, in Eastern and Central Europe. The two alliances functioned very differently; the Soviets always had much more control in the Warsaw Pact than the United States did in

NATO, though, as historians found when the Cold War was over, even the Soviets did not always get what they wanted from their allies.[9] The main point in terms of bipolarity, however, is that both superpowers had a disciplining status within their respective regions of control. The Soviets intervened militarily several times in support of that status, while the United States enforced discipline through other means.

Although there were many attempts during the Cold War at moving away from this relentless form of bipolarity, very few countries succeeded in doing so. India and China both sought security in pseudo-alliances with one of the superpowers, in spite of Nehru's and Mao's declarations of being nonaligned. So did many states that in the 1950s and '60s had embraced the Third World project. By the 1970s and early 1980s the world seemed more bipolar than ever, with key countries that had joined in the Third World—Indonesia, Egypt, Iraq—taking clear positions alongside one or the other of the superpowers. It could be argued that some of the main forces that undid the Cold War—anti-authoritarian revolutions, identitarian and religious movements, economic globalization—came from *outside* the international system and did not derive from changes within it.

Today's international system is not bipolar in any meaningful sense of the term, nor is it any longer unipolar. Rather, it is becoming increasingly multipolar. China is without doubt a rising great power and the United States is still the most powerful great power in military terms. But besides these two there are several other powers that are significant and relatively unrestrained by China and the United States. Russia, though in steep decline economically, has just shown this in its war of aggression against Ukraine. Although generally aligned with China, Russian president Vladimir Putin did not ask for China's permission before he ordered his momentous and ultimately disastrous invasion of Russia's southern neighbor. Neither does Putin's war depend on China's direct economic or military support. Putin's actions are a result of the relative autonomy Russia now has in its international affairs, very different from the Cold War, when the two superpowers aspired to determine matters of war and peace on a global scale.

India, another rising Asian power, sets its own foreign policy priorities, both with regard to its regional policies and further afield. The Ukraine war again serves as a good example. In spite of its increasingly close relationship with the United States, India has refused to condemn Russia's war in Ukraine. India even abstained on the United Nations resolution censuring Russia for its illegal annexation of four Ukrainian regions. Given India's membership in the Quadrilateral Security Dialogue, commonly known as the Quad—a strategic security framework linking India with the United States, Japan, and Australia—most US leaders had expected India to join the criticism of Russia's behavior. That India refused to do so is not just a result of Delhi's traditional links with Russia and its dependence on Russian military equipment. The government of Indian prime minister Narendra Modi made use of the Ukraine crisis to underline India's independent foreign policy, stressing how multipolarity was arriving whether the Americans liked it or not.[10]

Multipolarity also seems the order of the day in Latin America and in Europe. The two rival camps in Brazilian politics do not agree on much, but both have declared the dawn of a multipolar world in which Brazil refuses to take orders from the United States. In Europe, the countries of the European Union stress how the NATO alliance with the United States has helped isolate Russia and provide supplies for the defense of Ukraine. But it is highly unlikely that the European countries—even the United Kingdom—will join American attempts at economic and technological decoupling from China. The European Union is de facto allied with the United States, but less and less dominated by it.

Is it possible that increasing power discrepancies between the top two countries—the United States and China—and all other contenders will produce a new bipolar system, as argued elsewhere in this volume? While certainly possible, such a development for now seems highly unlikely. Long-term trends—economic, political, or demographic—do not seem to favor China and the United States over all other major powers. Both have severe domestic political challenges that will be hard to resolve without major disruptions. Economically, the global centers of growth are much more likely to be elsewhere, for instance, in South and Southeast Asia. Demographically, both countries may be challenged by forms of nativism that hinder migration while—especially in China's case—the native population's numbers will decline precipitously over the next generation. None of these trends seem to support a US-China bipolar world.

Another main difference between the Cold War and now is that the Cold War offered *two* distinct and mainly separate forms of economic systems. The Soviet Union and its allies did not want more of a role for themselves within global markets. They wanted to destroy the market-based system and replace it with a socialist system based on state economic planning. These ideas were not just variations on existing themes, as far as capitalist economies went. They were about destruction and replacement.[11]

The idea of "peaceful coexistence"—so often hailed by those who wanted to overcome Cold War bipolarity—was therefore a chimera as long as both superpowers insisted on the universal applicability of their respective ideas about development. Coexistence would entail one of them either giving up on the concept of the global superiority of its economic system or at least agreeing that it was only applicable to their own country. Such developments were highly unlikely until one of the superpowers—as happened to the USSR under Gorbachev—would get into critical and systemic economic difficulties.

Today the situation is very different. Although China and Russia have increased government control over their economies of late, both base their societies on market-driven economic exchange, and China is an eager and highly successful participant in global economic interaction. China's quarrel with the United States in economic terms is not caused by a revisionist wish to undo the existing system. On the contrary, it is caused by China's increasing success *within* that economic system, to the extent that China's gross domestic product in purchasing power parity terms has overtaken that of the United States. An increasing number of Americans feel that their country is being outcompeted in economic terms within the international framework created and upheld by the United States. Much of the resentment against China's rise is based on such ideas, rather than on any sense that the Chinese are out to destroy the global economic system.

A third important difference between the Cold War and now is the predominance of comprehensive and mutually opposing ideologies during the Cold War era versus the much lighter ideological footprint now. The Cold War was an epoch during which policy was determined by ideology to a remarkable degree compared to other historical international systems. These opposing ideologies went much beyond the issue of economic systems. They defined comprehensive universalist worldviews in terms of how people and countries should think, feel, and organize. First and foremost, they gave elites tools through which to view and understand the world. Ideologies defined how the world worked and why certain groups acted the way they did. They gave both direction and power to policy making.

Today ideologies still matter, but in a very different way than during the Cold War. None of the great powers, including the United States, which is by far the most ideological in its policy making, believe that the universal expansion of their own political, social, and economic systems is what should define their foreign policies. China and Russia, which are the great powers that define themselves as most adversarial to the United States, are not proposing alternative and comprehensive forms of government that have universal application. Rather, their regimes are obsessed with sovereignty for themselves and the expansion of their strategic power to their respective regions in Asia and Eastern Europe. Ideological preferences play a role, but within an interest-based foreign policy.

The most significant recent change in this regard is the policies of the United States. After the Cold War was over, the ideological element in American foreign policy changed very little. It could easily be argued that the war on terror and the wars in the Middle East came out of the same ideological framework that had animated US policies during the Cold War. The after-effects of the 2007–2008 global financial crisis made many Americans less inclined to support a universalist, ideologically driven foreign policy, and this critique was part of the electoral platform of Donald Trump. Trump was in many ways the first US post–Cold War president, who, in spite of the chaotic nature of his foreign policy, attempted to put US self-interest above ideological preferences. President Biden's policies, though reverting to some of the rhetoric of earlier ideological convictions, have kept a much narrower focus in foreign policy terms than any US postwar president before Trump. It is therefore likely that US preferences will continue to move away from universalist engagements and toward a more limited foreign policy in the future.

Similarities

There are of course also similarities between the Cold War and the posthegemonic world we live in today, though, in my view, the differences outweigh the similarities. Some of the similarities are aspects that have been inherited from the Cold War, which, after all, ended only one generation ago. It should also be stressed that some of these similarities are factors that almost all international systems have in common in one way or another, and which are therefore less consequential in terms of immediate comparison.

One similarity is obviously that the United States is the most powerful great power within the international system. Even if the current system is *not* bipolar, this matters. The fact that the United States was then and is now the most influential power is significant with regard to more than continuities (as noted above). It also implies that other powers are fearful of what the posthegemon can do to them or to their domestic or international aspirations. This is an important trait in current international affairs and is relevant for countries far beyond China and Russia. Likewise, smaller and less powerful countries often look to the United States for protection and support when threatened by regional great powers.

Another similarity is the predominance of capitalism as an economic system. Even though market forces—and especially finance capital—are now global and developed to a degree that was not the case during the Cold War, some of the fundamentals are similar to that era. The important difference that major countries and regions were then *outside* the capitalist system is of course significant, but it is also significant that the alliances between state power and capital operate more or less the same way today as they did back then, only now with a much larger group of countries within the same system. This also means that the United States, Europe, and China can use economic means to punish all those it disagrees with internationally.

As did the Soviets during the Cold War, the Chinese government, which is, at least in name, Communist, today sees the United States, and the West in general, as its enemies. Up until quite recently, Chinese leaders were careful and courteous in public and often declared their adherence to international norms. But in the party's internal messages, the line has for a long time been that the United States is planning to undermine China's rise through external aggression and internal subversion. "So long as we persist in CCP leadership and socialism with Chinese characteristics," says one 2013 inner-party communiqué, "the position of Western anti-China forces to pressure for urgent reform will not change, and they'll continue to point the spearhead of Westernizing, splitting, and 'Color Revolutions' at China."[12] The CCP's anti-Americanism bears a striking resemblance to the type Stalin promoted in the late 1940s.

A final similarity is that China is competing for predominance in Asia just as the Soviet Union sought predominance in Europe during the Cold War. The eastern Asian region is as important to the United States today as Europe was supremely important from the 1940s to the 1990s. The strong-arm methods China is using are similar to those used by the Soviets, with the added significance of market-based economic pressure, capability to match US military technology, and rapid growth in naval power. China has the capability to dominate eastern Asia within the coming decade in ways that the Soviet Union never achieved in Europe, even though some of the means that it is using are similar to those Moscow used during the Cold War.

Lessons

Although the differences between now and the Cold War are more important than the similarities, we still have many significant lessons that we can learn from an immediate past international system, not least with regard to how to keep great power peace. But before discussing these, let us at least note the other international system that today's posthegemonic world seems more similar to than the Cold War, namely great power relations at the end of the nineteenth century.

Back then we also saw a fast-rising power, Germany, confront a status quo power, Great Britain, which had been predominant for a very long time. Unlike the Cold War, this was a multipolar rather than a bipolar set of conflicts, with Russia, France, and Austria also playing significant roles. It was a period of great underlying instability, which led—some would say inadvertently—to the disaster of the First World War.

In terms of comparisons, it is particularly significant to look at the parallel between the Germany/Austria alliance back then and the China/Russia alliance that seems to be coming into being now. Germany then, like China today, was a rising great power with a rapidly increasing industrial and technological potential, restless within the existing international order. Germany's ally Austria was, like Russia today, an empire in decline, with significant quarrels with its neighbors and lots of pent-up internal conflict. Up to the summer of 1914, German leaders believed that they could manage Austria to their own advantage, in their rivalries with Britain, France, and Russia. Instead, what they got was a sequence of events in which Austrian concerns drove Germany toward war. After today's attack on Ukraine by Russia, China has to be very careful not to repeat that cycle of events.

As to lessons from the Cold War for today, forms of strategic misunderstanding played a major role in the escalation of conflict back then, and we should try to avoid making the same mistakes today. Both the United States and the Soviet Union overemphasized the aggressive intentions of the other and stressed irreconcilable domestic political, institutional, and cultural differences as justification for massive military buildups. Guided by their respective ideologies that stressed confrontation, both frequently misinterpreted the other's motives.[13]

Strategic misunderstanding was especially evident during crises. Washington, for example, thought the outbreak of the Korean War was a prelude to a Soviet global offensive, and therefore carried out an unprecedented mobilization that militarized its Cold War strategy. In both Vietnam and Afghanistan, fear of exploitation by the other side generated costly military interventions.

Today, the United States, China, and other great powers can work to better understand each other's strategic aims. This will not prevent all conflict; Russia's attack on Ukraine is an example of the kind of war that will lead to increased international tension even if we had understood Putin's motives better. But the sense that many Americans now have of China being out to replace the United States as the predominant global power and the belief that many Chinese have of the United States being intent on curtailing China's rise are assumptions that for the two leading great powers should be tested against concrete actions. Both Washington and Beijing must learn to rely on trustworthy analysis from experts who know the other side well and to avoid interpreting all rivalry in terms of worst-case scenarios.

The levels of mutual respect that are shown through personal diplomacy are essential parts of avoiding strategic misunderstanding. During the Cold War, leaders in the United States and the Soviet Union often used diplomatic means and personal contacts to convey respect of the other side as a great power, even as they worked to stymie its strategic designs. Such efforts made competition easier to manage and, ultimately, easier to resolve as ideological and political tensions began to ease. A degree of mutual respect also made it easier to pull back from the brink in some of the Cold War's most dangerous confrontations, such as the Cuban missile crisis in 1962 or the Indo-Pakistani war of 1971.

In the case of US-China relations during the Cold War, the real breakthrough came when US president Richard Nixon went to Beijing himself—making both him and his national security adviser, Henry Kissinger, revered figures in China, despite their being anti-Communists acting to advance their own country's national interest. Nixon and Kissinger frequently stressed their high regard for their hosts, despite vast differences in worldview, as did Mao Zedong and Zhou Enlai, who stuck to their principles even while honoring their guests. Such mutual respect facilitated the transition from hostility to normalization.

Technology today makes it more difficult to stick to principles while honoring guests. What leaders say in public (and often in private) is immediately available to both domestic and foreign audiences, making it all too easy to prioritize rhetoric that may satisfy one side's public opinion while appearing disrespectful and confrontational to the other. Even if the tone of conversations behind closed doors is civil, harsh public remarks—such as those made by both sides in Anchorage last March—make any compromise difficult. On such occasions, both sides should remember the value of conveying basic respect for the other's position as a great power, even while speaking out on matters of concern. And in planning high-level encounters—especially between the two countries' presidents—policy makers should choose both a setting and format with such objectives in mind.

In an intense rivalry, local conflicts can easily become entangled with great power interests—as happened in, among other flashpoints, Berlin, Cuba, Korea, and the Middle East during the Cold War. It took adept crisis management, by diplomats, military officers, and political leaders, to ensure that none of these confrontations led to global war.

Such crisis management relied on a number of steps by both sides, starting with the pursuit of limited and flexible objectives. During the Berlin crises, the Soviets did not try to move into West Berlin, or the United States and its allies into East Berlin. In the Cuban missile crisis, the Kennedy administration focused on withdrawal of Soviet nuclear missiles rather than overthrow of Fidel Castro or the total elimination of the Soviet presence in Cuba. Both sides must also leave space for the other to de-escalate, since unilateral de-escalation rarely happens when critical interests are at stake. In the Cuban missile crisis, US policy makers designed and implemented a maritime quarantine with particular caution, rather than following traditional naval blockade procedures, in order to allow Soviet de-escalation (while also promising, through backchannels, to withdraw US missiles from Turkey and not to invade Cuba). The Soviets, accordingly, could accept withdrawing their missiles from Cuba as an acceptable option given the risk of nuclear war.

In such crisis situations, communication was especially important: with emotions running high and high-level meetings off the table, there must be effective lines of communication to reduce the risk of miscalculation and identify shared crisis management objectives. Traditional diplomatic channels were often inadequate for such purposes, but backchannels—such as those used during the Cuban missile crisis—must be developed before the crisis begins. They must also be supplemented by effective command and control, and by efforts to manage relations with allies, to avoid third-party escalation. All major Cold War crises involved third parties, which often pursued their own objectives incompatible with de-escalation and crisis management. The only way to manage third-party policies and objectives was through direct communication between the two superpowers. The insights gained from such exchanges could also help each of them shape third-party behavior.

Crisis management is always difficult and inherently risky. Cold War policy makers learned over time that their best option was to do what they could to prevent crises from breaking out in the first place. On the strategic level, this involved dialogues, hotlines, and specific agreements on difficult issues such as Berlin. On the operational level, the two sides developed codes of conduct to regulate military encounters. Beijing and Washington seem to have learned some of these lessons, reflected in measures such as the Code for Unplanned Encounters at Sea and hotlines between defense establishments. Nevertheless, neither side is doing enough to facilitate crisis prevention and communication, in particular with regard to cyber issues and other new technologies.

During the Cold War, the potential for incremental improvement in great power relations was often neglected in favor of the pursuit of fundamental changes. Given the intense ideological conflict and sharp regional confrontations, such neglect was understandable. Yet it meant many lost opportunities, in areas from joint research and people-to-people exchanges to agreements on nonintervention in certain regions. The focus on ideology also prevented both sides from using leadership transitions to facilitate improvements rather than introducing new risks (by giving the impression of seeking short-term gain by testing a new leader or renegotiating past understandings).

These Cold War lessons can be very helpful for today's situation, not because the circumstances today are analogous to conditions back then, but because one should like to think that at least some learning from previous international systems is possible. If we are to be able to keep great power peace over the next couple of decades, the lessons from the Cold War should be quite helpful. But so are lessons from other international systems, both those relatively few that have dissolved peacefully and those that have ended in great power war. The past is always a powerful part of our own imagination. And given the often-disastrous outcomes of great power conflict in the twentieth century, we have a particular duty to use that imagination to propose better results for today's world.

Notes

1. I sometimes compare such historicist forms of thinking to a joke my granddad liked to tell about a drunk who looked under the streetlight for his lost keys rather than at the corner where he had lost them, because "this is where the light is." Psychologists call it the "streetlight effect"; see Samuel L. Popkin, *The Reasoning Voter: Communication and Persuasion in Presidential Campaigns* (University of Chicago Press, 1994), 92–95. For a critique from an investment perspective, see Ray Dalio, *Principles for Dealing with the Changing World Order: Why Nations Succeed and Fail* (Simon & Schuster, 2021), especially p. 72.

2. The quote often attributed to Carter is: "The language people speak in the corridors of power is not economics or politics. It is history." See Niall Ferguson, "Applying History in Real Time: A Tale of Two Crises," *Journal of Applied History* 1 (March 16, 2022): 1–18, https://doi.org/10.1163/25895893-bja10021.

3. See Yanming An, "The Idea of Cyclicality in Chinese Thought," *Dao* 20, no. 3 (September 1, 2021): 389–406, https://doi.org/10.1007/s11712-021-09787-8.

4. See G. W. Trompf, *The Idea of Historical Recurrence in Western Thought: From Antiquity to the Reformation* (University of California Press, 1992), 4–49.

5. Miguel Vatter, *Between Form and Event: Machiavelli's Theory of Political Freedom* (Springer Science, 2013), and, for Marx in a broader context, see Hayden V. White, *Metahistory: The Historical Imagination in Nineteenth-Century Europe* (Johns Hopkins University Press, 1973).

6. For imperial decline and its consequences, see Jane Burbank and Frederick Cooper, *Empires in World History: Power and the Politics of Difference* (Princeton University Press, 2010). For those who were excluded from the postcolonial frenzy of state making, see Lydia Walker, "Decolonization in the 1960s: On Legitimate and Illegitimate Nationalist Claims-Making," *Past & Present* 242, no. 1 (February 2019): 227–64.

7. For two different perspectives with concurring conclusions, see Odd Arne Westad, "Has a New Cold War Really Begun?," *Foreign Affairs*, March 3, 2018, https://www.foreignaffairs.com/articles/china/2018-03-27/has-new-cold-war-really-begun; Stephen M. Walt, "I Knew the Cold War. This Is No Cold War," *Foreign Policy*, March 12, 2018, https://foreignpolicy.com/2018/03/12/i-knew-the-cold-war-this-is-no-cold-war/.

8. The literature on historical cold wars other than the twentieth-century Cold War is not developed beyond occasional references. For the argument that there were *different* cold wars in the last century, see Lorenz M. Luthi, *Cold Wars: Asia, the Middle East, Europe* (Cambridge University Press, 2020).

9. See Laurien Crump, *The Warsaw Pact Reconsidered: International Relations in Eastern Europe, 1955–1969* (Routledge, 2015).

10. See Derek Grossman, "Modi's Multipolar Moment Has Arrived," *RAND* (blog), June 6, 2022, https://www.rand.org/blog/2022/06/modis-multipolar-moment-has-arrived.html.

11. There is a recent strain in the literature that claims the opposite, that the USSR would have conformed to at least parts of the capitalist global framework if it had not been purposefully excluded from them by the United States. See Oscar Sanchez-Sibony, *Red Globalization: The Political Economy of the Soviet Cold War from Stalin to Khrushchev* (Cambridge University Press, 2014) and, for a somewhat different take, Johanna Bockman, "Socialist Globalization against Capitalist Neocolonialism: The Economic Ideas behind the New International Economic Order," *Humanity: An International Journal of Human Rights, Humanitarianism, and Development* 6, no. 1 (2015): 109–28. The evidence for these views seems so far to be limited.

12. CCPCC General Office, "Communiqué on the Current State of the Ideological Sphere," approved by the central leadership and distributed April 22, 2013, *ChinaFile*, https://www.chinafile.com/document-9-chinafile-translation.

13. This part of the chapter is based on Li Chen and Odd Arne Westad. "Can Cold War History Prevent U.S.-Chinese Calamity?," *Foreign Affairs*, April 19, 2022, https://www.foreignaffairs.com/articles/china/2021-11-29/can-cold-war-history-prevent-us-china-calamity, but revised to reflect my own current views.

2

US-China Bipolarity and Conflictual Coexistence

Øystein Tunsjø

China's emergence as a peer competitor of the United States has triggered a new cold war debate.[1] China's leader Xi Jinping, US president Joseph Biden, and the United Nations general secretary António Guterres have all warned against a new cold war.[2] They are right to note that there is a new superpower rivalry and a bipolar international system.[3] However, the assumption that the world is entering a new cold war is misguided. If the contemporary bipolar system does not share the Cold War characteristics of the previous bipolar system, what, then, are the characteristics of this new bipolar system? Instead of a new cold war, it is argued that the United States and China are in a new era of conflictual coexistence where patterns of behavior differ from the Cold War and secondary states have more flexibility.

The Cold War was characterized by polarized economic blocs, embargoes, and blockades.[4] In contrast, the United States and China have interdependent economies and are linked through global value chains and transnational production networks. The Cold War was shaped by ideological contest and polarized institutions.[5] Today we see ideological pragmatism, technological connectivity, and multilateral cooperation. The Cold War was dominated by arms races, a balance of terror, and doctrines of massive retaliation and mutually assured destruction.[6] The new superpower rivalry fuels rearmament and a military buildup, but the intensity of balancing and arms racing is not as strong as during the Cold War.

The structural pressures compelling states to choose sides are less now than during the Cold War. An Iron Curtain is not descending over East Asia as it did in Europe during the origins of the previous superpower rivalry. Secondary states' alignment and room for maneuver differ, and the contemporary bipolar system is not polarizing states into two blocs.

Øystein Tunsjø, *US-China Bipolarity and Conflictual Coexistence*. In: *Not Just Another Cold War*.
Edited by: Bård Nikolas Vik Steen, Oxford University Press. © Oxford University Press (2025).
DOI: 10.1093/9780197799932.003.0003

Nonbloc members or nonaligned states will be more likely to support either superpower on specific issues rather than lending their support in general. However, the interconnectedness between China and US allies gives Beijing leverage that the Soviet Union did not possess. China has economic and technological influence that provides additional and different challenges for the United States and its allies compared to the primarily military and ideological toolbox that the Soviet Union relied upon. This adds to explaining why a new bipolar system is characterized by conflictual coexistence rather than a cold war.

The first part of this chapter establishes that the United States and China are the two superpowers in a new bipolar international system. The second part argues that the new superpower rivalry is better characterized by conflictual coexistence than the anachronistic Cold War analogy. The third part emphasizes that all bipolar structures do not necessarily have equal effects and examines the distinct geopolitical, military, economic, technological, and ideological interaction between the superpowers during the previous and contemporary bipolar system. The fourth part explains how conflictual coexistence affects secondary states' room for maneuver. The conclusion points to how this analysis refines Kenneth Waltz's structural realist theory[7] in accounting for bipolarity and its effects in the twenty-first century.

A New Bipolar System

Scholars cannot agree whether the international system is unipolar, bipolar, or multipolar.[8] If the latter was the case, and there was an ongoing great power rivalry, then the United States must at some point have been degraded from its superpower position to a great power. That has not happened. In a multipolar system there would have been three or more great powers that are roughly as powerful or somewhat in the same league, as was the case prior to the First and the Second World Wars and during centuries of great power competition and wars. That is not the case today.[9] Instead, the power gap between the United States and China and any third-ranking power is huge—and continues to grow. The contemporary international system is structurally distinct from the unipolar system. It is a bipolar system in which "no third power is able to challenge the top two."[10] In contrast to Westad's argument in this volume that the international system has become increasingly multipolar, there are two main reasons the international system has returned to bipolarity. First is the narrowing power gap between China and the United States. Second is the widening power gap between China and any other state.

From Unipolarity to Bipolarity

The United States is still the most powerful state in the world, but that is not sufficient for continued unipolarity. The power gap between the United States and China has narrowed considerably. The US economy was about fifteen times larger than China's in the early 1990s. In 2023, China's gross domestic product (GDP) was roughly 72% of the US economy. Measured in purchasing power parity (PPP), China is the largest economy in the world.[11] China has moved from having approximately 1% of the world economy in the early 1990s to having about 18% today. This economic rise has laid the foundation for China becoming the sole peer competitor of the United States. Never in the history of the rise and fall of great powers has one state become so powerful relative to all others in such a short period of time without the effects of a great power war (within a few years, the Second World War elevated the United States and the Soviet Union to a dominating power position and eliminated Germany and Japan as top-ranking states).

Brooks and Wohlforth, two of the staunchest defenders of the unipolar thesis, write that no other state is "a rough peer of the United States and China." They note that "China has indeed done a lot to shrink the gap in the economic realm, but it has done far less when it comes to military capacity and especially technology." In conclusion, they tweak their long-standing argument about unipolarity,[12] contending that the international system has become "partially unipolar."[13] The evidence for such a refinement is unconvincing.

Over the last three decades, China has become the world's factory and manufacturing hub, and steadily moved up the value chain in manufacturing and technology, increasingly threatening American dominance. China has climbed from having only 10 companies in 2001 on the Fortune Global 500 list of corporations worldwide measured in revenue to having most corporations on the list in 2022 (145 companies compared to 124 by the United States and as many companies as the United States within the top 10). China is the largest trading partner for more than half of the world, and its economy remains a key driver of global economic growth.[14]

Even if some would dispute the finding that China has become a global tech leader, it has clearly been catching up with the United States technologically.[15] Its technological progress and development have forced the United States to crack down on Chinese tech companies like Huawei and ZTE and China's technology access to semiconductors. To maintain its advantage and counter China, the United States launched the CHIPS and Science Act in August 2022.[16] A few months later the US Bureau of Industry and Security announced new export controls and sanctions on advanced computing and semiconductor manufacturing items to China, essentially seeking to strangle the Chinese chip industry.[17]

Building on the CHIPS and Science Act and the measures taken by the US Bureau of Industry and Security in 2022, President Biden issued an executive order in August 2023 declaring a "national emergency" to deal with the threat that countries of concern (China being the greatest concern) would develop sensitive technologies through certain US investments. In short, the White House issued regulations that prohibited investments exacerbating this threat.[18] These steps would not have been necessary if the international system was unipolar and the United States was unrivaled.[19] Clearly, the United States is increasingly concerned about China's growing technology capabilities, and this is unprecedented compared to the unipolar era.

Militarily, China dominates the Asian mainland. While China borders fourteen states, none can successfully invade China or pose an existential threat to China's security. Conversely, the Soviet Union was confronted by the United States and the North Atlantic Treaty Organization (NATO) in Europe, and during the second half of the Cold War, hostilities between China and the Soviet Union turned their border in the Far East into the most militarized border in the world. China contests the United States for control of the world's most important waterways in East Asia. US defense spending was roughly twenty times larger than China's in the early 1990s. In 2024, US defense spending was about two to three times larger than China's.[20] The percentage of GDP that the Soviet Union devoted to defense remained in the double digits throughout the Cold War. But spending close to 20% of its GDP on defense to compete with the United States was also a key factor contributing to the collapse of the Soviet Union. China has learned from the Soviet Union's mistake. It has not been willing to spend more than an average of roughly 2% of GDP on defense over the last three decades. Still, this has been enough to narrow the gap to the United States militarily.

China could have quadrupled its defense spending. In 2022, according to the Stockholm International Peace Research Institute (SIPRI), China's defense spending was $291 billion, and its share of China's GDP was 1.6%. US defense spending was $876 billion, and its share of the US GDP was 3.5%. If China spent four times more on defense, this would equal $1.164 billion and 6.4% of China's GDP. This would have resulted in China having a larger defense spending than the United States, but still a much lower defense spending as a percentage of its GDP than the Soviet Union. China's latent power is much larger than the Soviet Union's ever was, and China is more likely to present a greater challenge to the United States in the new bipolar system than the Soviet Union did in the previous bipolar system.

The lack of global power projection capability and US "command of the commons"[21] are often-used arguments to undermine the importance of the rise of China. But one should remember that the Soviet Union lacked global power projection capabilities in the 1950s and did not develop a large navy until the 1970s and launched its first aircraft carrier in 1975. Britain had a global navy in the 1950s and defeated Argentina in a war far from the British Isles during the Falklands War in 1982, but this did not define it as a superpower. China does not need global power projection to be considered a pole in a new bipolar system. Despite this, China has launched two aircraft carriers, has built a third, and is constructing a fourth.

China has as much global military, diplomatic, economic, and technological influence as the Soviet Union. China's military buildup, especially its rocket forces, its navy, and its cyber and space capabilities, challenges the balance of power in East Asia and undermines US power preponderance. Its capabilities in space, including satellites and its anti-satellite capabilities, challenge the security of US communication systems. The United States no longer enjoys hegemony and only partially commands the global commons.

The United States has a larger defense budget, but China can compensate by concentrating its military in East Asia. The United States was in continuous war for two decades in Afghanistan, in addition to prolonged warfare in Iraq, Libya, and Syria. China has lower global operating expenses for its armed forces. US wars in the greater Middle East sustained a central role for the army within the US military, but ground forces have a more limited role in balancing and warfighting in maritime East Asia. Conversely, China has been able to downsize the army and channeled more resources to the navy, rocket force, air force, cyber, and space, which are the branches of the military mostly involved in the US-China military rivalry in East Asia.

The United States has much more warfighting experience than China, but the United States has not been confronted with a peer competitor on the battlefield or engaged in any battle at sea. US wars in the greater Middle East have led to worn-out military capabilities and soldiers, which have increased expenses to veterans, salaries, pensions, and welfare. The costs of building ships and airplanes in China are still much lower than in the United States, and China's PPP also means lower maintenance costs. Many point to the fact that China has no real allies, and the United States has many. Still, it is difficult to tell which US allies are willing to go to war against China. At the same time, the United States remains committed to the security of its allies in other regions. These commitments eat into the defense budget and direct attention to other regions when crisis and wars occur. For example, the United States sent two aircraft carrier groups to the Middle East after the outbreak of war between Israel and Hamas in October 2023.

China can also take advantage of its geographical proximity to a potential war in East Asia. Compared to China's numerous bases on the mainland and favorable internal lines of communication, the United States needs to project and sustain military power across the Pacific to counterbalance China in Asia and East Asia waters. As Boulding has pointed out, "The law of diminishing strength, then, may be phrased as *the further, the weaker*; that is, the further from home any nation has to operate, the longer will be its lines of communications, and the less strength it can put in the field."[22] Once the US military reaches East Asia, China's anti-access/area-denial capabilities threaten the relatively few US military bases in the region and could destroy US ships and aircrafts operating in the vicinity of China's territory. The United States can compensate for China having a much larger navy in numbers of ships with more missile tubes on its submarines and surface fleet, more advanced technology, and better interoperability among US forces and with allies. However, China can counter this with the largest arsenal of short- and medium-range ballistic, cruise, and hypersonic missiles on the Chinese mainland, which will have strong effects in any military confrontation in maritime East Asia.

China does not require the same advanced military platforms, such as nuclear submarines and aircraft carriers, which the United States is dependent on to project military power halfway across the globe. Brooks and Wohlforth stress that the United States has sixty-eight nuclear submarines and China only twelve (this number includes both nuclear powered fast attack submarines (SSNs) and ballistic missiles submarines (SSBNs)). But

China does not need many nuclear attack submarines (it has six) as its main objective is to militarily dominate East Asia. Instead, it has developed about fifty advanced and quiet diesel submarines that are effective within the first island chain (South China Sea, Taiwan Strait, Yellow Sea, and East China Sea) and between the first and the second island chain (the Philippine Sea and the Western Pacific).

In its annual reports on the Chinese military, the Pentagon has pointed out that China is capable of producing complex weapons systems that are modern and technologically advanced—some examples include military artificial intelligence and other disruptive technologies, hypersonic and ballistic missiles, nuclear modernization, and cyber and space capabilities.[23] Wargames have increasingly showed that China is capable of putting up a good fight against the United States in East Asia.[24] The United States is no longer impregnable, many ships and aircrafts will be destroyed in a naval battle, and it is unclear how the United States would absorb such losses. China has become the world's largest shipbuilder, producing roughly half of the world's tonnage in 2023.[25] The US share of world shipbuilding is less than 1%.

China can replace more quickly not only ships but also personnel on ships by drawing on its huge maritime sector. In comparison to the Soviet Union, China is not only a leading land power but also a formidable maritime power with the world's largest navy measured in number of ships and the world's largest coast guard and fishing fleet, with a major merchant fleet and an enormous shipbuilding capacity. This matters because the United States and China are mainly confronting each other in the maritime domain and not on land like the United States and the Soviet Union did in Europe.

In a rather outdated view of world affairs in the nuclear age and a questionable view of China's ambitions, Brooks and Wohlforth argue that China has not "occupied vast territories across great distances" and "conquered key territory crucial to the global balance."[26] Occupying vast territories is indeed difficult when four of China's neighbors are nuclear states. This was not the case when the Soviet Union advanced toward Berlin during the end of World War II. More importantly, China's territorial ambitions are probably not to conquer vast territories. Instead, China is more likely to resemble US ambitions when it sought to become the dominant power within its region after gaining control of the North American continent. The United States did not prioritize the conquest of further territories in Canada or Mexico; instead, it wanted to push the British navy out of its region and take control of the waters and sea lanes of communications in the Western Hemisphere. Similarly, China wants to push the United States out of its region and take control of East Asian waters and sea lanes of communications in the Indo-Pacific. This is the core geopolitical challenge of the new bipolar system, shaping both the balance of power and international affairs.

China and the Rest

For many years, scholars and policy makers have been referring to the BRICS countries (Brazil, Russia, India, China, and South Africa) as a source of emerging multipolarity and diffusion of world power.[27] This view, however, is misleading.[28] China's nominal GDP is more than twice as large as the combined nominal GDP of Brazil, Russia, India, and South Africa. Russia, a state many point to when referring to multipolarity, has a GDP that is only about one-tenth of China's.[29]

China's defense budget is roughly four to five times larger than Russia's, although China only spends less than 2% of its GDP on defense, while Russia spends more than twice as much. In the aftermath of Russia's invasion of Ukraine, defense spending has probably increased to more than 6% of GDP. Still, Russia is far from catching up with China.[30] Instead, due to Western sanctions and Russia's military losses in the war in Ukraine, it is likely that the power gap between Russia and China will increase and make Russia more dependent on China. Even if states such as Germany, Japan, India, the United Kingdom, and France increase their defense spending in the years to come, the power gap between China and any third-ranking power is larger than that between China and the United States.

In a multipolar system there would be no need for the United States to balance China. Japan is the world's third-largest economy, and Russia and India have the world's third and fourth largest defense budgets, respectively. However, these states are unable to balance China. China's GDP and defense spending are larger than the combined GDP and defense spending of Russia, India, and all East Asian states. This resembles the situation in Europe at the origins of the previous bipolar system. Then, none of the European states could balance the Soviet Union and the United States was compelled to maintain a balance of power in Europe. Without US balancing, China would dominate Asia.

The world would look different if there was a multipolar system. In 2022, after Russia's attack on Ukraine, it was the United States that was balancing and deterring Russia. The United States provided by far the most military aid to Ukraine in 2022 and continues to be the leading country supporting Ukraine.[31] If the system was multipolar, European powers would more strongly balance Russia. Moreover, in contrast to China's dominating role in East Asia, Russia has a GDP slightly larger than Spain and smaller than Italy. If Germany spends 2% of its GDP on defense, it will alone have a defense budget that could go a long way toward matching Russia's. Accordingly, none of the European states are capable of dominating Europe.

Despite Russia's invasion of Ukraine and the outbreak of the largest war in Europe since the Second World War, the Pentagon concluded in its National Defense Strategy in October 2022 that the priorities were defending the homeland "paced to the growing multi-domain threat posed by the PRC." The Department of Defense emphasized "being prepared to prevail in conflict when necessary, prioritizing the PRC challenge in the Indo-Pacific, then the Russian challenge in Europe."[32] The United States is confronted by only one peer competitor in a new bipolar system, as the 2022 US National Security Strategy points out: "The post-Cold War era is definitively over," and China is "the only competitor with both the intent to reshape the international order and, increasingly, the economic, diplomatic, military, and technological power to advance that objective."[33]

A bipolar system is a system in which no third power can challenge the top two. It was the decline in Great Britain's relative power and the power gap between the Soviet Union and Great Britain that transformed the international system from multipolar to bipolar in the post–World War II period. In the first edition of *Politics among Nations*, Morgenthau discussed the United States, the Soviet Union, and Great Britain as great powers but noted that Great Britain was inferior to the other two powers. In his second edition, published in 1954, Morgenthau added, concerning the decline of the relative power of Great Britain, that the United States and the Soviet Union, "in view of their enormous superiority over the power next in rank, deserved to be called superpowers." Morgenthau argued that the United States and the USSR were not only much more powerful than the United Kingdom but also much more powerful than the traditional great powers under multipolar systems of the past. Thus, the United States and the USSR were defined as superpowers and not great powers.[34]

The distribution of capabilities and the power gap between these two top-ranking powers and the third-ranking power defined the origins of the bipolar system in the twentieth century. Today, there is a similar power gap between China and any third-ranking power. Moreover, China does not need to obtain power parity with the United States before the international system has shifted to a new polarity. Bipolarity is rarely symmetrical. As Westad also points out in this volume, power parity is not a requirement for bipolarity.[35] Perhaps a bipolarity initially tilted in the United States' favor will gradually move toward a bipolarity tilted in China's favor. The Soviet Union was never as powerful as the United States, but it was still regarded as a superpower and a pole in a bipolar international system. When we examine the distribution of capabilities in the contemporary international system,[36] we find that China and the United States are in a league of their own and much more powerful than any other state based on combined capabilities. This marks the return of bipolarity in international politics and defines the United States and China as superpowers in a new bipolar system.

Conflictual Coexistence

A key question in international politics is how the US-China rivalry will play out in the future. Some studies have pointed to the risk of war between the United States and China, drawing on analogies from great power wars during multipolar systems of the past and emphasizing the importance of power transitions.[37] However, these scholars have not analyzed US-China relations from Waltz's bipolar stability thesis or Gaddis's "long peace" argument on how the United States and the Soviet Union managed to go through forty years of superpower rivalry without going to war with one another.[38] The risk of a US-China war[39] is not the emphasis in this chapter, which instead examines how the embryonic US-China superpower dynamic has led to the development of a bipolar system with distinct patterns of behavior. The new bipolar system has unique characteristics influencing both the relationship between the superpowers and secondary states' autonomy in international politics. The post–Cold War unipolar era characterized by competitive coexistence is now replaced by a new US-China bipolar system characterized by conflictual coexistence, distinct from the Cold War patterns of behavior.

The United States and China compete, disagree, and confront each other over economic, technological, ideological, geopolitical, security, and military issues. However, despite deepening division and antagonism, interdependence and cooperation are also shaping US-China relations. The superpowers of the contemporary bipolar system are markedly more engaged

and interdependent and noticeably less independent than the superpow-·
ers under the previous bipolar system. This mix of conflict and coexistence
defines the new era of conflictual coexistence.

In *Foreign Affairs* in 1959, Nikita S. Khrushchev explained the policy
of peaceful coexistence.[40] It signifies in essence the repudiation of war as
a means of solving controversial issues and emphasizes commitment to
nonaggression. It also presupposes a renunciation of interference in the
internal affairs of other countries and an obligation on the part of all states to
desist from violating each other's territorial integrity and sovereignty in any
form and under any pretext whatsoever. Writing in *Foreign Affairs* in January 1960, and amazed by Khrushchev's interpretations, George F. Kennan
protested.[41] He argued that the Soviet Union did not abide by the principles
of peaceful coexistence and pointed to the record of the Russian revolutionary movement and the years of Soviet power over Eastern and Central
Europe.

The Chinese Communist Party promotes peaceful coexistence and win-
win cooperation, but whether China abides by these principles is disputed.
That debate is not the focus here; instead, the aim is to differentiate conflictual coexistence from peaceful coexistence. States have not renounced the use
of military force, and war is still used to solve controversial issues. Moreover,
aggression and coercion remain enduring aspects of international politics.
States are constantly interfering in other states' internal affairs. Sovereignty
is disputed and territorial integrity is violated. Conflict has not been repudi-
ated, and US-China relations have become more conflictual. At the same
time, coexistence has increased to a new level compared with the Cold
War era.

While there has been growing bipartisan consensus that the United States'
China policy must be tougher when confronted by the rise of China, not all
views have shifted from engagement to a new containment policy. Several
experts and policy makers have promoted a policy of "competitive coexistence."[42] The challenge with a competitive coexistence approach is that
everything in international politics involves competition—from superpower
and great power relations to emergency aid and securing Norway a seat on
the United Nations Security Council, from trade agreements, market access,
and arms sales to technological development and climate emissions. If all
state interaction includes elements of competition, then a policy of competitive coexistence is simply a reflection of international affairs and provides
limited analytical value added.

As there always will be competition between states in international politics, a new era of conflictual coexistence in US-China relations is characterized by more and escalating confrontational policies rather than existing competition. During periods of conflictual coexistence, states' interaction will move to a level that includes more conflict. That a period is shaped by conflictual coexistence indicates something more than competitive coexistence. There has not been a direct military conflict or war, but developments are moving in this direction.

The United States and China are still competing, but instead of running a marathon race where the aim is to outpace the other, they have moved toward a game more akin to rugby where contact is rough, and the objective is to prevent the other side's advance.[43] Other analogies of the distinction between competitive and conflictual coexistence could be between neighbors or in the labor market. Neighbors often compete in different areas, but when one neighbor builds a garage that limits the view of the other neighbor, then competitive coexistence could move to conflictual coexistence. The labor market is often characterized by competition, but this market can also escalate to a conflict involving a strike or a lockout. The period of engagement in US-China relations under unipolarity was marked by competitive coexistence shaped by liberalization, globalization, and marked mechanisms. The new bipolar era differs, and it is characterized by conflictual coexistence where security interests in many cases trump economic interests. The return of bipolarity compels the superpowers to emphasize relative gains and zero-sum thinking, as well as taking steps toward decoupling and derisking, but there will still be interdependence instead of independence.

At the same time, conflictual coexistence differs from the escalating confrontation and arms racing during the Cold War, since the most powerful states are far more intertwined economically, technologically, and geopolitically. Thus, we can distinguish between peaceful, competitive, and conflictual coexistence, and these different analytical approaches can explain, predict, and describe states' different behaviors and interactions.

Distinct Patterns of Behavior

There are no capitalist and communist blocs in the new bipolar system. In contrast to the Cold War, when the Soviet Union and the United States had limited trade relations and interaction, China is today a major force in the world economy.

Economic and Technological Connectivity

Globalization and strong economic interconnectedness will sustain a different economic order from the embargo and blockades witnessed in the economic relations between the United States and the Soviet Union. Today's transnational production networks, global supply chains, and economic interests were nonexistent between the Western and the Eastern blocs during the Cold War. Markets, investments, services, and production are interlinked in new and unprecedented ways, and China is a major driver of world economic growth.

The fact that the Soviet Union had little economic influence beyond its own bloc while China has extensive economic influence globally in a new bipolar system makes the US-China rivalry for economic domination fundamentally different from the Cold War era. Today's confrontation is not between two systems, the capitalist and the socialist. Instead, China and the United States coexist in the international economy. Since they are much more interlinked than the United States and the Soviet Union, the US-China economic and technological relationship is conflictual in new ways, as the tariffs and sanctions imposed in the so-called trade and tech war[44] demonstrates. The United States and China engage and confront each other over trade, market access, intellectual property rights, foreign direct investments, forced technology transfer, and many other issues—issues that did not affect US-Soviet bipolarity. US-China economic relations cannot be explained by the Cold War analogy. Instead, we should think of their interaction as conflictual coexistence.

China is changing the technology landscape through its position on internet sovereignty and the development of 5G, thereby creating new technology standards. China's market position in personal computers, smartphones, electric vehicles, e-commerce, and the digital economy have global effects and are distinct from the role of the Soviet Union. In early 2024, the United States was debating security risks related to TikTok, Chinese electrical vehicles, and Chinese cranes at US ports that could collect data, facilitate influence campaigns, provide China with competitive advantages, and give Beijing opportunities to sabotage US infrastructure and logistics. The Soviet Union never had such technological influence in the United States during the Cold War.

Competition for technological dominance, such as the nuclear and missile arms race or the competition in space and communications, characterized the Cold War. Nonetheless, the nature, speed, scope, and frequency of such competition have changed. The fourth industrial revolution[45] is rapidly altering the nature of competition and strategy for states in a new bipolar period. China's scientific achievements in bioinformatics, robotics, autonomous systems, artificial intelligence, and space are reshaping technology orders.[46]

Taylor Fravel demonstrates in this volume how the United States seeks to restrict China's access to critical technologies and confront China over the setting of standards in international bodies. The US-China "tech war" cuts across all domains and all sectors, involves a race for technological and military superiority, and is increasingly about values, information flows, trade, and global supply chains. Accordingly, the confrontation in the new arms race of the twenty-first century is more than traditional competition over missiles and nuclear capability. It is conflictual coexistence for dominance with broader implications than in the past.

Ideological Pragmatism and Institutional Orders

The sharply divided anti-communist/pro-capitalist and pro-communist /anti-capitalist polarity of the Cold War years reflected uncompromising ideological confrontation. The contemporary bipolar ideological rivalry is, in short, a confrontation between the democratic United States and authoritarian China. Surely a reflection of a real divide between them, the emphasis on ideological confrontation is nevertheless less apparent today. The mix of coexistence and conflict in contemporary US-China relations is distinct from the red menace scaremongering, propaganda campaigns, and apocalyptic rhetoric of the Cold War.

China does not seek worldwide revolution and does not export its ideology or communist system.[47] Soviet communists believed capitalism would inevitably be replaced by communism. China has demonstrated that it does not seek to overthrow the international order. Instead, it aims to benefit from many contemporary economical, technological, and institutional international orders. At the same time, China seeks to adjust these orders according to its preferences and interests and establish alternative China-led orders such as the Belt and Road Initiative and the Asian Infrastructure and Investment Bank.

In contrast to the Soviet Union, which dominated its own economic bloc with its own socioeconomic system and political structures, China benefits more from the existing global orders and has few incentives to overthrow them. Since China remains committed to existing international organizations, its ambitions and initiatives to develop alternative orders and institutions where Beijing has a more prominent role are likely to be more gradual than the Soviet Union's revolutionary approach. The new US-China superpower rivalry can become much more polarized and turned into a confrontation between two blocs or systems—democracy versus autocracy. However, this process is likely to be more gradual than during the previous superpower rivalry.

The Cold War was a contest between competing and in many ways mutually exclusive ideational interests that marginalized and polarized international institutions. The new superpower rivalry will have spillover effects on global and regional institutions and multilateralism. The technological rivalry is likely to fuel more confrontation and decoupling, as Fravel points out in this volume. However, in a world of conflictual coexistence, the new superpowers will also together confront such global issues as climate change, the environment, economic stability, terrorism, and proliferation of weapons of mass destruction. Moreover, as Kroeber and Dollar note in their chapters, China will remain dependent on international economic and technological linkages even as self-reliance and self-sufficiency become a strategic objective. In these circumstances, US-China interdependence will foster both coexistence and more conflict, unlike the unmitigated conflict of the Cold War. In addition, China works more closely with global and regional institutions, and is more socialized into multilateralism and the established international order, than the Soviet Union was.[48] At the same time, China's prominent global role also fuels conflict within orders ranging from trade and investments to technological development, and from the maritime domain to new domains such as cyberspace and space.

Secondary State's Room for Maneuver

The contemporary US-China rivalry may prove to be the defining rivalry of the twenty-first century. As a region, Asia will not be immune to what takes place in this rivalry. Nor will the rest of the world. With increased US-China confrontation, some scholars have examined whether East and Southeast Asia are drifting toward "two Asias" or a "dual structure," in which many states increasingly depend on China for trade, investments, and markets and look to the United States for guarantees of security.[49]

In a world of conflictual coexistence, the pressures compelling states to choose sides are less than during the Cold War. In recent years, and following China's more assertive posture, US regional allies such as South Korea, Japan, the Philippines, and Australia have increased cooperation and strengthened their alliance with the United States and between themselves in recent years. Nonetheless, these allies still sustain strong economic, technologic, and diplomatic ties with China. In contrast to the interaction between US allies and the Soviet Union, contemporary US allies sustain relations with both China and the United States, respectively. Although this pattern of behavior differs from the only modern historical example of bipolarity, namely the US-Soviet rivalry of the Cold War era, sustaining this balanced approach is not without its difficulties, as Stephen Walt's and Francois Heisbourg's respective contributions to this volume demonstrate.

Instead of US allies joining a new Coordinating Committee for Multilateral Export Controls (COCOM), which prevented trade with the Soviet Union and Warsaw Pact countries during the Cold War, US allies are today negotiating and signing investment and trade agreements with China. In November 2020, US allies and partners in East and Southeast Asia, and recently the United States' most important regional ally, Japan, joined China in the Regional Comprehensive Economic Partnership, the largest free trade agreement in history. The European Union (EU) concluded in December 2020 a comprehensive agreement on investments with China. So, despite the so-called US-China trade war, US allies have more autonomy in an era of conflictual coexistence to sign economic agreements with an adversary and peer competitor of the United States than they did during the Cold War period.

At the same time, the United States is pushing back, seeking to pressure allies to work more closely with the United States to combat China's trade and investment policies. In the aftermath of the Ukraine war, where China has showed its support for Russia through its diplomatic stand, by maintaining economic and technological ties, and by sustaining military cooperation, it is likely that there will be more Western unity when it comes to balancing Russia and China. The sanctions imposed on Russia have been unprecedented. Increased decoupling, protectionism, and stronger emphasis on self-sufficiency are to be expected. Western companies are waking up to the risks related to their investments and production in China.[50]

Nevertheless, it is highly unlikely that Western states will completely stop trading with or investing in China. Despite growing US-China confrontation over trade and disagreement between the EU and China, which prevented the EU Parliament's ratification of the comprehensive agreement on investment, large trade volumes between the United States and China and the EU and China have been sustained. China remains the most important trading partner for many European states and a top trading partner for the United States, and European and American businesses are still investing heavily in China. These trade relationships can be reversed and halted in a new era fueled by US-China superpower rivalry. The combined effects of the US-China trade and tech war and China's ties with Russia are becoming more of a concern for companies. However, it is unlikely that these developments will turn into a new cold war–type East-West divide with embargos and blockades.

Similar developments can be observed regarding behavior in international organizations. The Trump presidency created unprecedented and abnormal constraints in US ties with allies. Disagreements within the World Trade Organization, the World Health Organization, and the United Nations over issues such as trade, the COVID-19 pandemic, Iran, and climate mushroomed. However, some US allies demonstrated autonomy and willingness to undermine US interests when they joined China's Asian Infrastructure Investment Bank and participated in China's Belt and Road Initiative during the Obama administration. President Biden's ambition has been to improve US standing and work more closely with allies. Nonetheless, US allies are still likely to cooperate with China in several multilateral mechanisms and international organizations.

In ways unprecedented during the Cold War, secondary states will maximize economic and political gains from US-China economic and institutional rivalry. Many countries have banned China's Huawei from their telecommunications networks and are working on developing screening mechanisms that seek to block Chinese takeovers of technological innovations and prevent transfer of military or dual-use technology. At the same time, European and Asian governments and tech companies also fear that US sanctions—or too close alignment with the United States—will undermine business opportunities, which fuels disagreement among allies. Chip and processor producers in South Korea, Japan, and Taiwan are being pressured by Washington to move production to the United States, but many have resisted and there is still production going on in China. In many technological fields such as artificial intelligence, big data, quantum computing, and robotics, companies are arguing that cooperation with

China and Chinese companies is necessary to develop cutting-edge technology. However, such coexistence also fuels confrontation and conflicts of interest.

The new bipolar system is more likely to promote more autonomy for secondary states and permit them to maintain more equidistance to the superpowers than during the Cold War. Nonbloc members or nonaligned states will be more likely to support either superpower on specific issues rather than lending their support in general. US security partners, such as Indonesia, Thailand, Pakistan, Malaysia, and Singapore, have strengthened military cooperation with both the United States and China. India is cooperating more with the United States but has also increased cooperation with Russia and continues to cooperate with China. Moreover, there are costs related to closer military cooperation with the United States. China's economic retaliation against South Korea's deployment of the US Terminal High Altitude Area Defense (THAAD) missile system had consequences both for South Korea's economy and for its relationship with China. To restore ties with China, Seoul declared that there would be no additional THAAD deployments to South Korea, that it would not participate in US-Japan alliance cooperation, and that THAAD would not be integrated into the US missile defense system.[51]

China has used economic coercion and sanctions against other US regional allies. The effect has been strongest on South Korea and the Philippines, has been more mixed when it comes to Australia, and has had limited effect on Japan. The exercise of China's economic power has also compelled Malaysia and Singapore not to challenge China for fear they could incur the retaliation that the Philippines and South Korea faced. The role of trade in China's path to power underscores how the return of bipolarity and a new era of conflictual coexistence differ from the superpower rivalry and the role of secondary states during the Cold War.

The United States is now seeking to boost its deployments of intermediate-range ballistic missiles along the first island chain in East Asia. Such plans enhance deterrence and strengthen the defense of Japan, but Tokyo is likely to face more economic, political, and military pressure from China. While discussions have been ongoing for years, in 2024 there were no details on when and where missiles will be deployed.[52] US allies were subjugated to Soviet pressure during the Cold War, but Moscow lacked economic and technological leverage. Today, China has become the most important trading partner of many US allies and partners. Thus, secondary states are not similarly compelled to choose sides as during the Cold War but seek to maintain a balanced approach, manage risk, and hedge their bets under conditions of conflictual coexistence.

Conclusion

The structural effects of US-China bipolarity are distinct from US-USSR bipolarity. Twenty-first-century globalization and economic interdependence are vastly different from the polarization of the Cold War. The contemporary world is entering a fourth industrial revolution with new technologies contributing to interconnected supply chains and high-speed connectivity. There is no US-China ideological confrontation like the Cold War rivalry between capitalism and communism. No Iron Curtain is descending over contemporary East Asia.

Twenty-first-century geopolitics differ. The United States and the Soviet Union did not cross the static East-West divide in Europe for fear of triggering a nuclear third world war. The United States and China are not confronting each other in a military standoff on the Asia mainland. Instead, the two superpowers are militarily interacting in a more dynamic and unstable maritime domain of East Asia. This state of conflictual coexistence at sea heightens the risk of war between the contemporary superpowers compared with the Cold War period. The Cold War analogy does not capture the core characteristics and dynamics of the new US-China rivalry.

This argument challenges one of the leading theories in international politics, namely Waltz's understanding of structural realism. From a structural realist perspective, similar balancing behavior and stability are to be expected when the structure remains the same. Thus, the contemporary bipolar distribution of capabilities should provide compelling structural incentives for the US-China rivalry to replicate the US-Soviet rivalry. However, structural realism's theoretical emphasis on continuity across bipolar systems cannot explain why patterns of superpower behavior differ between two bipolar systems. A new geostructural realist theory better explains why the new US-China superpower balancing and stability differ from the US-USSR balancing and stability during the previous bipolar system.[53]

The distribution of capabilities between the two systems is roughly similar, but the contemporary bipolar system characterized by conflictual coexistence has distinct geopolitical, economic, and technological effects. This has implications for the superpowers stability and balancing, and secondary states' behavior, which differ from the Cold War bipolar system. Waltz argued that the superpowers during the Cold War were "markedly less interdependent and noticeably less dependent on the others than earlier great powers were."[54] In today's bipolar system, the superpowers are markedly more interdependent and noticeably less independent than the superpowers under the previous bipolar system. Moreover, the bloc organizational forms in the contemporary bipolar system differ from the US-Soviet Cold War bipolarity. Geopolitically, there was an East-West divide in Europe. There is no such geopolitical divide in today's bipolar system concentrated on East Asia. The bipolar system in the twentieth century was divided into incompatible ideologies of communism and capitalism. The twenty-first-century bipolar system is not based on equally mutually exclusive ideologies. Alliances and alignment are more flexible, and technological and economic cooperation is more extensive, under the current bipolar system.

The world has changed since the Cold War. While superpower rivalry is back, political, ideological, military, economic, geopolitical, and technological developments have altered the nature of strategic choices for and competition between states. Comparing two bipolar systems shows the different patterns of behavior between the Cold War and a new era of conflictual coexistence, which can strengthen the explanatory power of structural realism and reconfigure the theory to better account for variation in bipolar systems and structural effects.

Notes

1. Gideon Rachman, "A New Cold War: Trump, Xi and the Escalating US-China Confrontation," *Financial Times*, October 5, 2020, https://www.ft.com/content/7b809c6a-f733-46f5-a312-9152aed28172; Niall Ferguson, "The New Cold War? It's with China, and It Has Already Begun," *New York Times*, December 2, 2019, https://www.nytimes.com/2019/12/02/opinion/china-cold-war.html; Robert D. Kaplan, "A New Cold War Has Begun," *Foreign Policy*, January 7, 2019; W. R. Mead, "Beijing Escalates the New Cold War," *Wall Street Journal*, March 18, 2020, https://www.wsj.com/articles/beijing-escalates-the-new-cold-war-11584551652; Melvin P. Leffler, "China Isn't the Soviet Union. Confusing the Two Is Dangerous," *The Atlantic*, December 2, 2019, https://www.theatlantic.com/ideas/archive/2019/12/cold-war-china-purely-optional/601969/; Thomas J. Christensen, "There Will Not Be a New Cold War: The Limits of U.S.-Chinese Competition," *Foreign Affairs*, March 24, 2021, https://www.foreignaffairs.com/articles/united-states/2021-03-24/there-will-not-be-new-cold-war; Odd Arne Westad, "Has a New Cold War Really Begun? Why the Term Shouldn't Apply to Today's Great-Power Tensions," *Foreign Affairs*, March 27, 2018, https://www.foreignaffairs.com/articles/china/2018-03-27/has-new-cold-war-really-begun; Odd Arne Westad, "The Sources of Chinese Conduct: Are Washington and Beijing Fighting a New Cold War?," *Foreign Affairs*, September/October 2019, https://www.foreignaffairs.com/articles/china/2019-08-12/sources-chinese-conduct.

2. Xi Jinping, "Special Address by Xi Jinping, President of the People's Republic of China," *World Economic Forum*, January 25, 2021, https://www.weforum.org/events/the-davos-agenda -2021/sessions/special-address-by-g20-head-of-state-government-67e386f2d5/; Antonio Guterres, "UN Chief Guterres Warns against 'New Cold War,'" YouTube, September 23, 2020; Christina Wilkie, "Biden Sees No Need for 'New Cold War' with China," CNBC, November 14, 2022, https://www.cnbc.com/2022/11/14/biden-sees-no-need-for-a-new-cold-war-with-china-after-three-hour-meeting-with-xi-jinping.html.

3. Øystein Tunsjø, *The Return of Bipolarity in World Politics: China, the United States and Geostructural Realism* (Columbia University Press, 2018).

4. John L. Gaddis, *Strategies of Containment: A Critical Appraisal of American National Security Policy during the Cold War* (Oxford University Press, 1982).

5. Eric Hobsbawm, *The Age of Extremes: A History of the World, 1941–1991* (Random House, 1994); Odd Arne Westad, *The Cold War: A World History* (Basic Books, 2017).

6. Bernard Brodie, *Strategy in the Missile Age* (Princeton University Press, 1959); David E. Hoffman, *The Dead Hand: The Untold Story of the Cold War Arms Race and Its Legacy* (Bantam Doubleday, 2010).

7. Kenneth N. Waltz, *Theory of International Politics* (McGraw-Hill, 1979, reissued by Waveland Press, Inc, 2010).

8. "Did the Unipolar Moment Ever End? Foreign Affairs Asks Experts," *Foreign Affairs*, May 23, 2023, https://www.foreignaffairs.com/ask-the-experts/did-unipolar-moment-ever-end

9. Jo Inge Bekkevold, "No, the World Is Not Multipolar," *Foreign Policy*, September 22, 2023, https://foreignpolicy.com/2023/09/22/multipolar-world-bipolar-power-geopolitics-business-strategy-china-united-states-india/; Stephen G. Brooks and William C. Wohlforth, "The Myth of Multipolarity: American Power's Staying Power," *Foreign Affairs*, April 18, 2023, https://www.foreignaffairs.com/united-states/china-multipolarity-myth

10. Waltz, *Theory of International Politics*, 98.

11. International Monetary Fund, *World Economic Database: Select Country or Country Groups*, 2023, https://www.imf.org/external/datamapper/NGDPD@WEO/EU/CHN/USA

12. Stephen G. Brooks and William C. Wohlforth, "The Rise and Fall of the Great Powers in the Twenty-First Century: China's Rise and the Fate of America's Global Position," *International Security* 40, no. 3 (Winter 2015/2016): 7–53.

13. Brooks and Wohlforth, "The Myth of Multipolarity."

14. Lee Ying Shan, "China De-linking Talk Is Overdone and It's Still Key to the Global Economy, Asian Development Bank Says," CNBC, February 25, 2024, https://www.cnbc.com/2024/02/26/china-still-top-trading-partner-for-many-countries-says-adb.html

15. Jamie Gaida et al., *ASPI's Critical Technology Tracker*, March 2, 2023, https://www.aspi.org.au/report/critical-technology-tracker; Dagny Dukach, "Understanding the Rise of Tech in China," *Harvard Business Review*, September/October 2022, https://hbr.org/2022/09/understanding-the-rise-of-tech-in-china; Tarun Chhabra et al., "Global China: Technology," April 27, 2020, https://www.brookings.edu/collection/global-china-technology/ Although the US technology dominance is not what it used to be in the unipolar era, the United States still leads in science and technology. See United Nations Conference on Trade and Development, "Technology and Innovation Report 2023," https://unctad.org/system/files/official-document/tir2023_en.pdf.

16. White House, "Fact Sheet: Chips and Science Act Will Lower Costs, Create Jobs, Strengthen Supply Chains, and Counter China," August 9, 2022, https://www.whitehouse.gov/briefing-room/statements-releases/2022/08/09/fact-sheet-chips-and-science-act-will-lower-costs-create-jobs-strengthen-supply-chains-and-counter-china/.

17. US Department of Commerce, "Public Information on Export Controls Imposed on Advanced Computing and Semiconductor Manufacturing Items to the People's Republic of China (PRC)," Bureau of Industry and Security, October 7, 2022, https://www.bis.doc.gov/index.php/documents/about-bis/newsroom/press-releases/3158-2022-10-07-bis-press-release-advanced-computing-and-semiconductor-manufacturing-controls-final/file. See also Chris Miller, *Chip War: The Fight for the World's Most Critical Technology* (Scribner, 2022).

18. See "Executive Order on Addressing United States Investments in Certain National Security Technologies and Products in Countries of Concern," White House, August 9, 2023, https://www.whitehouse.gov/briefing-room/presidential-actions/2023/08/09/executive-order-on-addressing-united-states-investments-in-certain-national-security -technologies-and-products-in-countries-of-concern/; and "Background Press Call by Senior

Administration Officials Previewing Executive Order on Addressing U.S. Investments in Certain National Security Technologies and Products in Countries of Concern," White House, August 10, 2023, https://www.whitehouse.gov/briefing-room/press-briefings/2023/08 /10/background-press-call-by-senior-administration-officials-previewing-executive-order -on-addressing-u-s-investments-in-certain-national-security-technologies-and-products-in -countries-of-concern/.

19. Michael Beckley, *Unrivaled: Why American Will Remain the World's Sole Superpower* (Cornell University Press, 2018).

20. See Stockholm International Peace Research Institute (SIPRI) military expenditure database, https://www.sipri.org/databases/milex.

21. Barry Posen, "Command of the Commons: The Military Foundations of U.S. Hegemony," *International Security* 28, no. 1 (2003): 5–46.

22. Kenneth E. Boulding, *Conflict and Defense: A General Theory* (Harper & Brothers, 1962), 231.

23. US Department of Defense, "Military and Security Developments Involving the People's Republic of China: Annual Report to Congress," October 19, 2023, https://media.defense.gov/2023/Oct/19/2003323409/-1/-1/1/2023-MILITARY-AND-SECURITY-DEVELOPMENTS-INVOLVING-THE-PEOPLES-REPUBLIC-OF-CHINA.PDF

24. Mark F. Cancian et al., *The First Battle of the Next War: Wargaming a Chinese Invasion of Taiwan* (Center of Strategic and International Studies), January 9, 2023, https://csis-website -prod.s3.amazonaws.com/s3fs-public/publication/230109_Cancian_FirstBattle_NextWar .pdf?VersionId=XlDrfCUHet8OZSOYW_9PWx3xtc0ScGHn

25. "China Now Produces More Than Half of All Tonnage," *Maritime Executive*, December 17, 2023, https://maritime-executive.com/article/china-now-produces-more-than-half-of-all-new-tonnage

26. Brooks and Wohlforth, "The Myth of Multipolarity."

27. Oliver Stuenkel, *The BRICS and the Future of Global Order*, 2nd ed. (Lexington, 2020); Robert J. Lieber, "The Rise of the BRICS and American Primacy," *International Politics* 51 (2014): 137–54; Subhash C. Jain, ed., *Emerging Economies and the Transformation of International Business* (Edward Elgar, 2006); Jim O'Neill, *Building Better Global Economic BRICSs*, Global Economics Paper 66 (Goldman Sachs, November 2001).

28. Harsh V. Pant, "The BRICS Fallacy," *Washington Quarterly* 36, no. 3 (2013): 91–105.

29. International Monetary Fund, *World Economic Database*.

30. SIPRI and Pavel Luzin and Alexandra Prokopenko, "Russia's 2024 Budget Shows It's Planning for a Long War in Ukraine," Carnegie, October 11, 2023, https://carnegieendowment.org/politika/90753.

31. Jonathan Masters and Will Merrow, "How Much Aid Has the U.S. Sent Ukraine? Here Are Six Charts," Council on Foreign Relations, February 23, 2024, https://www.cfr.org/article/how-much-aid-has-us-sent-ukraine-here-are-six-charts.

32. US Department of Defense, "Military and Security Developments."

33. White House, *National Security Strategy*, October 2022, https://www.whitehouse.gov/wp-content/uploads/2022/10/Biden-Harris-Administrations-National-Security-Strategy-10.2022.pdf.

34. Hans J. Morgenthau, *Politics among Nations: The Struggle for Power and Peace* (Alfred A. Knopf, 1948), 271–74; Hans J. Morgenthau, *Politics among Nations: The Struggle for Power and Peace,* 2nd ed. (Alfred A. Knopf), 322–26.

35. Tunsjø, *Return of Bipolarity in World Politics*, chaps. 2–4, especially 84–93.

36. Waltz, *Theory of International Politics*.

37. G. Allison, *Destined for War: Can America and China Escape Thucydides's Trap?* (Houghton Mifflin Harcourt, 2017); C. Coker, *The Improbable War: China, the United States and the Continuing Logic of Great Power Conflict* (Hurst & Company, 2015); H. Kissinger, *World Order* (Penguin Press, 2014); J. J. Mearsheimer, *The Tragedy of Great Power Politics*, 2nd ed. (Norton, 2014); A. F. K Organski and Jacek Kugler, *The War Ledger* (University of Chicago Press, 1980).

38. Waltz, *Theory of International Politics*; Kenneth N. Waltz, "The Stability of a Bipolar World," *Daedalus* 93, no. 3 (Summer 1964): 881–909; Gaddis, *Strategies of Containment*; Tunsjø, *Return of Bipolarity in World Politics*.

39. Michael Beckley and Hal Brands, *Danger Zone: The Coming Conflict* (W. Norton, 2022); Øystein Tunsjø, "Another Long Peace?," *National Interest*, October 17, 2018, https://nationalinterest.org/feature/another-long-peace-33726.

40. Nikita S. Khrushchev, "On Peaceful Coexistence," *Foreign Affairs* 38, no. 1 (October 1959): 1–18.

41. George F. Kennan, "Peaceful Coexistence: A Western View," *Foreign Affairs* 38, no. 2 (January 1960): 171–90.

42. Andrew S. Erickson, "Competitive Coexistence: An American Concept for Managing U.S.-China Relations," *National Interest*, January 30, 2019, https://nationalinterest.org/fea ture/competitive-coexistence-american-concept-managing-us-china-relations-42852; Kurt M. Campbell and Jake Sullivan, "Competition without Catastrophe: How America Can Both Challenge and Coexist with China," *Foreign Affairs*, online August 1, September/October 2019, 96–110 https://www.foreignaffairs.com/china/competition-with-china-catastrophe-sullivan-campbell; Evan S. Medeiros, *Major Power Rivalry in East Asia*, Discussion Paper Series on Managing Global Disorder No. 3 (Council on Foreign Relations, 2021), https://www.cfr.org/report/major-power-rivalry-east-asia For an approach that emphasizes "competitive interdependence" see Ryan Hass, *Stronger: Adapting America's China Strategy in an Age of Competitive Interdependence* (Yale University Press, 2021).

43. Hass, *Stronger*, 65–66. For an argument that the new conflictual coexistence is shaped by a different sort of state competition see the case for "hypercompetition" in Ian Bowers and Øystein Tunsjø, "The Implications of Contemporary US-China 'Hypercompetition,'" *Washington Quarterly* 46, no. 4 (December 2023): 83–102.

44. This can hardly be labeled a "war" as US-China bilateral trade and investment remain high and the two superpowers are among each other's top trading partners. However, the trade relationship has become more confrontational compared to the more cooperative partnership during the post–Cold War era.

45. Klaus Schwab, *The Fourth Industrial Revolution* (Penguin Books, 2017).

46. Michael C. Horowitz, "Do Emerging Military Technologies Matter for International Politics?," *Annual Review of Political Science* 23 (2020): 385–400; James S. Johnson, "Artificial Intelligence: A Threat to Strategic Stability," *Strategic Studies Quarterly* 14, no.1 (Spring 2020): 16–39; Daniel W. Drezner, "Technological Change and International Relations," *International Relations* 33, no. 2 (2019): 286–303.

47. Christensen, "There Will Not Be a New Cold War."

48. Alastair Iain Johnston, "China in a World of Orders: Rethinking Compliance and Challenge in Beijing's International Relations," *International Security* 44, no. 2 (Fall 2019): 9–60; Alastair Iain Johnston, *Social States: China in International Institutions, 1980–2000* (Princeton University Press, 2008).

49. Robert S. Ross, "On the Fungibility of Economic Power: China's Economic Rise and the East Asian Security Order," *European Journal of International Relations* 25, no. 1 (2019): 302–27; Wang Dong, "Two Asias? China's Rise, Dual Structure, and the Alliance System in East Asia," in *Strategic Adjustment and the Rise of China: Power and Politics in East Asia*, ed. Robert S. Ross and Øystein Tunsjø (Cornell University Press, 2017), 100–134; Øystein Tunsjø, "U.S.–China Relations: From Unipolar Hedging toward Bipolar Balancing," in *Strategic Adjustment and the Rise of China: Power and Politics in East Asia*, ed. Robert S. Ross and Øystein Tunsjø (Cornell University Press, 2017), 41–68; John G. Ikenberry, "Between the Eagle and the Dragon: America, China, and Middle States Strategies in East Asia," *Political Science Quarterly* 131, no. 1 (2016): 9–43.

50. Editorial, "Western Companies Wake Up to China Risk," *Financial Times*, August 11, 2022. https://www.ft.com/content/0a03a58c-01ed-4b7e-8891-c9267f2dd7e6

51. Jo He-rim, "China Demands Korea Uphold 'Three Nos' policy," *The Korean Harald*, July 28, 2022, https://www.koreaherald.com/view.php?ud=20220728000666

52. Jeffrey W. Hornung, "Ground-Based Intermediate-Range Missiles in the Indo-Pacific: Assessing the Positions of U.S. Allies," (RAND), April 28, 2022, https://www.rand.or g/pubs/research_reports/RRA393-3.html; Ryo Nakamura and Ken Moriyasu, "U.S. to Deploy New Ground-Based Missiles to Indo Pacific in 2024," Nikkei Asia, December 3, 2023, https://asia.nikkei.com/Politics/International-relations/Indo-Pacific/U.S.-to-deploy-new-ground-based-missiles-to-Indo-Pacific-in-2024.

53. Tunsjø, *Return of Bipolarity in World Politics*.

54. Waltz, *Theory of International Politics*, 193.

II
THE ECONOMIC CONTEST

II.
THE ECONOMIC CONTEST

3

The Limits of China's Economic Rise

David Dollar

The issues of China's rise and US-China tension taken up in this book will be heavily influenced by how well China continues to do economically. After all, China's increasing influence in the world owes a lot to its remarkable economic performance, growing at 10% for thirty-plus years after initiating market-oriented reforms in 1978.[1] Recently China's growth rate has slowed down: some easing as the economy reached middle income was inevitable, but in China's case the drop-off has been very sharp. In the five years ending in 2008, China averaged nearly 12% growth; the most recent five years, half of that. It is impossible to predict how China will do in the next ten or twenty years because there are so many domestic and international unknowns. But we can examine the strengths and weaknesses of China's economy and identify the challenges that may hold back the country's rise.

Productivity in China is only one-quarter of US productivity (measured at purchasing power parity); hence, there is a lot more room for catch-up and convergence. Looking at historical precedents, Japan, South Korea, and Taiwan each took twenty to thirty years to go from one-quarter of US productivity to two-thirds. After that, convergence slowed down dramatically, essentially ending in Japan and Korea.[2] While history is a useful guide, China will not necessarily do as well. First, the earlier industrializers faced a very favorable, open global environment. China is now facing moves from the West to decouple in high-tech areas, as well as more general protectionism at home and abroad. Second, the East Asian industrializers had very good, market-oriented institutions and policies, which China is having difficulty replicating.

A number of recent studies focus on China's long-term growth potential, to 2030 and beyond. They generally agree that the key issue is total factor productivity (TFP) growth because demographics will ensure that the labor force declines and there are diminishing returns to China's extensive capital

David Dollar, *The Limits of China's Economic Rise*. In: *Not Just Another Cold War*. Edited by: Bård Nikolas Vik Steen, Oxford University Press. © Oxford University Press (2025). DOI: 10.1093/9780197799932.003.0004 investment. A study from the Lowy Institute extrapolates the recent down-ward trend in productivity growth in China and arrives at an estimate of overall gross domestic product (GDP) growth of 3.0% by 2030.[3] A simi-lar study from the Bank of Japan is more optimistic, drawing on historical examples to argue that productivity growth could rebound and GDP growth could reach 4.4% by 2030.[4] The significant difference in projected growth rate illustrates the difficulty of predicting TFP growth.

This chapter focuses on four factors, in particular, that will influence how well China realizes catch-up potential. First is the demographic challenge. Low fertility, aided by the one-child policy, means that the country's labor force has peaked and will now decline. China cannot do much to change its demographics at this point, but various policies could lead to better devel-opment and deployment of human capital. Second, China is fortunate to have a high savings and investment rate that funds its development. How-ever, there is mounting evidence of inefficiency in the allocation of capital and of sharply diminishing returns. Here the combination of state-owned banks lending to state-owned enterprises wastes a lot of capital, while most GDP is produced by a private sector with poor access to finance. Third, China faces a severe water crisis. Partly this is natural, as China has vastly more of the world's population than of the world's renewable water. But the natural shortage is exacerbated by heavy pollution, weak demand manage-ment, and restrictions on movement that keep an overly large population in the most water-constrained locations. The fourth issue is energy efficiency and carbon emissions. Climate change is exacerbating the water crisis in China, and the country is large enough that its own emissions are a main contributor. President Xi Jinping's pledge to reach carbon-zero by 2060 is, simply, not good enough. Unless China does an exceptional job han-dling these challenges, its growth rate is likely to slow and it will probably end up in a few decades modestly larger than the United States, but not overwhelmingly so.

The Demographic Challenge

China's demographics have been affected by its one-child policy. Fertility and hence population growth had been high in much of the pre-reform period, but fertility was already coming down when the one-child policy was introduced. As people's incomes grow and girls are educated, it is nat-ural for fertility to decline. This process was helped along by a strict policy of allowing urban couples to have only one child and most rural couples no more than two. The sharp decline in fertility gave rise to a "demographic dividend." The labor force was growing because of earlier population growth, there were as yet few old people, and now the youth cohort was declining in relative terms. As more and more of the population was of working age, this was a strong foundation for rapid growth.

Unfortunately, now the process is in reverse. The elderly population is increasing because of extended life expectancy, and the working-age population has peaked and is starting to decline. In general, it is hard to grow rapidly when the labor force is declining, but there is one important mitigating factor in China's case: rural-urban migration. China began economic reform in 1978 with only 18% of the population living in cities. This was enforced by a strict household registration (hukou) system that made it difficult for people to move around, especially limiting family movement from countryside to cities. China needed more urban workers but did not want to give up the control inherent in the hukou system. Hence was born the migrant worker system. Rural-registered adults could move to cities as long as they had jobs. They were not full urban residents entitled to social services or in many cases housing. Those who worked construction lived on the construction sites. Employees of large manufacturers lived in dormitories. If there was a downturn in the economy, migrants who lost their jobs were expected to return to their villages. Looking at who actually lives in cities (not hukou registration), the urbanization rate went from 18% to over 60% during the forty years since the start of economic reform. About three hundred million of this population are migrants. The migrant worker system had a certain economic efficiency as it allowed for the rapid growth of urban labor without burdening the government with the cost of expensive urban services.[5]

The urban prime-age population (twenty-five- to fifty-four-year-olds) increased from one hundred million to four hundred million over the thirty years from 1990 to 2020 (see Figure 3.1). Urban workers in industry and services are more productive than rural farmers, so this reallocation from low-productivity to high-productivity employment was a source of China's rapid growth. What happens now depends a lot on further prospects for rural-urban migration. The projections in the figure combine population projections for China with the assumption that the urbanization rate continues to rise, reaching 77% by 2050.[6] Under this assumption, the urban prime-age population will be stable for several decades but eventually decline.

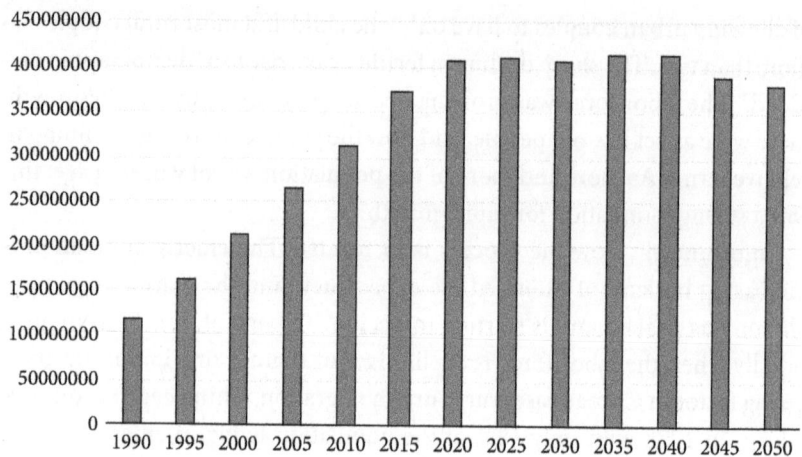

Figure 3.1 Urban Prime-Age Population (Twenty-Five- to Fifty-Four-Year-Olds)

From the point of view of growth, the important point is that rapid growth of the prime urban population ended right around 2020. The best China can do now is stabilize the urban workforce rather than see it immediately decline. It will probably take some further reform to achieve this. Reforms of the hukou system are focused on medium/small cities, but the rural migrants prefer large cities because they have the highest productivity and best job prospects. The medium/small cities have fewer jobs, and the employment that is available is not considered as valuable and might even be less desirable than a rural hukou, which entitles small-city residents to farmland, housing land, and rural benefits.[7]

China would get a positive impetus from eliminating the system and providing all urban residents with social services. This would make urban life more attractive and productive. There is also the issue of educational differences. Holders of rural hukou have 7.2 years of schooling on average, whereas the urban registered population has 10.4.[8] Also, the quality of rural education is poor. In China's export-oriented growth phase, rural workers who had been educated through lower middle school could move to urban factories and construction sites and be productively employed. But as China becomes a more developed economy and moves up the value chain, the labor market will need people with education and skills. There is a risk of mismatch between rural workers who are largely unskilled and the urban demand for labor in expanding high-tech sectors. Seriously addressing this issue will require more redistribution through the fiscal system. China currently has very little redistribution via taxes and transfers, leaving poor areas largely to fend for themselves in the financing and provision of services. Without more resources for rural social services, there is a danger of locking in a very high level of inequality, which tends to work against rapid growth by excluding much potential talent from fair access to education and jobs.

China could also facilitate migration and make agriculture more efficient through rural land reform. Farmers now have very incomplete use rights over their land, but they lose the right if the whole family moves to the city and does not farm the land. From the point of view of the rural economy, this prevents efficient increases in scale and mechanization. From the point of view of potential migrants, a system in which they could sell their rights would give them a "first pot of gold" to start their life in the city. A main source of inequality in China is rural-urban differences in productivity and living standards, as well as parallel differences between urban full residents and migrants. A pro-growth policy to achieve "common prosperity" would center on these issues of dismantling the hukou system, providing urban migrants with public services, increasing investment in rural education, and strengthening farmers' property rights over land.

Another aspect of the demographic challenge is that the elderly population is expanding rapidly. The number of people aged sixty-five years and older will roughly double from 200 million today to 400 million by 2049. Within the group, the fastest increase will be among the eighty-five-and-older cohort. That cohort will more than triple, from fewer than 50 million today to 150 million in 2049.[9] The elderly in general need more health care and social assistance, and caring for the "old-olds" is particularly resource intensive. China currently spends less on social services, as a share of GDP, than other G20 developing countries such as Turkey, Argentina, Russia, or Brazil, and far less than Organisation for Economic Co-operation and Development countries. China will have to spend significantly more resources taking care of the elderly. Taking care of the elderly also links up with the issue of rural-urban migration discussed previously. Many old people are living in the countryside, with their working-age children now in cities. Some of them would want to move to the cities if the opportunity arose, where they can be with their children and get good urban health care. Others will prefer to remain in the countryside but will need more assistance as they age. How China handles these challenges will have a big effect on human welfare as well as on the economy's growth potential.

The Allocation of Capital

During China's rapid growth phase, rural-urban migration moved labor from low-productivity agriculture to higher-productivity jobs in cities. An analogous reallocation took place with capital, but the shift was not geographic but rather from government-controlled enterprises to private ones. An important difference was that the overall capital stock was growing very rapidly—at about 10% per year throughout the reform period. So, the government did not have to actually take resources away from state firms. It just oversaw a process in which the private sector grew up around the state sector. When China joined the World Trade Organization in 2001, 65% of manufacturing assets were in the hands of state enterprises, with which they produced 50% of the output. Ten years later the state share had declined to 40% for assets and 25% for output.[10]

This shift was partly deliberate since in the 1990s China had legalized the domestic private sector and opened up to foreign private firms. But the extent of the shift was probably not deliberate. China's trade and investment reforms, combined with a robust global economy, led to an extraordinary surge in exports. Most of the direct exports came from foreign-invested firms, but they had quickly built backward linkages to Chinese private suppliers so that most of the value added in China's exports came from the domestic private sector. An export-oriented strategy was implicitly a pro–private sector strategy.

This phenomenon of an expanding private sector came to an end with the global financial crisis. The global economy and hence China's exports were weak for several years. This was compensated to some extent by rising consumption. Relative to exports, consumption relies more on services. Unlike manufacturing, China had left most of the important service sectors in the hands of state enterprises: telecom, airlines, media, finance. These state-dominated sectors all were increasing their share of the economy. Plus, the leadership decided that in manufacturing it would consolidate some of the state enterprises to make globally competitive firms in upstream sectors such as shipbuilding, steel, and chemicals. The trend toward a declining state share in manufacturing ended around 2010. As a result of these different factors, the state enterprise share of the total economy has been stable at around 25% for some time now.[11]

Part of China's response to the global financial crisis was also a massive program to stimulate the economy through infrastructure investment. This

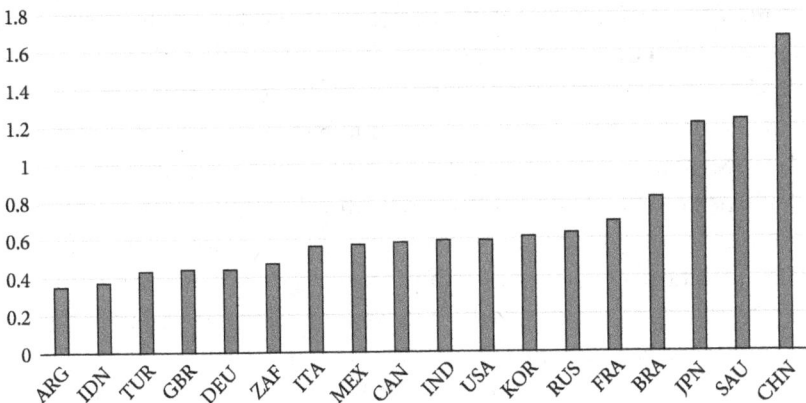

Figure 3.2 General Government Capital Stock, 2019 (Ratio to GDP, Purchasing Power Parity Terms)
Source: IMF Investment and Capital Stock Dataset, 2021

is also state-directed finance aimed primarily at transport and water projects. The big-ticket items were the development of a vast, high-speed rail network and huge South-North water transfer projects. China stands out among countries in having a huge infrastructure stock, about three times as large as in the United States relative to GDP (see Figure 3.2). The United States certainly has its infrastructure deficiencies, and much of China's infrastructure is impressive. But it now appears that China overinvested and that this is one factor in the growth slowdown. The initial lines of high-speed rail, for example, served densely populated corridors and are widely used; but more recent investments have extended the network into sparsely populated areas where there is little use. The water projects will be examined in detail in the next section, but in general they are expensive efforts that provide little benefit. It is telling that the Chinese government has overinvested in public capital and underinvested in public services. The agenda laid out in the previous section—of hukou reform, more services for migrants, more finance for rural communities, and care for the elderly—could be paid for by cutting back on wasteful infrastructure investment.

There is macro and micro evidence that the productivity of capital has declined in China. Some diminishing returns as capital is built up is natural, but in China's case the drop-off has been severe. At the macro level, the growth rate of the capital stock has been around 10% for a long time; for much of that period GDP growth was also at 10%. But with the same accumulation continuing, GDP growth has now declined to around 6% and looks likely to be headed lower. At the enterprise level, the real return to capital declined from 15% to 5% over the past twenty years. Comparative studies find capital productivity in private firms to be almost 100% higher than in state-owned ones; hence, one policy that would restore capital productivity would be to rein in state enterprises and favor the private sector, as occurred in the 1990s and 2000s.[12] China for the moment appears to be going in the other direction. As detailed in Arthur Kroeber's Chapter 4, the government has stepped up its industrial policy interventions aimed at seeding particular technologies such as semiconductors and electric vehicles.

Looking at the financial sector's role in allocating capital, China has a bank-led system in which four giant state-owned commercial banks dominate lending. State enterprises get a disproportionate share of financing, as do local government infrastructure projects. The capital markets are underdeveloped. Listing on the stock market is a bureaucratic affair that requires multiple approvals. It is difficult for private firms to list, and at the same time households are reluctant to put their savings into the market because it lacks transparency and seems like a gambling casino. Households keep considerable savings in the banks, which funds their lending. But households also have a striking 75% of their wealth in real estate.[13] Households hold apartments not just for living but also for investment and speculative purposes. This is probably another factor in the decline of capital productivity: empty apartments do not produce any GDP.

Real estate's role in the economy has increased over time. Its contribution to GDP has grown steadily from less than 10% at the beginning of housing reform in 1997 to over 30% in the past few years. As reference, the share in the United States reached 20% on the eve of the housing crisis in 2005, and in Spain the number hit 30% before its bubble burst. There are a number of indicators that signal the potential for a housing bubble in China that bursts. Most important, prices have gotten out of line with incomes. The ratio of house price to income is above 40:1 in Beijing and 30:1 in Shanghai, compared, for example, to less than 20:1 in London and closer to 10:1 in New York and San Francisco.[14] China's demographics are such that growth of the urban population will slow; and growth of household income is likely to slow as well as GDP growth moderates. Hence, the sustainability of the housing bubble in China is very much in question.

The underdevelopment of China's capital markets is clear from a number of metrics. The US and Chinese economies are now close in size (China's

GDP is 77% of the United States' at market exchange rates). Yet US capital markets are far larger: stock market capitalization is $26.2 trillion compared to China's $7.6 trillion (as of July 2021). The American bond market has $46 trillion capitalization, compared to $19 trillion for China. The differences arise because in the US firms that meet standards of profitability and transparency can go to the markets at their discretion, whereas in China access to stock and bond markets is at the discretion of regulators. China uses this discretion to help state enterprises get market funding and to favor certain private firms. The underdeveloped nature of these markets, along with the lack of transparency, means that capital markets are a minor choice for households in determining where to put their very considerable savings.

The reform agenda that would produce a more efficient allocation of capital is straightforward but politically difficult. Even with the consolidation that has taken place, there are still a lot of state enterprises owned at the local level, usually by city governments. China could reduce the number of sectors in which state-owned enterprises are allowed to operate and force local governments to divest others. Opening more sectors to foreign investment, as China has done with investment banking and electric vehicles, would be supportive as well. In the capital markets, firms that meet standards should be allowed to issue bonds and stocks. All of this is controversial because it would remove some of the government control over the allocation of capital. But it would give households savings vehicles other than real estate, thus diminishing the risk of a bubble; and by channeling resources to the most innovative and productive firms, it would be supportive of economic growth overall.

The Water Crisis

China in general is a natural resource–poor country relative to its population, and water is a classic example. With 20% of the world's population, China has only 6% of its renewable water resources. Renewable water per person is about 2,000 cubic meters per year, only one-quarter of the global average. Furthermore, the water is not distributed evenly around the country. Traditionally the North and South of the country are divided by the Yangzi River, with about half the population on each side. However, 80% of the water is in the South, leaving the North severely water stressed (see Figure 3.3).[15]

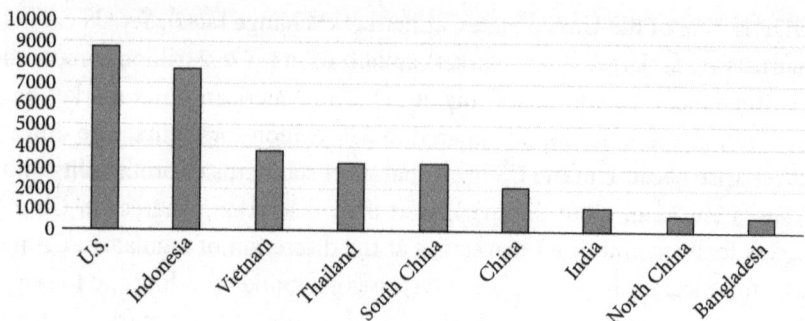

Figure 3.3 Renewable Water Resources per Person, 2017 (cubic meters)
Source: World Bank, World Development Indicators

Aside from natural shortage, China has been plagued by poor water policy. For a long time industrial and household waste was dumped untreated into rivers and lakes, resulting in severe water pollution. The Chinese government subsequently made an effort to require waste treatment and to invest in wastewater treatment plants for major cities. Still, as of 2017, 32% of monitored sections in major waterways were lower than class IV on China's five-point scale of water quality, indicating that the water was not suitable for human consumption. Among 5,100 monitored underground water sources, two-thirds were rated as poor or very poor. Similarly, six of nine major bays or coastal inlets have poor or very poor water quality. While China has made progress with treating wastewater from major cities and factories, there is still polluted runoff from small cities and from farms.[16]

While unpolluted water in China is extremely scarce, it is paradoxically not used very efficiently in production. China's water consumption per RMB 10,000 of industrial value added is two to three times higher than the average for upper-middle-income countries. In agriculture, the effective utilization rate of irrigation water is 0.52—that is, about half the water is completely wasted. Other upper-middle-income countries have utilization rates of 0.7 to 0.8.[17] One important factor in the inefficiency with which water is used is its low price. China has progressed from a near-zero price to prices that typically cover recurrent costs of water treatment and delivery. Pricing reform raised the rate of profit of urban water companies from −0.1% in 2005 to 1.6% in 2013. But such a low return means that prices do not reflect the enormous capital costs involved in water infrastructure, nor the scarcity cost of the resource.[18]

Water usage is also heavily affected by China's agricultural policies. The government aspires to be 95% self-sufficient in the grain that people eat. China imports vast quantities of soybeans to feed its swine herd, but the rice, wheat, and corn consumed by people is largely grown at home, with import quotas on grain and prices above the international market to ensure domestic production. These grains are water intensive, so the requirement of keeping most land for grain drives up the demand for water.[19] It is natural for a large country, a great power such as China, to want to produce most of its own food for security reasons. But modest fine-tuning of the policy would make a big difference for water use. For example, the government could allow farmers to shift more land from grain to water-saving crops such as various food trees, and import more rice, wheat, and corn (which is indirectly importing the water that China is scarce in). China would maintain a large agricultural sector, and land could be shifted back into grain if there were a war or other crisis in the global food trade. In the normal state, farmers would earn more income, and water use in agriculture would go down. In times of war or crisis, production could shift back to grain.

Climate change plays a key role in the water shortage crisis in China. For thousands of years, civilizations along the Yangzi and Yellow Rivers fed on the glacial meltwater from the Qinghai-Tibetan Plateau—also known as the "Third Pole." Once a stable source of river flow, the ice mass is now less capable of supplying glacial melt with fresh snow and ice, since global warming has raised the temperature of the glacial region by 3 to 3.5 degrees Celsius over the past half-century. Since the 1950s, 82% of China's glaciers have retreated and more than one-fifth of the ice cover has disappeared. Consequently, glacial runoff into the Yangzi alone has been reduced by 13.9% since the 1990s, lessening freshwater availability.[20]

Meanwhile, increasing temperatures have also changed atmospheric circulation. It has become more difficult for humid summer monsoons to reach northern and inland areas, resulting in more unreliable rainfall patterns. This abnormally dry weather has been experienced by Beijing in recent years: between October 2017 and February 2018, no precipitation, neither rain nor snow, was recorded in the metropolis. The 116-day drought is unprecedented.

As noted, the country's uneven resource distribution further exacerbates the scarcity problem: 80% of water is concentrated in South China, but the North is the core of some of the central government's national development plans. For instance, President Xi Jinping's JingJinJi Project initiated in 2014 integrates three heavily industrialized northern provinces—Beijing, Tianjin, and Hebei—as a single megalopolis to compete with other world-class economic regions such as the New York tri-state area. The estimated population of the regions combined is 130 million. Water is already insufficient in the North, and this intense development is only putting more pressure on water demand.

The pressing water shortage crisis has forced China to develop various water schemes to boost water availability in dry regions; the South-North Water Transfer Project (SNWTP) is the best known. Based on an idea traced back to the 1950s, the project is the largest and most expensive engineering work in the country; it is expected to cost $62 billion by completion in 2050, almost double the Three Gorges Dam Project. The SNWTP aims to alleviate the water shortage problem in northern China by moving water from the Yangzi River in the South through 1,500-kilometer-long canals. The East and Middle Routes—each taking ten years to build—have been in service since 2013 and 2014, respectively, and are capable of transferring 20.9 billion cubic meters of water each year. This amounts to less than 30 cubic meters per person in the North, less than a 4% increase in water availability; in other words, it is not transformative. The West Route is more complicated and is expected to be completed by 2050. However, the project raises environmental, social, and geopolitical challenges.[21]

As construction advances across the country, natural landscapes are harmed, leading to biodiversity loss. All three routes will change natural hydrology on an unprecedentedly large scale; the East Route raises the water level of the four lakes it passes through. There is also potential for southern aquatic species invading northern waters; increasing global temperatures are making waters at higher latitudes habitable for southern species, threatening the biodiversity of the water-receiving regions. The project may change hydrology and microclimate in the region; a ten-year study analyzing the potential climatic impacts of the Middle Route predicts that the sudden influx of water may alter local evaporation and precipitation rates by bringing more frequent convection (short and intense rain) to the area. Because rain patterns affect temperature, the researchers predict regional microclimates will be modified as the project progresses.[22]

The water supply of the Yangzi Basin in southern China relies on natural precipitation and glacial melt. As climate change accelerates Himalayan glacial retreat and brings abnormal weather, southern China may become equally vulnerable to water insecurity; already, southwest

China experienced a severe drought in 2011, which impacted the drinking and irrigation water of more than sixty million people. The SNWTP takes water from the Yangzi River and reduces its river discharge; a decline in groundwater may result in seawater flowing inland in dry seasons, contaminating the freshwater aquifers of the Yangzi Delta.

China's Southeast Asian neighbors are worried by China's response to its water issues. Chinese territory hosts the headwaters of many important regional rivers. For example, the Mekong originates from the Tibetan Plateau and flows through western China before reaching Myanmar, Laos, Thailand, Cambodia, and Vietnam. The Brahmaputra also flows across the boundary of China, Bangladesh, and India. Therefore, China's changes upstream can significantly impact the water of downstream countries.

China's neighbors fear its control of regional water resources and decry its reluctance to sign international agreements on cross-border water management. The country can seize water sources without any military force; because the rivers originate within its territory, they are seen as China's natural assets. The SNWTP reinforces this impression—despite the inclusion of transboundary rivers such as the Mekong, the Nu River, and the Brahmaputra in the West Route, China keeps the project unilateral without seeking input from the affected countries.

China's SNWTP is at best a short-term and partial solution, preventing the government from correcting man-made problems and creating new challenges in the intra- and international community. China's water policies link to growth in a number of ways. The giant investment in the South-North water transfer scheme is a classic example of a wasteful infrastructure project that provides little value. More important, the commitment to producing water-intensive grain in unsuitable locations consigns a large farmer population to low-productivity work. An alternative approach would involve more serious pollution cleanup efforts, economic pricing of water to encourage efficient use, and a shift of agricultural policy away from its emphasis on water-intensive grains to more focus on water-saving crops and more imports of grain. The issue of rural-urban migration raised earlier is also relevant to the water issue. As the country urbanizes, it would be rational for more of the population to shift to the South, which increasingly is where the water will be. With migration, a one-time movement of people will shift them from water-scarce to water-rich locales. With the South-North water diversion project, on the other hand, water has to be pumped every day in perpetuity to meet people's needs.

Energy and Climate Change

Energy is another area in which China is scarce in natural resources relative to its population. It is somewhat unfortunate that the only energy resource that China has in abundance is coal. In recent years China has gotten about two-thirds of its energy needs from coal, and 96% of that is mined domestically. China has major domestic petroleum and natural gas operations, but still limited relative to demand. In 2019, 56% of China natural gas use was domestically produced, and only 29% of its petroleum consumption was domestic. As a result, China is the world's largest importer of both petroleum and natural gas (having recently passed Japan for the number one spot in the gas market). Coal is the main energy source for industry and power generation. Petroleum is used primarily for powering vehicles. Natural gas is beginning to play a role in home heating and power generation, but starting from a low base. In setting energy policies China does not want to become too dependent on imported resources in case there is a disruption to world trade or, in the worst case, war. China has worked hard to diversify the sources of supply; it imports significant amounts of petroleum from Saudi Arabia, Russia, Iraq, the United Arab Emirates, Angola, and Brazil, for example.[23]

Aside from the reliance on coal, it is also the case that the Chinese economy is not very efficient in the use of energy. While the United States and China have economies of similar size, China uses much more energy: 151.6 quadrillion BTU in 2019 compared to American consumption of 100.4 quadrillion BTU. This partly reflects the stage of development, in which China has a large manufacturing sector and much construction activity, both of which tend to be energy intensive. The US economy is primarily services, so it can produce GDP with much less energy per unit than China. Aside from the structure of the economy, there are energy efficiency issues within each industry. In heavy sectors such as steel, aluminum, or chemicals, Chinese plants use more energy per unit of output than plants in the United States or Europe. These heavy sectors are dominated by state enterprises in China, and as noted above they tend to be much less efficient than private firms. China's different issues are all interrelated: more open, competitive sectors would result in more efficient firms and less energy use.

The combination of an energy-intensive development path and reliance on coal as the main energy source has severe environmental consequences.

In terms of local pollution, the heavy reliance on coal led Chinese cities to be among the most air-polluted in the world, with negative health consequences including premature death. Popular demand led to reductions in air pollution through the use of scrubbers on power plants and the shift from coal to gas in China's richest cities. In terms of global environment, China's energy path resulted in the country emerging as the world's leading emitter of greenhouse gases. In 2019 China accounted for 27% of global greenhouse gas emissions, more than the whole developed world combined.[24] Hence, China is one of the keys to reducing global emissions and limiting the global rise in temperature to 1.5 degrees Celsius.

China also has a strong incentive to cooperate because China will be the biggest loser from climate change according to the most recent report from the Intergovernmental Panel on Climate Change.[25] As noted in the previous section, Himalayan glaciers are melting, and the pace will depend on how rapidly and how far global temperatures rise. Another major exacerbating factor in Himalayan glacier melt is the soot that is emitted by industries in southwest China that drifts onto the glaciers in Tibet and increases dramatically the absorption of heat by the glaciers. If there is rapid melting, in the short run this will contribute to large seasonal variation in water flow in China's rivers and hence problems of flooding; in the long run the disappearance of the glaciers will create an even more severe water crisis in China and in South and Southeast Asian countries whose water flows primarily off the Tibetan Plateau. Temperature rise is also affecting rainfall in China, with more acute storms and flooding in the South and prolonged drought in the North. If greenhouse gas emissions are not curbed, the North China Plain could be hit by temperatures so extreme that they could make agriculture and human life there difficult. This raises serious questions about China's ability to feed itself in the future.

Aside from the issues of fresh water within China, there is the problem of sea level rise. Much of China's population and GDP is clustered in cities along the coast. Asian coasts are projected to see higher sea level rise than the global average. Chinese cities along the coast will be at increasing risk of storm surges and high waves caused by tropical cyclones of higher intensity. Updated projections find that, under a high emissions scenario, 340 million people worldwide live on land that will be underwater by mid-century. The greatest number of these people are in China. Much of Shanghai would be flooded in this scenario.[26] All the coastal cities will have to deal with flooding and saltwater incursion. Dealing with sea level rise will be an expensive proposition with needs for relocation and investments to manage the rise in water level.

As part of the United Nations process China has made various commitments on reducing carbon emissions. These are a good start but not enough to limit the temperature rise to no more than 1.5 degrees Celsius; they are more consistent with holding the rise to twice that level, for example, 3 degrees. The most important commitments from China are to reach zero net emissions by 2060 and to "strictly control" the increase in coal use over the next decade, reaching peak coal use and emissions by 2030.[27] Developed economies such as the United States, the European Union, and Japan have set a zero target by 2050. China's position is that it is a developing country and needs more time. But on this issue China itself is losing from the results of its policies. It would be in the country's interest to peak coal use immediately and start phasing it out, with the intention of reaching zero emissions by 2050. China has other good policies such as increasing targets for the share of power generated by renewables. China currently has more installed solar and wind power than any other country and plans to double this by 2030. The leaders see these technologies as important ones for the future and want to ensure that China has a prime place in developing and deploying them. China is also converting the vehicle fleet away from oil to electric, another technology that the leaders see as key to the future. (If the power is generated by coal, however, then shifting cars to electric does not make much difference, so the combination of moving away from coal and moving to electric vehicles is critical.)

The world as a whole is far from the path of emissions that would limit temperature rise to 1.5 degrees. With the current policies in place, emissions will not decline at all over the next few decades. The pledges that countries have made both pre- and post- Conference of the Parties 2026 (COP26) make a considerable difference and are estimated to result in cutting CO_2 emissions about in half by 2050, which is still not enough to reach the 1.5-degree target. To meet that target with confidence, emissions would have to start falling immediately and be down by about 40% by 2030. This is a global figure, but China is such a large part of this picture that such a global target would be impossible unless China starts reducing emissions immediately, rather than having them continue to grow over the next decade. The China path consistent with a global target of 1.5 degrees involves carbon emissions there starting to decline immediately and sharply declining until zero net emissions are reached in 2050.[28]

China in 2021 introduced a potentially powerful mechanism that would allow it to move efficiently to more stringent objectives for carbon reduction: an emission trading system (ETS). Initially the ETS involves 2,200 enterprises including all carbon-fueled power plants connected to the grid, as well as combined heat and power generators for large firms. Initially, emission permits are given out based on historical emissions and the total amount allowed leaves space for increasing emissions in the near term. This kind of gentle start-up is common in early stages of ETSs, and was experienced in Europe and California as they introduced emission trading. In China in the initial year of operation the carbon prices reflected this gentle start-up with prices per ton in the $6 to $9 range.[29]

Recent estimates indicate that prices would need to be closer to $100 per ton all around the world, and rising over time, if the 1.5-degree target is to be met. In China, the next steps for the ETS are clear: the sectoral coverage should be expanded beyond power to other energy-intensive sectors such as steel, aluminum, and chemicals; at least some permits should be auctioned off rather than given to incumbents; and most important, the total allowed emissions should be rapidly tightened, which will drive up the price and lead to a faster shift to a zero-carbon future. If eventually all permits are auctioned, this could become an important revenue source for the state to fund the social services highlighted in the first section as well as needed investments related to the environment.

The link from energy policy and climate change to economic growth is complicated. In the short run, a more ambitious program to reduce emissions could easily lead to slower economic growth as it involves replacing coal-fired plants that still have useful economic life. As we get toward the middle of the century, however, a 3-degree temperature rise is likely to have negative growth effects as resources are diverted to preventing storm surges and flooding and relocating people, water scarcity makes agriculture increasingly less productive, and extreme heat reduces human productivity.

Conclusion

Prospects for China's economy are mixed. On the plus side, it still has a lot of catch-up potential, a high savings rate to fund its investment, and trade agreements such as the Regional Comprehensive Economic Partnership that should provide better access to nearby economies. The convergence phenomenon only takes place among open economies, so it is important that China continue to open its economy to foreign trade and investment. Looking at the historical precedent of the other East Asian industrializers, China could continue to converge on the United States for at least another thirty years and reach 60% to 70% of US productivity. That would make China about three times larger than the United States in absolute economic size, so it would be a global superpower. It is not at all clear, however, that China will perform so well. First, the global environment is less favorable than that faced by the earlier industrializers, and tension in the US-China economic relationship is not likely to abate. Second, China has some distinct weaknesses that will work against convergence.

On the negative side, China's demographics will cause the overall labor force to shrink, which is a difficult environment for economic growth. While capital is abundant, the allocation shows a high degree of inefficiency, and correcting this will require a shift away from the state sector toward the private sector—a shift that is unpalatable for the current leadership. Instead of shifting resources to the private sector, the leaders have been cracking down on innovative firms. The country faces a water crisis that is only going to get worse with further industrial development and with climate change. China's energy policies are a prime cause of climate change.

A common theme running through these economic headwinds is that the Chinese economy is insufficiently market oriented. Labor productivity and wages are much higher in cities, especially the largest ones, compared to rural areas. Labor would naturally move more rapidly to cities if there were no restrictions. A market for land rights in rural areas would lead to more efficient agriculture and free up more labor to relocate to cities. A market-based financial system would allocate capital more efficiently and counteract diminishing returns. Firms that meet standards would go to the capital markets, without need for government "chops." A competitive banking system would lend more to private firms since they are more efficient and profitable. Water is similar to rural land: a system of clear property rights and market pricing would lead to more efficient use. China should naturally import more water-intensive grain, except that it is restricted by quotas. In the energy sectors, a realistic social price for carbon would lead to less coal use and more import of natural gas, more energy conservation, and more rapid expansion of renewables and electric vehicles.

China is unlikely to take all of the measures it needs to address its growth headwinds because they all involve less control for the state and more reliance on market mechanisms to allocate scarce resources. The current leadership has shown little inclination to use such mechanisms, relying instead on state and party control. Still, China is likely to do enough to grow at a medium pace for the next one to two decades. It only needs to grow at 4% to surpass the United States as the largest economy by about 2035. It would be surprising if they did not achieve that. The most likely scenario is that we are entering a period in which the US and Chinese economies will be about the same size. China may temporarily be modestly larger than the United States, but later in the century it would not be surprising if the United States returned as number one because the population difference will narrow significantly to more like 2:1 (from 4:1 today) and because the United States has many strengths such as a continual flow of immigrants, a vibrant private sector and capital markets, and abundant natural resources.

Notes

1. I would like to thank Louison Sall for excellent research assistance and Arthur Kroeber and Ken Lieberthal for helpful comments on an earlier draft.
2. R. Feenstra et al., "The Next Generation of the Penn World Tables," *American Economic Review* 105, no. 10, (October 2015): 3150–82 and updates.
3. R. Rajah and A. Leng, *Revising Down the Rise of China* (Lowy Institute, 2022).
4. T. Sasaki et al., "China's Long-Term Growth Potential: Can Productivity Convergence Be Sustained?," Working Paper Series (Bank of Japan, June 2021).
5. T. Huang, *Many Migrant Workers Are Excluded from China's Social Programs* (Peterson Institute for International Economics, 2020).
6. PopulationPyramid.net, *Population Pyramids of the World from 1950 to 2100: China*, December 2019.
7. C. Chen and C. Fan, "China's Hukou Puzzle: Why Don't Rural Migrants Want Urban Hukou?" *China Review* 16, no. 3 (2016): 9–39.
8. J. Yang et al., "An Analysis of Educational Inequality in China," *International Journal of Educational Development* 37 (July 2014): 2–10.
9. C. Bai and X. Lei, "Aging and Social Policy in an Era of Demographic Transition," in *China 2049: Economic Challenges of a Rising Global Power*, 69–92, ed. D. Dollar et al. (Brookings Press, 2020).
10. *Staff Report for the Article IV Consultation* (International Monetary Fund, December 2021).
11. A. Batson, *The State Never Retreats* (Gavekal Dragonomics, Deep China Report, October 2020).
12. *Staff Report for the Article IV Consultation.*
13. Y. Huang, "Constructing a Modern Financial System for China's Future," 113–34, in *China 2049: Economic Challenges of a Rising Global Power*, ed. D. Dollar et al. (Brookings Press, 2020).
14. *Rebalancing Act: From Recovery to High-Quality Growth* (World Bank, December 2021).
15. K. Leung, *Tackling China's Water Shortage Crisis,* Earth.org, July 2021. https://earth.org/tackling-chinas-water-shortage-crisis/.
16. *China: A Watershed Moment for Water Governance* (World Bank, 2018).
17. Ibid.
18. R. Rutkowski, *The Economics of H2O: Water Price Reform in China* (PIIE, 2019).
19. H. Feng and B. Li, "What Is the Redline Water Withdrawal for Crop Production in China?," *Sustainability* 12, no. 10, 4188 (2020).
20. S. Inglis, *Yangtze Headwaters Under Threat* (China Water Risk Organization, 2016).
21. K. Leung, *Tackling China's Water Shortage Crisis.*

22. F. Chen and Z. Xie, "Effects of Inter-Basin Water Transfer on Regional Climate: A Case Study of the Middle Route of the South-to-North Water Transfer Project in China," *Journal of Geophysical Research* 115, no. D11 (2010).
23. *China* (US Energy Information Administration, September 2020).
24. K. Larsen et al., *China's Emissions Exceeded Emissions from Developed Countries* (Rhodium Group, May 2021).
25. *Sixth Assessment Report* (Intergovernmental Panel on Climate Change, 2022).
26. S. Kulp and B. Strauss, "New Elevation Data Triple Estimates of Global Vulnerability to Sea-Level Rise and Coastal Flooding," *Nature Communications* 10, 4844 (2019).
27. *China: Country Summary* (Climate Action Tracker, November 2021).
28. *U.S. and China Climate Goals: Scenarios for 2030 and Mid-Century* (Asia Society Policy Institute, November 2020).
29. C. Busch et al., *Next Steps for China's Carbon Emissions Trading System to Improve Efficiency, Achieve Climate Goals* (Energy Innovation Policy and Technology, April 2022).

4

The "Venture Capital State"

Implications for China's Growth

Arthur R. Kroeber

Defining the likely evolution of the US-China strategic rivalry—the principal task of this book—requires judgments about how fast China's economy will continue to grow, and how China's leaders will use their economic power.[1] China's economic record since 1980 has been enviable: real gross domestic product (GDP) growth averaged around 10% a year from 1980 through 2012, and over the following decade it averaged around 6.5% a year. China has moved from backwater to the world's second largest economy, biggest manufacturer, and biggest trading nation. Its growth has enabled eight hundred million people to move out of extreme poverty, perhaps the single greatest improvement in human welfare in history.

Yet this growth also created significant stress in the global political and economic order. China lies outside the US alliance structure, has an authoritarian political system that sets it apart from the vast majority of upper-income countries, has an unusually high degree of state involvement in its economy, and has shown strong interest in influencing economies in the developing world through its Belt and Road Initiative of infrastructure finance.

These three facts—sustained fast growth, systemic difference, and rising global influence—have led some to worry that China's rise poses a threat to the stability of the global order. The specific concerns are that China's state-directed economy undermines a sense of fair competition; China could use its growing economic influence to export its authoritarian model of governance; and China's economic, political, and technological clout could undermine US leadership. These fears have mounted even though China achieved its growth in significant part by integrating with global economic institutions and practices.[2]

Arthur R. Kroeber, *The "Venture Capital State"*. In: *Not Just Another Cold War*. Edited by: Bård Nikolas Vik Steen, Oxford University Press. © Oxford University Press (2025). DOI: 10.1093/9780197799932.003.0005

The anxieties provoked by China's systemic differences with the US-led international order cannot be wished away. There is no realistic prospect that China will materially change its political or economic structures any time soon. Nor is it reasonable to expect that Chinese leaders will scale back their ambitions to translate economic strength into international influence. There is, however, much uncertainty about whether China will be able to maintain rapid growth in the coming decades, and what the structure of growth will be. In the most optimistic scenario, China's trend growth would slow to around 5% in the coming decade. This outcome would be roughly consistent with the growth performance of South Korea and Taiwan in the decade after they reached China's current level of real per capita income.

But achieving even that level of growth will require appropriate policies. On current policy settings, China risks an even larger growth slowdown in the coming decade, perhaps to below the 4% annual average that will be required for it to surpass the United States as the world's largest economy by the mid-2030s. The reason is that China's growth strategy relies too much on investments in technology-intensive industries and not enough on policies to improve the efficiency of resource use. Unless policies are changed, the likely consequence is that China will succeed in fostering some globally competitive technology industries (e.g., in semiconductors and new energy) but fail to generate the economy-wide productivity growth needed to sustain high rates of GDP growth. Strategic competition with the United States will persist under either the low- or the high-growth scenario, but the contours of that competition will differ greatly depending on China's economic trajectory.

Constraints on China's Growth, and Beijing's Policy Response

The basic constraints on China's growth are admirably summarized in David Dollar's contribution to this volume.[3] The labor force, which grew strongly for many years, is now shrinking as the population ages and (later this decade) begins to fall. In the past twenty years China relied heavily on increases to its physical capital stock (infrastructure, housing, and industrial plant) to drive growth, but the returns on these investments are now in steep decline. The rate of overall productivity growth has also been falling for many years.

Policy makers in the Chinese Communist Party (CCP) have long been aware of these problems and have evolved a range of strategies to sustain growth and national strength in a period of demographic decline and falling returns to investment in housing and infrastructure. The core strategy is one of intensive technological upgrading, in which the state identifies priority sectors and then creates a range of incentives for both public and private capital to invest in those sectors. The underlying idea is that technological upgrading will deliver the productivity gains needed to sustain high-speed economic growth.

On closer inspection, this strategy has not one but at least three objectives:

1) *Productivity improvement in the interests of maximizing economic growth.*
2) *Technological upgrading and the maintenance of a large manufacturing share of GDP.* Economic policy makers not only want to boost China's technological level but also tend to define "technology" essentially as hardware products or systems and believe that maintaining a high manufacturing share of GDP is necessary for technological progress, social stability, and national power.
3) *Self-reliance in key technologies.* China remains heavily reliant on imported technologies, notably but by no means exclusively semiconductors. Explicit and implicit technology sanctions by the United States since 2016 have crippled several large Chinese companies, have prevented Chinese firms from acquiring technology by cross-border mergers or acquisitions, and may impede technology-related investments by international companies in China. Facing ever-tighter constraints on their ability to import technology, Chinese leaders are increasingly focused on developing domestic substitutes.

One risk is that these different objectives may come into conflict. To the degree that China's strategy is one of "technological upgrading," rather than productivity per se, policy makers may tend to focus on industrial policy to the exclusion of more general efforts to boost productivity. These more general policies include market regulation, competition and bankruptcy rules that would speed the exit of unprofitable firms, and the development of a more efficient financial system that would direct capital to its most effective uses. Policy makers could also fall prey to a kind of magical thinking in which "high technology" automatically produces productivity growth.

In reality, the production of technology—which should be defined broadly to include not just semiconductors, advanced machinery, and other physical objects but any sort of know-how that makes things work better—does not increase productivity by itself, but only does so when conditions in the broader economy allow for its rapid diffusion and efficient and effective use.

Similarly, self-reliance may not be consistent with the productivity and technology-upgrading goals. Self-sufficiency could be achieved by adopting just-good-enough or second-best technologies that lie well behind the global technological frontier. By definition, these technologies should be produced by "reliable" companies that are domestically owned, immune to acquisition, and protected from competition. Without the discipline imposed by the threat of bankruptcy, takeover, or diminished profits, such companies are unlikely to maximize either productivity or technological competence. These are the well-known pitfalls of an "import substitution" strategy (practiced by India and many Latin American countries through the 1980s), in which technology imports are blocked in favor of locally produced goods.[4]

To this list of concerns we may add one more factor, which is not strictly speaking part of China's development agenda but could constrain its economic success. This is the evident desire of President Xi Jinping to regulate the economy far more tightly. This intent has been expressed in several major campaigns during Xi's tenure: an anti-corruption drive that began as soon as he took power in 2013 and which has led to the punishment of tens of thousands of officials; a financial derisking campaign that began in late 2016 and continues under the slogan of preventing the "disorderly expansion of capital"; a crackdown on major internet companies that began in late 2020; and a 2021 call for China's economic goal to be "common prosperity," or equitable growth.

Each of these campaigns can be justified in various ways. The overall goal of creating clearer, more consistently enforced regulations, and reducing the space for regulatory arbitrage and undue financial risk-taking, is appropriate for China's stage of development. So too is the objective of inclusive growth, where income gains are distributed equitably. But these campaigns have been enforced in an indiscriminate and heavy-handed way, and have also been used to punish Xi's political enemies, curb the power of large private companies, and increase the state's influence throughout the economy. Taken together, they can be viewed either as a needed corrective to decades of unregulated growth that spawned corruption, inequality, waste of resources, and financial risks[5] or as overreach by a government that has decided to prioritize political control over economic growth. This drive for control betrays a suspicion of bottom-up innovation driven by response to consumer or private sector preferences—rather than the industrial policy goals of the state—and a reluctance to permit a much-needed liberalization of the financial system.

The rest of this chapter will examine in more detail the challenge of raising productivity, the CCP's economic strategy, and the chances that this strategy will succeed in raising productivity, raising China's technological level, and increasing national self-sufficiency in strategic sectors.

The Productivity Challenge

China's basic economic challenge is that the forces that drove growth over the past decades are fading, and new sources of growth must be found. This problem can be expressed in various ways, but for the purposes of this chapter we will describe it with a simple growth accounting equation, in which annual GDP growth is the sum of three things: the growth in the **labor** force, the growth in the capital stock, and total factor productivity (TFP).[6] Capital investment can be further divided into business investment, housing investment, and public investment (mainly infrastructure). TFP is not a direct measurement (like total output per hours worked), but a residual: it is the amount of GDP growth left over once the capital and labor inputs have been computed.

Calculating the capital and productivity contributions to growth requires some assumptions; as a result, there is a range of estimates for China's historic rates of productivity growth. But in recent years several studies have converged around a broad story about the changes in China's economic growth since it began market-oriented reforms in 1979.[7]

In the first decade or so (1978–1989), China enjoyed massive gains from both labor and productivity. The labor force grew quickly because a population boom of babies born from the early 1960s to the mid-1970s came of working age and found plenty of employment opportunities in the newly liberalized agriculture, manufacturing, and construction sectors. Productivity grew both because workers shifted from relatively low-productivity rural occupations to higher-productivity urban jobs (e.g., in export manufacturing) and because control of production shifted from relatively inefficient state enterprises to relatively more efficient private or quasi-private companies. During this period, new capital investment played a supporting role. This pattern roughly continued in the 1990s, with a strong burst of productivity growth following the resumption of economic reforms in late 1991, which led to a wave of foreign investment in manufacturing.

The 1997 Asian financial crisis, whose ripple effects hurt China, spurred a spate of reforms that led to strong productivity gains. These included a massive restructuring of state-owned enterprises that opened up more space for private firms; urban housing privatization that unleashed pent-up demand for physical housing and housing services; financial reforms that freed banks to finance new industries; and China's December 2001 entry into the World Trade Organization, which forced domestic market liberalization and set off another big wave of foreign investment.

But China's growth equation changed in two important ways in the 1997–2008 decade. First, the contribution from employment growth fell dramatically, as the absorption of surplus rural labor into the modern economy neared completion. And second, the contribution from physical capital investment soared. This reflected both the housing boom and a massive program of infrastructure investments—expressways, ports, and telecoms and power networks—launched to stimulate growth in the wake of the Asian crisis and to support the strong industrial growth of the early 2000s.

Following the 2008 global financial crisis, the equation shifted again, with a sharp drop in productivity growth and even more reliance on physical capital, as annual construction of urban housing more than doubled and the central and local governments resorted to infrastructure spending to cushion the impact of every economic downturn. The changes in China's growth equation over the past four decades are summarized in Table 4.1.

Table 4.1 Composition of GDP growth in China, 1978–2017

Annual percentage point contribution, average over decade			
	1978–1987	1988–1997	1998–2007	2008–2017
---	---	---	---	---
Labor	2.9	2.8	0.8	0.1
Human capital*	0.7	0.8	0.4	0.4
Physical capital	2.3	2.8	5.5	6.4
Productivity	4.1	3.6	3.3	1.3
Total GDP growth	**10.1**	**10.0**	**10.0**	**8.3**

*Health and education.
Source: World Bank *Innovative China: New Drivers of Growth* (2019).

Put another way, in the first twenty years of China's reform era, about 40% of economic growth came from productivity and less than 30% came from additions of physical capital. In the decade after the Asian crisis, the productivity contribution fell to about a third and the capital share rose to 60%. And in the decade after the 2008 global crisis, capital spending accounted for nearly 80% of China's growth, while the productivity share fell to just 16%. Preliminary data show that in the years since 2017, the pattern has intensified, with virtually all of China's growth coming from capital spending.[8]

Two other features of the post-2008 decade bear mention: debt and the structure of investment. From the late 1990s until 2008, China's overall debt-to-GDP ratio rose only modestly, in part because GDP growth was so fast. But from 2008 to 2018, the national debt ratio nearly doubled, from around 140% to 260% of GDP (it now stands at close to 300%).[9] This rise reflects both the increased reliance of local governments and state-owned enterprises on debt to fund big capital projects, and rising consumer debt, mainly mortgages. China's debt-to-GDP ratio is not excessive by the standards of advanced economies, but it is quite high relative to China's level of income. Since late 2016, policy makers have put a high priority on controlling debt and reducing financial risk. The desire to prevent the debt-to-GDP ratio from rising much further is thus an important constraint on policy: rapid credit growth can no longer be permitted.

The second feature is that the structure of physical capital formation has shifted dramatically away from the business sector and toward housing and infrastructure (see Table 4.2). As recently as 2010, annual capital spending was about evenly split between business investment and housing/infrastructure. But by the second half of the 2010s, housing/infrastructure investment was more than double business investment, which had actually fallen as a share of GDP. This was a problem: numerous studies show that the return on investment on infrastructure is far lower than in past decades, and the rate of housing construction that prevailed until 2021 was well above the underlying rate of demand. Virtually all productivity growth in the economy comes from the business sector, while the contribution from housing and infrastructure (which was substantially positive before the global financial crisis) may now be negative.[10]

In 2022–2023 housing construction volumes fell by about half, prompted by a credit tightening whose aim was to cut construction down closer to

Table 4.2 Contributions to capital formation

% of GDP	2010	2015–2019
Business	21%	15%
Housing and infrastructure	24%	31%

Source: Adapted from R. Rajah and A. Leng. *Revising Down the Rise of China* (Lowy Institute March 2022) and R. Herd Policy Research Working Paper No. 9317 (World Bank 2020).

the underlying level of real demand and to shrink real estate's share of the economy. (Including both direct and indirect effects, residential real estate probably accounted for about 25% of GDP before the recent crash.) This massive housing contraction, combined with an otherwise anemic recovery after the pandemic, led to predictions that China's era of rapid growth has come to a permanent end and that it risks a "lost decade" similar to Japan in the 1990s.[11]

Such forecasts are premature. For one thing, China's level of income and demographic structure more closely resemble Japan in 1980, not 1990 when the "lost decade" began. There are other major structural differences, and it could be argued that China's property crash is an effort by Beijing to avoid Japan's fate by forcing the sector to contract before a naturally occurring collapse generated even worse economic damage. Nonetheless, it is clear that a major source of past growth has been permanently shut down. The challenge for the future is clear. For China to maintain rapid GDP growth of 4% to 5% a year in the coming years, much more growth needs to come from productivity. Yet productivity growth in the past decade has declined sharply. How can this trend be reversed?

The Development Strategy: A "Venture Capital State"

In response to this challenge, economists inside and outside of China typically recommend[12] a broad set of reforms, encompassing, among other things:

- a more aggressive shift from state to private ownership, especially in services;
- reforms to *hukou* (residence permit) and land rights to raise rural incomes, improve labor mobility, and drive consumption;

- liberalization of the financial sector to increase the role of capital markets; and
- fiscal reforms, notably the imposition of a property tax, hardening the budget constraints for local governments, and improving the efficiency of central-local transfers.

During the past decade, piecemeal efforts have been made in many of these areas, but overall progress has been modest. State ownership of the economy has remained almost constant at 25% to 30% of GDP since the late 1990s, exposing a preference of the CCP for a level of state ownership far higher than any advanced economy.[13] While the private sector remains active and vigorous, especially in manufacturing, the harsh crackdown on internet platform companies since 2020 has reinforced a pattern of state constraints on large-scale private firms and on economic activity driven by response to consumer demand. Reforms to *hukou* and rural land rights have been minimal, and there remains a focus on state-guided population movement. Financial liberalization was aggressive from 2009 to 2016, but since then it has gone into reverse, thanks in part to the campaign to reduce financial risk. While risk reduction was needed, the result was excessive centralization of finance in state-controlled banks. Some fiscal reforms were carried out in 2014–2015, but the basic problems remain entrenched: local governments rely too much on land sales revenue and enjoy "soft budget constraints"—that is, the expectation that any deficits they run will ultimately be funded by the central government.

Instead of emphasizing these kinds of reforms, Xi Jinping's government has focused on industrial policy, on the theory that productivity growth will be driven by heavy investment in a swathe of high-technology sectors. The ultimate aim was articulated in the 2016 "Outline of the National Innovation-Driven Development Strategy":

> By 2050, China shall be established as a world science and technology innovation superpower. . . . [T]echnology and talent will become the most important strategic resources for national strength, and innovation will become a core factor in policy formulation and system arrangements. Increases in labor productivity and social productive force will rely mainly on technological progress and overall innovation.[14]

To achieve this goal, China has adopted an approach that we can loosely compare to that of a venture capital fund. The state identifies a set of sectors that offer high potential returns, puts some of its own money into those sectors, but also tries to mobilize capital from other sources: private and state companies, and domestic and foreign institutional investors (the "limited partners" in this analogy). At least in principle the winners in each sector will be determined by market competition, not state favoritism. An implicit assumption is that not every single sectoral bet needs to pay off for the strategy to succeed. Just as a private venture capital fund might back twenty companies in the hopes of finding one big success, state goals can be achieved if a sufficient proportion of sectors produce high returns and big companies, even if some sectors see little or no progress. In theory, this is not a return to central planning, but a model that harnesses a large and vibrant market in the service of strategic goals set by the state.[15]

This model did not spring fully formed out of the heads of planners during the Xi Jinping era. Rather, as Barry Naughton has pointed out, it built upon a series of earlier plans and strategies that, starting in 2006, gradually put industrial policy at the center of China's development strategy.

The initial building block was the 2006 Medium- and Long-Term Plan for Science and Technology Development, which laid out a strategy for developing China's domestic technological capacities and introduced the goal of "indigenous innovation" (*zizhu chuangxin*), which implied an intent to reduce China's reliance on imported technology. This plan also unveiled sixteen "mega-projects," in which the state would directly invest tens of billions of dollars to develop major technologies. These included high-end semiconductors and machine tools, nuclear power plants, a GPS-style satellite navigation system, passenger aircraft, hypersonic missiles, and health and environmental protection systems.

This was followed by the 2010 strategic emerging industries (SEI) initiative, which identified seven high-tech areas for priority support. This list was later expanded to eight areas comprising twenty major industries, including semiconductors, commercial aircraft and satellites, renewable energy technology, biopharmaceuticals, and new materials.[16]

These strategies and commitments were already in place before Xi Jinping's government took power in 2013. Under Xi, they have been deepened and refined. The first refinement came with the Made in China 2025 program announced in 2015, which built on the SEI target industry list, and also laid out objectives for improving the efficiency of Chinese manufacturing in general, for instance, through more aggressive adoption of information technology. The plan was accompanied by a set of ambitious targets for Chinese firms' share of domestic and global technology markets. This element proved controversial and was widely viewed in the United States and Europe as evidence of intent by Beijing to use subsidies and forced technology transfer to enable Chinese companies to wrest market share from Western incumbents. Responding to this criticism, China removed references to "Made in China 2025" from official documents, but the underlying policies remain in place.

Two other refinements relate not to target sectors but to concept and implementation. At the conceptual level, the Innovation-Driven Development Strategy of 2016 put technological upgrading at the heart of long-run economic development and made clear that the main source of future productivity gains should be technology, rather than structural or market reforms.

At the implementation level, funding sources were diversified, most visibly with the launch of government-sponsored industrial guidance funds, beginning with a US$29 billion semiconductor fund in 2014. The idea behind these funds was that, instead of the government directly subsidizing companies in target sectors, it could seed professionally managed funds. These funds would have a mandate to raise money from other sources, invest the proceeds in a range of technology companies, and bear responsibility for delivering a profit on the whole portfolio. Within a few years more than two thousand such funds were set up by central and local governments, with a combined—and quite implausible—fundraising target of over US$1.7 trillion, or 11% of 2020 GDP.

The actual funds raised were, most likely, far below these aspirational figures. Outside the semiconductor sector[17] (and perhaps not even there), we have little firm evidence on what these funds have directly achieved.[18] The larger point is that these funds are just part—and not the biggest part—of a web of support for favored industries, which includes tax incentives, access to finance and land at below-market prices, and implicit transfers from private sector companies. This total support has recently been estimated at around 1.8% of GDP annually from 2017 to 2019, three to four times higher than comparable spending in other major economies.[19] The guidance funds also serve a signaling function, incentivizing corporations and the domestic capital markets to invest more in the sectors preferred by the government.[20]

The concepts of "technology" and "innovation" embedded in these various strategy and policy documents are overwhelmingly biased to the production of physical technology-intensive goods. Virtually no acknowledgment is given to the production of intangibles or innovation that is driven by consumer demand and results in improved delivery of services such as finance, health care, or education.

This bias is a feature and not a bug of Chinese policy under Xi. The Fourteenth Five-Year Plan, published in March 2021, set a target of keeping the manufacturing share of GDP "basically stable" (at around 26%, higher than any other major economy), bucking a long-term trend of decline.[21] Any doubt over the primacy of physical production was dispelled by the massive regulatory assault on consumer internet firms beginning in November 2020. It began with the cancellation of a US$35 billion initial public offering by China's leading financial technology firm, Ant Financial, which would have been the largest initial public offering in history. But it soon expanded to encompass tighter regulations on virtually all of China's major online platforms, in sectors including e-commerce, ride hailing, entertainment, and education. Some sectors faced modest adjustments, but others suffered major restrictions that impaired their long-term profitability, and the for-profit online education sector was shut down entirely. By mid-2022, the share prices of most of the surviving firms were down 50% to 80% from their precrackdown levels. As of April 2024, a few names had staged modest recoveries, but the internet is no longer seen as a strong growth sector.

This campaign was interpreted by some as an attempt to reassert state control over the economy and squash the private sector. This is not true: most of China's private sector lies outside the internet, was unaffected by the crackdown, and by some measures continues to increase its share of the economy.[22] Less debatable is that, to the degree that the state guides China's economic development, it offers massive encouragement and support to physical production, while curbing the fastest-growing consumer service sectors.

A final observation is that the "venture capital state" model is tied to a somewhat amorphous economic strategy called "dual circulation," which was announced in 2020, evidently in response to the trade tariffs and technology restrictions launched by the US government under President Donald Trump. The general idea is that China should continue to take advantage of "external circulation" (trade and investment flows with the rest of the world) but should hedge against an increasingly hostile international environment by putting more emphasis on "internal circulation" (domestic production and demand). In practice, this has meant more policy support for technology hardware firms, especially in critical areas such as semiconductors where China is especially vulnerable to potential export controls by the United States. It is, in effect, a policy to create self-sufficient domestic supply chains in strategic sectors.[23]

To sum up, China's leaders have adopted a development model targeting the manufacture of technology-intensive goods as the main source of future productivity growth. This policy extends and intensifies policy trends dating back at least to 2006. The conception of "technology" is relatively narrow, focusing almost exclusively on the production of physical goods, and policy makers have adopted the goal of keeping the manufacturing share of GDP high. The government has built financing mechanisms that bear some formal resemblance to venture capital funds and has encouraged the participation of capital markets and private companies. But the strategy assigns a large role to top-down guidance from state policy makers and a smaller one to bottom-up innovation. Finally, the technology-upgrading drive is closely tied to policies to create self-sufficiency in key technologies.

This strategy thus addresses three goals: technological upgrading for its own sake, raising productivity growth, and achieving greater self-reliance in technologies deemed to be strategically important. The question we now want to answer is how successful the strategy will be in meeting these goals.

Assessment of the Development Strategy

The discussion so far should suggest many reasons to be skeptical of China's "venture capital state" strategy. Yet it is worth first acknowledging the positive side of the ledger.

First, the last three decades have been littered with critiques that China's economic policies were too top-down and statist, and insufficiently focused on market-oriented reforms. In hindsight, these critiques consistently underestimated China's growth potential, innovative capacity, and ability to productively absorb capital inputs. China's size, complexity, and flexible governance mean that formally statist policies may often leave plenty of room for bottom-up dynamism. Pessimistic forecasts may be more firmly grounded today, but they have a bad record. An optimistic case for China's growth—say, 5% annual GDP growth for the next decade, putting it on track to surpass the United States as the world's biggest economy in the early 2030s—can plausibly be made on the grounds that China's TFP is still less than half that of the United States, so plenty of catch-up potential remains, and that the gains from investing more physical capital may not yet be exhausted.[24]

Second, Chinese industrial development can be effective—in terms of creating new industries, companies, and markets—even if it is very wasteful.[25] This pattern is arguably evident in renewable energy sectors such as solar and wind power, batteries, and electric vehicles, all of which were on the original SEI list of 2010. To promote these industries, China has deployed hundreds of billions of dollars of subsidies. The financial rate of return on these subsidies may be quite low, but Chinese firms are now global leaders in all segments of the solar value chain and dominant at home in wind power. China has by far the world's largest electric vehicle market—making it an irresistible lure for investment for leading-edge companies such as Tesla— and its battery firms are globally competitive. One key point here is that even if China's annual GDP growth slows markedly, say, to 2% to 3% in the next several years, its impact on global supply chains and patterns of industrial development could still be very large, due to its demonstrated ability to scale up new industries.

Third, it is perfectly legitimate, and perhaps wise, for the Chinese government to craft a development strategy with goals other than simply maximizing TFP. Chinese leaders observe that the United States—which in the name of efficient capital allocation allowed the manufacturing share of its economy to fall roughly by half since 1990, in favor of finance and internet services—is riven by social problems such as rising income inequality, political polarization, and drug addiction. Meanwhile countries such as Germany and South Korea, which have striven to maintain a larger industrial base, display more equality and social stability. The industrial policies adopted by the Biden administration, which explicitly reject the past focus on market-led financial efficiency in favor of state-led investment in manufacturing, are a tacit admission that China's growth model may be worth emulating.[26]

All that said, on net China's development strategy now looks more flawed than at any point in the last quarter-century. In the most general terms, China's economic success has stemmed from the CCP's ability to balance its two principal objectives: (1) political control and social stability and (2) rapid economic growth. At most times one could easily identify high-growth sectors that were being liberalized: agriculture in the 1980s; small-scale manufacturing in the 1990s; housing, automobiles, and telecom services in the 2000s; and finance and internet-based consumer services in the 2010s. Today, virtually every major sector is subject to tighter regulation. And after years of taking a relatively hands-off approach to private companies, the CCP is trying to institutionalize political channels of control such as party committees, or "golden shares" that confer review or veto rights over key business decisions.[27]

More concretely, the "venture capital state" strategy focuses heavily on production of technological goods and embeds an assumption that this in and of itself will generate the productivity gains needed to sustain high-speed growth. Most recent research, however, suggests that the lion's share of productivity gains come not from the production of high-tech goods but from the market mechanisms that (1) enable these goods to be diffused and deployed effectively and (2) ensure that resources can be reallocated to their most efficient users.

Of particular significance are competition and bankruptcy rules that enable high rates of new company formation and dissolution. China scores well on company formation: the number of business entities more than doubled—from 60 million to 140 million—in the six years after a 2014 reform that lowered barriers to company registration. (It is worth noting that the large majority of these are individually owned microenterprises; the increase in new corporations has been much slower.)

China thus offers a very dynamic environment for start-ups; but once companies get bigger, the picture gets cloudier. In advanced economies, the majority of business sector productivity gains come either from the exit of unprofitable firms or from the reallocation of resources from less productive to more productive firms. One careful study of China's manufacturing sector found that the productivity contribution from market exit and reallocation of resources is essentially zero.[28] It will be very hard for China to stop the slide in its productivity growth, let alone reverse it, unless it can create more vigorous ways of culling unprofitable firms from the market and reallocating resources from less efficient to more efficient firms.

The political obstacles are immense. As noted above, the overall state share of economic output has remained static at 25% to 30% since the late 1990s, even though study after study have shown that private firms deliver far higher returns on assets and equity than their state competitors. The inexorable corollary is that state firms consume resources (finance, energy, land) at a rate very disproportionate to their output. Even in sectors (such as manufacturing) where the aggregate private sector share of output is growing, the largest companies remain overwhelmingly state owned. Aggressively promoting resource reallocation and the exit or downsizing of unprofitable firms would inevitably hit the state sector very hard, and there is no evidence that the CCP leadership has any appetite to give up the control over resource allocation, economic direction, and political patronage that would come with such a trimmed-down state sector.

The state's role as a resource gatekeeper is especially vexing. The decade after the global financial crisis saw a wave of financial innovation that spawned a host of nonstate payment and funding channels, many of them focused on the needs of consumers, smaller enterprises, and rural households. The campaigns against financial risk and internet service companies were justified by real regulatory concerns, but their net effect has been to halt financial innovation and consolidate control of financial flows in large financial institutions that are almost entirely state owned, and hence subject to political influence in their lending decisions. State-owned banks and insurance companies are also the main buyers of corporate bonds. State domination of the financial sector is another reason that reallocation of capital from less to more efficient users will not likely be a big driver of productivity growth in the coming decade.

The development strategy that I have labeled (with some poetic license) the "venture capital state" has no obvious solutions to these problems; the resemblance between China's model and real-life venture capital is more formal than substantive. The industrial guidance funds, superficially modeled on venture capital funds, are basically dressed-up subsidy channels, lacking most of the disciplines and incentives that made venture capital such an important part of the American innovation engine. These include the staging of financial support based on clear milestones (and the withdrawal of funding when milestones are not met), the venture capital's contribution of not just finance but also management expertise and connections to networks of entrepreneurs in distantly related fields that can spur unexpected innovations, and the willingness to finance genuinely eccentric or disruptive ideas that come with some cost to established industries or social arrangements.[29]

My overall assessment is therefore that, absent complementary reforms in finance and competition policy, China's industrial policy strategy will probably not generate much of a productivity boost. The current policy trajectory most likely will lead China on a path of steadily (though not catastrophically) declining GDP growth.

The outlook for the strategy's second goal—technological upgrading—is more optimistic. Over the past fifteen years China's industrial policies have contributed to some notable successes, including the renewable energy examples cited above; the Beidou global navigation system, a credible alternative to GPS; integrated circuit design (though not fabrication); nuclear power plant technology, of which China is now poised to pass Russia as the main global exporter; satellite and space technology; and hypersonic missiles. Given the abundance of financial resources, the country's massive and growing technical talent pool, and China's unique economies of scale, it is reasonable to assume that Chinese firms will gain mastery in other technological areas as well.

On the self-sufficiency goal, there is little doubt that China will be able to produce domestic substitutes for some of the goods it now imports. But the more complex the technology, the less able China will be to achieve full self-reliance. The production chains for most technology-intensive goods are now highly dispersed around the world and rely on specialized components and materials that tend to be produced in countries with strong comparative advantages or resource endowments that cannot be replicated elsewhere.

Taking semiconductors as an (admittedly extreme) example, the full value chain—which encompasses specialized materials, chemicals, customized fabricating equipment, design capabilities, software, and capital-intensive manufacturing plants that require huge amounts of engineering know-how to run properly—is spread over more than a dozen countries. The United States, which has the most comprehensive capabilities in this industry, accounts for less than half the global value chain (China has about 5%) and remains entirely dependent on other countries in several key areas.[30]

From a productivity standpoint, this dependency is a good thing. Making use of goods and services best made elsewhere frees a country to specialize in the things it can make most efficiently. More technically, a recent International Monetary Fund study found that as much as a quarter of China's productivity growth in the early 2010s came from spillovers of technology developed in other countries, notably the United States and Japan. (In absolute terms, the US benefit from technology developed outside the United States was even higher.)[31] Pushing too hard for self-sufficiency in too many areas most likely will retard China's economic growth and technological progress.

Conclusion: Implications for the US-China Rivalry and Global Governance

What does all this mean for the problem I posed at the outset—the fear that China's growth and systemic difference threaten the stability of the global order—and for the issue addressed by the volume, the trajectory of the US-China strategic rivalry? I offer six observations.

First, we should not assume that China will inevitably surpass the United States as the world's biggest economy by the 2030s, as extrapolations from growth trends before the COVID pandemic generally suggested. In his contribution to this volume, David Dollar argues it is fairly likely China will overtake the United States in the 2030s, although it could later fall behind again as demographic headwinds exert a heavier toll. I am more pessimistic, believing there is only about a 50% chance of China overtaking the United States, and then only if there are significant policy changes in the next few years. The current policy mix indicates that China's growth will decelerate, since there is not a convincing recipe for productivity increases that can offset demographic decline and the gradual exhaustion of the capital-intensive growth model.[32]

Second, even if China's growth slows substantially and it fails to catch up with the US economy in total size, it is likely to increase its capabilities in many technology-intensive sectors. This in turn will amplify concerns in Washington and European capitals that Chinese technology firms will become more effective competitors for US and European incumbents and that China will use its technological prowess to extend its political (and perhaps military) influence and propagate authoritarian values around the world. At the time of writing (April 2024), this concern is already evident in a host of US and European policies. The Biden administration imposed a series of export and investment controls designed to prevent China from acquiring key technologies, especially semiconductors and artificial intelligence.[33] The European Union has partially followed the United States in these efforts (notably through controls on semiconductor machine tools) and instigated around ten investigations of subsidies in Chinese manufacturing and is likely to impose tariffs on Chinese electric vehicles as a result.

Third, US-led efforts to constrain China's technological capabilities are likely to be somewhat successful in semiconductors (and in applications, such as artificial intelligence and quantum computing, that rely on ultra-high-performance chips) but mostly unsuccessful in most other sectors. Semiconductors are a unique technology both in their complexity and in the way that the United States and its allies control key supply chain chokepoints. Green energy provides an opposite example: China is the technological leader in most renewable energy equipment (solar, wind, batteries, electric vehicles, and electricity transmission infrastructure) and controls most of the key supply chokepoints (notably in critical minerals). In most technological sectors, China should be able to achieve progress based on its ability to mobilize large-scale investments and the competitive strengths of its manufacturing ecosystem.

Fourth, under either a higher-growth (4% to 5% a year) or a lower-growth (2% to 4%) scenario, China will continue to be viewed as a systemic rival by the United States and its allies, because in both cases China's technological capabilities are likely to rise substantially, and the slowdown in growth will not be bad enough to undermine the domestic legitimacy of the authoritarian CCP regime. However, the higher-growth scenario would be significantly less stable than the low-growth scenario. With high growth, China's capacities would rise more quickly, and its leaders would be bolder in efforts to reshape the global geopolitical order, and international institutions, in ways that they believe serve CCP interests and that would be seen as deeply threatening by the United States. The slower-growth scenario would by no means be tension-free, but Chinese leaders would have less credibility in promoting China's political-economic model as an alternative to Western models and would have to devote more time and energy to managing domestic stability. A slower-growing China with no prospect of ever overtaking the US economy in absolute size would also be somewhat less threatening to Washington, which might eventually conclude that it was safe to manage the bilateral relationship in a less confrontational manner. But efforts to constrain China's technological progress, especially in areas relevant to military capacity, would continue.[34]

Fifth, the persistent US-China strategic rivalry must be understood in the context of a global environment that is far more complex than in the Cold War era. Economic interdependence is far greater, and the scope for middle and small powers to play the two major powers against each other for their own benefit is much broader.[35] In his contribution to this volume, Taylor Fravel makes the important observation that the United States and China do not lead two competing blocs, but rather two overlapping networks of economic and security ties, within which most countries have a strong interest and a strong capability to maintain deep relations with both major powers.[36] The logic of nonexclusive networks, not of exclusive blocs, will govern global affairs in the coming years.

Finally, it is worthwhile—indeed, essential—to consider the ways in which this persistent competition between overlapping networks can be managed in a way that is beneficial for global welfare. Strategic competition is inevitable, but a zero-sum rivalry perpetually skirting the edge of war is not. This is not mainly about finding areas where the United States and China can directly cooperate; the chief task is for leaders—not just in the United States and China but in middle powers as well—to craft "rules of the road" that will achieve the maximum level of economic interdependence consistent with the preservation of clearly defined national security objectives.

Notes

1. I am grateful to the detailed work by my Gavekal Dragonomics colleagues Andrew Batson and Dan Wang, whose research has informed many of my views, and to Bert Hofman, Simon Rabinovitch, and participants in the 2022 Nobel Symposium for comments on an earlier draft.
2. The view of China as systemic rival is explicit in numerous US and European policy documents, notably the Trump administration's December 2017 National Security Strategy (https://trumpwhitehouse.archives.gov/wp-content/uploads/2017/12/NSS-Final-12-18-2017-0905.pdf); the Biden administration's October 2022 National Security Strategy (https://www.whitehouse.gov/wp-content/uploads/2022/10/Biden-Harris-Administrations-National-Security-Strategy-10.2022.pdf), which highlights the competition between democracies led by the United States and autocracies led by China and Russia; and the European Commission China strategy ("EU-China: A Strategic Outlook," March 12, 2019, https://commission.europa.eu/system/files/2019-03/communication-eu-china-a-strategic-outlook.pdf). Since China and the United States and its allies have always had widely divergent political systems, we may ask why this was not a problem from 1980 until around 2015 and then became a major problem thereafter. The basic answer is that so long as China's economy was relatively small and complementary to that of the United States and its allies, systemic political differences could be overlooked in favor of other strategic goals. Systemic differences became more salient as China's economy grew larger and more competitive with the advanced industrial democracies, and as Xi Jinping broke with the low-key foreign policy stance of prior Chinese leaders and sought to translate China's economic power into global political influence. See Arthur R. Kroeber, "The Economic Origins of US-China Strategic Competition," in *Cold Rivals: The New Era of US-China Strategic Competition*, 172–202, ed. Evan Medeiros (Georgetown University Press, 2023).
3. David Dollar, "The Limits to China's Economic Rise," this volume.
4. A review of the many problems of import substitution, and revival of interest in this strategy, is Douglas Irwin, "The Rise and Fall of Import Substitution," Working Paper 20-10 (Peterson Institute of International Economics, July 2020), https://www.piie.com/publications/working-papers/rise-and-fall-import-substitution.
5. Yuen Yuen Ang, *China's Gilded Age: The Paradox of Economic Boom and Vast Corruption* (Cambridge University Press, 2020). Ang notes that the heavy-handed and top-down approach of corruption control may be self-defeating.
6. In the subsequent tables there is a fourth component, "human capital," which the World Bank now uses to assess the contribution of improvements in health and education to the quality of the workforce (https://www.worldbank.org/en/publication/human-capital). In

the Chinese context, this component is relatively small and fairly stable. So for the purposes of this discussion I will focus on the changing shares of labor, physical capital, and TFP.

7. *Innovative China: New Drivers of Growth* (World Bank and Development Research Center of the State Council, 2019); Roland Rajah and Alyssa Leng, "Revising Down the Rise of China" (Lowy Institute, March 2022), https://www.lowyinstitute.org/sites/default/files/RAJAH%20LENG%2C%20Revising%20Down%20Rise%20of%20China%2C%20PDF%20v3.pdf.

8. Personal communication from Martin Raiser, World Bank country director for China, May 2022. For 2018–2020, physical capital accounted for 4.7 percentage points of China's average annual 5% GDP growth, while TFP contributed 0.2 percentage points and employment –0.4 percentage points. Because this period is short and contains the pandemic year of 2020, when much normal economic activity was artificially suppressed, I have omitted it from the trend comparison.

9. Bert Hofman, "How Fast Can China Grow?," presentation at the Harvard University Fairbank Center for Chinese Studies, April 27, 2022, https://www.youtube.com/watch?v=OITot9CQlYI.

10. Richard Herd, "Estimating Capital Formation and Capital Stock by Economic Sector in China: The Implications for Productivity Growth," Policy Research Working Paper No. 9317 (World Bank, 2020), 25, https://openknowledge.worldbank.org/handle/10986/34126.

11. Adam S. Posen, "The End of China's Economic Miracle," *Foreign Affairs*, September–October 2023, https://www.foreignaffairs.com/china/end-china-economic-miracle-beijing-washington.

12. For instance, Dollar, "The Limits to China's Economic Rise," and Hofman, "How Fast Can China Grow?"

13. Andrew Batson, "Some Facts about China's State Capitalism," in *Chinese State Capitalism: Diagnosis and Prognosis*, 9–14, ed. Scott Kennedy and Jude Blanchette (Center for Strategic and International Studies, October 2021), https://csis-website-prod.s3.amazonaws.com/s3fs-public/publication/211007_Kennedy_Chinese_State_Capitalism.pdf.

14. Center for Security and Emerging Technology. Central Committee of the Communist Party of China and the PRC State Council, "Outline of the National Innovation-Driven Development Strategy," May 19, 2016, https://cset.georgetown.edu/publication/outline-of-the-national-innovation-driven-development-strategy/.

15. This discussion owes much to excellent work by Barry Naughton, who describes the development approach as "grand steerage." Barry Naughton, *The Rise of China's Industrial Policy, 1978–2020* (Universidad Nacional Autónomia de Mexico, 2021), https://dusselpeters.com/CECHIMEX/Naughton2021_Industrial_Policy_in_China_CECHIMEX.pdf. See also "The Incubator State: Xi Jinping's Bold Plan for China's Next Phase of Innovation," https://www.economist.com/finance-and-economics/2022/04/16/xi-jinpings-bold-plan-for-chinas-next-phase-of-innovation.

16. A complete list of the SEI priority sectors is in Naughton, *The Rise of China's Industrial Policy, 1978–2020*, 60–61.

17. The National Integrated Circuit Industry Investment Fund has now raised about US$55 billion since its inception, of which at least US$39 billion has been invested in semiconductor fabrication. The Semiconductor Industry Association in the United States estimates that total government support for China's semiconductor industry will be around US$150 billion during the 2014–2030 period. See "State of the US Semiconductor Industry 2021" (Semiconductor Industry Association, September 2021), https://www.semiconductors.org/wp-content/uploads/2021/09/2021-SIA-State-of-the-Industry-Report.pdf.

18. According to Wei Shaojun, director of Tsinghua University's Institute of Microelectronics and a leading authority on China's semiconductor industry, National Integrated Circuit Industry Investment Fund investments have succeeded in increasing China's self-sufficiency in a number of key chip categories from near zero in 2017 to 7% to 20% by 2021. Wei Shaojun, WeChat post, August 17, 2022, https://mp.weixin.qq.com/s/5vDMyGGAmMgizsPW-P10ew. But the future of the fund is in doubt following the summer 2022 arrest of its head, and seven other industry officials, for corruption. "Corruption Is Sending Shockwaves through China's Chipmaking Industry," *MIT Technology Review*, August 5, 2022, https://www.technologyreview.com/2022/08/05/1056975/corruption-chinas-chipmaking-industry/.

19. Gerard DiPippo et al., "Red Ink: Estimating Chinese Industrial Policy Spending in Comparative Perspective" (Center for Strategic and International Studies, May 2022), https://csis-website-prod.s3.amazonaws.com/s3fs-public/publication/220523_DiPippo_Red_Ink.pdf?LH8ILLKWz4o.bjrwNS7csuX_C04FyEre.

20. Thomas Gatley, "How Markets Multiply Subsidies," Gavekal Dragonomics research note, September 7, 2021, https://research.gavekal.com/article/how-markets-multiply-subsidies/.

21. Nathaniel Taplin, "Why China Worries About Losing Manufacturing," *Wall Street Journal*, March 9, 2021, https://www.wsj.com/articles/why-china-worries-about-losing-manufacturing-11615275559.

22. Tianlei Huang and Nicholas R. Lardy, "Is the Sky Really Falling for Private Firms in China?," Peterson Institute for International Economics, October 14, 2021, https://www.piie.com/blogs/china-economic-watch/sky-really-falling-private-firms-china; Tianlei Huang and Nicholas R. Lardy, "China's Tech Crackdown Affects Only a Small Share of Its Digital Economy and Total GDP," Peterson Institute for International Economics, October 20, 2021, https://www.piie.com/research/piie-charts/chinas-tech-crackdown-affects-only-small-share-its-digital-economy-and-total; Tianlei Huang and Nicolas Véron, "The Private Sector Advances in China: The Evolving Ownership Structures of the Largest Companies in the Xi Jinping Era," Working Paper 22-3 (Peterson Institute for International Economics, March 2022).

23. "China's 'Dual Circulation' Strategy Means Relying Less on Foreigners," *The Economist*, November 5, 2020, https://www.economist.com/china/2020/11/05/chinas-dual-circulation-strategy-means-relying-less-on-foreigners.

24. See, for instance, Hofman, "How Fast Can China Grow?," and Loren Brandt et al., "China's Productivity Slowdown and Future Growth Potential," Policy Research Working Paper No. 9298 (World Bank, 2020), https://openknowledge.worldbank.org/handle/10986/33993.

25. Scott Kennedy, "The Fat Tech Dragon: Benchmarking China's Innovation Drive" (Center for Strategic and International Studies, August 2017), https://www.csis.org/analysis/fat-tech-dragon.

26. Robert Lighthizer, US trade representative under President Trump in 2017–2020 and a likely senior economic official in any future Republican administration, is even more explicit that the United States should abandon a pure free market, free trade approach and use high tariffs and industrial policy to engineer a revival of American manufacturing. Robert Lighthizer, *No Trade Is Free: Changing Course, Taking on China, and Helping America's Workers* (Broadside Books, 2023).

27. Chang-Tai Hsieh, "State-Connected Private Firms in China," and William Norris, "The Party in the Boardroom," in Kennedy and Blanchette, eds., *Chinese State Capitalism*.

28. Brandt et al., "China's Productivity Slowdown and Future Growth Potential."

29. For a detailed discussion of how private venture capital funds work, see Sebastian Mallaby, *The Power Law: Venture Capital and the Making of the New Future* (Penguin Press, 2022). A discussion of the importance of international linkages in technology development is in Jonathan Woetzel et al., *China and the World: Inside the Dynamics of a Changing Relationship* (McKinsey Global Institute, July 2021), 68*ff.*, https://www.mckinsey.com/featured-insights/china/china-and-the-world-inside-the-dynamics-of-a-changing-relationship.

30. Dan Wang, "The Quest for Semiconductor Sovereignty," Gavekal Dragonomics research note, April 20, 2021, https://research.gavekal.com/article/quest-semiconductor-sovereignty/; "Strengthening the Global Semiconductor Supply Chain in an Uncertain Era" (Boston Consulting Group and Semiconductor Industry Association, April 2021), https://www.semiconductors.org/wp-content/uploads/2021/05/BCG-x-SIA-Strengthening-the-Global-Semiconductor-Value-Chain-April-2021_1.pdf.

31. Diego A. Cerdeiro et al, "Sizing Up the Effects of Technological Decoupling," Working Paper 2021/069 (International Monetary Fund, March 2021), https://www.imf.org/en/Publications/WP/Issues/2021/03/12/Sizing-Up-the-Effects-of-Technological-Decoupling-50125.

32. A good summary of the factors that could lead China to surpass the United States, or not, is Eric Zhu and Tom Orlik, "When Will China Rule the World? Maybe Never," Bloomberg News, July 5, 2021, https://www.bloomberg.com/news/features/2021-07-05/when-will-china-s-economy-beat-the-u-s-to-become-no-1-why-it-may-never-happen?sref=69A1tQL7.

33. Gregory C. Allen, "Choking Off China's Access to the Future of AI" (Center for Strategic and International Studies, October 11, 2022), https://www.csis.org/analysis/choking-chinas-access-future-ai.

34. An alternative view is that a weaker and slower-growing China would be more aggressive and destabilizing, either because its leaders would seek to exploit a narrow window of opportunity to increase their global influence or because they would use foreign adventurism and appeals to nationalist pride to shore up regime legitimacy as the economic basis of legitimacy erodes. See Hal Brands and Michael Beckley, *Danger Zone: The Coming Conflict with China* (W. W. Norton, 2022). I believe this view misunderstands the fundamentally conservative and risk-averse nature of the CCP party-state. As economic growth slows, the energies of the state are more likely to be directed inward, to the maintenance of domestic stability, than on risky international ventures.

35. Jeongmin Seong et al., *Geopolitics and the Geometry of Global Trade* (McKinsey Global Institute, January 2024), https://www.mckinsey.com/mgi/our-research/geopolitics-and-the-geometry-of-global-trade.

36. M. Taylor Fravel, "Technological Competition and the US-China Rivalry," this volume.

III

THE MILITARY BALANCE

5

China

Regional Power or Global Superpower?

Robert S. Ross

Just as US and Soviet Cold War policies reflected their twentieth-century competition over the balance of power in Europe, the trend in US and Chinese security policies in the twenty-first century will reflect US-China competition over the East Asian balance of power. Nonetheless, the US-China competition will not be Cold War II. East Asia is very different than Europe. As a maritime theater, it has its own geopolitical conditions, with distinct implications for the character of the US-China competition and for the likelihood that China will emerge as the world's next global naval power.

The rise of China and the US-China power transition have led to fundamental changes in the East Asian balance of power. Over the past decade, China has emerged as an East Asian naval power that now contends with the United States over the regional security order. This change in the distribution of power has led to a transformation in Chinese security policy, as it seeks greater security on its maritime perimeter, and to the realignment of secondary powers. It has also led to the reformulation of US defense policy and to the emergence of the Indo-Pacific strategy. As Øystein Tunsjø and Odd Arne Westad argue in their chapters, China and the United States contend in a bipolar East Asia.

Thus far, the US-China power transition has been a regional development. Even as China has developed greater naval presence in distant regions, the effect of China's rise on balance-of-power politics has been limited to the East Asian theater. But as China's economy and maritime capabilities continue to grow faster than the United States' economy and maritime capabilities, the potential exists for China to emerge as a global maritime power that can determine security affairs over the globe, including in the Indian Ocean, the western Pacific Ocean, and the polar regions.

Robert S. Ross, *China*. In: *Not Just Another Cold War*. Edited by: Bård Nikolas Vik Steen, Oxford University Press. © Oxford University Press (2025). DOI: 10.1093/9780197799932.003.0006

This chapter argues that in the twenty-first century China's global naval presence will grow, but it will not become a global maritime power. It considers the geopolitical constraints on China evolving from a regional maritime power to a global naval power, with a status similar to the United Kingdom's status as a global power in the nineteenth century and to the United States' status as a global power since the end of World War II. It considers the implications of the necessary permissive global conditions that enable development of global maritime power for Chinese global expansion, of the long-term trend in US-China relative capabilities, and of the geopolitical characteristics of the US defense strategy in the Indo-Pacific for China's ability to extend its great power naval capabilities beyond East Asia.

The first part of this chapter examines the trend in US-China capabilities and the long-term implications for the East Asian balance of power and for China's potential to develop a naval force for worldwide power projection. The second part of the chapter considers the global geopolitical constraints on China's ability to become a global naval power. The third part of the chapter examines the likely trend in the US-China balance of power for China's ability to expand beyond East Asia. The fourth part of the chapter examines the geopolitics of the US defense strategy and the implications for China's ability to disperse its forces to distant regions. The final section of the chapter briefly examines the implications of the US-China competition in East Asia for the global maritime order and for security affairs outside East Asia.

The East Asian Power Transition

In the past, Chinese neighbors, particularly Russia/Soviet Union in Northeast Asia and the United States, with its military presence in Indochina until 1973, constrained China's naval development by challenging China's land borders. But since the turn of the twenty-first century, none of China's fourteen neighbors have been able challenge Chinese territorial integrity. In Northeast Asia, Russia's declining population and deteriorating infrastructure in its Far East diminish any likelihood of a Russian challenge to Chinese security. Its war in Ukraine has accelerated its decline vis-à-vis China. The Indian challenge to Chinese security in the Himalayas remains manageable with China's current ground force capacities. Thus, free from land threats to its security, China has been able to focus its resources on developing its naval capabilities to contend with post–World War II US naval superiority in East Asia.[1]

Over the past decade, the rise of the Chinese navy has transformed the East Asian balance of power. China's improved naval capabilities have ended US maritime dominance and challenged US regional security interests. Bipolarity is the dominant trend in East Asian security affairs.[2] The Chinese and American response to this power transition informs their respective security policies and will determine the intensity of US-China great power competition.

China now operates nearly seventy attack submarines and commissions nearly three submarines each year.[3] In 2023, the US Department of Defense estimated that the People's Liberation Army Navy already operated 370 major ships, not including its 60 Houbei missile patrol ships. It estimated that by 2030 the Chinese navy could operate 435 ships.[4] China's fleet is also modern. In 2017, over 70% of its fleet was modern.[5] Although much of China's fleet is composed of smaller coastal water ships, including corvette missile ships, these ships can be effective for "swarming" tactics in the South China Sea. Moreover, China is rapidly expanding its fleet of submarines and large surface combat ships. Whereas China can produce three submarines each year, in 2023 the US Navy reported that it can deliver approximately one submarine each year.[6] Among its many destroyers in construction, each year China can produce three 052 Luyang III destroyers and two 055 Renhai destroyers. It is also developing a next-generation frigate, the 054B. These are modern ships equipped with anti-ship and anti-air cruise missiles. The Renhai destroyer has 112 missile tubes. Overall, the US Navy can deliver, at most, two destroyers per year.[7]

China's DF-21C and DF-26 intermediate-range conventional ballistic missile can target US access to air and naval facilities in South Korea, Japan, the Philippines, Singapore, and Malaysia.

Meanwhile, despite the rise of the Chinese navy and America's evident concern for the trend in the East Asian balance of power, the US Navy is getting smaller. In recognition of the cost of maintaining up-tempo presence operations with an aging fleet and of long-term budget constraints, the US Navy is seeking to "divest to invest." Chief of Naval Operations Admiral Michael Gilday has argued that maintaining the current fleet would be a case of "throwing good money after bad" and make the United States weaker vis-à-vis China.[8] In 2020, the size of the active US fleet was 293 ships. The nonpartisan Congressional Budget Office reports that if the navy's shipbuilding budget were simply the average of its budget over the prior thirty years, corrected for inflation, and it maintained its aircraft carrier and ballistic submarine construction schedules, in 2045 the active naval fleet would decline to 237 ships.[9] By 2028, the number of US attack submarines will likely decline to 41 ships.[10]

The United States retains significant technological advantages over China that contribute to its military capabilities, but China's technology base is improving. In an interconnected world of global supply chains and cyber communications, it is difficult for the United States to maintain control over advanced military technologies. In many cases, China has developed technologies that are competitive with or better than US technologies, including communication technologies, artificial intelligence, and high-speed computing.[11]

Moreover, technology is an unreliable foundation for competition with China. The Pentagon is developing the Joint All-Domain Command and Control (JADC2) system, but it may not compensate for fewer ships. The Pentagon has struggled to develop secure communications for the JADC2.[12] US naval officers report that electronic warfare in East Asia is a "contested space" and that in some areas the United States is "behind its rivals."[13] In 2023, the Central Intelligence Agency determined that China's cyber capabilities may enable it to "seize control" of U.S. satellites and to "deny" and "render ineffective" US satellites for surveillance and targeting of Chinese naval platforms.[14] The US Space Development Agency reports that Chinese cyber attacks on ground stations "can take out all of [our] satellites" from ground systems. It also reports that Chinese ground-based laser systems can challenge US communication systems.[15] The Pentagon is similarly concerned that Chinese lasers could disable US satellites. It acknowledges that there is "nothing we can do in space" if US "networks . . . are vulnerable to attack."[16]

China does not possess naval parity, much less superiority. But it possesses an effective anti-access/area-denial (A2/AD) capability. Because of the few channels enabling access to maritime East Asia, China's undersea and surface capabilities can impose significant costs on US wartime efforts to enter East Asian seas through the few chokepoints in the first island chain and through Japan's Ryukyu Islands. As early as 2016, the US Navy no longer expected to wage surface warfare inside East Asian waters.[17] In 2018, Admiral Philip Davidson, commander of the US Indo-Pacific Command, observed that "China is now capable of controlling the South China Sea in all scenarios, short of war with the United States."[18] In 2021, Secretary of Defense Lloyd Austin advocated maintaining an "edge" over China, even as the "gap" has "closed significantly."[19]

Over the next decade, China will likely be able to sustain its ship production rate at current levels, so that this trend in the US-China balance will continue, with an ongoing decline in US capabilities.[20] Moreover, budget constraints present a persistent challenge to the US ability to increase ship production. Annual US budget increases primarily aim to support greater compensation for soldiers and sailors and to offset other inflationary pressures.

Despite America's great wealth, as an advanced industrial country, its social welfare policies constrain budget flexibility and the ability to significantly increase defense spending. In 2018, the federal government allocated 70% of its budget to entitlement programs and interest payments on the federal debt. Funding for these programs cannot be reduced without congressional legislation. Political imperatives determine that Congress will not reduce spending on social welfare programs. Regarding the remaining 30% of the budget, the discretionary budget, the Pentagon receives 55%, not including funding for nuclear weapons and the coast guard. The remainder of the discretionary budget contributes to such national priorities as health care, education, and infrastructure development, leaving little room for expansion of the defense budget.[21]

The structure of the US defense budget similarly constrains the US ability to contend with China's naval buildup. Despite the large size of the US defense budget, in its 2021 budget the US Navy allocated only 28% of its spending to acquisitions, including for new ships. This amount reflects the high cost of the US voluntary military, including the cost of salaries, housing, and benefits, as well as the cost of operations and maintenance of an aging fleet.[22]

In contrast to US budget constraints, China's military budget is not constrained by high personnel costs, the costs of an aging fleet, or sustaining worldwide deployments and operations. Its defense budget is smaller than the US defense budget, but its navy's acquisition budget is proportionally larger than the US Navy's acquisition budget. China's official defense budget is 1.7% of its gross domestic product (GDP); the US official defense budget is 3.7% of its GDP.[23] Whereas China has dozens of shipyards that can build naval ships, the United States has just two shipyards that build surface ships, down from eight in 1990. In 2022, China possessed nearly a 50% share of global ship construction; the United States possessed less than a 1% share.[24]

Over the next decade, the combination of US budget constraints and continued growth of the Chinese navy suggests that China could develop sufficient naval capabilities to consolidate its security in East Asia as well as develop a global power projection navy. Its navy has already begun to develop access to port facilities on the Indian Ocean and the West Pacific, suggesting an interest in developing a global naval presence.

Geopolitical Constraints on Global China

China's ability to develop global naval power will, in part, reflect America's ability to make the East Asian balance of power its primary security concern. In history, global naval powers, including the United States, possessed naval hegemony in their own regions. This allowed them to disperse their fleets to distant regions. Because the United States possesses maritime hegemony in the Western Hemisphere, it can prioritize resistance to Chinese regional hegemony to sustain regional bipolarity, requiring China to concentrate its naval capabilities in East Asian waters, rather than project worldwide naval power.

The United Kingdom and the United States developed global naval power under unique geopolitical circumstances. In both cases, the absence of a competing naval power in their respective home theaters enabled each to disperse their naval capabilities across the globe. In the British case, from the end of the Napoleonic Wars to the early twentieth century, Europe's continental great powers were all preoccupied with developing armies to defend their land borders against other continental powers. They thus lacked the resources to construct large navies that could contend with the British navy and cross the English Channel, an effective moat defending the British Isles. This permissive environment enabled the United Kingdom to become a global naval power.

But after 1900 the rapid growth of the French and Russian navies and then of the German navy compelled the British navy to retrench from the Caribbean and from Northeast Asian waters to its coastal waters and the Mediterranean. Great Britain thus relinquished its status as a global naval power.[25]

Since the early twentieth century the United States has enjoyed similar geopolitical circumstances to those that enabled the United Kingdom to rise to global naval power. Since the British conceded US preeminence in the Caribbean at the turn of the twentieth century, the United States has faced neither a land power nor a maritime power in the Western Hemisphere that could challenge its security. It has enjoyed "remarkable security."[26] Once the United States decided to exercise global naval power after World War II, hemispheric hegemony enabled it to distribute its naval capabilities in distant waters.

For China to distribute its forces outside East Asia, it too will require naval superiority in its home theater. But unlike the United Kingdom in the early twentieth century, in the twenty-first century there is little likelihood that the United States will have to retrench from East Asia to concentrate its naval forces in its home theater to contend with a great power competitor. And there is little likelihood that a land power or a naval power will emerge in Europe that will require the United States to sustain a large naval presence in European waters to participate in the European balance of power. Thus, the United States, given its continental and maritime hegemony in the Western Hemisphere and the absence of European threats to its security, will be free to concentrate its naval forces in East Asia to contend with China in the regional balance of power and constrain China from dispersing its forces in distant theaters.

If the US Navy can maintain great power status in a divided East Asia, the Chinese navy, similar to the British navy following the emergence of the French, Russian, and German navies in the early twentieth century, will be preoccupied with the East Asian balance of power.

US Military Constraints and Chinese Naval Expansion

Despite the seeming US inability to extract itself from European and Middle Eastern conflicts, over time the continued growth of Chinese capabilities will require the US Navy to focus its declining capabilities on East Asia to contend with the Chinese navy. China may well become the superior naval power in East Asian waters, but the United States simply requires sufficient capabilities to threaten Chinese forces in East Asia should China disperse its capabilities over multiple regions. Despite the ongoing decline of the US Navy, its focus on the rise of China has required it to transform its budget and acquisition strategies, so that over the next decade, the trend in the US-China balance of power will begin to stabilize. The United States will remain an East Asian maritime great power in East Asian bipolarity, constraining Chinese global expansion.[27]

China's rise reflects both its impressive economic growth since 1978 and its ability to prioritize its naval spending on ship construction. But both of these advantages will wane over the coming decade. First, China's economic growth rate has already begun to decline and will likely continue to do so over the next decade. This trend will entail declining central government revenue available for defense spending. Second, Chinese spending on ship production has benefited from the low cost of maintenance and operations for Chinese ships. Because China has decommissioned many of its older ships, its maintenance costs are low. But as China's navy ages and its ships spend more time at sea, its maintenance budget will increase, at the expense of its shipbuilding budget.

But China's rise reflects not only American budget constraints and China's economic growth and lean defense budget but also American reliance on and overuse of its aging and declining fleet to maintain the pace of its naval presence operations to signal its resistance to China's rise in East Asia, while increasing its presence in other regions.[28]

For the past ten years, faced with China's challenge to US maritime hegemony and its East Asian alliance system, the United States has increasingly relied on frequent high-profile naval and air operations to signal its resolve to resist China's rise. Each year the US Navy conducts frequent and publicized operations and overflights, including its freedom of navigation operations. Davidson said that these operations "reassure our allies and partners of our commitment."[29] This trend picked up in 2020. In the first five months of 2020, US aircraft, including B-52 bombers, carried out forty flights near Chinese waters, more than three times the pace of 2019.[30]

The United States has also increased the frequency and size of its joint naval exercises with its regional security partners. To reassure South Korea, the Philippines, and Japan of its resolve, the navy conducts high-profile bilateral and multilateral exercises in the South China Sea, including with India and Australia.[31]

US transits through the Taiwan Strait reflect a similar effort to establish resolve. There is a consensus among US and Taiwan civilian and military leaders and analysts that China does not have the capability to carry out an amphibious landing on Taiwan, that it will not have that capability for at least five years, and that there is no indication that China is preparing to attack Taiwan.[32] In 2024, the former head of intelligence plans for China and the China Strategic Focus Group for the US Pacific Command argued that China will not have the amphibious capability to invade Taiwan through at least 2030. Moreover, China lacks the air support capabilities to protect its ships during lengthy operations necessary to deploy troops in the island.[33]

In 2021, the US Department of Defense explained that the Chinese military had increased its air and naval activities near Taiwan, including in its air defense identification zone (ADIZ), to enhance its deterrence posture and "to signal its displeasure at warming Washington-Taipei ties."[34] In July 2018, the US Navy began frequent transits through the strait. In 2018, the US Navy made three transits through the strait; in 2019, it made nine transits; and in 2020, it made thirteen transits. Nearly two years later, in May 2020, China's first aircraft incursion into Taiwan's ADIZ occurred.[35]

These presence operations have required the United States to keep older ships in service and at sea longer than planned and to defer maintenance of older ships to operate them for extended periods. Once its ships return to the United States for maintenance, they endure extended time waiting for space in shipyards for repair. In 2021, the navy reported that the condition of its surface fleet and submarines had "degraded."[36]

US aircraft carriers are pressed to meet the high demand for their presence in multiple regions, but the navy has been able to fulfill only 50% of the demands, with only half of its carriers available for operations. Reliance on older ships has affected the readiness of attack submarines. Extended deployments with deferred maintenance have led to more ships experiencing mechanical problems at sea and spending greater time being repaired.[37] The Department of Defense expressed concern that during wartime conditions China would be able to repair and put back to sea damaged ships faster than the United States.[38] Recent naval incidents attest to the stress on sailors and their increasing inability to perform at a high level. The commander of the navy's surface fleet argued that to restore personnel readiness, the navy requires "fewer obligations. It is hard to see things any other way."[39]

The US Navy in Transition

Alarmed at the shifting naval balance and at America's allocation of its defense budget to operating and maintaining older ships, the naval leadership is determined to reform the navy to allow for the development of a larger, modern, and relevant navy for contending with the Chinese navy. After an era of prolonged stagnation and misallocation of spending on twentieth-century surface ships, the naval leadership plans that over the next decade the navy will begin to emerge and then develop a navy more capable of contending with China's navy.[40] The reorientation of the US Navy will coincide with the slower growth of the Chinese navy, so that the pace of China's rise will decline and the great power balance will stabilize into a bipolar order.

As part of its plan to "divest to invest," the US Navy's 2025 budget request calls for funding construction of six ships but for decommissioning nine battle force ships and decommissioning nineteen ships altogether. From 2022 to 2027, the navy anticipates inactivating nearly eighty ships. These decommissioned ships include older ships that have already been kept in service longer than planned. It also includes the navy's newest class of surface ships, the littoral combat ships, which have yet to reach their half-life but are not appropriate for naval competition with China and large cruisers.[41] The navy has argued that these older ships are not safe and not worth the cost of upgrades and that maintaining its current fleet size with older ships will raise maintenance costs and undermine readiness. On the other hand, the savings from shrinking the fleet would allow investment in fleet modernization and more effective platforms.[42]

While focusing on future warfighting capabilities rather than on current fleet size, the navy is also developing a revised approach to warfighting that responds to Chinese strengths. It is transitioning away from larger and more expensive surface ships, including aircraft carriers and carrier task forces, and toward developing more submarines and smaller surface ships, including drone platforms, which allow for "distributed lethality," to adjust both to the vulnerability of large platforms and to the size of the Chinese navy and its ability to concentrate its capabilities to overwhelm ship defenses. In this context, the navy plans for a reduced carrier-based sortie rate.[43]

The US Navy is also adjusting to the decline of the US shipbuilding industry and maintenance facilities by cooperating with Asian countries. In 2020, it reached an agreement with the Italian company Fincantieri to construct up to ten of its next-generation frigates. In line with the navy's planning for future wars, these frigates will be small ships equipped with thirty-two missile launch cells.[44] The US Navy has also secured access to Indian maintenance facilities and is in discussion with Japan and South Korea to gain regular access to their maintenance facilities.[45]

East Asian Maritime Geography and American Defense Policy

The rise of the Chinese navy has transformed the East Asian balance of power. But global naval power depends on more than the size of a navy and the regional balance of power. It also depends on the region's geopolitical characteristics and the implications for great power competition. The regional geography of the US-China naval competition enables the US defense strategy to constrain China's ability to extend its naval presence to distant regions and become a global naval power.

Just as the first island chain enables China to develop an effective A2/AD strategy that constrains American access to East Asian seas despite not possessing maritime superiority or even parity, that same geography enables the United States to develop an A2/AD capability to contain China's navy within the first island chain, even if China eventually develops a relatively larger and more modern navy.[46] Alfred Mahan observed that the development of sea power requires numerous deep harbors that provide access to the oceans. China possesses numerous harbors, but they offer access to East Asia's internal seas; China does not have any harbors on the Pacific Ocean.[47]

With expanded US access to air and naval facilities in the Indian Ocean and in the West Pacific, US maritime encirclement of East Asia will constrain China's ability to disperse its forces worldwide to support global naval power. This is the essence of the US Indo-Pacific strategy, the strategic component of the Japan–Australia–India–United States "Quad." The 2021 US Department of Defense's Global Policy Review called for improved military infrastructure across the Western Pacific and in Australia. As a former US general explained, "How are you going to keep the Chinese navy bottled up inside, if not the first . . . island chain?"[48] With its A2/AD capabilities, the United States can maintain military superiority in the waters surrounding East Asian seas.

The 2014 US-Australia Force Posture Agreement calls for increased US presence at Australia's Darwin air force base in Northern Territory, including rotational deployments of US Marines and enhanced US communication facilities, and for expanded runways and ramp space at the Learmonth and Tindal bases, contributing to US operations in the Indian Ocean south of the first island chain. Australia will upgrade four northern military bases and expand access for rotational US aircraft deployments. It has also discussed extended deployments of US nuclear-powered submarines in Australia. In 2012, Canberra and Washington opened discussions on US use of Cocos Island, south of Indonesia, for drone surveillance operations, and in 2016 Australia announced plans to expand the airfield on Cocos Island for anti-submarine warfare.[49] The Australia, United Kingdom, and United States (AUKUS) partnership and development of an Australian nuclear-powered attack submarine underscore the importance of Australia in US defense policy.

India's presence west of the Malacca Strait similarly contributes to US maritime containment of China. The Obama administration named India a "major defense partner," and between 2008 and 2016 the value of Indian military imports from the United States surged from $1 billion to $15 billion.[50] The United States and India reached a Logistics Exchange Memorandum of Agreement, enabling regular US access to India military facilities for fueling and logistic support.[51] During the Trump administration, the United States and India signed the Communications Compatibility and Security Agreement, enabling improved intelligence sharing of military developments. In 2020, India agreed to purchase twenty-four anti-submarine helicopters, and in 2021 it agreed to buy Predator drones.[52] The Indian and US navies carry out joint anti-submarine exercises and share intelligence on Chinese submarine operations. Indian upgrades of anti-submarine warfare and air combat facilities on the Andaman and Nicobar Islands, including construction of its fourth air base and its third naval facility, will contribute to the US ability to contain Chinese naval capabilities within the South China Sea and to project US air power into the South China Sea. In 2021, a US military aircraft refueled for the first time on the Andaman and Nicobar Islands.[53]

In Papua New Guinea, the United States supports Australian expansion of the deep-water Lombrum Naval Base in the Indian Ocean, southeast of the Philippines. US chief of naval operations Admiral John Richardson described Lombrum redevelopment as a "terrific opportunity" and said that "we look forward to identifying opportunities where we can support that," including with US naval access.[54] In 2023, United States and Papua New Guinea negotiated the Defense Cooperation Agreement, and Papua New Guinea agreed to full US military access to Lombrum and to its naval facilities at Port Moresby.[55]

Japan remains the cornerstone of US strategy in East Asia. US naval forces based at Yokosuka can patrol east of the few transit points between the East China Sea and the Western Pacific. In 2022 Japan and the United States agreed to expand Japanese military presence on the islands along these chokepoints. They have also established an extensive Sound Surveillance System (SOSUS) network in the channels between the Nansei Islands and the Pacific Ocean, strengthening containment of the Chinese navy within the East China Sea.[56] The US Marines plan to deploy mobile anti-ship missiles on the Ryukyu Islands, astride the chokepoints between the East China Sea and the West Pacific.[57]

The United States is also cooperating with the Philippines to expand naval facilities on Batanes Island. Batanes is the northernmost Philippines island, located at the southern end of the Bashi Strait. US military presence on Batanes will facilitate its monitoring of Chinese ships entering the West Pacific.[58]

The United States is also developing expanded air and naval facilities in the Western Pacific. In 2021, it reached agreement with Micronesia to build a base and to post a permanent military presence on the islands. In 2020, in response to the vulnerability of Guam to Chinese missiles, the Pentagon began upgrading air facilities on Tinian Island and Wake Island. Australia is funding military infrastructure development in the Solomon Islands. The United States has also expressed interest in expanded military presence at the air and naval facilities in Palau. In 2020, Mark Esper became the first US secretary of defense to visit Palau. Secretary of the Navy Kenneth Braithwaite then visited Palau and the Pentagon completed renovation and began use of Palau's Angaur Airstrip. In 2022, the Pentagon announced plans for the development of an air and naval defense radar system in Palau.[59]

The End of Global Maritime Power

The presence of a global naval power from Great Britain in the early nineteenth century through the United States in the early twenty-first century suggests that in every era in international politics there is a global naval power. But global naval power requires particular geopolitical conditions in great power competition to enable dispersal of a fleet from a great power's home region to multiple distant regions. These conditions do not exist in US-China relations.

The rise of China will require the US Navy to retrench from European and Middle Eastern waters to concentrate its fleet in the West Pacific and the Indian Ocean. Along with the transformation of US naval capabilities, retrenchment will enable the United States to contain the Chinese fleet within East Asian waters and ensure its ability to resist a Chinese naval challenge in the Pacific Ocean. This strategic transition toward East Asia first emerged during the Clinton administration, when the United States began transferring naval platforms from Europe to Asia. The Obama administration's "pivot" to Asia reinforced this trend, and it accelerated during the Trump administration. Despite the Russian invasion of Ukraine and the recent expansion of US ground force presence in Europe, the Biden administration has continued this policy. Since the Clinton administration, the United States has deployed each new US air and naval platform first to East Asia.[60]

Just as was the case for the United Kingdom at the turn of the twentieth century and its concern for rival European navies, the rise of China in East Asia and the declining number of US naval platforms require the United States to yield its status as a global maritime power with strategic influence in multiple regions. The United States' diminishing global presence is already reflected in the politics of the Middle East and in Europe, as countries prepare for a reduced US role in their regional affairs. In the Middle East, Saudi Arabia has begun to distance itself from the United States and improve relations with China, reflecting its diminished concern for US authority in the Middle East.[61] Similarly, reduced confidence in the US commitment to regional stability is affecting regional alignments throughout the region.[62]

In Europe, after an extended period of declining defense budgets since 2014, there has been a determined increase in defense spending. Overall, European defense spending increased by over 25%, faster than the rate of economic growth. During this same period, German and French defense spending increased by approximately 30%. There is a long way to go before Europe can provide for its own security, but the trend reflects European uncertainty over America's ability to contend with the rise of China in East Asia and provide security for Europe.[63] Moreover, the consequential decline of Russian military capabilities as a result of the prolonged war in Ukraine will enable Europe to carry a greater burden of European security and thus require less US military presence in Europe, facilitating US concentration of its forces in Asia.

China will not succeed the United States as a global maritime power for the twenty-first century. China's navy will establish a growing global presence; it has already reached logistics and basing agreements with countries around the globe, and its ships will be omnipresent in support of Chinese global economic and nontraditional security interests.[64]

But China's global presence will not expand to enable China to become a global maritime power that can influence regional balances of power or local security affairs outside East Asia. Rather, long-term US-China naval parity will require China to concentrate the bulk of its naval platforms in the East Asian theater, limiting it to an observer role in distant regions. China will be no more a global maritime power in the twenty-first century than France and Germany were from the 1890s to World War II; their navies sailed the world, but they focused their resources on defense in continental Europe.

The world has seldom seen a contest between two naval powers in a bipolar maritime theater. But the emergence of China and the United States as rival naval powers competing in East Asian waters will give rise to an era in which there is no longer a global naval power. This will transform the security policies of states throughout the world. It may usher in an era of greater regional conflict and instability as secondary powers are less deterred by the threat of great power retaliation against the use of force. But US retrenchment and Chinese preoccupation with East Asian security may also enable other regions to decouple from great power politics, enabling reduced tension and polarization and greater attention to economic development and multilateral cooperation.

Notes

1. Robert S. Ross, "Sino-Russian Relations: The False Promise of Russian Balancing," *International Politics* 57, no. 5 (2020), 834–84.
2. Øystein Tunsjø, *The Return of Bipolarity in World Politics: China, the United States, and Geostructural Realism* (Columbia University Press, 2018).
3. *Military and Security Developments Involving the People's Republic of China 2020* (US Department of Defense, 2020), 42, 45, https://media.defense.gov/2020/sep/01/2002488689/-1/-1/1/2020-dod-china-military-power-report-final.pdf.
4. *Military and Security Developments Involving the People's Republic of China 2023* (US Department of Defense, 2023), https://media.defense.gov/2023/oct/19/2003323409/-1/-1/1/2023-military-and-security-developments-involving-the-peoples-republic-of-china.pdf; *China Naval Modernization: Implications for U.S. Navy Capabilities—Background and Issues for Congress*, RL33153 (Congressional Research Service, May 15, 2023), 210–11, https://sgp.fas.org/crs/row/RL33153.pdf.
5. See the discussion in Eric Heginbotham et al., *The U.S.-China Military Scorecard Forces, Geography, and the Evolving Balance of Power, 1996–2017* (Santa Monica: Rand, 2015).
6. Megan Eckstein et al., "How the US Plans to Expand Its Submarine Industrial Base for AUKUS," Defense News, March 15, 2023, https://www.defensenews.com/naval/2023/03/15/how-the-us-plans-to-expand-its-submarine-industrial-base-for-aukus/; Justin Katz, "As AUKUS Looms, US Navy Sub Leaders Sound Alarms at Home," *Breaking Defense*, November 22, 2022, https://breakingdefense.com/2022/11/as-aukus-looms-us-navy-sub-leaders-sound-alarms-at-home/.
7. Brad Lendon and Haley Britzky, "US Can't Keep Up with China's Warship Building, Navy Secretary Says," CNN, February 22, 2023, https://www.cnn.com/2023/02/22/asia/us-navy-chief-china-pla-advantages-intl-hnk-ml/index.html; Justin Katz, "Citing Industry Capacity, Navy's Gilday Throws Cold Water on Three Destroyers per Year," *Breaking*

*Defense,*September 14, 2022, https://breakingdefense.com/2022/09/citing-industry-capacity-navys-gilday-throws-cold-water-on-three-destroyers-per-year/; "Luyang III/Type 052D—Program," Globalsecurity.org, https://premium.globalsecurity.org/military/world/china//luyang-iii-program.htm; Liu Zhen, "China Confirms New Guided-Missile Frigate Is Being Developed," *South China Morning Post,* September 1, 2023, https://www.scmp.com/news/china/military/article/3233094/china-confirms-new-guided-missile-frigate-being-developed.

8. Courtney Mabeus, "CNO Gilday Says with Current Budget, Cutting Ships Necessary for Navy Long-Term," USNI News, July 20, 2021, https://news.usni.org/2021/07/20/cno-gilday-says-with-current-budget-cutting-ships-necessary-for-navy-long-term.

9. "An Analysis of the Navy's Fiscal Year 2016 Shipbuilding Plan" (Congressional Budget Office, October 2015), 20, https://www.cbo.gov/sites/default/files/114th-congress-2015-2016/reports/50926-shipbuilding-2.pdf.

10. "An Analysis of the Navy's Fiscal Year 2019 Shipbuilding Plan" (Congressional Budget Office, October 2018), 8, https://www.cbo.gov/system/files/2019-01/54564-FY19Shipbuilding.pdf; David B. Larter, "As the US Navy Scrambles to Field More Missiles in Asia, a Tough Decision Looms for Aging Cruisers," Defense News, April 12, 2021, https://www.defensenews.com/naval/2021/04/12/as-the-us-navy-scrambles-to-field-more-missiles-in-asia-a-tough-decision-looms-for-aging-cruisers/#.YHWM4-NZvqw.mailto.

11. See, for example, Robert D. Atkinson, "The Hamilton Index: Assessing National Performance in the Competition for Advanced Industries" (Information Technology & Innovation Foundation, June 8, 2022), https://itif.org/publications/2022/06/08/the-hamilton-index-assessing-national-performance-in-the-competition-for-advanced-industries/.

12. Michael Marrow, "'Network-Centric' Security 'Killing Us' on JADC2 Initiatives: USAF General," *Breaking Defense,* July 11, 2023, https://breakingdefense.com/2023/07/network-centric-security-killing-us-on-jadc2-initiatives-usaf-general/#:~:text=WASHINGTON%20%E2%80%94%20While%20the%20Air%20Force,of%20security%20is%20killing%20us.%E2%80%9D.

13. Colin Demarest, "INDOPACOM's Aquilino Seeks More Electromagnetic Resources for the Pacific," Defense News, April 20, 2023, https://www.defensenews.com/electronic-warfare/2023/04/20/indopacoms-aquilino-seeks-more-electromagnetic-resources-for-pacific/; Michael Marrow, "US 'Behind' in Electronic Warfare, and Personnel Are the Key to Catching Up: EW Officer," *Breaking Defense,* April 20, 2023, https://breakingdefense.com/2023/04/us-behind-in-electronic-warfare-and-personnel-are-the-key-to-catching-up-ew-officer/; Colin Demarest, "Electronic Warfare Is New Frontier for US Missile Defense Agency," C4ISRNET, March 28, 2023, https://www.c4isrnet.com/electronic-warfare/2023/03/28/electronic-warfare-is-new-frontier-for-us-missile-defense-agency/ Sydney J. Freedberg Jr., "'Let's Bring That Margin Back': China, Russia Too Close for Comfort in Electronic Warfare, Say Generals," *Breaking Defense,* December 13, 2023, https://breakingdefense.com/2023/12/lets-bring-that-margin-back-china-russia-too-close-for-comfort-in-electronic-warfare-say-generals/.

14. Mehul Srivastava, "China Building Cyber Weapons to Hijack Satellites, Says US Leak," *Financial Times,* April 21, 2023, https://www.ft.com/content/881c941a-c46f-4a40-b8d8-9e5c8a6775ba.

15. Audrey Decker, "Satellite Ground Stations Are Vulnerable, US Warns," Defense One, April 24, 2023, https://www.defenseone.com/threats/2023/04/sda-stresses-need-protect-satellites-ground-stations/384786/; Sandra Erwin, "Space Force: We Expect to See 'Interfering, Blinding" of Satellites during Conflict," Space News, March 15, 2023, at https://spacenews.com/space-force-we-expect-to-see-interfering-blinding-of-satellites-during-conflict/. On ground station hacking during the Ukraine war, see Maggie Smith and Jason Atwell, "A Solution Desperately Seeking Problems: The Many Assumptions of JADC2" (Modern War Institute, May 3, 2022), https://mwi.usma.edu/a-solution-desperately-seeking-problems-the-many-assumptions-of-jadc2/.

16. Doug Cameron, "Pentagon Prepares for Space Warfare as Potential Threats from China, Russia Grow," *Wall Street Journal,* March 28, 2023, https://www.wsj.com/articles/pentagon-prepares-for-space-warfare-as-potential-threats-from-china-russia-grow-62a0623b.

17. Interview, senior US Pacific fleet officer, September 2016.

18. Hannah Beech, "China's Sea Control Is a Done Deal, 'Short of War with the U.S.,'" *New York Times*, September 20, 2018, https://www.nytimes.com/2018/09/20/world/asia/south-china-sea-navy.html.

19. Advance Policy Questions for Lloyd J. Austin, Nominee for Appointment to be Secretary of Defense, Senate Armed Services Committee, 9, January 19, 2021, https://www.armed-services.senate.gov/imo/media/doc/Austin_APQs_01-19-21.pdf; Mallory Shelbourne, "SECDEF Nominee Austin Affirms Threat from China, Will 'Update' National Defense Strategy," USNI News, January 19, 2021, https://news.usni.org/2021/01/19/secdef-nominee-austin-affirms-threat-from-china-will-update-national-defense-strategy.

20. Jack Bianci et al., "China Choices: A New Tool for Assessing the PLA's Modernization" (Center for Strategic and Budgetary Assessments, 2022), https://csbaonline.org/uploads/documents/CSBA8310_(Chinas_Choices_report)_FINAL_web.pdf.

21. Anna Malinovskaya and Louise Sheiner, "The Hutchins Center Explains: Federal Budget Basics" (Brookings Institution, December 13, 2018), https://www.brookings.edu/blog/up-front/2018/12/13/the-hutchins-center-explains-federal-budget-basics/.

22. *Highlights of the Department of the Navy FY 2018 Budget* (US Department of the Navy), 6, 2017,https://www.secnav.navy.mil/fmc/fmb/Documents/18pres/Highlights_book.pdf.

23. "Military Expenditure (% of GDP)" (World Bank), https://data.worldbank.org/indicator/MS.MIL.XPND.GD.ZS.

24. Caitlin M. Kenney, "The U.S. Needs More Military Arms Makers, Says Pentagon No. 2," Defense One, February 15, 2022, https://www.defenseone.com/business/2022/02/us-needs-more-military-arms-makers-says-pentagon-no-2/362041/; "China's Shipbuilding Sector Sees Rise in Deliveries, New Orders," Hellenic Shipping News Worldwide, March 7, 2023, https://www.hellenicshippingnews.com/category/shipping-news/shipbuilding-news/; "America's Commercial Shipbuilding Industry Is Nearly Gone," FreightWaves, January 22, 2021, https://www.freightwaves.com/news/freightwaves-classics-americas-commercial-shipbuilding-industry-is-nearly-gone. On Chinese shipbuilding, see Andrew S. Erickson, ed., *Chinese Naval Shipbuilding: An Ambitious and Uncertain Course* (Naval Institute Press, 2017).

25. Aaron L Friedberg, "Britain and the Experience of Relative Decline, 1895–1905," *Journal of Strategic Studies* 10, no. 3 (1987), 331–62.

26. Howard K. Beale, *Theodore Roosevelt and the Rise of America to World Power* (Johns Hopkins University Press, 1956), 144–47; Harold H. Sprout and Margaret T. Sprout, *The Rise of American Naval Power, 1776–1918* (Princeton University Press, 1939), 211–12, 252, 255.

27. Øystein Tunsjø, *The Return of Bipolarity in World Politics: China, the United States, and Geostructural Realism* (Columbia University Press, 2018).

28. On the effect of US presence operations of the navy's declining fleet, see Robert S. Ross, "Reluctant Retrenchment: America's Response to the Rise of China," *Naval War College Review* 76, no. 4 (Autumn 2023).

29. *Naval Doctrine Publication 1: Naval Warfare*, April 2020, https://cimsec.org/wp; Command before the Senate Armed Services Committee on U.S. Indo-Pacific Command Posture, March 9, 2021, 12, https://www.armed-services.senate.gov/imo/media/doc/Davidson_03-09-21.pdf; Ed Adamczyk, "U.S. Air Force Sends F-22s to Western Pacific as Message to China," UPI, July 16, 2021, https://www.upi.com/Defense-News/2021/07/16/f22-usaf-guam-marianas-exercise-China/6291626457191/.

30. Kristin Huang, "US-China Tensions in South China Sea Fuelled by Increase in Military Operations," *South China Morning Post*, May 10, 2002, https://www.scmp.com/news/china/military/article/3083698/us-china-tensions-south-china-sea-fuelled-increase-military; Ralph Jennings, "U.S. Adding Air Power to Naval Operations in Disputed South China Sea," VOA News, March 24, 2021, https://www.voanews.com/usa/us-adding-air-power-naval-operations-disputed-south-china-sea-0.

31. See, for example, Dzirhan Mahadzir, "U.S., Australia, Japan Drill with the Philippines in South China Sea; China Flies Military Drone Near Taiwan," USNI News, August 27, 2023, https://news.usni.org/2023/08/27/u-s-australia-japan-drill-with-the-philippines-in-south-china-sea-china-flies-military-drone-near-taiwan; Nobuhiko Tajima, "Japan to Join U.S.- Philippine Joint Exercise in South China Sea," *Asahi Shimbun*, March 31, 2024, https://www.asahi.com/ajw/articles/15215558.

32. Natasha Bertrand and Oren Liebermann, "China, Taiwan Tensions Spark Debate inside Biden Admin as Democrats Push for More Forceful Response," CNN, October 16, 2021, https://www.cnn.com/2021/10/15/politics/china-taiwan-tension-debate-biden-response/index.html; "China Unlikely to Try to Militarily Seize Taiwan in Near Future, Top U.S. General," Reuters, November 3, 2021, https://www.reuters.com/world/china/china-unlikely-try-militarily-seize-taiwan-near-future-top-us-general-2021-11-03/; "China Military May Be Capable of War against Taiwan and Allied Forces by 2027," Focus Taiwan, June 4, 2022, https://focustaiwan.tw/cross-strait/202206040009; Sarah Wu, "Taiwan Says Odds of War with China in Next Year 'Very Low,'" Reuters, October 20, 2021, https://www.reuters.com/world/asia-pacific/taiwan-says-odds-war-with-china-next-year-very-low-2021-10-20/#:~:text=TAIPEI%20(Reuters)%20%2D%20The%20odds,claims%20sovereignty%20over%20the%20island.

33. J. Michael Dahm, *Beyond Chinese Ferry Tales: The Rise of Deck Cargo Ships in China's Military Activities, 2023*, China Maritime Report No. 35 (China Maritime Studies Institute, US Naval War College, February 2024), https://digital-commons.usnwc.edu/cgi/viewcontent.cgi?article=1034&context=cmsi-maritime-reports; Owen R. Cote Jr., "One If by Invasion, Two If by Coercion: US Military Capacity to Protect Taiwan from China," *Bulletin of the Atomic Scientists* 78, no. 2 (2022), 65–72.

34. *Military and Security Developments Involving the People's Republic of China* (Office of the Secretary of Defense, US Department of Defense, 2021), 99, https://media.defense.gov/2021/Nov/03/2002885874/-1/-1/0/2021-CMPR-FINAL.PDF.

35. Caitlin Doornbos, "US Navy Ends 2020 with Another Taiwan Strait Transit," *Stars and Stripes*, December 31, 2020, https://www.stripes.com/us-navy-ends-2020-with-another-taiwan-strait-transit-1.656979; "Two U.S. Navy Ships Pass through Taiwan Strait, Opposing China," Reuters, November 28, 2018, https://www.reuters.com/article/us-usa-china-taiwan-military/two-us-navy-ships-pass-through-taiwan-strait-opposing-china-idUSKCN1NX2NF; "China Condemns U.S., Canada for Sending Warships through Taiwan Strait," Reuters, October 17, 2021, https://www.reuters.com/world/asia-pacific/us-canadian-warships-sailed-through-taiwan-strait-last-week-2021-10-17/.

36. Megan Epstein, "Navy 'Struggling' to Modernize Aging Cruiser Fleet as Tight Budgets Push Pentagon to Shed Legacy Platforms," USNI News, April 5, 2021, https://news.usni.org/2021/04/05/navy-struggling-to-modernize-aging-cruiser-fleet-as-tight-budgets-push-pentagon-to-shed-legacy-platforms; David B. Larter, "Surface Ship Readiness Continues to Struggle, US Navy Inspections Show," Defense News, March 3, 2021, https://www.defensenews.com/naval/2021/03/03/surface-ship-readiness-continues-to-struggle-navy-inspections-show/#.YEJJbcv3JT8.mailto.

37. "Military Readiness: Department of Defense Domain Readiness Varied from Fiscal Year 2017 through Fiscal Year" (US Government Accountability Office, April 2021), https://www.gao.gov/assets/720/713622.pdf; Hope Hodge Seck, "Navy Has Choice: More Ships or Fewer Missions, Surface Commander Says," Military.com, January 10, 2018, https://www.military.com/dodbuzz/2018/01/10/navy-has-choice-more-ships-or-fewer-missions-surface-commander-says.html; Megan Eckstein, "No Margin Left: Overworked Carrier Force Struggles to Maintain Deployments after Decades of Overuse," USNI News, November 12, 2020, https://news.usni.org/2020/11/12/no-margin-left-overworked-carrier-force-struggles-to-maintain-deployments-after-decades-of-overuse#:~:text=Decades%20of%20Overuse-,No%20Margin%20Left%3A%20Overworked%20Carrier%20Force%20Struggles%20to,Deployments%20After%20Decades%20of%20Overuse&text=For%20two%20years%2C%20in%202018,percent%2and%20then%2016%20percent.

38. Paul McLeary, "In War, Chinese Shipyards Could Outpace US in Replacing Losses; Marine Commandant," *Breaking Defense*, June 17, 2020, https://breakingdefense.com/2020/06/in-war-chinese-shipyards-can-outpace-us-in-replacing-losses/; *Navy Ships: Timely Actions Needed to Improve Planning and Develop Capabilities for Battle Damage Repair*, U.S. Government Accountability Office, June 2, 2021, https://www.gao.gov/products/gao-21-246

39. David B. Larter, "Surface Navy Boss: To Fix the Fleet, Reduce Commitments and Give Us More Ships," Defense News, January 9, 2018, https://www.defensenews.com/digital-show-dailies/surface-navy-association/2018/01/09/surface-boss-to-fix-the-fleet-reduce-commitments-and-give-us-more-ships/; Megan Eckstein, "VADM Rowden Calls Naval

Surface Group Western Pacific an Advocate for Ship Training Needs," USNI News, January 9, 2018, https://news.usni.org/2018/01/09/30486;

40. See Admiral Gilday's statement at Caitlin M. Kenney, "Navy Fleet Plan Needs 3–5% Annual Budget Increases for the Next Two Decades," Defense One, July 27, 2022, https://www.defenseone.com/policy/2022/07/navy-fleet-plan-needs-3-5-annual-budget-increases-next-two-decades/375038/.

41. "Report to Congress on the Annual Long-Range Plan for Construction of Naval Vessels for Fiscal Year 2025" (Office of the Secretary of the Navy, March 2024), https://s3.documentcloud.org/documents/24487775/rtc-pb25-shipbuilding_plan.pdf; Mallory Shelbourne, "New Navy Budget Seeks 6 Battle Force Ships, Decommissions 19 Hulls in FY 2025," USNI News, March 13, 2024, https://news.usni.org/2024/03/11/new-navy-budget-seeks-6-battle-force-ships-10-decommissions-in-fy-2025; Heather Mongilio, "Navy Wants to Decommission 39 Warships in 2023," USNI News, August 15, 2022, https://news.usni.org/2022/08/15/navy-wants-to-decommission-39-warships-in-2023; "Report to Congress on the Annual Long-Range Plan for Construction of Naval Vessels for Fiscal Year 2023" (Office of the Secretary of the Navy, April 2022), 21–22, https://media.defense.gov/2022/Apr/20/2002980535/-1/-1/0/PB23%20SHIPBUILDING%20PLAN%2018%20APR%202022%20FINAL.PDF.

42. Megan Eckstein, "Navy Offers a New Argument for Decommissioning Cruisers: They're Not Safe," Defense News, March 9, 2022, https://www.defensenews.com/naval/2022/03/09/navy-offers-a-new-argument-for-decommissioning-cruisers-theyre-not-safe/; Marcus Weisgerber, "Top Navy Admiral: Fleet Size Doesn't Always Matter," Defense One, April 4, 2022, https://www.defenseone.com/policy/2022/04/top-navy-admiral-fleet-size-doesnt-always-matter/363974/.

43. T. S. Rowden, "Surface Force Strategy: Return to Sea Control" (US Navy, 2016), 9–10, 18, https://apps.dtic.mil/sti/pdfs/AD1024229.pdf; "Report to Congress on the Annual Long-Range Plan for Construction of Naval Vessels for Fiscal Year 2023," 5, 9; Cancian, "U.S. Military Forces in FY 202: Navy," Center for Strategic & International Studies, November 2, 2021, https://www.csis.org/analysis/us-military-forces-fy-2022-navy

44. David B. Larter, "The US Navy Selects Fincantieri Design for Next-Generation Frigate," Defense News, April 30, 2020, https://www.defensenews.com/breaking-news/2020/04/30/the-us-navy-selects-fincantieri-design-for-next-generation-frigate/; Fincantieri, "Fincantieri to Build the Second Constellation-Class Frigate for the US Navy," May 21, 2021, https://www.fincantieri.com/en/media/press-releases/2021/fincantieri-to-build-the-second-constellation-class-frigate-for-the-us-navy/.

45. Aaron-Matthew Lariosa, "India to Take on Future U.S. Navy Ship Maintenance per Agreement," USNI News, September 14, 2023, https://news.usni.org/2023/09/14/india-to-take-on-future-u-s-navy-ship-maintenance-per-agreement; John Geddie and Tim Kelly, "U.S. Wants Japanese Shipyards to Help Keep Warships Ready to Fight in Asia," Reuters, January 19, 2024, https://www.reuters.com/world/asia-pacific/us-eyeing-japanese-shipyards-warship-overhauls-says-us-ambassador-2024-01-19/; Leilani Chavez, "South Korea, US Explore Joint Ship, Weapons Maintenance Opportunities," Defense News, February 6, 2024, https://www.defensenews.com/naval/2024/02/06/south-korea-us-explore-joint-ship-weapons-maintenance-opportunities/.

46. Owen R. Cote Jr., "Assessing the Undersea Balance," SSP Working Paper WP11-1 (Massachusetts Institute of Technology, 2011), http://web.mit.edu/ssp/publications/working_papers/Undersea%20Balance%20WP11-1.pdf.

47. A. T. Mahan, The Influence of Sea Power upon History, 1660–1783 (Dover Publications, 1987), 35–36.

48. David Makichuk, "US Marines Are Bringing Ship Killer to the Pacific," Asia Times, September 30, 2021, https://asiatimes.com/2021/09/us-marines-are-bringing-a-ship-killer-to-the-pacific/.

49. Anthony De Ceglie, "Government Eyes Troops for Christmas, Cocos Islands," West Australian, November 16, 2016, https://thewest.com.au/news/australia/government-eyes-troops-for-christmas-cocos-islands-ng-ya-123549; "Australian Defence Force Posture Review" (Australian Government, March 30, 2012), 26, http://www.defence.gov.au/oscdf/adf-posture-review/docs/final/Report.pdf; Australian Government, Department of Defence, "Contract Awarded for Cocos (Keeling) Islands Runway Upgrade," January 31, 2020, https://www.

minister.defence.gov.au/minister/melissa-price/media-releases/contract-awarded-cocos-keeling-islands-runway-upgrade.

50. Jeff Smith and Alex Werman, "Assessing US-India Defense Relations: The Technological Handshake," *The Diplomat*, October 6, 2016, https://thediplomat.com/2016/10/assessing-us-india-defense-relations-the-technological-handshake/.

51. K. Alan Kronstadt and Shayerah Ilias Akhtar, "India-U.S. Relations: Issues for Congress," R44876 (Congressional Research Service, June 19, 2017), 14–16, https://fas.org/sgp/crs/row/R44876.pdf.

52. "US Approves Anti-Submarine Helicopter Sale to India," *Straits Times*, April 3, 2019, https://www.straitstimes.com/world/united-states/us-approves-anti-submarine-helicopter-sale-to-india.

53. "With INS Kohassa, India Set to Get Fourth Airbase in the Andamans," *Hindustan Times*, January 24, 2019, https://www.hindustantimes.com/india-news/with-ins-kohassa-india-set-to-get-fourth-air-base-in-the-andamans/story-XzsZdOBW0ruBgZ9a7eWlzM.html; Sanjeev Miglani, "India Navy set to Open Third Base in Strategic Islands to Counter China," January 23, 2019, https://www.reuters.com/article/us-india-navy-base/india-navy-set-to-open-third-base-in-strategic-islands-to-counter-china-idUSKCN1PH17Y/; Darshana M. Baruah, "Sister Islands in the Indian Ocean Region: Linking the Andaman and Nicobar Islands to La Réunion," *War on the Rocks*, March 20, 2019, https://warontherocks.com/2019/03/sister-islands-in-the-indian-ocean-region-linking-the-andaman-and-nicobar-islands-to-la-reunion/.

54. Stephen Dziedzic, "US to Partner with Australia, Papua New Guinea on Manus Island Naval Base," ABC (Australia), November 16, 2018, https://www.abc.net.au/news/2018-11-17/us-to-partner-with-australia-and-png-on-manus-island-naval-base/10507658?pfmredir=sm; Rod McGuirk, "With China Rising, CNO Praises Australian Decision to Expand Naval Base in Papua New Guinea," *Navy Times*, November 1, 2018, https://www.navytimes.com/home/left-column/2018/11/01/with-china-rising-cno-praises-australian-decision-to-expand-naval-base-in-papua-new-guinea/; Alan Boyd, "Spy vs Spy as China Eyes US-Oz Sea Defense Moves," *Asia Times*, March 2, 2020, https://asiatimes.com/2020/03/spy-vs-spy-as-china-eyes-us-oz-sea-defense-moves/.

55. "United States Starts Defense Cooperation Agreement Negotiations with Papua New Guinea" (Office of the Spokesperson, US Department of State, February 11, 2023), https://www.state.gov/united-states-starts-defense-cooperation-agreement-negotiations-with-papua-new-guinea/; "US Military Will Have 'Unimpeded' Access to Papua New Guinea Bases under New Security Deal," *The Guardian*, June 15, 2023, https://www.theguardian.com/world/2023/jun/15/us-military-will-have-unimpeded-access-to-papua-new-guinea-bases-under-new-security-deal.

56. Desmond Ball and Richard Tanter, *The Tools of Owatatsumi Japan's Ocean Surveillance and Coastal Defence Capabilities* (ANU Press, 2015).

57. "A Concept for Stand-in Forces" (US Marine Corps, Department of the Navy, December 2021), https://www.hqmc.marines.mil/Portals/142/Users/183/35/4535/211201_A%20Concept%20for%20Stand-In%20Forces.pdf?ver=MFOzu2hs_IWHZlsOAkfZsQ%3D%3D#:~:text=A%20Concept%20for%20Stand%2Din%20Forces%20deals%20with%20rivals%20who,and%20sustain%20it%20over%20time.

58. Pia Lee-Brago, "Batanes Seaport to Be Funded by US," *Philippine Star*, March 12, 2024, https://www.philstar.com/headlines/2024/03/12/2339913/batanes-seaport-be-funded-us.

59. US Department of Defense, "Readout of Secretary of Defense Dr. Mark T. Esper's Meeting with the President of the Republic of Palau and Other Members of his Cabinet," August 28, 2020, AMTI, athttps://www.defense.gov/News/Releases/Release/Article/2328409/readout-of-secretary-of-defense-dr-mark-t-espers-meeting-with-the-president-of/; Brief (Center for Strategic and International Studies, June 15, 2023), https://amti.csis.org/strategic-upgrades-in-the-pacific/; US Army, "U.S. Military Lands C130 on Newly Renovated Angaur Airfield in Palau," September 8, 2020, https://www.army.mil/article/238873/u_s_military_lands_c130_on_newly_renovated_angaur_airfield_in_palau.

60. Robert S. Ross, "US Grand Strategy, the Rise of China, and US National Security Strategy for East Asia," *Strategic Studies Quarterly* 7, no. 2 (Summer 2013): 20.

61. Frank Tang, "China a 'Very Important Customer', Says Saudi Arabia, as Global Oil Supply Worries Grow," *South China Morning Post*, May 31, 2022, https://www.scmp.com/economy/

china-economy/article/3179717/china-very-important-customer-says-saudi-arabia-global-oil; Zachary Cohen, "US Intel and Satellite Images Show Saudi Arabia Is Now Building Its Own Ballistic Missiles with Help of China," CNN, December 23, 2021, https://www.cnn.com/2021/12/23/politics/saudi-ballistic-missiles-china/index.htm.

62. Tom Hussain, "With US Distracted by Russia's Ukraine War and China, Economics and an Emboldened Iran Drive Middle East Powers to Redraw Alliances," *South China Morning Post*, March 27, 2021, https://www.scmp.com/week-asia/politics/article/3171848/us-distracted-russias-ukraine-war-and-china-economics-and?utm_source=email&utm_medium=share_widget&utm_campaign=3171848.

63. German Defence Spending, Trading Economics, Statista, https://tradingeconomics.com/germany/military-expenditure; Defence Data 2019–2020: Key Findings and Analysis (European Defence Agency, 2021), 4, https://eda.europa.eu/docs/default-source/brochures/eda—defence-data-report-2019-2020.pdf; French Defence Spending, Trading Economics, Statista, https://www.statista.com/statistics/1293422/france-defense-expenditure/#:~:text=In%202021%2C%20France%20spent%20approximately,with%2043.5%20billion%20U.S.%20dollars.

64. Andrea Ghiselli, *Protecting China's Interests Overseas: Securitization and Foreign Policy* (Oxford University Press, 2021).

6

Will US-PRC Military Competition Go Global?

Why Russia's Invasion of Ukraine Matters

Thomas J. Christensen

In the preceding chapter, Robert Ross argues convincingly that military competition between the People's Republic of China (PRC) and the United States will largely take place in the East Asia region for many years to come. China lacks power projection capabilities, at least in the conventional realm, for direct and sustained confrontation of the United States or US allies outside the region. Despite this limiting factor, we might still witness a Sino-American strategic competition in areas far from China that could escalate into local military conflicts. As Øystein Tunsjø has argued, the Soviet Union could not project conventional military power far from home for most of its existence, but that did not prevent the Soviet-American confrontation from going global and becoming militarized on various continents.[1] Like the Soviets, Beijing could arm or train proxies and allies to fight in more distant regions against US proxies or allies, or even against US forces themselves.

How and whether the regional military competition in East Asia will morph into a global one in this fashion will hinge as much on the political and economic nature of US-PRC strategic competition as it does on the details of China's military modernization or the size of the overall gap between American and Chinese national military power. Three key questions must be addressed: Will Sino-American competition take on a more explicitly ideological tone over time? Will globalization move in reverse and will the United States and its allies and partners decouple from the Chinese economy? And will two opposing alliance blocs form around the world along these political dividing lines?

Thomas J. Christensen, *Will US-PRC Military Competition Go Global?*. In: *Not Just Another Cold War*. Edited by: Bård Nikolas Vik Steen, Oxford University Press. © Oxford University Press (2025).
DOI: 10.1093/9780197799932.003.0007

In the years before Russia's invasion of Ukraine, the US-China strategic competition seemed unlikely to evolve into a US-Soviet-style Cold War. The answer to all of the questions above appeared likely to be "no." There were three interrelated reasons:

First, the PRC under Xi Jinping and the United States, especially under Donald Trump, were not actively exporting their national ideological models abroad. The ideological differences between Beijing and Washington still mattered in exacerbating bilateral mistrust, but there was no competition to spread those models around the world.

Second, globalization and the creation of transnational production chains linked China tightly to the United States and its allies and partners in the economic sphere in ways that made it hard to imagine the formation of the kinds of separate economic blocs that we witnessed during the Cold War. China's dependence on the United States and its allies meant that Beijing was unlikely to try to undermine their democracies.

Third, for reasons related to the first two factors above, US allies and partners would be unlikely to sign up to a US-led containment strategy against China with all of its military and economic components. For its part, China continues to lack a robust network of allies and partners.

Therefore, the world seemed unlikely to split starkly between a China-led coalition and a US-led coalition in the way that international politics played out in the first two decades of the US-Soviet Cold War.[2]

The Russian invasion of Ukraine and how it unfolded require a reconsideration of those questions. The invasion and its aftermath might unleash forces that override the stabilizing forces listed above, or, alternatively, it might prove to be a stress test, if you will, demonstrating the strength of those factors in preventing a new Cold War. It is still too early to know, but this chapter will explore what to watch to determine whether the Russian invasion has started a process that will lead to a new Sino-American Cold War.

Why Russia's Invasion Matters

By exploiting his close relationship with China's Xi Jinping and ordering the invasion of the capital of a neighboring democracy, Putin amplified the view of a world divided between democracies and autocracies, compelled Beijing to side more explicitly with the latter, and thereby dragged China into a more confrontational stance with the United States and its allies, on whom Beijing still depends for continued economic growth.

In the years before the invasion, some important changes were already occurring. The Sino-American trade war and the ban on certain technology exports to China and the damage done to supply chains by the global pandemic called into question the future of global interdependence. In 2021, US foreign policy under Joseph Biden became more ideological than it was under President Trump. At least in its rhetoric, the United States would return to a more traditionally principled American foreign policy by promoting the spread of democracy and renewing criticism of the authoritarian leaders with whom Donald Trump seemed so comfortable.

Still, after the wearying conflicts in Iraq and Afghanistan and four years of "America First" sloganeering, it seemed unlikely that Biden's declared struggle of "democracy versus authoritarianism" would take on military dimensions, and Secretary of State Blinken explicitly stated that Washington was not seeking to undermine the Chinese government at home.[3] Moreover, the prospect of the United States rallying allies into an anti-China alliance seemed small. Before Russia's invasion of Ukraine, Chinese security experts felt confident that the advanced economies aligned with the United States, regardless of regime type, would be reluctant to align tightly to contain China's economic growth and expanding international influence. Key US allies like Japan and South Korea, they argued, are just too dependent on the Chinese economy. They sustained their economic interactions with China and in some cases even deepened them, despite Trump's protectionism and the pandemic (see tables 6.1, 6.2, and 6.3 below). Chinese observers also took courage in the lack of cohesion in the US-led alliance system caused by historical and political tension between countries like Japan and South Korea and the United States and postcoup Thailand. Moreover, some potential strategic partners of the United States, especially Vietnam, are not democratic and there is a strong legacy of nonalignment among other potential US partners, like India, Malaysia, and Indonesia.[4]

None of this would likely hold, however, if the PRC began actively exporting its ideology by undermining existing foreign democracies in the vein of what Putin's Russia has attempted in Eastern Europe, and/or if economic nationalism and geopolitics undermined the transnational supply chain in ways that made the separation of Cold War–style blocs appear more affordable. The events of February 2022 opened up pathways that could lead in that direction over time. And since then we have seen an increase in US government limits on high-tech transfers to China, especially in high-end semiconductors and semiconductor manufacturing equipment; Washington's coaxing of allies and partners like South Korea, the Netherlands, Japan, and Taiwan to join in the embargo; a significant warming of Japan-Korea relations; and growing links between the North Atlantic Treaty Organization (NATO) alliance and the US allies in the Asia Pacific with the creation of the Australia, United Kingdom, and United States (AUKUS) technology sharing arrangement and the attendance of Japan and South Korea at high-level NATO meetings.

While Putin was attending the Beijing Olympics, he and Xi offered a detailed statement of their deep partnership, which they proclaimed had "no limits."[5] Despite the rhetoric regarding its unlimited potential, the Sino-Russian partnership is still far from a formal alliance, even taking into account the joint military exercises conducted during President Biden's May 2022 trip to Japan. It is still hard to imagine Chinese forces joining the Russian military in a future war over Ukraine or Russian forces joining the People's Liberation Army (PLA) in a conflict across the Taiwan Strait, even one that involved the United States. However, the joint statement was significant all the same. In ways that echoed Cold War rhetoric, it publicly linked Xi Jinping with his avowed "best friend," Vladimir Putin, in ways that focused on their "non-Western" (read: nondemocratic) form of government and the threat posed to them by "Western" (read: US and European) efforts to export "color revolutions." In a manner reminiscent of the Cold War, the statement also excoriated efforts to strengthen the US-led alliance systems in both Europe and Asia.[6]

The February 4th statement became truly consequential when, on February 24, Putin apparently surprised Beijing by launching a massive invasion of Ukraine, designed, however poorly, to overthrow and replace the democratically elected government of Volodymyr Zelenskyy. Prior to the invasion, Beijing had dismissed as inaccurate, propagandistic, or both Washington's public and private warnings and intelligence briefings that Russia was preparing for such an invasion.[7] Xi and his advisors chose instead to believe Putin, not Putin's adversaries in Washington. News articles, citing a leaked US intelligence document, suggested that Xi was aware of and perhaps even approving of Putin's plans for aggression and simply asked him to wait until after the Beijing Winter Olympics to carry them out.[8] Various statements by high-level officials, including then PRC ambassador to the United States

Qin Gang and state councilor for foreign affairs Wang Yi, rejected claims in the US media that Beijing had advance knowledge and supported the invasion or that China was preparing to transfer arms to Russia. Beijing's utter failure to evacuate PRC citizens and diplomats in Ukraine in advance seem consistent with that narrative.[9]

Several aspects of the invasion and its aftermath must have come as an unpleasant surprise to Beijing. They include the Russian drive on the Ukrainian capital, Kyiv; the strength of the Ukrainian resistance; the poor performance of Russian forces; the unity of the US allies in Europe and Asia in severely sanctioning Russia in response; and the United States and NATO allies nimbly providing Ukraine with essential military equipment and vital intelligence in a timely fashion.

It appears that Putin exploited Xi by locking him in publicly to an enhanced partnership before committing a brazen act of aggression. If that aggression were to fail, Russia could then ask China to provide support for the Russian economy and, most important, Putin's political survival. One is reminded of the way that, in spring 1950, Stalin and Kim Il-sung manipulated Mao Zedong into supporting the latter's invasion of South Korea, thus sparking a large international war on China's doorstep for which China had to pick up the bill once that invasion failed and United Nations forces intervened and crossed the thirty-eighth parallel heading north. The lengthy war would eventually cost the PRC a million casualties and deprive Mao of his dream of unification of the mainland with Taiwan as Truman reversed his earlier hands-off stance toward the Chinese Civil War across the Taiwan Strait.[10]

Beijing refuses to condemn Russian actions and rebroadcasts Putin's propaganda about the alleged precipitating causes of the conflict (the United States and its support for NATO expansion). Chinese officials have even sometimes retweeted Moscow's smear campaign about Nazis in Zelenskyy's government.[11] Beijing has also been harshly critical of the sweeping trade and financial sanctions levied on Russia by almost all advanced economies of the world and especially of the threat of "secondary sanctions" by the United States and Europe against any economy that violates the sanctions on Russia by providing prohibited forms of support to Moscow.[12]

Top Biden administration officials, including the president and national security advisor, have made clear to their Chinese counterparts that not just the United States, but several other leading economies, would sanction China and restrict exports to China if Beijing were to choose to flout the international sanctions on Moscow by backfilling Russian needs created by those sanctions. Secretary of Commerce Gina Raimondo threatened to cripple key Chinese tech companies that are dependent on US inputs and know-how if they were to violate allied embargoes on the transfer of semiconductors to Russia. National Security Advisor Jake Sullivan said that China would face "real costs" if it were to sell lethal military equipment to Russia during the war.[13] Janet Yellen has similarly threatened Chinese banks with secondary sanctions if they were to transfer hard currency to Russia and direct sanctions if Beijing tried to use force to compel Taiwan to accept unification.[14]

Especially early in the war, Beijing was walking a tightrope. On the one hand, Beijing has long considered indirect or secondary sanctions to be illegal and the threat to use them to be destabilizing. On the other hand, Beijing has apparently taken threats of secondary sanctions seriously and seems loathe to be subject to them. According to public statements by US officials, Beijing, in general, has avoided violating the international sanctions on Russia, especially as they apply to the sale of weapons to Russia at a time when Russian demand for them is great.[15] China continues, however, to provide succour to Russia's economy, for example, by buying large amounts of energy, albeit by using renminbi rather than hard currencies, for trade credits for fear of triggering financial sanctions.[16] Especially since US allies and partners in Europe and Asia themselves purchased energy from Russia after the invasion, such Chinese purchases are not actionable. Since late 2023 US government officials have begun to complain that, while China has still refused Russian requests for arms sales in areas such as artillery shells and armed drones, Beijing has been making economic transfers that strengthen the Russian defense industrial base so that Russia can produce more of its own weapons for the grinding war with Ukraine.[17] In December 2023, the Treasury Department sanctioned several Chinese companies and nationals involved in coordinating the sale of Chinese-manufactured technologies with clear military application like high-resolution observation satellite imagery and advanced electronics to Russia.[18] Beijing appears, then, to be walking close to the line of triggering further sanctions by the United States and, perhaps, some other highly developed economies concerned about Ukraine's survival.

There are then scenarios that could produce spirals of tension between China and the advanced economies currently sanctioning Russia. Most of those economies are participating in severe export controls on Russia, amounting to an embargo, on a range of products like semiconductors and commercial aircraft and parts. These measures could do serious damage to the Russian economy over time. It is natural for Russia to turn to China to supply such products. But, as Secretary Raimondo reminded us, China itself is still heavily dependent on US and European technologies in these key economic sectors.[19] Beijing therefore will continue to run risks to its own economy if it chooses to fulfill certain Russian requests.

Still, the Chinese Communist Party (CCP) and President Xi in particular have strong domestic political reasons to want to prevent Russia's complete failure in Ukraine. The fall of Putin that might follow such a failure, especially since it would have occurred under pressure from liberal democracies, would be a disaster of the first order for the CCP. Leninists are concerned primarily with domestic security. CCP elites must concern themselves with demonstration effects of a coup or "color revolution" in Russia. Beijing also does not want to lose a major political ally on the international stage with which China actively opposes American and European efforts to promote democracy. Moreover, there would be little guarantee that a successor Russian state would not be more pro-European and anti-China even if it remained authoritarian. In any protracted conflict with the United States over Taiwan, Beijing might want to turn to Russia to provide it with needed resources, especially oil. Russia's willingness to do so will depend in part on the regime in power in Moscow at the time.

The good news for Beijing is that it would be very difficult for the United States to rally partners for sanctions on the PRC for its general support of Russia. In this way, the Russian invasion might provide a test case of how economic globalization can prevent the division of the world into starkly divided blocs in the twenty-first century. After the invasion, the Biden administration worked quickly and effectively to put together a broad coalition of advanced economies to sanction Russia. This was no easy task even though Russia was the clear culprit in the war. Some countries, like Germany and Finland, are paying a high cost to stand up to Putin. Getting countries to sanction China simply for supporting Russia, however, would be an order of magnitude more difficult. The nearly certain Chinese retaliation against those countries could cause large-scale economic pain as China is a much larger economic player than Russia. Moreover, no matter how distasteful China's backfilling of international sanctions on Russia might appear, that policy will not spark the same intense emotional and political reaction as Russia's killing of Ukrainian soldiers and civilians in their sovereign territory.

Was Globalization Already Dying?

Since globalization and transnational production chains are a major buffer against a new Cold War, it is worth asking if this variable has significantly changed in the years before the Russian invasion. Donald Trump's trade war with China, several countries' nervousness about reliance on Chinese telecommunications infrastructure, the global pandemic's disruption of supply chains, and the growth of economic nationalism around the world, especially in China itself, might call into question the robustness of the globalization factor in preventing a new Cold War. These phenomena have, to date, only had a limited impact on globalization and transnational production chains. They have mostly affected certain technological sectors and certain bilateral relationships. Comparing statistics from before and after these events reveals this. In 2014, China was heavily dependent on the United States and its allies and partners and therefore would be very reluctant to harm relations with those countries by trying to harm their political systems and spread authoritarianism. If one removed Hong Kong from the list, eight out of ten of China's largest economic partners were the United States and its treaty allies and security partners. In 2021, the year before the Russian invasion, things were largely unchanged on this score.[20] In 2021, six out of eight of China's top international trade partners were still the United States and its allies and security partners.[21] Moreover, in certain key economic sectors, like advanced semiconductors, the PRC remained highly dependent on those US allies and partners. Trade has dropped as a percentage of China's gross domestic product (GDP) in the interim years, but it remains a very important part of Chinese economic well-being.

US allies and partners, particularly those in East Asia, also remained highly dependent on China. This will make it hard for the United States to build and sustain a coalition to sanction China even if China were to ignore US threats of secondary sanctions and begin to sell weapons to Russia, as North Korea has. Table 6.1 shows where China ranked in 2018 for these countries in terms of export markets and sources of imports. The picture was very similar in 2021 (Table 6.2).

Table 6.1 China's economic importance to the United States, US allies, and potential security partners in East Asia in 2018 (unit: billions USD)[a]

2018	Exports to China (global rank)	Imports from China (global rank)	Total trade with China (export, import)	% of total trade	% of GDP	China's ranking (export, import)
United States	120 (3)	539 (1)	659	16	3	(3, 1)
Japan	144 (1)	175 (1)	319	21	6	(1, 1)
Republic of Korea	162 (1)	106 (1)	268	24	17	(1, 1)
Australia	87 (1)	58 (1)	145	29	10	(1, 1)
Malaysia	36 (1)	44 (1)	80	17	23	(1, 1)

[a]Data from United Nations COMTRADE database, World Bank national accounts, and OECD National Accounts.

Table 6.2 China's economic importance to the United States, US allies, and potential security partners in East Asia in 2021 (unit: billions USD)[a]

2021	Exports to China (global rank)	Imports from China (global rank)	Total trade with China (export, import)	% of total trade	% of GDP	China's ranking[b] (export, import)
United States	151 (3)	506 (1)	657	16	3	(3, 1)
Japan	163 (1)	185 (1)	348	25	7	(1, 1)
Republic of Korea	138 (1)	163 (1)	301	27	15	(1, 1)
Australia	130 (1)	72 (1)	202	36	7	(1, 1)
Malaysia	46 (1)	55 (1)	101	21	27	(1, 1)

[a]Data from United Nations COMTRADE database, World Bank national accounts, and OECD National Accounts.
[b]Data from United Nations COMTRADE database, World Bank national accounts, and OECD National Accounts.

As one can see, even US-China bilateral trade remains robust despite the damage done by the tariff wars. US-China tensions have damaged US-China economic relations dramatically in certain sectors, especially Chinese investment into the United States, which has plummeted since Trump's inauguration in 2017. As shown in Table 6.3, robust trade between China and the United States continues, however, and Secretary of Treasury Janet Yellen recognized that the Trump tariffs on Chinese imports may be hurting the United States more than the PRC. This provides a kind of test case for the powerful influence of globalization despite domestic political and national security incentives to reduce that influence.[22]

In 2023 trade links were still impressively robust between these actors despite increased global geopolitical tensions; Beijing's own statist, protectionist economic policies; and China's often abrasive diplomacy toward its economic partners. US-China trade has dropped somewhat since 2021, and trade between South Korea and China and between Japan and China took a fairly significant hit in 2023. Total Japan-China trade in 2023 decreased by 16.6% from 2022.[23] Overall trade between South Korea and China declined 12.6% from the previous year, with South Korean exports to the United States surpassing exports to China on a month-to-month basis in December 2023.[24] And not shown here is that South Korean investment into China fell precipitously in the last two years.[25]

Still, this data carries mixed lessons for our purposes. Rising geostrategic competition and attendant political tensions have negatively impacted China's economic links with the United States and US allies and partners like

Table 6.3 China's economic importance to the United States, US allies, and potential security partners in East Asia in 2023 (unit: billions USD)

2023	Exports to China (global rank)	Imports from China (global rank)	Total trade with China (export, import)	% of total trade	% of GDP	China's average ranking (export, import)
United States	147 (3)	448 (2)	595	11	2	(3, 2)
Japan	117 (2)	160 (1)	277	19	6.5	(2, 1)
Republic of Korea	128 (1)	142 (1)	270	21	15	(1, 1)
Australia	120 (1)	71 (1)	191	29	11	(1, 1)
Malaysia	42 (1)	56 (1)	98	17	24	(1, 1)

Sources: UN COMTRADE United Nations https://comtradeplus.un.org/; Trading Economics https://tradingeconomics.com/.

Japan and South Korea. However, so far a robust economic interdependence still exists among these actors. Transnational production chains are complex and difficult to unwind. And when they do unwind, they do not tend to do so in straightforward ways. For example, US tariffs on imports from China in place since 2018 have accelerated a preexisting trend in which China is selling intermediate parts for assembly of final products to countries like Vietnam and Mexico. As a result, China's exports to those countries have skyrocketed, as have US imports from those countries. The mutual dependence of the United States and the PRC persists, but in a different and less direct form, and the US trade deficit with the world was at a record high in 2022.[26]

Chinese and American Ideological Export

Increasing Chinese "influence operations," attempts to alter politics and policies in liberal democracies, seemingly run counter to the argument that economic forces deter Beijing from exporting authoritarianism. The influence attempts are real and pose important challenges to liberal institutions and the spread of democracy. The basic realities on that score, however, have not yet changed in recent years. Beijing's efforts in this realm remain focused on reducing foreign criticism of CCP rule at home and preventing countries from siding with the PRC's opponents in sovereignty disputes in the East China Sea, in the South China Sea, and across the Taiwan Strait. While Chinese wolf-warrior diplomats and media have often mocked "Western democracy" for its shortcomings, this is generally in response to foreign criticism of CCP governance at home on topics from COVID cover-ups and lockdowns, to suppression of democracy in Hong Kong, to the forced detention of young Uighurs in Xinjiang. There does not seem to be a concerted PRC effort to overthrow democracies or support anti-democratic forces in existing democracies in the way that Chairman Mao and Soviet leaders did in the first half of the Cold War and that Putin's Russia does today.

China indeed exports surveillance technologies, trains foreign governments in internet censorship, and pressures foreign journalists and academics not to criticize Beijing. These Chinese practices are very concerning to anyone who believes in universal values like freedom of expression and freedom from government oversight. They seem, however, to pose a bigger threat to the spread of democracy to currently authoritarian polities than a Cold War–style threat to existing nonauthoritarian states. Institutions in liberal democracies like universities and media outlets, however, should remain especially vigilant in defending against these CCP efforts even if they do not yet rise to the level of the US-Soviet Cold War or even to the level of Russia attempting to undermine democracy in Ukraine, Georgia, and the Baltic States. The places where Beijing has actively tried to destroy democracy on an institutional level—Hong Kong and Taiwan—appear to be the exceptions, not the rule. Beijing claims that these areas are special because they are part of China's sovereign territory.[27]

Beginning in 2023 there were some signs that Beijing was starting to engage in Russian-style online influence attempts designed to sow general doubts in the US public about the credibility and effectiveness of the US government. For example, messages traced back to China on social media spread false rumors that the wildfires on the Hawaiian island of Maui had been set by the US military.[28] This nascent behavior warrants our attention as it goes beyond the defensive undermining of those voices abroad who are critical of CCP rule at home or the PRC's expansive sovereignty claims.

The Biden administration has enhanced US security cooperation with China's democratic neighbors through the "Quad" (India, Japan, Australia, and the United States) and brought the United Kingdom more into the Asian security realm with AUKUS, a pact focusing on the cooperative development of nuclear-powered submarines. In August 2023 President Biden hosted President Yoon of South Korea and Prime Minister Kishida in a historic trilateral summit that has fostered an unprecedented level of trilateral interaction between the governments of the three allies.[29] Also, President Yoon and Prime Minister Kishida have attended NATO summits, further linking the US-led alliance system in Asia with that of Europe.[30] There is little doubt that these efforts are part of the ongoing strategic competition with China. In these contexts, the Biden administration has indeed made broad proclamations about the nature of the twenty-first century that sound like a Cold War divide: the battle between authoritarianism and democracy.[31] Still, even in its own strategy statements, the Biden administration has said that fostering domestic political change in the PRC is no longer a stated goal of the United States. Instead, Washington seeks to shape China's external environment.[32] That seems more like standard great power competition than an ideological Cold War.

The Russian Invasion of Ukraine and the Prospect of US-PRC Conflict over Taiwan

Through a series of indirect effects, the brazen invasion of democratic Ukraine by an authoritarian Russia could help spark a direct conflict between the United States and the PRC far from Ukraine, in the Taiwan Strait. If such a war were to occur, then a new Cold War that could move US-PRC military competition beyond East Asia seems much more imaginable. Key events that change the overall tenor of security relations around the world permeate international history. As alluded to earlier, the Korean War was just such an event. For the United States and the PRC, the Cold War, as we came to know it, began in Korea. When the war broke out, the United States reinserted itself in the Chinese Civil War by sending naval forces into the Taiwan Strait and declaring that Taiwan's status in relation to mainland China was "undetermined" pending a peace treaty involving all the major combatants in World War II. Such a treaty has never been signed between Japan and Russia. Washington's position on Taiwan's sovereign status remains.[33]

As with the Russian invasion of Ukraine, the Korean War and its escalation affected events far from Korea by fully mobilizing the United States for the Cold War. The US defense budget tripled from June 1950 to January 1951, and Washington sent most of those new resources to other areas of the world considered strategically more important than Korea to American security, such as the European states in the new NATO alliance. At a more abstract level, the Korean War seemed to support the conclusions of a stark, Manichean assessment of a world divided between Communist and free blocs that was outlined in the National Security Council Paper NSC-68, a national security document drafted in spring 1950 but initially shelved by Truman until after the Korean War began.[34]

Something roughly analogous may have happened in February 2022. During the Beijing Olympics, Putin convinced Xi Jinping to issue the aforementioned statement of an unlimited partnership. Russia had amassed significant forces on the Russian and Belarussian borders with Ukraine. US officials warned China privately and the rest of the world publicly that Putin had every intention of invading Ukraine. Beijing apparently disagreed with the private warnings from US officials. Instead, Chinese propaganda parroted the Russian claims that Washington was slandering Moscow and mocked US intelligence failures of the recent past, including the false claims regarding weapons of mass destruction in Saddam Hussein's Iraq.[35] When

Putin launched his massive invasion and drive on Kyiv on February 24, Xi Jinping and his advisors refused to condemn the invasion, or even call it an invasion. PRC officials blamed the United States and NATO for creating the tensions that led to the conflict. Public statements suggested, however, that they were both surprised and worried about the invasion.[36]

Beijing had reason for worry. After organizing massive multilateral sanctions against Russia, US leaders focused on China's relations with Russia. President Biden and National Security Advisor Jake Sullivan warned their Chinese counterparts that violation of those sanctions would lead to crippling secondary sanctions on China.[37] Perhaps more important, the Russian invasion of Ukraine amplified the Biden administration's preexisting view of international politics as a struggle between authoritarianism and democracy and the threat posed to America by an authoritarian China.

Predictably, Taiwan has been at the center of these developments. Tensions across the Taiwan Strait were already high before the Russian invasion, with Beijing refusing to open dialogue with Taiwan since democratically elected leader President Tsai Ing-wen from the traditionally pro-independence Democratic Progressive Party (DPP) took office in 2016. In the following years, Beijing used economic pressure and frequent military exercises to try to intimidate Taiwan into accepting Beijing's terms for cross-strait relations. As discussed further below, the military pressure campaign intensified after Speaker of the House Nancy Pelosi visited Taiwan in August 2022. Beijing also worked hard to convince Taiwan's diplomatic partners to switch sides and recognize the PRC instead of the Republic of China (ROC) on Taiwan.

While PRC officials insisted that Russia-Ukraine relations are fundamentally different than relations across the Taiwan Strait, Americans on both sides of the political divide saw the relationships as very much of a type. Biden administration officials were eager to preempt any perception that their resolve to assist in Taiwan's defense was in doubt because NATO had failed to deter Russian aggression against Ukraine or to intervene directly when deterrence failed. Articles in the US media suggested that the Russian invasion of Ukraine might be a model for a PRC invasion of Taiwan and argued that such an attack could take place soon because the United States and its allies were distracted by events in Europe.[38] For some combination of strategic and domestic reasons, the Biden administration warned China publicly not to doubt US resolve to support Taiwan.[39]

In Taiwan, official and public commentators drew parallels between the struggles of a free Ukraine against an authoritarian Russia and Taiwan's struggles to remain free under increasing PRC economic and military pressure on the island. Those in the traditionally pro-independence DPP camp took courage in the highly successful initial Ukrainian resistance to the Russian invasion, while former Kuomintang (KMT) president Ma Ying-jeou emphasized that the United States and its allies were afraid to engage directly a nuclear-armed Russia. Therefore, he warned, they were unlikely to come to Taiwan's defense against the PRC if pro-independence forces were to provoke a cross-strait conflict.[40]

Even before the Russian invasion, but especially after it, American commentators suggested that Washington should end the strategy of "strategic ambiguity" toward cross-strait relations. By keeping both sides guessing about the conditions under which the United States would intervene, Washington has used ambiguity for decades to deter both the PRC from forcing unification with the island and pro-independence forces on Taiwan from adopting provocative actions that might spark an otherwise avoidable war. Recent critics of this long-standing policy called instead for "clarity," a firm and unconditional commitment to Taiwan's defense if it were attacked by the mainland.[41] Former Japanese prime minister Shinzo Abe weighed in before his tragic assassination, calling for the United States to clarify its commitment to Taiwan in ways that would break from the traditional US "one China" policy dating back to 1979.[42] During a visit to Taipei by a bipartisan group of senators and congressional representatives to Taiwan, Taiwan officials, including President Tsai, and the US legislators themselves similarly invoked the lens of authoritarianism versus democracy and the example of the Russian invasion of Ukraine to argue for a tighter alliance among democracies.[43]

Former leading Trump administration officials also sounded out on Taiwan policy following Russia's invasion. Former secretary of state Mike Pompeo travelled to Taiwan and called for renewed US formal recognition of the government there, severed in 1979 as part of US normalization with the PRC.[44] In April, former national security advisor John Bolton went further, calling for the basing of significant numbers of US forces in Taiwan in peacetime in a manner reminiscent of the US-ROC alliance from 1954 to 1979, the abolition of which was another PRC condition for normalization. He cited the failure of US deterrence in Ukraine to underscore the necessity for a fundamentally new US approach to Taiwan.[45] It will be difficult now for Republican candidates to stray very far from such postures in the lead-up to the 2024 presidential and congressional elections.

Then on May 23, 2022, in Tokyo at a press briefing with Prime Minister Kishida, President Biden for the third time publicly stated that the United States was fully committed to come to Taiwan's defense if the PRC were to attack Taiwan. In his response to a reporter, Biden made direct links between the Russian war on Ukraine and any potential PRC attack on Taiwan. He suggested that American resolve was very much now on the line in the Taiwan Strait, stating that the Russian invasion made the "burden even stronger [sic]" for the United States to defend Taiwan.[46] As after previous off-the-cuff remarks, Biden's White House staff quickly walked the president's statement back, stating that it did not signify a change in US policy toward cross-strait relations in the direction of clarity over ambiguity. But that effort seems less credible now that the Russian invasion of Ukraine solidified the view in the United States that democracies are in a global struggle against an axis of authoritarian states and that Taiwan and Ukraine are of a piece.

From an analytic perspective, such a clear US commitment to Taiwan would be very poor strategy. It would be unlikely to enhance deterrence but instead might spark the war that it is aiming to prevent. A return to something resembling the US-ROC alliance appears worse than unnecessary. CCP elites on the mainland already take the current US security relationship with Taiwan seriously even though it falls short of a formal alliance. Documents that are central to the US one-China policy, especially the 1979 Taiwan Relations Act, already underscore the US interest in a peaceful settlement of cross-strait differences and the grave concern with which the United States would view any PRC use of force. The United States has also continued to sell arms and offer training to Taiwan forces, and the US military prepares often for potential conflicts with the PRC over Taiwan. For these reasons, despite US strategic ambiguity, CCP military and civilian elites already expect the United States to intervene in any cross-strait conflict and actively plan to counter that US intervention if Beijing decides to use force. US resolve to intervene is apparently not at issue under existing policy. While some Americans might have doubts about whether the United States would actually intervene, elites in Beijing do not seem to share those doubts, and it is their perceptions that matter most for deterrence.

For several reasons, deterrence in the Taiwan Strait may in fact be stronger now given the largely failed initial Russian invasion of Ukraine. Chinese leaders must be surprised and concerned by the intensity of the Ukrainian resistance and sobered by the notion that Putin's generals might have sold him a bill of goods about how easily and quickly they could topple and replace Zelenskyy's regime in Kyiv. The effectiveness of asymmetric tactics by mobile, well-equipped Ukrainian forces against a superior foe must give hope and additional political capital to those on Taiwan who agree with the long-standing recommendations of US officials: Taiwan should develop similar asymmetric capabilities and tactics to prepare for a PRC invasion of the island by acquiring mobile coastal defenses and air defenses, stockpiling weapons, and preemptively creating defense in depth with reservists and an expanded civil defense force.[47]

Moreover, one long-standing nonmilitary deterrent to mainland use of force against Taiwan has been the economic damage that such a conflict would inflict on the mainland's own economy. President Biden's impressive rallying of advanced economies to sanction Russia following the invasion and to threaten secondary sanctions on nations that violate them must be quite sobering to CCP elites as they consider the potential massive economic fallout of PRC aggression toward Taiwan.

The adoption of a US policy of strategic clarity toward Taiwan is more than just unnecessary—it could be dangerous. Deterrence requires not just credible threat of a painful response if the target of deterrence behaves in a proscribed manner; the deterring state must also assure the target that if it does not behave in the proscribed manner, its key interests will not be harmed anyway. If such assurances are not credible, deterrence will fail just as easily as if the threats themselves were not credible.[48] Any US policy that recognizes Taiwan's independent sovereignty or seems to restore the US-ROC alliance as part of a deterrent strategy would seem to permanently separate Taiwan from mainland China, an outcome that is anathema to the CCP's legitimacy at home. Under those conditions, the PRC would likely use force even if Beijing was uncertain of the outcome of the ensuing war. Mainland experts also know that Taiwan citizens' estimation of the likelihood of US military intervention on Taiwan's behalf greatly influences their support for pro-independence political positions on Taiwan. Mainland analysts therefore take some courage in the worst-case analysis of their counterparts on Taiwan. Under conditions of US strategic ambiguity, Taiwan elites must entertain the possibility that the United States might not intervene in a timely fashion if Taiwan were to spark a conflict by adopting pro-independence policies that run against traditional US prohibitions to unilateral changes to the status quo.

In 2024 there will be a US presidential election and consequential races for the House and Senate. Republican Party candidates seem increasingly likely to take a hard-line position on US support for Taiwan's defense, and President Biden's multiple apparent gaffes in his public description of US policy toward Taiwan might make it even more difficult for him or other Democratic Party congressional candidates to distance themselves from a similarly rigid posture during the campaign. In Taiwan, the ruling, tradition-ally pro-independence party, the DPP, remains more popular than its main opposition, the KMT, which has supported a more accommodating stance toward mainland China, as evidenced in the successful 2024 presidential campaign of Vice President Lai Ching-te. While the former DPP president, Tsai Ing-wen, was quite moderate toward the mainland, she came under crit-icism within her own party for not pushing pro-independence initiatives more forcefully. Lai has a reputation for being more outspoken in support of Taiwan independence. His campaign for the presidency and his acceptance speech in January 2024, however, were both marked by moderation in a way consistent with Tsai's presidency. Still, mainland analysts are likely correct that an explicit and unconditional US commitment to intervene in support of Taiwan in a conflict with the mainland will feed into Taiwan politics in a way that encourages more support for assertions of Taiwan's independent sovereignty.

The January 2024 Taiwan election occurred in the context of a general sense in Beijing that, especially since the Trump administration took office, the stated US one-China policy has been progressively "hollowed out."[49] The concern is that Washington might be moving toward treating Taiwan as a sovereign state and an ally again for the first time since 1979. Tai-wan has been included in US government national defense documents in lists of "countries" and mentioned alongside non-NATO allies in public statements by officials. Beginning in the Trump years, the US government eased some internal restrictions on US government officials' contacts with Taiwan's officials, designed initially to avoid conveying an official status to US-Taiwan ties. Language about aspects of the US one-China policy that Beijing found reassuring—like no support for Taiwan independence and openness to any peaceful resolution of cross-strait difference—has, at times, been left out of public US government recaps of the one-China pol-icy. To their great credit, in the final year of President Biden's first term in office, it appears that top officials have grasped the shortcomings in previous statements and have begun making more fulsome descriptions of the traditional US one-China policy that include these long-standing elements.[50]

Some PRC analysts believe that the purpose of US support for Taiwan has morphed into an effort to weaken the PRC as a nation.[51] In their view, US policy makers now view Taiwan as a tool of a broader containment strategy against a rising China rather than as a partner warranting protection from coercion for its own sake. In congressional testimony one senior Department of Defense official called Taiwan a "critical node" in the Asian island chain, the loss of which to the PRC would undermine the ability of Washington to defend America's regional allies.[52] This suggests that peaceful settlement of cross-strait differences is not the core goal of the United States; permanent denial of Taiwan to the PRC is. After the Russian invasion of Ukraine, Defense Secretary Austin fed into this Chinese logic when he said that a core US goal in supporting Ukraine's war effort was not just to help Ukraine, but to raise the costs of the war to Russia and thereby weaken it as an adversary nation.[53]

Exacerbating Beijing's concerns was the September 2022 introduction in the Senate of a bipartisan bill, the Taiwan Policy Act. The bill sought to formalize and put into law many of the recent adjustments in US policy toward Taiwan that Beijing finds to be at odds with the US-PRC normalization agreement. It added a few new ones, including providing Taiwan direct military aid rather than just selling weapons, something that had not occurred since the US broke the alliance with the ROC on Taiwan in 1979–1980 as part of the normalization of relations with the PRC.[54] While the bill was never passed into law in its original form, key elements of it, including federal military funding for weapons transfers to Taiwan, were adopted in other legislation.[55]

The frustrations in Beijing about this perceived trend in US policy toward Taiwan preceded the fateful visit of Speaker of the House Nancy Pelosi to Taipei in early August 2022 and magnified the predictably negative reaction to that visit. There had already been hints in Track 2 dialogues that some elites in mainland China thought a strong military signal to Taipei and Washington might be in order some time before the 2024 elections. The visit to Taiwan by the US federal government's third-ranking official became the occasion for such a dramatic signal: a large-scale and unprecedented military exercise very near Taiwan, to include ballistic missile firings over the island just after the Speaker departed. The military pressure on Taiwan, to include frequent PLA air exercises in Taiwan's air defense identification zone and routine crossing of the median line in the Taiwan Strait by PLA military assets, continues into the time of this writing.[56] For our purposes here, it is notable that, during her visit, Speaker Pelosi and Taiwan officials linked the threat to democracies posed by authoritarian states, the Russian invasion of Ukraine, and the need for Washington to upgrade its support for Taiwan.[57]

These links between the Russian invasion of Ukraine and instability across the Taiwan Strait are perhaps the most likely manner in which that invasion might transform the preexisting US-PRC strategic competition into something like a US-Soviet Cold War. The Russian invasion magnified a simple "autocracy versus democracy" interpretation of international politics in the United States, as did Beijing's reaction to that invasion: refusing to condemn the brutal Russian assault, instead blaming the United States and NATO expansion as the cause of the war. The US failure to deter the initial invasion of Ukraine and domestic pressures during the 2024 electoral campaign could lead politicians and executive branch officials to promote a clearer and more direct US commitment to Taiwan. This could in turn lead Beijing to react with further military pressure on Taiwan, intensifying the ongoing tensions in the Taiwan Strait.

Chinese officials and analysts have tried to draw distinctions between Ukraine's relations with Russia and Taiwan's relationship with the mainland. They emphasize their claim that Taiwan is part of China, not a separate sovereign nation.[58] Xi Jinping has placed his party's legitimacy and his own personal prestige on the great rejuvenation of the Chinese nation and considers progress on Taiwan's unification with the mainland a prerequisite to achieving that goal.[59] Upgrading of the US relationship with Taiwan and the apparent restoration of the US-ROC alliance would be anathema to this core mission and an affront to Xi and the CCP more generally. For these reasons, a clear US commitment to Taiwan in the future, especially if accompanied by diplomatic recognition or the stationing of significant US forces on the island by a future US administration, rather than deterring the PRC, would greatly increase the likelihood of a military attack on Taiwan and an ensuing US-PRC conflict.

Such a conflict would create intense US-China hostilities for many years to come and would severely damage the transnational production chain that I have argued has been a force for peace in the region and a buffer against the creation of two Cold War blocs. The PRC would almost certainly try to blockade Taiwan as part of military operations against the island, and the United States would likely interfere with commerce in and out of mainland China in various ways in response. Even if Washington, for some reason, did not consciously adopt such a strategy, military conflict in the area itself would do severe damage to normal commercial relations between China and the rest of the world.

US allies like Japan, South Korea, and Australia, all highly dependent on commercial relationships with China, would have very difficult choices to make about their future relations with China and the United States. Many actors would still want to avoid economic warfare with China even under these conditions, given their dependence on the Chinese economy. More-over, some of them take positions closer to Beijing's on cross-strait relations than do the United States, simply recognizing Taiwan as part of China. Still, in this war, unlike the Russia-Ukraine war, the PRC would clearly be a bel-ligerent, not just an enabler. The scenes of bloodshed and the endangerment of these countries' expatriates on Taiwan would make it easier for the United States to insist that these countries limit economic interaction with mainland China.

Success in that US coalition-building effort would hinge on whether these third parties blamed Beijing or Washington for the outbreak of hostilities. Context matters. One of the downsides of the Pelosi visit for the United States and Taiwan was that it made it easier for Beijing to pin the blame for its provocative and destabilizing military exercises on the United States. The PRC thereby reduced the diplomatic price it paid in Asia and beyond for sending signals to Washington and Taipei about PRC willingness to fight over Taiwan. But even if third parties were to blame the United States for any future Sino-American conflict around Taiwan and even if the threat of US secondary sanctions was not enough to dissuade them from maintain-ing economic relations with China, the clashes between the two nations' militaries near mainland ports would likely deter most commerce anyway. China's international commerce would suffer immensely.

A US-PRC conflict could also interfere with oil shipped to China from the Middle East, on which China's economy depends. Under these cir-cumstances, Beijing would likely turn to Russia to backfill some minority percentage of China's lost energy supplies. Beijing might also ask Russia to supply vital intelligence on the global movement of US military assets. The PRC-Russia relationship thereby would move a few steps closer to becoming a true alliance, and many of the stabilizing links between the US alliance system and China will have suffered severe harm.

Conclusion

If there were a US-PRC conflict over Taiwan, one can also imagine intense conflict around the world between pro-US and pro-PRC political forces. In a compelling book, Øystein Tunsjø has argued that the current world, like the Cold War era, is already bipolar, with two great powers whose national strength far outstrips that of any other great power in the world. Tunsjø takes heart, however, in the fact that the United States and its allies are facing off with China primarily at sea in East Asia rather than on land, as NATO and the Warsaw Pact did in Europe in the Cold War. Maritime dominance is difficult to both establish and sustain, and crises over maritime disputes often lack the destabilizing first-mover advantage of crises over land disputes. This, combined with the PRC's lack of global military power projection, means that crises might be quite frequent but are less likely to escalate into general war than were crises in the Cold War.[60]

This exclusively regional, maritime focus might not survive a US-PRC conflict over Taiwan. A rapid decoupling of the economies of the United States and some of its allies and partners from mainland China, and a tightening of an authoritarian axis between Russia and China, would reduce the economic costs of a global ideological struggle between democracy and authoritarianism. One could imagine conflicts around the world between proxies of a US-led coalition and of a PRC-led one, with Russia as a junior partner to Beijing. Many of these conflicts could be on land, not at sea, and therefore carry more escalatory potential.

For many years, China will lack the military power projection to intervene directly in conflicts in far-flung parts of the planet; but it already has the wherewithal to train, equip, and provide intelligence to friendly anti-American forces anywhere on the planet. As Tunsjø argues in his book, the Soviet Union also generally lacked conventional power projection in distant parts of the world but was able to use proxies to exert influence around the world. Such proxy wars always risked escalation to direct great power conflict, especially if a great power seeks to interdict the assistance sent by its adversaries to those adversaries' regional proxies (think Cuba in 1962).

Cold Wars do not necessarily remain cold. For this and many other reasons, we should avoid starting a new one if possible.

Notes

1. Øystein Tunsjø, *The Return of Bipolarity in World Politics: China, the United States, and Geostructural Realism* (Columbia University Press, 2018).
2. See Thomas J. Christensen, "There Will Be No New Cold War: The Limits of U.S.-PRC Strategic Competition," *Foreign Affairs*, March 22, 2021; "No New Cold War: Why U.S.-Strategic Competition Will Not Be Like the U.S.-Soviet Cold War" (ASAN Institute, September 2020), http://en.asaninst.org/contents/no-new-cold-war-why-us-china-strategic-competition-will-not-be-like-the-us-soviet-cold-war/.
3. Secretary Antony Blinken, "The Administration's Approach to the People's Republic of China," US Department of State, May 26, 2022, https://www.state.gov/the-administrations-approach-to-the-peoples-republic-of-china/.
4. Yang Jiemian, "Bu Hui you Xin de Lengzhan" [There cannot be a new cold war] (Shanghai Institute of International Studies, November 22, 2018). Supporting Yang's view is Christopher Scott, "China Hysteria Falls on Deaf Ears in Europe," *Asia Times*, March 22, 2019. Hiroaki Nakanishi, the chairman of Hitachi, agrees, stating: "It's impossible for Japan to exist if we treat [China] as an enemy. . . . Maybe they can do that in America, but it doesn't work like that in Japan." Demonstrating Nakanishi's point, Japan's reaction to the U.S.-China trade war was to trade more with China in 2018 than in previous years. See Peter Landers, "Japan's Top Business Group: China Isn't an Enemy," *Wall Street Journal*, February 2, 2019; Shin Kawashima, "Is Japan Pulling Its Companies Out of China?," *The Diplomat*, May 11, 2020, ProQuest, https://www.wsj.com/articles/japans-top-business-group-china-isnt-an-enemy-11549037591; also see Kazuki Nakamura, "Is the Japanese Public on Board with the 'New Era' of China-Japan Relations?," *The Diplomat*, June 10, 2020, https://www.thediplomat.com/2020/06/is-the-japanese-public-on-board-with-the-new-era-of-china-japan-relations/.
5. "Factbox: Moscow-Beijing Partnership Has 'No Limits,'" Reuters, February 4, 2022, https://www.reuters.com/world/china/moscow-beijing-partnership-has-no-limits-2022-02-04/.
   For the full February 4, 2022, statement in translation see https://www.airuniversity.af.edu/Portals/10/CASI/documents/Translations/2022-02-04%20China%20Russia%20joint%20statement%20International%20Relations%20Entering%20a%20New%20Era.pdf.
6. Xi first referred to Putin as his "best friend" at a June 2019 summit in Moscow; see Scott Neuman, "As Relations with U.S. Sour, Xi Describes Putin as 'Best Friend' at Moscow Meeting," National Public Radio, June 6, 2022, https://www.npr.org/2019/06/06/730200317/as-relations-with-u-s-sour-xi-describes-putin-as-best-friend-at-moscow-meeting.
7. Edward Wong, "U.S. Officials Repeatedly Urged China to Help Avert War in Ukraine," *New York Times*, February 25, 2022, https://www.nytimes.com/2022/02/25/us/politics/us-china-russia-ukraine.html.
8. Edward Wong and Julian E. Barnes, "China Asked Russia to Delay Ukraine War until after Olympics, U.S. Officials Say," *New York Times*, March 2, 2022, https://www.nytimes.com/2022/03/02/us/politics/russia-ukraine-china.html.
9. Ambassador Qin Gang, "Chinese Ambassador: Where We Stand on Ukraine," *Washington Post*, March 15, 2022, https://www.washingtonpost.com/opinions/2022/03/15/china-ambassador-us-where-we-stand-in-ukraine/; Stuart Lau, "China Insists It's 'Not a Party' to Russia's War with Ukraine," *Politico*, March 14, 2022, https://www.politico.eu/article/china-is-not-party-russia-war-on-ukraine-foreign-minister/.
10. Thomas J. Christensen, *Worse than a Monolith: Alliance Politics and Problems of Coercive Diplomacy in Asia* (Princeton University Press, 2011), chap. 2.
11. Simone McCarthy and CNN's Beijing Bureau, "China's Promotion of Russian Disinformation Indicates Where Its Loyalties Lie," CNN, March 10, 2022, https://www.cnn.com/2022/03/10/china/china-russia-disinformation-campaign-ukraine-intl-dst-hnk/index.html. Also see the tweet from PRC diplomat Li Yang [@Li_Yang_China]. "Surprisingly, the US Stands with the Neo-Nazis! Is the US Willing to See This Scene?," Twitter, April 6, 2022, https://twitter.com/Li_Yang_China/status/1511513980136615938?s=20.

12. Lorne Cook et al., "China Rejects Sanctions as Ukraine War Tops Summit Agenda," Associated Press, April 1, 2022, https://apnews.com/article/russia-ukraine-business-beijing-economy-europe-f904dfdf7f17cf1259b34d91d226d353.

13. Jasmine Wright and Paul LeBlanc, "US Says China Will Face 'Real Costs' If It Provides Lethal Aid to Russia for War in Ukraine," CNN, February 26, 2023, https://edition.cnn.com/2023/02/26/politics/jake-sullivan-ukraine-russia-china-cnntv/index.html#:~:text=US%20national%20security%20adviser%20Jake,presents%20real%20complications%20for%20Beijing.

14. James Politi, "US Threatens to Punish Third Parties Helping Moscow Evade Sanctions," *Financial Times*, March 25, 2022, https://www.ft.com/content/867dc0d2-fb7b-461e-9e54-0c545ccd8c47; Alex Leary and Lingling Wei, "White House Says Biden Warned China's Xi of Consequences if Beijing Supports Russia on Ukraine," *Wall Street Journal*, March 18, 2022, https://www.wsj.com/articles/biden-xi-talk-as-u-s-threatens-actions-if-china-backs-russia-in-ukraine-war-11647611124; Ana Swanson, "Chinese Companies That Aid Russia Could Face U.S. Repercussions, Commerce Secretary Warns," *New York Times*, March 8, 2022, https://www.nytimes.com/2022/03/08/technology/chinese-companies-russia-semiconductors.html; Christopher Condon, "Yellen Says U.S. Would Use Sanctions If China Invaded Taiwan," Bloomberg, April 6, 2022, https://www.bloomberg.com/news/articles/2022-04-06/yellen-says-u-s-would-use-sanctions-if-china-invaded-taiwan.

15. On May 9, then press secretary Jen Psaki said, "I don't think we have seen to date a breaking of the sanctions [by China] at this point in time." See White House, "Press Briefing by Press Secretary Jen Psaki, May 9, 2022," May 9, 2022, https://www.whitehouse.gov/briefing-room/press-briefings/2022/05/09/press-briefing-by-press-secretary-jen-psaki-may-9-2022/. On March 10, Treasury Secretary Janet Yellen stated: "I've not seen evidence that China is providing Russia with any significant workaround for our sanctions." See "CNBC Transcript: United States Treasury Secretary Janet Yellen Speaks with CNBC's 'Closing Bell' Today," CNBC, March 10, 2022, https://www.cnbc.com/2022/03/10/cnbc-exclusive-cnbc-transcript-united-states-treasury-secretary-janet-yellen-speaks-with-cnbcs-closing-bell-today.html. On the early fallout on PRC-Russia relations, see Cate Codell and Ellen Nakashima, "Beijing Chafes at Moscow's Requests for Support," *Washington Post*, June 2, 2022, https://www.washingtonpost.com/national-security/2022/06/02/china-support-russia-ukraine/.

16. "Russia Coal and Oil Paid for in Yuan Starts Heading to China," Bloomberg, April 6, 2022, https://www.bloomberg.com/news/articles/2022-04-07/russian-coal-and-oil-paid-for-in-yuan-to-start-flowing-to-china.

17. Jake Sullivan, "On-the-Record Regional Press Call by APNSA Jake Sullivan on the National Security Supplemental," White House, February 20, 2024, https://www.whitehouse.gov/briefing-room/press-briefings/2024/02/20/on-the-record-regional-press-call-by-apnsa-jake-sullivan-on-the-national-security-supplemental/. The 2024 Annual Threat Assessment of the US intelligence community also highlights China's support of Russia's defense industrial base through providing dual-use materials, weapons components, and a threefold increase in PRC exports of goods with potential military applications. See "Annual Threat Assessment of the U.S. Intelligence Community" (Office of the Director of National Intelligence, February 2024), 8, https://www.odni.gov/files/ODNI/documents/assessments/ATA-2024-Unclassified-Report.pdf.

18. US Department of the Treasury, "Treasury Imposes Sanctions on More Than 150 Individuals and Entities Supplying Russia's Military-Industrial Base," December 12, 2023, https://home.treasury.gov/news/press-releases/jy1978.

19. Ana Swanson, "Chinese Companies That Aid Russia Could Face U.S. Repercussions, Commerce Secretary Warns," *New York Times*, March 8, 2022, https://www.nytimes.com/2022/03/08/technology/chinese-companies-russia-semiconductors.html.

20. Data on China's top trading partners from the 2014 China Statistical Yearbook can be found at https://www.stats.gov.cn/sj/ndsj/2014/indexeh.htm.

21. Data on China's top trading partners from the 2021 China Statistical Yearbook can be found at https://www.stats.gov.cn/sj/ndsj/2021/indexeh.htm.

22. Secretary Janet Yellen, "Transcript of Press Conference from Secretary of the Treasury Janet L. Yellen in Bonn, Germany," US Department of the Treasury, May 18, 2022, https://home.treasury.gov/news/press-releases/jy0793.

23. Noriyuki Suzuki, "Japan Trade Deficit Halves to 9.3 Trillion Yen in 2023 on Record Exports," *Kyodo News*, January 24, 2024, https://english.kyodonews.net/news/2024/01/33292599c342-update1-japan-trade-deficit-halves-to-93-tril-yen-in-2023-on-record-exports.html.

24. Kotaro Hosokawa, "South Korea Records Its First Trade Deficit with China in 31 Years," Nikkei Asia, January 1, 2024, https://asia.nikkei.com/Economy/Trade/South-Korea-records-its-first-trade-deficit-with-China-in-31-years.

25. Sam Kim and James Mayger, "South Korea's Investment Flow to China Falls Most on Record," Bloomberg, March 12, 2024, https://www.bloomberg.com/news/articles/2024-03-15/south-korea-direct-investment-flow-to-china-falls-most-on-record; US Census Bureau, "Top Trading Partners," https://www.census.gov/foreign-trade/statistics/highlights/topcm.html; Yuri Kageyama, "Japan Slips into a Recession and Loses Its Spot as the World's Third-Largest Economy," AP News, February 15, 2024, https://apnews.com/article/japan-economy-2023-gdp-893d53deba654c4924e4924f0b321cc5; World Economics, "GDP Annual Growth Rate," https://www.worldeconomics.com/GrossDomesticProduct/GDP-Annual-Growth-Rate/Malaysia.aspx#:~:text=Real%20GDP%20in%20Malaysia%20is,%2DPacific%2C%20ahead%20of%20Taiwan.

26. Thomas J. Christensen, "Mutually Assured Disruption: Globalization, Security, and the Dangers of Decoupling," World Politics, 2024 (75th Anniversary edition, on-line only), https://muse.jhu.edu/article/918726; Ana Swanson, "America's Trade Deficit Surged in 2022, Nearing $1 Trillion," New York Times, February 7, 2023, https://www.nytimes.com/2023/02/07/business/economy/us-trade-deficit.html; "Joe Biden's China Strategy Is Not Working," The Economist, August 10, 2023, https://www.economist.com/leaders/2023/08/10/joe-bidens-china-strategy-is-not-working.

27. Moreover, Xi told foreign leaders in 2017 that China would not "'export' a China model, nor ask others to 'copy' Chinese methods." See "China Will Not 'Export' Chinese Model," Xinhua, December 1, 2017, www.xinhuanet.com/english/2017-12/01/c_136793833.htm. A State Council white paper in 2019 further stated: "It is the right of every sovereign state to choose its own development path. . . . [China] does not 'import' foreign models, nor 'export' the Chinese model, and will never require other countries to replicate its practices." See "Full Text: China and the World in the New Era" (State Council of the People's Republic of China, September 27, 2019), 27, https://english.www.gov.cn/archive/whitepaper/201909/27/content_WS5d8d80f9c6d0bcf8c4c142ef.html.

28. David E. Sanger and Steven Lee Myers, "China Sows Disinformation about Hawaii Fires Using New Techniques," New York Times, September 11, 2023. For more about Beijing's increasing use of disinformation and influence campaigns worldwide, see Joshua Kurlantzick, Beijing's Global Media Offensive (Oxford University Press, 2022).

29. For more, see White House, "FACT SHEET: The Trilateral Leaders' Summit at Camp David," August 18, 2023, https://www.whitehouse.gov/briefing-room/statements-releases/2023/08/18/fact-sheet-the-trilateral-leaders-summit-at-camp-david/.

30. Ministry of Foreign Affairs of Japan, "Outcome of Prime Minister Kishida's Attendance at the NATO Summit Meeting," July 12, 2023, https://www.mofa.go.jp/erp/ep/page7e_000023.html; Ministry of Foreign Affairs of the Republic of Korea, "President Yoon Pledges to Share More Military Intel with NATO," July 14, 2023, https://lby.mofa.go.kr/eng/brd/m_5674/view.do?seq=320841&srchFr=&amp%3BsrchTo=&amp%3BsrchWord=&amp%3BsrchTp=&amp%3Bmulti_itm_seq=0&amp%3Bitm_seq_1=0&amp%3Bitm_seq_2=0&amp%3Bcompany_cd=&amp%3Bcompany_nm=.

31. President Joe Biden, "Remarks by President Biden on America's Place in the World," White House, February 4, 2021, https://www.whitehouse.gov/briefing-room/speeches-remarks/2021/02/04/remarks-by-president-biden-on-americas-place-in-the-world/.

32. See Blinken, "The Administration's Approach to the People's Republic of China."

33. Thomas J. Christensen, Useful Adversaries: Grand Strategy, Domestic Mobilization, and International Conflict, 1947–58 (Princeton University Press, 1996), chap. 5.

34. Christensen, Worse than a Monolith, chap. 2.

35. For example, see Zhao Lijian [@zlj517], "Disinformation Magician," Twitter, February 18, 2022, https://x.com/zlj517/status/1494825404195950592; Li Yang [@Li_Yang_China], "Look, This Is the Weapon of Mass Destruction Captured by the United States in Iraq!!!," Twitter, March 2, 2022, https://x.com/Li_Yang_China/status/1499287565903405058.

36. Ambassador Qin Gang, "Chinese Ambassador: Where We Stand on Ukraine," Washington Post, March 15, 2022, https://www.washingtonpost.com/opinions/2022/03/15/china-ambassador-us-where-we-stand-in-ukraine/; Lau, "China Insists It's 'Not a Party' to Russia's War with Ukraine."

37. White House, "Readout of President Joseph R. Biden Jr. Call with President Xi Jinping of the People's Republic of China," March 18, 2022, https://www.whitehouse.gov/briefing-room/statements-releases/2022/03/18/readout-of-president-joseph-r-biden-jr-call-with-president-xi-jinping-of-the-peoples-republic-of-china-2/; "Biden Adviser Warns China Will Face Consequences If It Helps Russia Evade Sanctions," *The Guardian*, March 13, 2022, https://www.theguardian.com/us-news/2022/mar/13/jake-sullivan-biden-national-security-adviser-china-russia.

38. For example, see Evan Osnos, "What Is China Learning from Russia's Invasion of Ukraine?," *The New Yorker*, February 24, 2022, https://www.newyorker.com/news/daily-comment/what-is-china-learning-from-russias-invasion-of-ukraine; Elbridge Colby and Oriana Skylar Mastro, "Ukraine Is a Distraction from Taiwan," *Wall Street Journal*, February 13, 2022, https://www.wsj.com/articles/ukraine-is-a-distraction-from-taiwan-russia-china-nato-global-powers-military-invasion-jinping-biden-putin-europe-11644781247?mod=Searchresults_pos1&page=1.

39. See Alex Thompson and Camille Gus, "Biden Vows to Defend Taiwan with US Military If China Invades," *Politico*, May 23, 2022, https://www.politico.eu/article/us-would-intervene-militarily-if-china-invaded-taiwan-biden/; Keoni Everington, "Taiwan and Ukraine Not Same, US to Ensure Chinese Invasion 'Never Happens,'" *Taiwan News*, April 15, 2022, https://www.taiwannews.com.tw/en/news/4508152.

40. See Lee Hsin-fang et al., "Military Conscription Changes Mulled," *Taipei Times*, March 18, 2022, https://www.taipeitimes.com/News/front/archives/2022/03/18/2003774996; Flor Wang and Wang Cheng-chung, "'Peace Has No Losers': Former President Ma," Focus Taiwan, February 28, 2022, https://focustaiwan.tw/cross-strait/202202280008.

41. For example, see Richard Haass and David Sacks, "American Support for Taiwan Must Be Unambiguous," *Foreign Affairs*, September 2, 2020, https://www.foreignaffairs.com/articles/united-states/american-support-taiwan-must-be-unambiguous.

42. Shinzo Abe, "Op-Ed: The U.S. Must Make Clear to the World It Will Defend Taiwan against Chinese Invasion," *Los Angeles Times*, April 12, 2022, https://www.latimes.com/opinion/story/2022-04-12/china-taiwan-invasion-united-states-policy-ambiguity.

43. "U.S. Lawmakers Signal Support for Taiwan in Visit," National Public Radio, April 15, 2022, https://www.npr.org/2022/04/15/1093003540/us-lawmakers-signal-support-for-taiwan-in-visit.

44. Lauly Li et al., "Pompeo Urges Washington to Recognize Taiwan as Sovereign Nation," Nikkei Asia, March 4, 2022, https://asia.nikkei.com/Politics/International-relations/Pompeo-urges-Washington-to-recognize-Taiwan-as-sovereign-nation.

45. John Bolton, "Remarks at the Global Taiwan National Affairs Symposium 海內外臺灣國是會議 XI," YouTube, April 16, 2022, https://www.youtube.com/watch?v=osp0SSlvccg; Bolton's address starts at 27:01.

46. President Joe Biden, "Remarks by President Biden and Prime Minister Kishida Fumio of Japan in Joint Press Conference," White House, May 23, 2022, https://www.whitehouse.gov/briefing-room/speeches-remarks/2022/05/23/remarks-by-president-biden-and-prime-minister-fumio-kishida-of-japan-in-joint-press-conference/.

47. For example, see Ben Blanchard, "Analysis: Taiwan Studies Ukraine War for Own Battle Strategy with China," Reuters, March 8, 2022, https://www.reuters.com/business/aerospace-defense/taiwan-studies-ukraine-war-own-battle-strategy-with-china-2022-03-09/; Task Force on U.S.-China Policy, "Avoiding War over Taiwan" (Asia Society, October 12, 2022), https://asiasociety.org/sites/default/files/2022-10/2022-avoiding-war-over-taiwan.pdf.

48. Thomas C. Schelling, *Arms and Influence* (Yale University Press, 2008).

49. For example, see Wang Wenbin, "Meifang ying jiang Yige Zhongguo Yuanze buzhebukou de luodao shichu" [The U.S. should fully implement the One-China principle], Zhonghua Renmin Gongheguo Waijiaobu, August 17, 2022, https://www.fmprc.gov.cn/gytwwtdlc/fyrbt_131928/202208/t20220817_10744892.shtml.

50. For example, see Sarah Beran, "Digital Press Briefing with Sarah M. Beran, National Security Council Senior Director for China and Taiwan Affairs, Daniel J. Kritenbrink, Assistant Secretary of State for East Asian and Pacific Affairs, and Brian Nichols, Assistant Secretary of State for Western Hemisphere Affairs," US Department of State, November 17, 2023, https://www.state.gov/digital-press-briefing-with-sarah-m-beran-national-security-council-senior-director-for-china-and-taiwan-affairs-daniel-j-kritenbrink-assistant-secretary-of-

state-for-east-asian-and-pacific-affai/; White House, "Background Press Call by Senior Administration Officials Previewing the President's Upcoming Bilateral Engagement," November 9, 2023, https://www.whitehouse.gov/briefing-room/press-briefings/2023/11 /09/background-press-call-by-senior-administration-officials-previewing-the-presidents-upcoming-bilateral-engagement/. For more on the reiteration of long-standing US policy by Biden administration officials, see Bonnie S. Glaser et al., "Taiwan and the True Sources of Deterrence," *Foreign Affairs*, November 20, 2023, https://www.foreignaffairs.com/taiwan/ taiwan-china-true-sources-deterrence.

51. For example, see State Council Information Office, "US Plays with Fire by Using 'Taiwan Card' to Contain China: Spokesperson," May 24, 2022, http://english.scio.gov.cn/ pressroom/2022-05/24/content_78233964.htm; Teddy Ng, "Beijing Berates US for 'Trying to Include Taiwan in Strategy to Contain China,'" *South China Morning Post*, February 22, 2022, https://www.scmp.com/news/china/diplomacy/article/3167977/beijing-berates-us-trying-include-taiwan-strategy-contain.

52. Assistant Secretary Ely Ratner, "Statement by Dr. Ely Ratner Before the 117th Congress Committee on Foreign Relations," US Senate, December 8, 2021, https://www.foreign.senate.gov/ imo/media/doc/120821_Ratner_Testimony1.pdf.

53. See Secretary Lloyd Austin, "Secretary of State Antony J. Blinken and Secretary of Defense Lloyd J. Austin III Remarks to Traveling Press," US Department of Defense, April 25, 2022, https://www.state.gov/secretary-antony-j-blinken-and-secretary-lloyd-austin-remarks-to-traveling-press/.

54. Taiwan Policy Act of 2022, https://www.congress.gov/bill/117th-congress/senate-bill/4428. For more on the bill's progression, see Rebekah Metzler, "Senate Panel Advances Bill to Bolster US Security Assistance to Taiwan," CNN, September 14, 2022, https://edition.cnn.com/2022/ 09/14/politics/us-senate-panel-bill-security-assistance-taiwan/index.html.

55. "Taiwan: Defense and Military Issues" (Congressional Research Service, updated March 1, 2024), https://crsreports.congress.gov/product/pdf/IF/IF12481#:~:text=117%2D263) %20for%20the%20first,in%20grant%20assistance%20through%20FY2027.

56. "Toward a Fourth Taiwan Straits Crisis?" (Center for Strategic and International Studies, August 4, 2022), https://www.csis.org/events/toward-fourth-taiwan-strait-crisis.

57. Nancy Pelosi, "Why I'm Leading a Congressional Delegation to Taiwan," *Washington Post*, August 2, 2022, https://www.washingtonpost.com/opinions/2022/08/02/nancy-pelosi-taiwan-visit-op-ed/; Lin Fei-fan, "It's Time the Free World Commits to the Defense of Taiwan," *Washington Post*, August 12, 2022, https://www.washingtonpost.com/opinions/2022/08/12/ china-taiwan-democracy-defense-free-world/.

58. For example, see Foreign Minister Wang Yi, "State Councilor and Foreign Minister Wang Yi Meets the Press," Ministry of Foreign Affairs of the People's Republic of China, March 7, 2022, https://www.mfa.gov.cn/eng/wjbzhd/202203/t20220308_10649559.html.

59. President Xi Jinping, "Wei Shixian Minzu Weida Fuxing Tuijn Zuguo Heping Tongyi Er Gongtong Fendou" [Working together to realize rejuvenation of the Chinese nation and advance China's peaceful reunification], Taiwan Affairs Office of the State Council, January 2, 2019, http://www.gwytb.gov.cn/wyly/201904/t20190412_12155687.htm.

60. Øystein Tunsjø, *The Return of Bipolarity in World Politics: China, the United States, and Geostructural Realism* (Columbia University Press, 2018).

IV

THE TECHNOLOGICAL RIVALRY

7

Technological Competition
and the US-China Rivalry

M. Taylor Fravel

The growing rivalry between the United States and China coincides with a period of rapid technological change sometimes described as the "Fourth Industrial Revolution." Technological developments in this era include robotics, autonomous systems, and the Internet of Things, among many others. This combination of major and structural simultaneous changes—a power transition in the international system amid the dawn of a new technological era—is rare and, at least in modern times, unprecedented. The United States and China are competing not only for relative power position but also to remain at the frontier of new technological developments. These competitions are interdependent, as technological advancements and innovations are likely to serve as new sources of national wealth and new instruments of military power that can further bolster a state's relative power position.

Based on these trends, this chapter examines how the current rapid pace of technological change will impact the escalating rivalry between China and the United States. Will it make the rivalry more intense, make it less intense, or simply reflect the underlying competition? Specifically, this chapter examines technology as the focus of competition between the two states. If states view technological advantage as critical to their relative position in the rivalry, as a key source of future wealth or military power, then it should be viewed as increasingly zero sum and increase the stakes in the rivalry.

Several findings emerge from the analysis. First, technology has become an increasingly central object of competition between the United States and China. US efforts to curb China's development of certain technologies have shaped Chinese perceptions of US intentions and hostility. As efforts to limit China's access to these technologies continues, which is likely, these actions will increase the intensity of the rivalry, especially when compared with

M. Taylor Fravel, *Technological Competition and the US-China Rivalry*. In: *Not Just Another Cold War*. Edited by: Bård Nikolas Vik Steen, Oxford University Press. © Oxford University Press (2025).
DOI: 10.1093/9780197799932.003.0008

the role of technological competition in the Cold War. Second, technological competition has elevated the role of US allies and other closely aligned states, many of whom as technological powers are key actors in efforts to limit China's access to certain technologies, such as by enforcing export controls.

This chapter proceeds as follows. The first section reviews the context, namely technological competition in the Cold War and the Fourth Industrial Revolution. The next section provides an overview of the US-China "tech war" that began around 2019. The third examines the crux of the current competition: US efforts to restrict China's access to critical technologies through export controls and investment screening. The fourth section probes the impact of the technological competition on the rivalry, focusing on China's perceptions of US intentions. The penultimate section assesses the broader implications of technological competition for the US-China rivalry in the coming decade.

Technological Competition in the Cold War and the Fourth Industrial Revolution

To set the stage for discussion of technological competition in the US-China rivalry, this section reviews the role of technological competition in the Cold War and the characteristics of the Fourth Industrial Revolution. This brief review yields two conclusions. First, unlike in the Cold War, especially the early part of the Cold War, technological competition in the US-China rivalry bears even more directly on the generation of wealth and latent military power and is therefore broader in scope. The second is that the characteristics of the Fourth Industrial Revolution suggest that the speed and intensity of technological competition will be much greater than during the Cold War.

Cold War Technological Competition

In considering the role of competition over technology in the US-China rivalry today, it is helpful to review the essential features of technological competition between the United States and the Soviet Union during the Cold War. Three aspects are perhaps most salient.

First, the Cold War occurred between two exclusive political, military, and economic blocs, in which economic activity and technological exchange between them was highly regulated and relatively limited. To be sure, there was still some high-technology trade and scientific exchange between the United States and the Soviet Union. Nevertheless, broadly speaking, exchanges were strictly controlled and limited through institutions like the Coordinating Committee for Multilateral Export Controls (COCOM) that was created at the dawn of the Cold War as part of an economic embargo of the socialist bloc.[1]

Second, the Cold War technological competition was predominantly military in nature. At its height, the size of the Soviet economy was at most only half the size of the United States and probably smaller.[2] As such, the Cold War technological competition was focused on gaining a military advantage. This is made clear by the stated goals of COCOM, which was to "deny the export of strategic technology to the Warsaw Pact in order to deny access to technologies that increased the effectiveness of their respective *militaries*" (emphasis added).[3] Technological acquisition was motivated by military gain. For example, one of the most high-profile cases involving Western technology was the Toshiba-Kongsberg case. Between 1980 and 1984, the Soviet Union purchased robotic propeller milling machines from Toshiba and sophisticated computer equipment from Kongsberg, which substantially enhanced Soviet submarine technology by enabling the production of quieter submarine propellers.[4]

Third, the Cold War competition largely occurred in a closed innovation system, where "state organizations create and control high-end military technologies"[5] such as nuclear weapons, intercontinental ballistic missiles, jet fighters, and precision-guided munitions.

The current US-China rivalry differs in all three respects. First, despite some decoupling—such as US efforts to discourage allies and partners from using Huawei equipment—current US-China competition is not one between two exclusive blocs, but rather between two overlapping networks, with members adjusting their alignment based on their own values, security considerations, or material interests.[6]

Second, China today combines the military challenge of the Soviet Union during the Cold War with the economic challenge of Japan in the 1980s.[7] US technological competition with China reflects both economic and military concerns. For instance, in a 2021 report on Chinese military power, the US Department of Defense observes that "the PRC's military modernization objectives are commensurate with, and part of, Beijing's broader national development aspirations." Even in a report focused on China's military capabilities, the Department of Defense notes that China's technological development "[presents] economic challenge to nations that export high-tech products," highlighting both commercial and military concerns.[8]

This is in part being driven by the type of technologies involved in the competition, most notably artificial intelligence (AI), which is a general-purpose technology that brings substantive economic as well as military advantages. General purpose technologies are distinct from dual-use technologies—which characterized many Cold War technologies—in that they not only have civilian and military uses but also widespread applications in both arenas.[9] Ultimately, it is the interaction between this suite of technologies and the nature of strategic competition—predominantly military in the Cold War, and military and economic today—that drives the character of technological competition.

Third, and finally, technological advancement occurs in an open innovation system. This is characterized by popular access, with a much broader range of actors involved in innovation, such as professionals, hobbyists, and commercial entities.[10] The US Department of Defense notes that "the commercial sector increasingly drives breakthroughs in advanced dual-use technologies."[11]

The Fourth Industrial Revolution

Klaus Schwab, the founder of the World Economic Forum, popularized the term "Fourth Industrial Revolution" in 2015. This revolution is characterized by a combination of technologies that "blur the lines between the physical, digital, and biological spheres."[12] These technologies include, among others, AI, robotics, the Internet of Things, autonomous vehicles, 3D printing, nanotechnology, biotechnology, materials science, energy storage, and quantum computing.

Technologies of this industrial revolution are considered revolutionary because of their speed, their scope, and how they transform systems of production, management, and government. First, technologies such as computing power are developing exponentially, in contrast to the linear pace of previous industrial revolutions. Additionally, these technologies have a much broader scope in terms of impact and use. AI, for example, has applications ranging from self-driving cars to lethal autonomous weapons. The combination of technologies of the Fourth Industrial Revolution is also potent, such as using 3D manufacturing with gene editing to produce living tissue for tissue repair and regeneration. Finally, these technologies engender new systems of production and governance that will likely have profound social and political effects. Compared with traditional manufacturing, for example, digital companies face lower marginal costs, enabling firms to generate more revenue with fewer employees. The three largest companies in Silicon Valley achieved much higher market capitalization with about ten times fewer employees than their counterparts in Detroit in the 1990s.[13] Social scientists have cautioned that these new systems of production and management, such as the rise of platform firms that seek market dominance, could have deleterious effects for inequality, welfare, investment, productivity, and ultimately social and political tensions.[14]

How will the speed, scope, and system transformation of the Fourth Industrial Revolution shape technological competition? First, the speed of technological development suggests that competition will be intense because mastering key technologies brings significant first-mover advantages such as network effects and lock-in, as is the case with semiconductors. Conversely, losers will also lose more quickly, further creating incentives to compete to reach the technological frontier. Intensity means that countries will be inclined to view competition as zero sum and be willing to use antagonistic instruments to blunt the development of others.

Second, the broad scope of these technologies increases the breadth of competition. Because of their diverse applications, competition will occur across a wide range of sectors, instead of being limited to the military realm. Moreover, a broader range of actors will be involved, from competition for talent over individuals to targeting commercial firms that are pioneers in general purpose technologies like AI.

Finally, the transformation of production and governance systems enabled by these technologies creates an impulse to view competition as one between different societal systems, namely, which system is better suited to foster innovation and manage its socioeconomic and political impacts. In a sense, this enlarges the breadth of competition to the point where it might be all-encompassing, in which domestic policies on investment, labor, welfare, and even political values are seen as instruments of competition. For this reason, US-China competition is increasingly described as a competition among systems.[15]

The US-China "Tech War"

In international relations, enduring or strategic rivalries among states revolve around the importance of the underlying stakes, such as contested territory or status. Unlike most enduring or strategic rivalries that scholars study, however, the US-China rivalry is also part of a much larger power transition that will play out over the next few decades.[16] A key element of national power in this rivalry will be the ability to develop and harness new technologies part of the Fourth Industrial Revolution as means to increase national wealth and military power and thus prevail in the rivalry. If an important element of national wealth and power was how much territory a state controlled in the nineteenth century and how much it could manufacture and produce in the twentieth century, it will be whether states can occupy and control the "commanding heights" of new technologies in this century.

Technology has already become a central object of competition in the US-China rivalry and is poised to grow in importance. China has proclaimed ambitious technological goals, while the United States has already sought to prevent or degrade China's efforts to become a leading technological power in specific industries and sectors. Evidence of such competition is apparent in the growing emphasis on technology transfer concerns, among other areas.

Along with the phrase "trade war," it is increasingly common to read about a "tech war" in the US-China context. As shown in Figures 7.1 and 7.2, the use of the phrase in English media and in Chinese academic journals has increased in the past few years, to the point where it reflects an important dynamic of the relationship. A turning point was US concerns about China's potential to dominate 5G communications technology and the potential for the leading Chinese firm in this area, Huawei, to use its equipment and networks not only to dominate this technology and reap great economic gains but also to facilitate espionage by the Chinese government. More generally, it occurred amid concerns in the United States about China's technological ambitions, as expressed in documents like "Made in China 2025."[17] China's large-scale, relentless, and systematic efforts to acquire these technologies over the past two decades, through lawful means such as open-source research and technology transfer programs as well as unlawful ones such as theft and industrial espionage, had generated increased concerns about the stakes.[18]

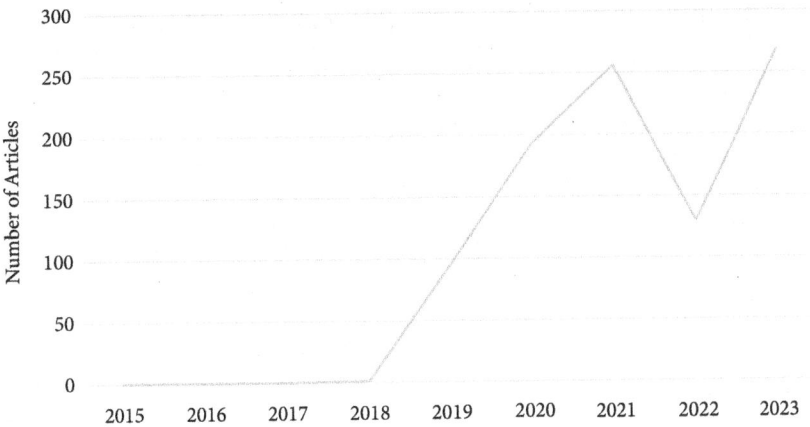

Figure 7.1 Mentions of "US-China Tech War," 2015–2023

Source: Factiva

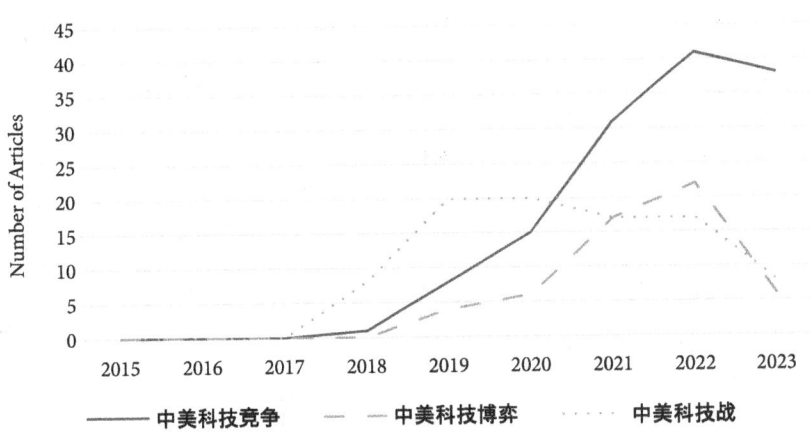

Figure 7.2 US-China Tech "Competition," "Game," and "War" in China Academic Journals database, 2015–2023

Source: China Academic Journals database

The United States and China have highlighted many of the same technologies as critical for each nation to develop, which reflects the breadth of the technological competition. Table 7.1 lists technologies identified in China's Fourteenth Five-Year Plan Outline, issued in March 2021, and by the US National Science and Technology Council, issued in February 2022 (updating a 2020 list).[19] The overlap in technologies each country identifies as critical is substantial, and many of these technologies are also associated

Table 7.1 Comparison of US and Chinese Critical Technologies Lists

	US list	China list
Advanced Computing*	Yes	Yes – Included as frontier technology
Advanced Engineering Materials*	Yes	Yes –High-end new materials under manufacturing
Advanced Gas Turbine Engines	Yes	Yes – Jet engines and gas turbine engines under manufacturing
Advanced Manufacturing*	Yes	Yes – Additive manufacturing and smart manufacturing under manufacturing
Advanced & Networked Sensing and Signature Management	Yes	Yes – Included as exploration frontier technology
Advanced Nuclear Energy Technologies*	Yes	No[a]
Artificial Intelligence*	Yes	Yes – Included as frontier technology
Autonomous Systems and Robotics*	Yes	Yes – Smart manufacturing and robotics under manufacturing
Biotechnology*	Yes	Yes – Included as frontier technology
Communication and Networking Technologies*	Yes	Yes – 5G and 6G[b]
Directed Energy	Yes	No
Financial Technologies	Yes	Yes – Blockchain as part of the digital economy
Human-Machine Interfaces*	Yes	Yes – FT brain science
Hypersonics	Yes	No
Quantum Information Technologies*	Yes	Yes – Included as frontier technology
Renewable Energy Generation and Storage*	Yes	Yes
Semiconductors and Microelectronics	Yes	Yes – Included as frontier technology
Space Technologies	Yes	Yes – Included as exploration frontier technology
Medical and Public Health Technologies	No[c]	Yes – Included as medical sciences frontier technology
Brain Science and Brain-Inspired Intelligence Technology*	No[d]	Yes – Included as brain science frontier technology

Note: Grey highlights denote technologies that are unique to either the US or China list. An asterisk denotes inclusion in Schwab's list of technologies of the 4th Industrial Revolution. China's 14th FYP plan includes seven important "frontier technologies," which are noted above.
[a]Energy infrastructure (Table 6) includes coastal nuclear energy, which is narrower than technologies like fusion and space nuclear power on the US list.
[b]Yes, but Chinese list excludes satellite communications or spectrum management from US list.
[c]US list includes 'health-sector sensing' under Advanced Networked Sensing and Signature Management and several sub-categories under Biotechnologies.
[d]US list has sub-category "brain-computer interfaces" under Human-Machine Interfaces, which does not cover the same range of technologies as the Chinese frontier technology, which includes more medical uses. The US issued an update to the 2022 list in February 2024, which included a subcategory of neurotechnology that may overlap with the Chinese category.
Sources: US Critical and Emerging Technologies List, China 14th Five-Year Plan and 2035 Long Term Goals Outline.

with the Fourth Industrial Revolution. Although many other advanced economies are also targeting the development of these same technologies, their development plays a special role in the US-China power transition because they are viewed as critical to generating economic and military advantages.

Unsurprisingly, both governments now highlight the importance of technology to each nation. In a series of speeches in April 2021, Chinese leader Xi Jinping noted that "technological innovation has become the primary arena for international strategic competition [博弈], competition for the commanding heights of technology has reached new levels of intensity."[20] Moreover, "as a core matter of overall development and national security, we have to target AI, quantum information, integrated circuitry, advanced manufacturing, health sciences, brain sciences, biological sciences, aerospace, deep sea/deep land exploration etc., put in place a set of strategic and stable technological development programs, target the commanding heights of future technologies and manufacturing."[21]

In October 2021, the US National Counterintelligence and Security Center (under the Directorate of National Intelligence) issued a report entitled *Protecting Critical and Emerging US Technologies from Foreign Threats*. The report noted specific sectors such as AI, biotechnology, quantum technology, semiconductors, and autonomous systems as sectors "where the stakes are potentially greatest for U.S. economic and national security. These sectors produce technologies that may determine whether America remains the world's leading superpower or is eclipsed by strategic competitors in the next few years."[22] Similarly, CIA director William Burns highlighted technology as "the main arena for competition and rivalry with China."[23] Eric Schmidt, the former CEO of Google and chair of the National Security Commission on Artificial Intelligence, testified in 2021 that "the threat of Chinese leadership in key technology areas is a national crisis and needs to be dealt with directly, now." Moreover, "a national strategy should focus on fundamental technologies with broad impact on national competitiveness and security. A priority shortlist should include AI, 5G, microelectronics, biotechnology, and quantum computing."[24]

Export Controls and Investment Restrictions in the Tech War

As the United States and China compete in similar sectors, a core element of technological competition is US efforts to deny China access to cutting-edge US technologies that might enhance China's capabilities in these sectors.

This primarily occurs through the export control process but also involves restrictions on US investments in Chinese companies. That is, the United States seeks to prevent sensitive or critical technologies from being sold or licensed to Chinese organizations and seeks to prevent US institutions and individuals from investing in Chinese firms developing these technologies. Of course, China has been subject to a variety of US export controls since the 1989 demonstrations and massacre in Tiananmen Square (particularly regarding military technologies). What changed around 2019 was a much more expansive use of export controls to prevent the transfer of technologies that are linked directly not only with national security concerns but also with China's efforts to develop indigenous capacity and leadership in these sectors in ways that might challenge the dominance of US and aligned states. The export control and investment tools available to the US government are vast and potentially open-ended in the criteria for their use, which indicates that this aspect of the technological competition is likely to grow in the future, further intensifying this aspect of the US-China rivalry.

The first and most important set of tools focuses on export controls. The most important tool comes from the US Commerce Department's Bureau of Industry and Security (BIS) and its Export Administration Regulations (EAR). The BIS maintains a list of technologies it seeks to restrict, which are described in the Commerce Control List (CCL). Any US firm or institution seeking to export items on the CCL requires a license to do so.

A separate list, the "Entity List," contains the names of foreign parties including individuals, businesses, research institutions, or government organizations that face extra scrutiny in terms of what may be exported or licensed to them. Specifically, designated entities are "prohibited from receiving some or all items subject to the EAR unless the exporter secures a license."[25] The criteria for inclusion in the list are broad, namely, "engaging in activities contrary to U.S. national security and/or foreign policy interests." Entities are added to the list by Executive Order, based on a determination by the End-User Review Committee composed of representatives from the Commerce, State, and Treasury Departments. Any US firm or organization that seeks to sell, license, or transfer technologies to a designated entity must obtain a license from the BIS "for the export, reexport and/or transfer (in-country) of specified items." Importantly, re-exports, or products made in third countries but with US components above a *de minimus* threshold, are also covered by the EAR and subject to licensing requirements.

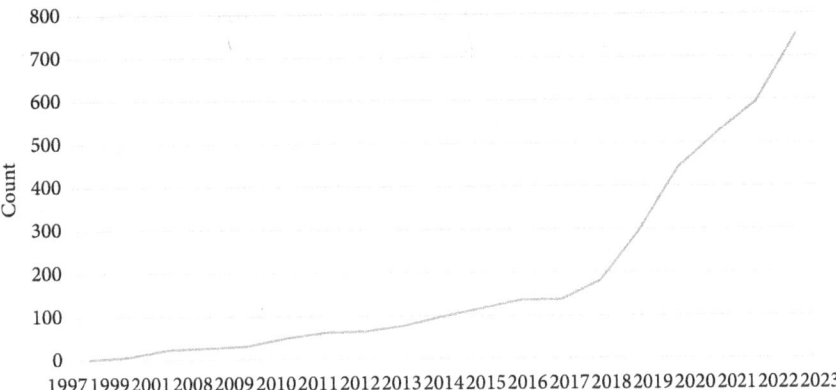

Figure 7.3 Cumulative People's Republic of China Entities Added to the Entity List, 1997–2023
Source: BIS

An increasingly more prominent tool relating to export controls is the Foreign Direct Product Rule (FDPR). This rule seeks to block the sale or transfer of products that were made or designed with US technology but manufactured or produced in third countries in facilities that use restricted US technology.[26] In essence, it expands the number of actors that would need to comply with US export controls and allows the United States to govern what can be sold or transferred to Chinese entities by firms or organizations beyond the United States.

The Entity List has become an important tool for limiting access to cutting-edge US technology. As of March 2024, 762 Chinese entities are on the Entity List, which accounts for 29% of the total, up from 20% in 2018. As shown in Figure 7.3, the number of designated Chinese entities increased significantly between 2019 and 2023. Technologies now covered by the inclusion of leading Chinese tech firms on the Entity List include telecommunications, AI, video surveillance, and drones, among others.

The second set of tools consist of investment screening and restrictions, both of investments into the United States and investments by US firms in Chinese companies. The Committee on Foreign Investment in the United States (CFIUS) is the main investment screening tool, whose scope of review has increased significantly in the past few years. To regulate investment in Chinese firms, the Department of the Treasury established the Non-SDN Chinese Military-Industrial Complex Companies List in June 2021 to prevent US investment into China's military-industrial complex. It currently lists sixty-eight "Communist Chinese Military Companies," based on their ties to the People's Liberation Army (PLA), role in China's defense industries, or broader national security implications for the United States, such as surveillance technologies, and prohibits trading their securities or those of subordinate entities. Most designated companies on the list (some of which are part of the same parent company) focus on aerospace and telecommunications and, to a lesser extent, electronics manufacturing and AI.[27]

Finally, other tools have also been employed to limit China's access to US technologies or to provide support for Chinese firms. These include a "covered list" from the Federal Communications Commission, which bans the use of telecommunications and other equipment by US firms from all major Chinese manufacturers in US networks. Sectors targeted include video surveillance and software in addition to telecommunications. The United States has employed also import restrictions, federal government procurement restrictions, and visa restrictions.[28] As this brief review indicates, the United States has targeted core industries and technologies including telecommunications (especially 5G), semiconductors, AI, digital cameras, drones, cybersecurity, and supercomputing. Below, efforts to limit China's access to technology in some of these sectors is reviewed.

Supercomputing. The United States began restricting exports in supercomputing to China before the current "tech war," back in 2015. The initial rationale was to limit the development of China's nuclear weapons program and weapons development programs, such as hypersonic weapons. Nevertheless, the Entity List has been used extensively to limit China's ability to access US technology related to supercomputing. Designated entities include seven of China's national supercomputing centers, some universities like the PLA's National University of Science and Technology, the Shanghai High-Performance Integrated Circuit Design Centre, and companies involved in making chips for China's supercomputing efforts such as Sunway Microelectronics and Tianjin Phytium, among several others.[29] As a recent report concludes, "It effectively opposes Chinese supercomputing as a whole—a general-purpose technology with innumerable civilian uses."[30]

5G/Telecommunications. The United States effort to limit China's development of 5G communications technology has focused largely on the Chinese company Huawei. Indeed, no single Chinese organization has been the target of more efforts to restrict its access to US technology than Huawei.

In August 2018, Section 889 of the National Defense Authorization Act prohibited the US federal government from purchasing telecommunications equipment from multiple Chinese firms, including Huawei, and then the United States sought to extradite the company's chief financial officer Meng Wanzhou in December 2018 while she was transiting through Canada. Although her extradition was based on allegations that Huawei had violated US export control laws by selling products to Iran, it became intertwined with broader concerns about the company. In May 2019, Huawei and 68 subsidiaries were placed on the Entity List, with another 46 added in August 2019 and 38 more in August 2020, bringing the total to over 150 or roughly 20% of all China-related entities on the list.[31] Notably, the FDPR was altered to specifically target Huawei by seeking to restrict its access to "foreign-manufactured items that are produced utilizing US-origin manufacturing or testing equipment or that are based on Huawei designs that are, themselves, a product of US-origin software and technology."[32] Huawei is also listed as a Chinese military company and thus denied access to US investment.

Semiconductors. China has long-standing aspirations to be a leading, independent player in semiconductors, which in turn will play a critical role in almost every other advanced sector of the Fourth Industrial Revolution, from AI to telecommunications. China's largest company in this space is the Semiconductor Manufacturing International Corporation (SMIC), which aspires to be a foundry on par with Taiwan Semiconductor (TSMC) and Samsung, as well as "fabless" design firms such as Huawei's HiSilicon subsidiary.

The US approach in semiconductors unfolded in two phases. First, the United States placed SMIC and other Chinese semiconductor firms on the Entity List, primarily to deny them access to cutting-edge design and manufacturing tools but still permitting the ability to purchase equipment to manufacture "commodity" chips. For example, SMIC's entry on the Entity List states that the BIS would maintain a "presumption of denial for items uniquely required for production of semiconductors at advanced technology nodes (10 nanometers and below, including extreme ultraviolet technology)" but pursue other licenses on a case-by-case basis.[33] Thus, the goal was to keep SMIC one or two generations behind leading firms like TSMC and Samsung, which are now manufacturing on scale at the 7-nanometer level and pursuing 3- and 2-nanometer capabilities. SMIC is also listed as a Chinese military company and thus denied access to US investment.

The second phase began in October 2022, when the United States issued a much broader set of export controls. Their goal was to limit China's ability to produce semiconductors at scale at the 14-nanometer level and below. These new controls are designed not only to ensure that firms like TSMC maintain a permanent lead over China but also to limit China's ability to become a global leader in the area of semiconductors. The new rules will block China's access to high-end chips (especially those used in AI), US-made chip design software, US-made semiconductor manufacturing equipment, and US-built components.[34] As one analyst notes, "These actions demonstrate an unprecedented degree of U.S. government intervention to not only preserve chokepoint control but also begin a new U.S. policy of actively strangling large segments of the Chinese technology industry—strangling with an intent to kill."[35]

In October 2023, the United States strengthened these measures in a move some analysts described as making "the yard bigger and the fence higher."[36] This was in part in a response to reports that China has found ways of circumventing the 2022 controls.[37] In brief, the 2023 update put a broader range of chips and semiconductor manufacturing equipment under control, for example, placing high-performance gaming chips and lower-performance datacenter chips under US export controls. It also expanded geographical coverage of its export controls to prevent diversion from third countries and foreign subsidiaries of Chinese multinationals, adding forty-three countries to US controls.[38]

Artificial Intelligence. In the area of AI, the United States has targeted leading Chinese firms. In October 2019, the Commerce Department placed AI firms Yitu Technologies, Megvii Technology, SenseTime, and iFlyTek on the Entity List for their role in the crackdown on human rights in Xinjiang.[39] In addition to Yitu, Megvii, and SenseTime, Cloudwalk Technology and Ximen Meiya Pico were listed as Chinese military companies and thus denied access to US investment. The October 2022 US action on semiconductors covers high-end chips used in AI and thus implicates this sector as well.

Quantum Computing. Although the export controls tend to focus on existing technologies, new and emerging technologies can also be included. In 2021, the BIS proposed a new export control classification number to "control quantum computers and related electronic assemblies and components including specified qubit devices and circuits and quantum control components and measurement devices."[40] In November 2021, the BIS added five Chinese firms involved in quantum computing to the Entity List.

Impact of Technological Competition on the US-China Rivalry

The growing role of technological competition impacts the US-China rivalry in several ways. US efforts to restrict China's access to US and allied cutting-edge technology coincided with several other factors that, taken together, have shifted Chinese perceptions of US intentions. These include the initiation of the trade war in July 2018, the increased focus on Xinjiang and Hong Kong in 2019, and the increased emphasis on Taiwan in 2020. As shown in Figure 7.4, references to "containing China" (遏制中国) in Chinese media sources have appeared with increasing frequency from 2015 to 2023, accelerating with the initial US moves against Huawei and increasing use of the Entity List that began in 2019. Of course, technological competition was not the only factor, but it was an important one.

Chinese writings on the role of technology in US-China relations often reach this conclusion. Zhu Feng and Ni Guihua from Nanjing University, for example, describe the United States as pursuing a "four-pronged approach to suppressing China [打压中国]." One is high-tech decoupling.[41] The other three are human rights, economics, and security. They describe the Biden administration as "projecting a comprehensive containment strategy against China and trying to harass and even block China's industrial upgrading, so as to secure longer US dominance over China's power and particularly impede on China's military modernization process," thereby linking technology and security.

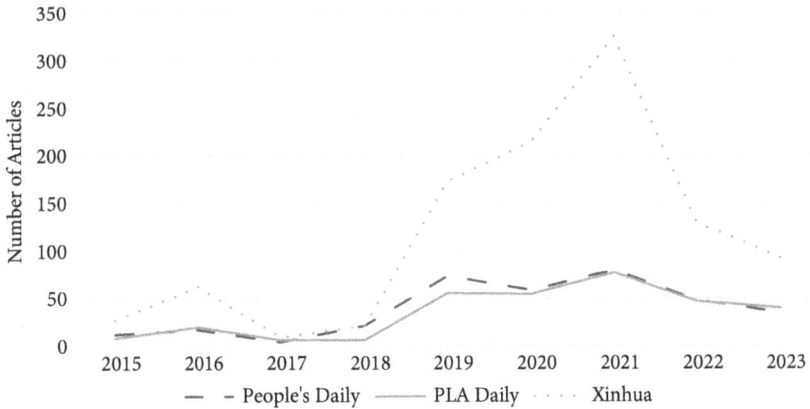

Figure 7.4 Articles with "Containing China" in Chinese Media

Source: PLA Daily, People's Daily, Xinhua (via Factiva)

Similarly, one scholar at Nankai University describes the United States as seeking to maintain "a dominant position in the field of science and technology," which the "US regards as the key to maintaining economic security, military security, and thus maintaining its hegemony." Thus, the Trump administration embarked on a suite of policies to "stall" the rapid rise of China's scientific and technological strength and continue to ensure US global dominance in the field of science and technology, which the Biden administration continued.[42]

Likewise, Chi Zhipei from the Central University of Finance and Economics describes the US approach as "fully shifted to a containment strategy." He describes the Fourth Industrial Revolution as having elevated the importance of technology as a future determinant of national power, leading the United States to seek to maintain its position of strength in high-technology areas, in part by "suppressing and preventing technology pursuers."[43]

Similar statements now appear in China's diplomacy. For example, in commenting on the Indo-Pacific Economic Framework, Foreign Minister Wang Yi asked rhetorically, "Does the US want to help the world economy recover, or will it continue man-made decoupling, erect technological barriers, and disrupt supply chains?"[44] In his first phone call after the October 2022 semiconductor export control policy was introduced, Wang Yi said, "The US side should stop its containment and suppression of China and not create new obstacles to bilateral relations."[45]

China has pursued several general policy responses to US actions.[46] One has been to accelerate efforts to improve China's "indigenous innovation" and self-reliance so that it can gain the ability to manufacture core technologies, to reduce dependence on foreign inputs and components and enhance supply chain security and stability. After the ZTE's placement on the Entity List shortly before the eruption of the "tech war," which threatened the company's viability, Xi Jinping in 2018 emphasized indigenous innovation, stating that "core technologies are important instruments of the state" (核心技术是国之重器) for the first time.[47] More recently, the Fourteenth Five Year Plan called for "science and technology self-reliance, . . . self-improvement," and "strategic support for national development."[48] The plan also calls for "significant subsidies for commercial technology applications and investments in new technology infrastructure"[49] as well as increased funding in seven frontier technologies (see Table 7.2). Similar themes were echoed in the work report from the Twentieth Party Congress in October

2022. Overall, spending on research and development is planned to increase 7% per year.

Implications for the US-China Rivalry

The preceding analysis yields several implications. First, the role of US export controls in the US-China technological competition is likely to increase, as the United States seeks to be able to cement US advantages in key areas. China sees itself as lagging behind the United States and other countries in critical sectors. According to a study from the Institute of International Strategic Studies at Peking University, "China is playing catch up in many areas, 'running together' in limited areas, and ahead in extremely few areas."[50] Similarly, a series of thirty-five articles published in 2018 in China's main science newspaper, *Science and Technology Daily* (科技日报), highlighted technological "chokepoints" where China was dependent on imports of critical technologies.[51] Thus, these areas are likely to remain at the forefront of US export controls and investment restrictions. Table 7.2 lists some of these areas where this aspect of technological competition may be most intense in the coming decade.

Second, the nature of the US export control regime suggests that it is poised to grow even more as a tool in the technological competition, so long as US-origin firms own or are developing technologies that China desires. The US government has wide discretion for designating entities as threats to national security, and there are few barriers to increasing the number of designated Chinese entities. In addition, the waivers or licenses that have been granted to permit the export of certain technologies can be revoked. Concerns about China's "military-civil fusion" program could lead to even more firms either being placed on the Entity List or being designated as Chinese military companies to block investment by US firms. The scope of US export controls, especially the FDPR, may also increase, with similar consequences for the rivalry. Finally, as the US reaction to the Russian invasion of Ukraine demonstrates, the Entity List could also be used to punish other foreign policy behaviors. To the degree that the United States continues to use these tools and expand the technologies or Chinese entities involved, they will further harden perceptions of hostile intentions and intensify the growing US-China rivalry.

Table 7.2 US-China technology balance

Sector	Balance	Sources
Aerospace	US advantages • Space transport and travel, satellites, exploration, materials, electronics, and propulsion • Civilian aviation • High-end bearing steel, aviation design software, aviation-grade steel, and aircraft engine nacelles (engine housing)	PKU Report; *Keiji Ribao* assessment
Artificial Intelligence	US advantages • Computing and algorithms • Original, groundbreaking research • Talent: 88% of Chinese AI students stay in the United States to work; only 10% return to China China advantages • Big data (facial/voice recognition, computer vision, etc.) • Overtook the United States in AI journal citations in 2020 • Projected to overtake the United States in 1% most cited papers by 2025	PKU Report; Allison and Schmidt; *2021 AI Index Report*
Biotechnology	US advantage	PKU Report; Moore
Hypersonics	Peer or slight Chinese advantage; United States successfully tested ARRW (an HGV) in May 2022	Congressional Research Service Report
Operating Systems and Industrial Software	US advantage in operating systems like Android and Apple Chinese weaknesses in electronic design automation software (useful for microchips)	PKU Report; Allison and Schmidt; *Keiji Ribao* assessment
Quantum	Peer or Chinese advantage, but technology itself is not mature yet	CRS Report; Garisto
Semiconductors	US advantage	PKU Report; *Keiji Ribao* assessment

Telecommunications	Chinese advantage, especially in 5G patents	PKU Report; Pohlmann and Buggenhagen
	As of November 2021, Huawei and ZTE account for 13.52% and 9.83% of 5G patent families globally, respectively, compared to Qualcomm at 9.97% and Apple at 1.7%	
	However, China is still reliant on foreign chips	

Sources: 2021 AI Index Report, Human-Centered Artificial Intelligence, Stanford University, 2021; Congressional Research Service, "Emerging Military Technologies: Background and Issues for Congress," R46458, April 6, 2022; Graham Allison and Eric Schmidt, "Is China Beating the U.S. to AI Supremacy?" (Belfer Center, August 2020); Daniel Garisto, "China Is Pulling Ahead in Global Quantum Race, New Studies Suggest," *Scientific American,* July 15, 2021; Institute of International and Strategic Studies Research Group (北京大学国际战略研究院课题组) "技术领域的中美战略竞争:分析与展望" [Sino-US strategic competition in the domain of technology: analysis and prospects] (Peking University, February 2022) (PKU Report); Scott Moore, "China's Role in the Global Biotechnology Sector and Implications for U.S. Policy" (Brookings Institution, April 2020); Ben Murphy, "Chokepoints: China's Self-Identified Strategic Technology Import Dependencies" (Center for Science and Emerging Technology, May 2022) (*Keiji Ribao* assessment); Tim Pohlmann and Magnus Buggenhagen, "Who Leads the 5G Patent Race" (IPlytics, November 2021).

Third, like sanctions, it is much easier for any entity to be designated and added to the Entity List than it is for them to be removed. Amid increasing US-China rivalry, national security rationales in US policy making related to China are likely to become even more prominent. Demonstrating that an entity, which was deemed to threaten US interests, no longer poses a threat will likely be a hard argument to sustain in many cases. The example of ZTE, a Chinese telecommunications hardware manufacturer, is instructive, as it took twelve months and fines upward of US$1.2 billion for the case to be resolved, which revolved primarily around ZTE's sales of prohibited items to Iran and not broader national security concerns in the US-China rivalry.[52] Similarly, the removal of Chinese entities will also likely be constrained by US domestic politics, as doing so can be easily portrayed as being "soft" on China, especially in Congress, a dynamic that is unlikely to improve and much more likely to worsen amid deep polarization in the United States on many domestic policy issues.

Fourth, in the technological competition, the importance of US allies and other aligned and "likeminded" states will become increasingly important to deny China access to critical technologies. The new US-European Union (EU) Technology and Trade Council (TTC) is a case in point. Its purpose is to maintain US and EU leadership in science and technology and manage differences relating to privacy and regulation. Many of the working groups formed under the TTC address issues such as standards, supply chain security, semiconductor competitiveness, data governance, export controls, and investment screening.[53] In the future, the United States could pursue similar arrangements with allies in Asia such as Japan or South Korea. Thus, allies and states who share US concerns regarding technology are important assets for the United States in this aspect of the technological competition. This is especially true regarding standards, where the United States along with the economies of key allies have a dominant presence in the main standards development organizations.

Fifth, the externalities or market distortions created by these policies, especially in export controls and investment restrictions, will be important to monitor. The largest beneficiary of actions against Huawei may very well be ZTE. Reduced exports by US firms to China may reduce funds available for future research and development. For this reason, before October 2022, the United States sought only to restrict semiconductor technology below 10 nanometers, allowing the export or sales of less sophisticated, commodity semiconductors and related technology to China to continue, thus generating revenue for further research and development by American firms that produce these chips or related manufacturing technologies. The delisting of Chinese technology firms from US markets does prevent their access to US capital, but many can raise capital in other markets. Indeed, the CHIPS and Science Act is designed in part to compensate for potential lost revenue from sales to China.

Sixth, some bifurcation or partial decoupling between the United States and China in the technology arena is inevitable. How wide the split becomes, however, is difficult to predict. As technology continues to advance, the rivalry creates strong US incentives to limit China's ability to advance, suggesting that a continuing bifurcation will grow over time. Alternatively, perhaps, as current cutting-edge technologies mature and become commodified, the restrictions on those technologies might ease, limiting the degree of bifurcation.

Conclusion

Looking ahead, a central feature of the growing global competition between the United States and China will be the competition of technological advantage. The stakes are high. Technology will confer advantages not only in the development of military power but also in national wealth more generally. The technologies of the Fourth Industrial Revolution are all general-purpose technologies. Paradoxically, in a competitive environment, competition over these technologies creates stronger incentives to limit access to those deemed to be critical technologies. China is seeking to become a technological superpower, and the United States is increasingly focused on preventing China from fulfilling this ambition. The US export controls and investment restrictions reviewed in this chapter will play a central role.

Notes

1. Brendan Thomas-Noone, "What the Cold War Can Teach Washington about Chinese Tech Tensions," *Brookings* (blog), January 12, 2021, https://www.brookings.edu/techstream/what-the-cold-war-can-teach-washington-about-chinese-tech-tensions/.
2. "Soviet Economy: Assessment of How Well the CIA Has Estimated the Size of the Economy" (Government Accountability Office, September 1991), https://www.gao.gov/assets/nsiad-91-274.pdf.
3. Rand C. Lewis, "COCOM: An International Attempt to Control Technology" (Defense Institute of Security Assistance Management Wright-Patterson AFB OH, January 1, 1990), https://apps.dtic.mil/sti/citations/ADA497085.
4. Stephen Kelly, "Curbing Illegal Transfers of Foreign-Developed Critical High Technology from CoCom Nations to the Soviet Union: An Analysis of the Toshiba-Kongsberg Incident," *Boston College International and Comparative Law Review* 12, no. 1 (December 1, 1989): 181.
5. Audrey Kurth Cronin, *Power to the People: How Open Technological Innovation Is Arming Tomorrow's Terrorists* (New York, NY: Oxford University Press, 2020), 23.
6. Kaan Sahin, "The Tech Cold War Illusion," DGAP, January 6, 2020, https://dgap.org/en/research/publications/tech-cold-war-illusion; Adam Segal, "A Fluid Cold War: US, China, and the Competition over Digital Technology," *Hérodote* 184–85, no. 1–2 (January 2022): 271–84.
7. Tai Ming Cheung, "The Emergence of the Chinese Techno-Security State: United States-China Great Power Competition," Minerva Research Initiative, August 13, 2019, https://minerva.defense.gov/Owl-In-the-Olive-Tree/Owl_View/Article/1932846/the-emergence-of-the-chinese-techno-security-state-united-states-china-great-po/.
8. *Military and Security Developments Involving the People's Republic of China 2021*, Annual Report to Congress (Department of Defense, November 3, 2021).
9. Michael Horowitz, "Artificial Intelligence, International Competition, and the Balance of Power," *Texas National Security Review* 1, no. 3 (May 2018): 36–57, https://doi.org/10.15781/T2639KP49.
10. Cronin, *Power to the People.*
11. *Military and Security Developments Involving the People's Republic of China 2021*, 147.
12. Klaus Schwab, "The Fourth Industrial Revolution," *Foreign Affairs*, December 12, 2015, https://www.foreignaffairs.com/articles/2015-12-12/fourth-industrial-revolution.
13. Klaus Schwab, *The Fourth Industrial Revolution*, 1st US ed. (Crown Business, 2016). For example, Silicon Valley (2014): $1.09 trillion with 137,000 employees; Detroit (1990): $36 billion with 1.2 million employees.
14. Jacob S. Hacker et al., eds., *The American Political Economy: Politics, Markets, and Power* (Cambridge University Press, 2021); K. Sabeel Rahman and Kathleen Thelen, "The Rise of the Platform Business Model and the Transformation of Twenty-First-Century Capitalism," *Politics & Society* 47, no. 2 (June 1, 2019): 177–204, https://doi.org/10.1177/0032329219838932.

15. For instance, see Anthony Blinken, "The Administration's Approach to the People's Republic of China," US Department of State, May 26, 2022, https://www.state.gov/the-administrations-approach-to-the-peoples-republic-of-china/.

16. Michael P. Colaresi et al., *Strategic Rivalries in World Politics: Position, Space and Conflict Escalation* (Cambridge University Press, 2008), https://doi.org/10.1017/CBO9780511491283.

17. The ten core areas identified in this document are "new generation information technology (IT), high-end computer numerical control (CNC) machines and robots, aerospace, marine engineering and high-tech ships, advanced rail transport, fuel efficient and new energy vehicles, electric power generation, agricultural machinery, new materials, and biotech and high-performance medical devices. See "Notice of the State Council on the Publication of 'Made in China 2025'" (Center for Security and Emerging Technology, March 10, 2022), 19–22, https://cset.georgetown.edu/publication/notice-of-the-state-council-on-the-publication-of-made-in-china-2025/.

18. On China's efforts to acquire technologies, see William C. Hannas et al., *Chinese Industrial Espionage: Technology Acquisition and Military Modernization*, Asian Security Studies (Routledge, 2013); William C. Hannas and Didi Kirsten Tatlow, eds., *China's Quest for Foreign Technology: Beyond Espionage*, Asian Security Studies (Routledge, 2021).

19. For the Chinese list, see "CSET Original Translation: China's 14th Five-Year Plan" (Center for Security and Emerging Technology, May 13, 2021), 12–13, https://cset.georgetown.edu/publication/china-14th-five-year-plan/. For the US list, see "Critical and Emerging Technologies List Update" (National Science and Technology Council, February 2022), https://www.whitehouse.gov/wp-content/uploads/2022/02/02-2022-Critical-and-Emerging-Technologies-List-Update.pdf.

20. Xi Jinping, "习近平:在中国科学院第二十次院士大会、中国工程院第十五次院士大会、中国科协第十次全国代表大会上的讲话" [Xi Jinping: speech at 20th Academician Conference of China Academy of Sciences, 15th Academician Conference of China Academy of Engineering, and 10th National Congress of China Association for Science and Technology], Xinhua, May 28, 2021, http://www.xinhuanet.com/politics/leaders/2021-05/28/c_1127505377.htm.

21. Ibid.

22. *Protecting Critical and Emerging US Technologies from Foreign Threats* (US National Counterintelligence and Security Center, February 2021), https://www.dni.gov/index.php/ncsc-newsroom/item/2254-ncsc-fact-sheet-protecting-critical-and-emerging-u-s-technologies-from-foreign-threats.

23. "Transcript: NPR's Full Conversation with CIA Director William Burns," NPR, July 22, 2021, https://www.npr.org/2021/07/22/1,017,900,583/transcript-nprs-full-conversation-with-cia-director-william-burns.

24. Eric Schmidt, "Emerging Technologies and Defense: Getting the Fundamentals Right," Senate Committee on Armed Services, 2021, https://www.armed-services.senate.gov/imo/media/doc/Schmidt_02-23-21.pdf.

25. Bureau of Industry and Security, "Lists of Parties of Concern," accessed June 14, 2022, https://www.bis.doc.gov/index.php/policy-guidance/lists-of-parties-of-concern.

26. James Mulvenon, "Seagate Technology and the Case of the Missing Huawei FDPR Enforcement," *Lawfare* (blog), June 6, 2022, https://www.lawfareblog.com/seagate-technology-and-case-missing-huawei-fdpr-enforcement.

27. US Department of the Treasury, "Non-SDN Chinese Military-Industrial Complex Companies List (NS-CMIC List)," accessed June 14, 2022, https://home.treasury.gov/policy-issues/financial-sanctions/consolidated-sanctions-list/ns-cmic-list.

28. On these restrictions, see Bateman, *U.S.-China Technological "Decoupling,"* 15–16.

29. Jane Zhang and Che Pan, "Who Are China's Blacklisted Supercomputer Groups?," *South China Morning Post*, sec. Tech, April 9, 2021, https://www.scmp.com/tech/tech-war/article/3,128,963/chinas-blacklisted-supercomputer-organisations-who-are-they-and-what.

30. Bateman, *U.S.-China Technological "Decoupling,"* 61.

31. Kim Caine and Stefan Reisinger, "US Expands Existing Restrictions on Exports to Huawei and Broadens Entity List Scope," *Norton Rose Fullbright* (blog), August 31, 2020, https://www.nortonrosefulbright.com/en-us/knowledge/publications/e775a355/us-expands-existing-restrictions-on-exports-to-huawei-and-broadens-entity-list-scope.   https://www.

nortonrosefulbright.com/en-us/knowledge/publications/e775a355/us-expands-existing-restrictions-on-exports-to-huawei-and-broadens-entity-list-scope.

32. Ibid.

33. Bureau of Industry and Security, "Addition of Entities to the Entity List, Revision of Entry on the Entity List, and Removal of Entities from the Entity List," Federal Register, December 22, 2020, https://www.federalregister.gov/documents/2020/12/22/2020-28031/addition-of-entities-to-the-entity-list-revision-of-entry-on-the-entity-list-and-removal-of-entities.

34. Gregory C. Allen, "Choking Off China's Access to the Future of AI: New U.S. Export Controls on AI and Semiconductors Mark a Transformation of U.S. Technology Competition with China" (Center for Strategic and International Studies, October 11, 2022), https://www.csis.org/analysis/choking-chinas-access-future-ai.

35. Ibid.

36. Hanna Dohmen and Jacob Feldgoise, "Explainer: The Commerce Department's October 2023 Export Control Update," *Center for Security and Emerging Technology* (blog), December 4, 2023, https://cset.georgetown.edu/article/bis-2023-update-explainer/.

37. Tim Fist et al., "Chinese Firms Are Evading Chip Controls," *Foreign Policy* (blog), June 21, 2023, https://foreignpolicy.com/2023/06/21/china-united-states-semiconductor-chips-sanctions-evasion/.

38. Dohmen and Feldgoise, "Explainer"; William Alan Reinsch et al., "Insight into the U.S. Semiconductor Export Controls Update," Center for Strategic and International Studies, October 20, 2023, https://www.csis.org/analysis/insight-us-semiconductor-export-controls-update; Emily Benson, "Updated October 7 Semiconductor Export Controls," Center for Strategic and International Studies, October 18, 2023, https://www.csis.org/analysis/updated-october-7-semiconductor-export-controls.

39. Bureau of Industry and Security, "Addition of Certain Entities to the Entity List," Federal Register, October 9, 2019, https://www.federalregister.gov/documents/2019/10/09/2019-22,210/addition-of-certain-entities-to-the-entity-list; "List of China's Blacklisted AI Firms by Washington," *AFP*, October 13, 2019, https://www.breakingasia.com/china/list-of-chinas-blacklisted-ai-firms-by-washington/amp/.

40. For the rule, see Bureau of Industry and Security, "View Rule," Reginfo.gov, 2021, https://www.reginfo.gov/public/do/eAgendaViewRule?pubId=202,104&RIN=0694-AH75.

41. Zhu Feng and Ni Guihua, "拜登政府对华战略竞争的态势与困境" [The situation and dilemma of the Biden administration's strategic competition with China], *Taiping anquan yu haiyang yanjiu* 亚太安全与海洋研究, no. 1 (2022): 1–18.

42. Huang Zhaolong, "特朗普政府时期美国科技战略解析" [Analysis of US science and technology strategy during Trump administration], *Nankai xuebao (zhexue shehui kexue ban)*, no. 3 (2022): 86–94.

43. Chi Zhipei, "美国对华科技遏制战略的实施与制约" [The implementation and restriction of US science and technology containment strategy to China], *Taipingyang xuebao* 28, no. 6 (2020): 27–42.

44. Chinese Ministry of Foreign Affairs, "王毅：要对美国的'印太经济框架'划一个大大的问号" [Wang Yi: a big question mark on the "Indo-Pacific Economic Framework" of the United States], May 22, 2022, https://www.mfa.gov.cn/wjbzhd/202205/t20220522_10690866.shtml.

45. "Top China Envoy Lashes Out at US Export Curbs in Blinken Call," Bloomberg, October 30, 2022, https://www.bloomberg.com/news/articles/2022-10-31/blinken-speaks-with-china-s-top-diplomat-in-latest-sign-of-thaw.

46. This paragraph draws on Adam Segal, "Seizing Core Technologies: China Responds to U.S. Technology Competition," *China Leadership Monitor*, no. 60 (Summer 2019), and Adam Segal, "China's Move to Greater Self Reliance," *China Leadership Monitor*, no. 70 (Winter 2021).

47. Quoted in Segal, "Seizing Core Technologies," 4.

48. Quoted in Segal, "China's Move to Greater Self Reliance," 2.

49. Ibid.

50. Institute of International and Strategic Studies Research Group [北京大学国际战略研究院课题组], "技术领域的中美战略竞争：分析与展望" [Sino-US strategic competition in the domain of technology: analysis and prospects] (Institute of International and Strategic Studies, Peking University, February 2022).

51. Ben Murphy, "Chokepoints: China's Self-Identified Strategic Technology Import Dependencies" (Center for Science and Emerging Technology, May 2022).

52. Kerry Contini and Olivia Colvill, "US Government Removes ZTE Corporation and ZTE Kangxun from Entity List," *Sanctions & Export Controls Update* (blog), March 29, 2017, https://sanctionsnews.bakermckenzie.com/u-s-government-removes-zte-corporation-and-zte-kangxun-from-entity-list/.
53. US Department of Commerce, "U.S.-EU Joint Statement of the Trade and Technology Council," May 16, 2022, https://www.commerce.gov/news/press-releases/2022/05/us-eu-joint-statement-trade-and-technology-council.

8

Technological Change and the Intensifying US-China Security Dilemma

Henrik Stålhane Hiim

China and the United States appear deadlocked in an increasingly fierce superpower rivalry. Both states view the other as harboring hostile intentions and fear that its influence and security will suffer at the hands of its competitor. Leaders in the United States have described China as having "the intent to reshape the international order" and have initiated major military efforts—as well as economic and diplomatic ones—to check Chinese aggression or even expansion.[1] Chinese leaders point to "external attempts to blackmail, contain, blockade and exert maximum pressure on China."[2] The rivalry between the two superpowers is playing out in several areas, including in the realm of technology.

The security dilemma is a crucial driver of the intensifying competition between China and the United States. The security dilemma refers to situations where a state with defensive intentions takes efforts to enhance its own security that others view as threatening. This in turn triggers other states to take countermeasures, such as building military capabilities. As a result, a spiral of tension and military competition—which may even lead to armed conflict—ensues.[3] As several scholars have highlighted, there are clear signs of such dynamics informing and exacerbating the China-US rivalry.[4]

Technological shifts can have a strong effect on security dilemma dynamics. As Taylor Fravel demonstrates in the previous chapter, US attempts to curb China's technology development efforts contribute to strengthening Chinese perceptions of hostility. Drawing on classical theories, this chapter highlights how the state of military technology, and whether it favors offense or the defender, can impact security dilemma dynamics. At the outset, East Asia is strongly defense dominant, which dampens the security dilemma

Henrik Stålhane Hiim, *Technological Change and the Intensifying US-China Security Dilemma*. In: *Not Just Another Cold War*. Edited by: Bård Nikolas Vik Steen, Oxford University Press. © Oxford University Press (2025). DOI: 10.1093/9780197799932.003.0009 and makes general war less likely. Both actors possess nuclear weapons, and the maritime geography of East Asia greatly complicates power projection. Unfortunately, recent shifts in military technology may blunt the impact of this defense dominance and exacerbate spiral dynamics.

The chapter points to two primary pathways to a more intense security dilemma. First, the advent of advanced precision-strike technology—coupled with the maturation of missile defense technology—is undermining nuclear stability. US deployments of nuclear and conventional counterforce weaponry exacerbate Chinese concerns about its capability to retaliate. This has contributed to China's expansion of its nuclear forces, which the United States in turn views with alarm. Moreover, both countries are fielding new nuclear weapons capabilities that the other fears could be employed in a limited first nuclear strike. As a result, a nuclear security dilemma is emerging between the two superpowers.

Second, the low likelihood of general war in East Asia may somewhat paradoxically increase the likelihood of a limited war.[5] Indeed, both China and the United States appear to believe—as US policy makers phrase it—that a Taiwan contingency is their "pacing scenario" and that a limited war is a distinct possibility.[6] In a conventional, limited war in East Asia, technological shifts have led to potential advantages of striking first, or an offense advantage.[7] In particular, as Avery Goldstein has highlighted, both states may have major incentives to strike first against the command, control, communications, computers, intelligence, surveillance, and reconnaissance (C4ISR) networks that modern militaries are strongly dependent on to fight effectively.[8] There are several ways of targeting such networks, including through cyber- and electronic warfare or conventional precision strike. In this chapter, I focus particularly on the space domain, which is critical for C4ISR networks, and counterspace capabilities that may target space assets.

This chapter proceeds as follows. First, I outline origins and regulators of the US-China security dilemma, and why the security environment at large is defense dominant. In the second section, I highlight why technological shifts are nevertheless contributing to an intensifying nuclear security dilemma. In the third section, I highlight why a limited war is far from unthinkable, and how technology such as counterspace weaponry generates potential first-strike incentives in such a conflict. In the conclusion, I highlight why the security dilemma between the United States and China will be hard to mitigate, and why military competition is likely to remain severe.

The Origins and Regulators of the
US-China Security Dilemma

In recent years, China's rapid economic growth and extensive military modernization have generated uncertainty in the United States and sparked concerns that China may harbor aggressive intentions. As a result, the United States is modernizing its military forces and developing operational concepts designed to counter China. Chinese leaders, in turn, see these steps as threatening. Perceptions of hostility—which may aggravate security dilemma dynamics—also abound: whereas the United States has described China as "revisionist," Chinese leaders believe the United States is developing a coalition designed to "contain" China.

That security dilemma dynamics may be at work, and that it may aggravate tensions between the United States and China, has been recognized by at least some US practitioners.[9] Chinese analysts have traditionally been more skeptical about applying the security dilemma concept to US-China relations, because it implies that Chinese behavior contributes to spirals and negative outcomes.[10] In recent years, however, Chinese analysts have started to argue that security dilemma dynamics are influencing their relationship with the United States.[11] Also among the broader publics, scholars have found perceptions that are consistent with the logic of the security dilemma, with the same action being perceived as defensive when taken by your own country, but offensive when taken by the other actor.[12]

According to Randall Schweller, the security dilemma is the result of "misplaced fear that others harbor aggressive designs" and only applies in situations where both states have mainly defensive goals.[13] Some observers argue that China's intentions are revisionist, and that US-China competition therefore is not the result of a security dilemma.[14] This is overstated: China's long-term intentions are unknowable. Moreover, as recent research by Alastair Iain Johnston demonstrates, claims of full-fledged revisionism, and that China is seeking to overthrow the so-called liberal international order, cannot be supported empirically.[15] To be clear, there are several examples of limited Chinese revisionism. China has long been discontented with the territorial status quo in the South China Sea and has during the last decade pushed its claims aggressively, including through its island-building spree.[16] China's goal of reunification with Taiwan, potentially through use of force, is perhaps the most clear-cut example of at least limited Chinese revisionism. Nevertheless, as Thomas Christensen has highlighted, China's leaders may have at least partly defensive motivations, as they "fear Taiwan's permanent independence from the Chinese nation" and regard "deterring this outcome a defensive strategy."[17] More broadly, even if China is conditionally revisionist, security dilemma dynamics may still apply. Even states with limited revisionist intentions may have reasons to be concerned about their security more broadly and about the intentions of others.[18]

The security dilemma is a byproduct of anarchy in the international system, and is therefore challenging, if not impossible to fully eliminate. Nevertheless, there are many factors or regulators that may ameliorate or intensify security dilemma dynamics.[19] These include perceptual regulators: as Charles Glaser notes, "the effects of structure are mediated through states' perceptions, whether accurate or not."[20] Recently, more scholarship has emerged on the importance of perceptual regulators of the security dilemma, including in China-US dynamics. For example, Alastair Iain Johnston has highlighted that "security dilemmas are socialization experiences," where shifts in identifies can intensify (or ameliorate) such dynamics.[21] These processes—such as the emergence of a master narrative of rivalry— are aggravating China-US tensions.[22] Although the extent to which ideology influences both China's and the United States' behavior and thus the current superpower rivalry is contested (see Chapters 1, 2, 10 and 14 in this volume), perceptions of ideological hostility can certainly worsen security dilemmas.

In addition, the actions of third parties may influence security dilemma dynamics, giving rise to "security trilemmas" or "nested security dilemmas."[23] In East Asia, North Korea's nuclear program has contributed significantly to the United States bolstering missile defense efforts, which again raises concern in China.[24] Along somewhat similar lines, the diffusion of precision-strike technology to US allies in the region may lead to Chinese concerns about the military balance, as well as about the survivability of its nuclear arsenal in the event of a US-led preemptive strike against it.[25]

As for material regulators and military technology, Robert Jervis's classic account of the security dilemma highlights two key variables, namely the offense-defense balance, and offense-defense distinguishability. If defensive weapons generate an advantage—meaning that it is "easier to protect and to hold than it is to move forward, destroy, and take"—the security dilemma is dampened, since status quo actors can tend to their security relatively easily without threatening others.[26] Conversely, if there is an offensive advantage, efforts to secure oneself will be perceived as threatening to other states.

Geography and technology are key determinants of the state of the offense-defense balance. In addition, the distinguishability between offensive and defensive weapons may regulate the intensity of the security dilemma. In situations where they are separable, status quo actors may arm themselves in ways that are different from aggressors. By contrast, if they are harder to distinguish, it is challenging for a defensive state to credibly signal that its military capabilities are not meant for infringing on the security of others.[27]

In the current US-China security environment, there is still a significant defense dominance. Perhaps most importantly, nuclear weapons lead to strong defense dominance as long as both actors have a second-strike capability. According to Jervis and other scholars of the nuclear revolution, the existence of second-strike nuclear forces therefore significantly ameliorates the security dilemma.[28] In an environment where aggression may be met with devastating retaliation—and where states have no means to defend themselves against this retaliation—aggression is futile.

In addition, geography renders maritime East Asia, which is where the China-US rivalry is most intense, strongly defense dominant. In essence, the "stopping power of water" greatly complicates power projection and offensive operations.[29] As Robert Ross has highlighted, the combination of a defensive geography and a power distribution characterized by stable bipolarity "will contribute to regional peace and order" and "mitigate the impact of the security dilemma."[30] Along similar lines, Jennifer Lind has highlighted that the potency of weapons platforms such as anti-ship missiles contributes to further reinforce the defense dominance of the region.[31]

However, even if nuclear weapons and geography likely diminish fears among both actors of general war, they do not eliminate security dilemma dynamics. There are indications—at least from China's point of view—that the United States has not fully accepted the nuclear revolution and China's possession of secure second-strike forces. As a result, a nuclear security dilemma is emerging, reinforced by technology such as precision-strike platforms and improving missile defense. Moreover, neither geography nor nuclear weapons preclude the outbreak of a more limited conflict, such as over Taiwan or in the South China Sea. As I outline in more detail below, particularly the United States appears to have offensive operational concepts that aggravates the security dilemma.[32] In a conflict, new technology and both sides' strong dependence on potentially vulnerable C4ISR networks may further provide incentives to strike first.

Technological Change and the US-China
Nuclear Security Dilemma

At the outset, nuclear weapons may greatly ameliorate security dilemma dynamics. If both actors in a potential conflict dyad have a secure second-strike capability, nuclear weapons greatly stabilize relations. Under mutual deterrence, the prospect of catastrophic retaliation makes the cost of using offensive weapons prohibitively high.

Pursuit of certain capabilities may undermine nuclear stability and contribute to reinforcing the security dilemma. Counterforce capabilities—that is, weapons that may destroy or deplete the nuclear forces of an adversary—may undermine stability by making states uncertain about their ability to retaliate. Somewhat counterintuitively, counterforce capabilities do not only include offensive weapons, such as nuclear or conventional strike platforms with high precision, but also defensive capabilities, such as missile defense. Pursuit of offensive and defensive counterforce capabilities in tandem may produce concern: states may fear that adversaries could employ offensive weapons to strike their arsenal and then rely on missile defense systems to mop up any surviving nuclear weapons.

Although nuclear deterrence arguably still has a stifling effect on the China-US security dilemma at large, there are signs of nuclear security dilemma dynamics emerging between them. Traditionally, China has sought to develop a relatively small force, premised on a strategy of "assured retaliation."[33] However, China's building of three large silo fields indicates that it is now vastly expanding its force of intercontinental ballistic missiles (ICBMs). According to the US Department of Defense, China now has five hundred operational nuclear warheads, which is twice as many as in 2020. By 2030, they expect the stockpile to double again, with China possessing "over 1,000 operational nuclear warheads, most of which will be fielded on systems capable of ranging the CONUS [continental United States]."[34]

Although there are other potential explanations for its nuclear expansion—such as great power prestige—several analysts have highlighted how Chinese concerns about the survivability of its nuclear forces is a very likely driver.[35] Studies conducted prior to the buildup have demonstrated that China's second-strike capability for years was quite feeble.[36] Although China in recent years has developed a nascent nuclear triad, its ballistic missile submarines are reportedly struggling with noise levels and are therefore likely vulnerable to US anti-submarine warfare, whereas its bombers would have to venture far into the Eastern Pacific before they would have the continental United States within range. Land-based missiles will therefore remain the backbone of China's nuclear forces, and its silo-building efforts may be the result of a perceived urgent need to bolster its second-strike capability.[37]

China's worries about survivability are likely at least partly informed by a revolution in missile guidance technology and remote sensing, which enable states to hold nuclear arsenals more efficiently at risk. Because of this revolution in precision-strike capabilities, states may increasingly even threaten the nuclear arsenals of others through conventional weapons.[38] For Chinese leaders, the combination of more potent US nuclear counterforce weapons, the prospect of highly precise US missiles deployed in East Asia, and continued US investments in more advanced missile defense have provided a strong rationale for bolstering its nuclear forces.[39] That the silo fields are located deep inland and out of range of US conventional precision-strike weapons may indicate that China has held concerns about conventional counterforce.

Unsurprisingly, US civilian and military leaders do not see China's nuclear expansion as defensive. Some of the statements by US leaders are hyperbolic, such as Air Force Secretary Frank Kendall's claim that China could be headed for a "first-strike capability" with an expanded ICBM force, or former commander Charles Richard of the US Strategic Command's claim that an expanded force could "execute any possible nuclear employment strategy."[40] Even if the projection of a thousand warheads by 2030 materializes—and the US intelligence community has frequently overestimated the expansion of Chinese nuclear force in the past—China will still be far behind the United States and Russia, which both have almost four thousand warheads in their stockpiles.[41] Another fear held by US leaders is that a more robust nuclear "shield" could make China more confident that it could safely engage in limited aggression, most notably against Taiwan. Even though there is little evidence in Chinese sources of such a goal, the "shield" hypothesis remains plausible.[42] More broadly, it appears as if US military leaders fear the prospect of facing two, rather than one, nuclear great powers and the implications this will have for nuclear targeting.[43] A Chinese nuclear expansion will greatly challenge the US ability to maintain a degree of damage limitation against China and potentially dispel notions of nuclear primacy, particularly in the face of two nuclear-armed adversaries.[44]

In addition, both states are increasingly concerned about the prospects of limited nuclear first use in the event of a conflict. These fears are at least partly informed by the revolution in precision-strike technology.

The Chinese strategic rocket force is fielding an increasing number of the dual-use DF-26 ballistic missile, which provides China with a theater-range nuclear precision-strike capability. Although the primary purpose of the nuclear-armed DF-26s may be to bolster regional deterrence, US analysts fear China could use it for limited first use in the event of a conflict.[45] The fact that there is no concrete evidence of China moving away from its no first-use (NFU) policy does not soothe US concerns, with US military leaders stating that they could "drive a truck through" Chinese NFU pledges.[46] China, on the other hand, fears that it is the United States that is seeking to lower the threshold for nuclear employment, and viewed the 2018 Nuclear Posture Review and its emphasis on new lower-yield nuclear weapons with alarm.[47] Chinese leaders appear to fear that the United States could rely on lower-yield nuclear weapons against its forces in a Taiwan conflict.[48] Although there is little concrete evidence available, some analysts believe China could seek to rely on capabilities such as the DF-26 as a tit-for-tat escalation management tool in the event of US threats of limited nuclear use.[49] Indeed, although they are still few in number, some Chinese experts have argued in favor of developing nonstrategic nuclear weapons to have a response option vis-à-vis the United States.[50]

Moreover, concern about the survivability of its nuclear arsenal appear to bolster China's search for advanced conventional weapons that can hold US missile defense capabilities at risk. Chinese analysts have discussed relying on kinetic and nonkinetic counterspace platforms, conventional precision-strike weapons, and other capabilities to target US missile defense systems, rather than focusing only on improving the penetrability of Chinese missiles. Tong Zhao has highlighted how some Chinese experts have called this approach "system penetration" or "system confrontation," and that China should potentially target interceptors, space-based sensors, ground-based radars, and command, control, and communication networks.[51] As he further notes, such an approach could clearly exacerbate security dilemma dynamics, as such capabilities may appear threatening for the United States in conventional conflict scenarios as well.[52] In addition, China is developing other advanced weapons. Its reported test of a fractional orbital bombardment system that carried a hypersonic glide vehicle in July 2021 caused alarm in the United States, with some US analysts fearing that the system could be used in a decapitation strike, or against bombers, with little or no warning time.[53] The US Department of Defense, however, has acknowledged that China's development of this and other advanced delivery systems is "in part due to long-term concerns about United States missile defense capabilities as well as to attain qualitative parity with future worldwide missile capabilities."[54]

Finally, the security dilemma is reinforced by the "entanglement" of nuclear and conventional weapons, where "militaries' nuclear and nonnuclear capabilities are becoming dangerously intertwined."[55] Because of this entanglement, conventional capabilities can be seen as a threat to the other side's nuclear forces. For example, scholars have debated whether the entanglement of Chinese nuclear and conventional missile forces, and the United States targeting these forces in a conflict, may create risks of inadvertent escalation.[56] Inadvertent escalation risk is a variant of security dilemma dynamics, as it describes a process where hostilities increase without the adversaries having an intent to escalate the conflict.[57]

In principle, arms control discussions could dampen the nuclear security dynamics at play between the United States and China. In November 2023, China and the United States held the first arms control talks in years, but unfortunately, the talks did not yield any concrete results. Although limited steps such as a missile launch notification regime may be possible to achieve, there is little reason to be optimistic about the prospects for agreements that include concrete constraints, such as numerical limits. The still-major discrepancy in arsenal size, the United States' unwillingness to accept parity, China's interest in constraints on nonnuclear weapons such as missile defense, and the perception among many in the United States that it needs a nuclear posture that can deter China and Russia simultaneously contribute to complicating arms control.[58] In addition, cynicism and mutual suspicion run strong. Although trust is not necessarily a prerequisite for arms control, many in China even appear to distrust the process, seeing arms control as a "trap" where the United States seeks to lock China into a position of inferiority rather than as a mechanism to mutually enhance security.[59]

In sum, although nuclear weapons arguably still significantly dampen the prospects of a conflict between the United States and China, there are signs of a nuclear security dilemma dynamics emerging. These dynamics are driven by concerns about counterforce, limited first use, and nuclear weapons being used as a shield for aggression. The complexity of the dilemma and the strong mutual suspicion between the superpowers make it very challenging to mitigate these dynamics.

Counterspace Weapons and First-Strike Incentives

Despite the defense dominance generated by nuclear weapons and East Asia's maritime geography, a limited military conflict between the United States and China is far from unthinkable. In fact, as Øystein Tunsjø has argued, a limited conflict between China and the United States is probably more likely than a limited conflict in Europe between the superpowers during the Cold War ever was. Whereas an initially limited war on land in Europe would likely have escalated quickly, the prospects for keeping a war limited in maritime East Asia is greater.[60] In other words, the so-called stability-instability paradox, where stability at the highest strategic level leads to instability by making limited conflict appear safe to fight, is arguably more intense in the current superpower rivalry than it was during the Cold War.[61] Both states are preparing actively for a limited war. Although there are several areas where a limited conflict may erupt, the most serious—and perhaps most likely—is a Taiwan Strait contingency. As Scott Kastner and Bruno Tertrais outline in this volume, the Taiwan Strait remains a serious potential flashpoint, and a war could in the worst case lead to nuclear employment.[62]

In addition, although the maritime nature of East Asia creates a strong defense dominance at the outset, the United States is—because of its alliance relationships—highly dependent on being able to project power to the region. As Jennifer Lind highlights, this defense dominance makes power projection challenging, with the result that the United States has sought to generate massive military power to offset this disadvantage. Moreover, to overcome the challenges brought by China's so-called anti-access/area-denial (A2/AD) capabilities, the United States is "operationally on the offense" when it seeks to project power to East Asia.[63] To be sure, other scholars claim current US operational approaches are unnecessarily offensive. Rather than breaking through China's A2/AD bubble—including through potentially striking targets on the Chinese mainland and jamming or spoofing Chinese sensors—they argue that the United States should invest in a "defensive defense" approach to mitigate the security dilemma, including by having US allies invest in A2/AD capabilities of their own.[64] So far, however, the United States appears to have maintained its more offensive operational approach.

In the event of a limited conflict in the Taiwan Strait, technological shifts are producing areas where there are significant potential first-strike incentives, which contributes to security dilemma dynamics. As noted, military effectiveness is increasingly tied to C4ISR networks that states may have incentives to target early in a conflict.[65] Although there are several ways to target such networks, such as cyberweapons, electronic warfare, or conventional precision strike, I focus on counterspace capabilities in this chapter. In a limited conflict, both China and the United States may have major incentives to employ such capabilities early. These incentives further aggravate the security dilemma.

In recent years, both China and the United States have emphasized the critical role of space, and how it is likely to figure in a future war. The United States has defined space as a "warfighting domain," which requires "enterprise-wide changes to policies, strategies, operations, investments, capabilities, and expertise for a new strategic environment."[66] Similarly, the most recent Chinese defense white paper states that "Outer space is a critical domain in international strategic competition."[67] Both states claim that the other actor represents a threat to space security, which strongly indicates that security dilemma dynamics is in play.[68]

Bolstering their ability to fight a war in the space domain, both China and the United States are rapidly developing capabilities that will enable strikes against space assets. China's interest in counterspace capabilities were first dramatically on display in 2007, when it shot down one of its own aging satellites, generating significant space debris as a result. China has continued to invest in direct-ascent weapons, which may hold at risk satellites in low earth orbit. According to the US Department of Defense, China "probably intends to pursue additional ASAT weapons capable of destroying satellites up to geosynchronous Earth orbit."[69] In addition, China has developed co-orbital systems with possible counterspace roles, as well as directed energy, electronic warfare, and likely cyber capabilities that may target space-based assets.

The United States fields one acknowledged counterspace system that relies on electronic warfare, but it "also has multiple other operational systems that could be used in counterspace roles."[70] Moreover, as Brian Weeden and Victoria Samson highlight, spurred largely by the broader rivalry with China (as well as Russia), there is increasingly debate in the United States about developing new counterspace systems. Through such capabilities, the United States may hope to both deter adversaries from attacking US assets and deny adversaries the use of space assets in a conflict.[71] China's increasing reliance on space assets will likely only spur further debate among US planners and policy makers. Moreover, demonstrating the increasing importance of the space domain to the US military, the United States founded the Space Force as a distinct service branch in 2019.

Whether to employ kinetic counterspace capabilities at the outset of a conflict would be a complex trade-off for both states. On the one hand, there are significant benefits associated with a strike against space assets. Chinese military analysts regard the dependence of the heavily networked US military on space-based assets for warfighting effectiveness as a vulnerability, highlighting that US (as well as Russian) "strategic intelligence, military communications, navigation and positioning, [and] weather information" mainly come from "space information systems."[72] As Kevin Pollpeter argues, in a conflict, the PLA may strike first "to achieve an asymmetric advantage against a superior US force in order to delay its entry and keep it away from the conflict zone."[73] For the United States, he argues that striking space-based assets early could "defeat China's ability to locate, track, and target US bases and naval ships with long-range precision strike platforms."[74]

On the other hand, there are clear risks and costs associated with kinetic counterspace strikes. Most importantly, any attack would invite retaliation from the adversary, and thus lead to loss of your own space-based assets. In addition, kinetic strikes may produce space debris, which can again cause a cascade effect that could damage your own satellites. For these reasons, the threshold for employing particularly kinetic weapons that permanently damage the space assets of an adversary is likely to be relatively high. Even in serious limited conflicts—most notably a Taiwan scenario—both China and the United States would take serious risks if they employed such weapons. Beyond the risk of retaliation, both China and the United States would need to consider the vulnerability of the systems. In the case of the United States, the Global Positioning System (GPS) is often regarded as relatively vulnerable, whereas other functions are becoming much less vulnerable, not least because of the resiliency and redundancy offered by megaconstellations.[75]

Whether they would employ kinetic counterspace weapons would partly depend on the conflict scenario. In a Taiwan scenario, China would—because of its geographical proximity—be less dependent on space-based systems for C4ISR functions than in a conflict around the Spratly Islands. China could potentially rely on other platforms, such as ground-based or airborne radars, for situational awareness.[76] Moreover, because of the importance of Taiwan, China's willingness to run significant risks would likely be high. Nevertheless, even in a Taiwan scenario, a loss of space-based assets would be a disadvantage for the PLA in its efforts to defeat Taiwan's forces in the early stages of conflict before US forces could arrive in the theater.[77] In addition, it remains an open question how well China's forces would be able to adapt to operating without the support of space assets, compared to US forces.

One possible way to address this tension for both states is to develop a greater array of nonkinetic capabilities.[78] According to a recent report by the Center for Strategic and International Studies, China is "greatly increasing its development, testing, and fielding of non-kinetic physical and electronic counterspace weapons." Indeed, Chinese analysts have claimed that "soft kill and reversible damage are the future development direction" in counterspace technologies.[79] More broadly, according to Fiona Cunningham, China has adopted a "calibrated escalation" space force posture where it seeks to limit the intensity of attacks to be able to manage the escalation process.[80] Investment in nonkinetic counterspace capabilities matches a posture designed to calibrate escalation. Temporarily denying US space assets—and avoiding the creation of space debris—is less escalatory than permanently damaging satellites. Although they may be less escalatory, the development of nonkinetic counterspace capabilities may reinforce first-strike incentives. Precisely because they create lower risk of escalation, the threshold for employing such capabilities is lower. In some cases, it may be challenging to attribute the source of attacks, making temptations to employ these capabilities even greater.

Despite these caveats, the potential incentives for kinetic first strikes—and the concern it is creating among both superpowers—are real. It is far from clear whether both China and the United States would resist the temptation to strike first in a conflict. As Kevin Pollpeter highlights about the PLA, while "strategic writings indicate a cautious approach to space warfare, writings on the operational level of war suggest a predilection for strong offensive actions at the beginning of a conflict."[81] Moreover, counterspace capabilities have limited offense/defense distinguishability. For both the United States and China, developing counterspace capabilities is a way to bolster space deterrence, and as noted above, China is developing counterspace weapons to target US missile defense. Unfortunately, the counterpart regard these capabilities as offensive.

Conclusion

Technological shifts are aggravating the security dilemma between China and the United States. Although mutual nuclear deterrence and the

188 HENRIK STÅLHANE HIIM

challenges of projecting power in maritime East Asia contribute strongly to overall defense dominance—thereby lessening the likelihood of general war—it does not eliminate the dilemma. First, the mutual nuclear deterrence relationship between China and the United States appears increasingly tenuous. Partly the result of the advent of advanced precision—strike technology, coupled with maturing missile defense technology, China is increasingly concerned about its second—strike capability and is moving to expand and modernize its nuclear forces. The nuclear expansion has caused a strong reaction in the United States. Moreover, both countries are fielding new capabilities that its counterpart fears could facilitate limited first nuclear use in a conflict. As a result, a nuclear security dilemma is emerging between the United States and China.

Second, the overall defense advantage of the region may somewhat counterintuitively increase the risk of a limited war. In a limited war—for example, over Taiwan—new technology is increasingly producing first-strike incentives for both parties. Such incentives are salient in the space domain. By targeting the space assets of its adversary, both parties may believe they could secure a significant advantage during the next phases of a conflict. Such incentives may be especially strong for China, which could partially replace space-based C4ISR assets with other alternatives in a Taiwan scenario, and which sees the heavily networked nature of the US military as an Achilles heel.

Technological developments and first-strike incentives are certainly not the only sources of the security dilemma between the United States and China. Perceptual regulators also reinforce security dilemma dynamics between China and the United States. In the United States, China is frequently seen as "revisionist," a view that reinforces security dilemma dynamics. Similarly, Chinese elites tend to see the United States with strong suspicion. Moreover, the actions of third parties matter as well. If countries aligned with the United States or China acquire weapons that the other superpower perceives as threatening, it may reinforce security dilemma dynamics.

In sum, the security dilemma between the United States and China is complex, increasingly fierce, and therefore difficult to mitigate. Although defense dominance strongly limits the risk of general war at the outset, the security dilemma dynamics are likely to remain severe, and may even deepen. This not only will contribute to arms competition and rivalry but could even increase the likelihood of an armed conflict between the superpowers.

Notes

1. White House, "National Security Strategy," October 2022, 8, https://www.whitehouse.gov/wp-content/uploads/2022/10/Biden-Harris-Administrations-National-Security-Strategy-10.2022.pdf.

2. Xi Jinping, "Hold High the Great Banner of Socialism with Chinese Characteristics and Strive in Unity to Build a Modern Socialist Country in All Respects," Report to the 20th National Congress of the Communist Party of China, October 16, 2022, 3. See also, for example, Su Jingxiang, "美国对中国的遏制战略" [The United States' containment strategy towards China], *China-US Focus*, April 15, 2021, http://cn.chinausfocus.com/foreign-policy/20210415/42248.html.

3. Robert Jervis, "Cooperation under the Security Dilemma," *World Politics* 30, no. 2 (1978): 167–214, https://doi.org/10.2307/2009958; Charles L. Glaser, "The Security Dilemma Revisited," *World Politics* 50, no. 1 (1997): 171–201, https://www.jstor.org/stable/25054031.

4. See, for example, Adam P. Liff and G. John Ikenberry, "Racing toward Tragedy?: China's Rise, Military Competition in the Asia Pacific, and the Security Dilemma," *International Security* 39, no. 2 (2014): 52–91; Evan S. Medeiros, "The Changing Fundamentals of US-China Relations," *Washington Quarterly* 42, no. 3 (2019): 93–119, https://doi.org/10.1080/0163660X.2019.1666355.

5. Øystein Tunsjø, *Return of Bipolarity in World Politics: China, the United States, and Geostructural Realism* (Columbia University Press, 2018).

6. See Terri Moon Cronk, "Testimony: DOD Is Laser Focused on China Pacing Challenge, Meeting Our Commitments under the Taiwan Relations Act," *DOD News*, December 8, 2021, https://www.defense.gov/News/News-Stories/Article/Article/2867003/testimony-dod-is-laser-focused-on-china-pacing-challenge-meeting-our-commitment/. On how the Taiwan scenario is key to Chinese military planners, see Joel Wuthnow and M. Taylor Fravel, "China's Military Strategy for a 'New Era': Some Change, More Continuity, and Tantalizing Hints," *Journal of Strategic Studies* 46, no. 6–7 (2023): 1149–84.

7. Jervis, "Cooperation under the Security Dilemma," 188.

8. Avery Goldstein, "First Things First: The Pressing Danger of Crisis Instability in U.S.-China Relations," *International Security* 37, no. 4 (2013): 67–68.

9. Jeffrey A. Bader, *Obama and China's Rise: An Insider's Account of America's Asia Strategy* (Brookings Institution Press, 2013), 150.

10. Alastair Iain Johnston, "Beijing's Security Behavior in the Asia–Pacific: Is China a Dissatisfied Power?," in *Rethinking Security in East Asia: Identity, Power, and Efficiency*, ed. Jae-Jung Suh et al. (Stanford University Press, 2004), 76.

11. See, for example, 尹继武 [Yin Jiwu], "国际安全困境的缓解逻辑:一项理论比较分析" [The logic of the regulation of security dilemma: a comparative study], 教学与研究 [Jiaoyu yu Yanjiu] 1 (2021): 101–12.

12. See Joshua D. Kertzer et al., "Perspective Taking and the Security Dilemma: Cross-National Experimental Evidence from China and the United States," unpublished manuscript, https://jkertzer.sites.fas.harvard.edu/Research_files/SCS_KQB_Web.pdf.

13. Randall L. Schweller, "Neorealism's Status-Quo Bias: What Security Dilemma?," *Security Studies* 5, no. 3 (1996): 117, https://doi.org/10.1080/09636419608429277.

14. See, for example, Ronan Tse-Min Fu et al., "Correspondence: Looking for Asia's Security Dilemma," *International Security* 40, no. 2 (Fall 2015): 186–87, https://www.jstor.org/stable/43828299.

15. Alastair Iain Johnston, "China in a World of Orders: Rethinking Compliance and Challenge in Beijing's International Relations," *International Security* 44, no. 2 (2019): 9–60.

16. However, China did also engage in coercive diplomacy against other claimants during the 1970s, 1980s, and early 1990s.

17. Thomas J. Christensen, "The Contemporary Security Dilemma: Deterring a Taiwan Conflict," *Washington Quarterly* 25, no. 4 (2010): 12, https://doi.org/10.1162/016366002760252509.

18. Ibid.

19. For an excellent analysis of the regulators of the security dilemma, see Shiping Tang, "The Security Dilemma: A Conceptual Analysis," *Security Studies* 18, no. 3 (2009): 587–623, https://doi.org/10.1080/09636410903133050.

20. Glaser, "The Security Dilemma Revisited."

21. Alistair Iain Johnston, "Stability and Instability in Sino–US Relations: A Response to Yan Xue-tong's Superficial Friendship Theory," *Chinese Journal of International Politics* 4, no. 1 (2011): 19, https://doi.org/10.1093/cjip/por003.
22. Adam Breuer and Alistair Iain Johnston, "Memes, Narratives and the Emergent US–China Security Dilemma," *Cambridge Review of International Affairs* 32, no. 4 (2019): 429–55, https://doi.org/10.1080/09557571.2019.1622083.
23. Linton Brooks and Mira Rapp-Hooper, "Extended Deterrence, Assurance, and Reassurance in the Pacific during the Second Nuclear Age," in *Strategic Asia 2013-14: Asia in the Second Nuclear Age*, ed. A. J. Tellis et al. (National Bureau of Asian Research, 2013), 266–300; George J. Gilboy and Eric Heginbotham, "Double Trouble: A Realist View of Chinese and Indian Power," *Washington Quarterly* 36, no. 3 (2013): 125–42.
24. Eleni Ekmektsioglou and Ji-Young Lee, "North Korea, Missile Defense, and U.S.-China Security Dilemma," *Pacific Review* 35, no. 4 (2020): 587–16, https://doi.org/10.1080/09512748.2020.1862285.
25. Zhao Tong, "Conventional Long-Range Strike Weapons of US Allies and China's Concerns of Strategic Instability," *Nonproliferation Review* 27, no. 1–3 (2020): 109–22.
26. Jervis, "Cooperation under the Security Dilemma," 187.
27. Ibid., 199–206.
28. Robert Jervis, *The Meaning of the Nuclear Revolution* (Cornell University Press, 1989); see also Kenneth N. Waltz, "Nuclear Myths and Political Realities," *American Political Science Review* 84, no. 3 (1990): 730–45, https://doi.org/10.2307/1962764.
29. John J. Mearsheimer, *The Tragedy of Great Power Politics* (W. W. Norton, 2014), 83–137.
30. Robert Ross, "The Geography of the Peace: East Asia in the Twenty-First Century," *International Security* 23, no. 4 (1999): 117.
31. Jennifer Lind, "Geography and the Security Dilemma in Asia," in *The Oxford Handbook of the International Relations of Asia*, ed. Saadia Pekkanen et al. (Oxford University Press, 2014), 719–36, https://doi.org/10.1093/oxfordhb/9780199916245.013.0037.
32. Eugene Gholz et al., "Defensive Defense: A Better Way to Protect US Allies in Asia," *Washington Quarterly* 42, no. 4 (2019): 171–89.
33. Taylor Fravel and Fiona Cunningham, "Assuring Assured Retaliation: China's Nuclear Posture and U.S.-China Strategic Stability," *International Security* 40, no. 2 (2015): 7–50.
34. US Department of Defense, "Military and Security Developments Involving the People's Republic of China: 2023," 111, October 19, 2023, https://media.defense.gov/2023/Oct/19/2003323409/-1/-1/1/2023-military-and-security-developments-involving-the-peoples-republic-of-china.pdf.
35. See David Logan and Philip Saunders, *Discerning the Drivers of China's Nuclear Force Development: Models, Indicators, and Data* (National Defense University Press, 2023); Henrik Stålhane Hiim, "The Last Atomic Waltz: China's Nuclear Expansion and the Persisting Relevance of the Theory of the Nuclear Revolution," *Contemporary Security Policy* 45, no. 2 (2023): 239–64.
36. Wu Riqiang, "Living with Uncertainty: Modeling China's Nuclear Survivability," *International Security* 44, no. 4 (2020): 84–118.
37. Henrik Stålhane Hiim et al., "The Dynamics of an Entangled Security Dilemma: China's Changing Nuclear Posture," *International Security* 47, no. 4 (2023): 173–80.
38. Scott D. Sagan and Allen S. Weiner, "The Rule of Law and the Role of Strategy in U.S. Nuclear Doctrine," *International Security* 45, no. 4 (Spring 2021): 126, https://doi.org/10.1162/isec_a_00407; Keir A. Lieber and Daryl G. Press, "The New Era of Counterforce: Technological Change and the Future of Nuclear Deterrence," *International Security* 41, no. 4 (2017): 9–49, https://doi.org/10.1162/ISEC_a_00273; see also Ian Bowers and Henrik Hiim, "Conventional Counterforce Dilemmas: South Korea's Deterrence Strategy and Stability on the Korean Peninsula," *International Security* 45, no. 3 (2021): 7–39.
39. See Hiim et al., "The Dynamics on an Entangled Security Dilemma."
40. Marcus Weisgerber, "Air Force Secretary Warns of China's Burgeoning Nuclear Arsenal, Reveals B-21 Detail," Defense One, September 20, 2021, https://www.defenseone.com/threats/2021/09/air-force-secretary-warns-chinas-burgeoning-nuclear-arsenal-reveals-b-21-detail/185486/; John Vandiver, "'Breathtaking Expansion': US Strategic Command Leader Expects Further Revelations of China's Nuclear Weapons Advancement," Stars and Stripes, October 18, 2021, https://www.stripes.com/theaters/europe/2021-10-18/china-us-russia-nuclear-weapons-hypersonics-stratcom-3283272.html.

41. Kelsey Davenport, ed., "Nuclear Weapons: Who Has What at a Glance," Arms Control Association, January 2022, https://www.armscontrol.org/factsheets/Nuclearweaponswhohaswhat.
42. Taylor Fravel et al., "China's Misunderstood Nuclear Expansion," *Foreign Affairs*, November 10, 2023, https://www.foreignaffairs.com/china/chinas-misunderstood-nuclear-expansion.
43. Andrew F. Krepinevich Jr., "The New Nuclear Age: How China's Growing Nuclear Arsenal Threatens Deterrence," *Foreign Affairs* 101, no. 3 (2022): 92–104.
44. On the debate about whether the United States should pursue damage limitation and maintain nuclear primacy, see Brendan Rittenhouse Green et al., "Correspondence: The Limits of Damage Limitation," *International Security* 42, no. 1 (Summer 2017): 193–207, https://doi.org/10.1162/ISEC_c_00279.
45. On the role of the DF-26, see Cunningham and Fravel, "Dangerous Confidence?," 91–92; David C. Logan, "Are They Reading Schelling in Beijing? The Dimensions, Drivers, and Risks of Nuclear-Conventional Entanglement in China," *Journal of Strategic Studies* 46, no. 1 (2023): 39–40. For apparent concern that China could retort to limited nuclear first use, see US Department of Defense, "2018 Nuclear Posture Review" (Office of the Secretary of Defense, 2018), 32, https://media.defense.gov/2018/Feb/02/2001872886/-1/-1/1/2018-nuclear-posture-review-final-report.pdf.
46. Committee on Armed Services, *Hearing for the United States Senate*, February 13, 2020, 61, https://www.armed-services.senate.gov/imo/media/doc/20-04_02-13-2020.pdf.
47. See, for example, Li Bin, "Will US Nuclear Posture Review See a Return to Hegemony?," Carnegie Endowment for International Peace, January 26, 2018, https://carnegieendowment.org/2018/01/26/will-us-nuclear-posture-review-see-return-to-hegemony-pub-75359.
48. US Department of Defense, "Military and Security Developments Involving the People's Republic of China: 2021," 93, November 3, 2021, https://media.defense.gov/2021/Nov/03/2002885874/-1/-1/0/2021-cmpr-final.pdf.
49. Zhao Tong, "China's Silence on Nuclear Arms Buildup Fuels Speculation on Motives," *Bulletin of the Atomic Scientists*, November 12, 2021, https://thebulletin.org/2021/11/chinas-silence-on-nuclear-arms-buildup-fuels-speculation-on-motives/#post-heading.
50. Pan Zhenqiang, "A Study of China's No-First-Use Policy on Nuclear Weapons," *Journal for Peace and Nuclear Disarmament* 1, no. 1 (2018): 129, https://doi.org/10.1080/25751654.2018.1458415.
51. Zhao Tong, "Narrowing the U.S.-China Gap on Missile Defense: How to Help Forestall a Nuclear Arms Race" (Carnegie Endowment for International Peace, 2020), 47–50, https://carnegieendowment.org/2020/06/29/narrowing-u.s.-china-gap-on-missile-defense-how-to-help-forestall-nuclear-arms-race-pub-82120.
52. Ibid., 56.
53. Center for Global Security Research, *China's Emergence as a Second Nuclear Peer: Implications for US Nuclear Deterrence Strategy*, A report of a study group convened by the Center for Global Security Research at Lawrence Livermore National Laboratory, 2023, https://cgsr.llnl.gov/content/assets/docs/CGSR_Two_Peer_230314.pdf.
54. US Department of Defense, "Military and Security Developments Involving the People's Republic of China: 2023," 111.
55. James M. Acton, "Why Is Nuclear Entanglement So Dangerous?," Q&A, Carnegie Endowment for International Peace, January 23, 2019, https://carnegieendowment.org/2019/01/23/why-is-nuclear-entanglement-so-dangerous-pub-78136.
56. Logan, "Are They Reading Schelling in Beijing?"
57. Barry Posen, *Inadvertent Escalation: Conventional War and Nuclear Risks* (Cornell University Press, 1991), 12–16.
58. See, for example, Madelyn R. Creedon et al., Congressional Commission on the Strategic Posture of the United States, 2023, https://armedservices.house.gov/sites/republicans.armedservices.house.gov/files/Strategic-Posture-Committee-Report-Final.pdf.
59. Henrik Hiim and Magnus Langset Trøan, "Hardening Chinese Realpolitik in the 21st Century: The Evolution of Beijing's Thinking about Arms Control," *Journal of Contemporary China* 31, no. 133 (2022): 86–100, https://doi.org/10.1080/10670564.2021.1926095.
60. Tunsjø, *Return of Bipolarity in World Politics*, 126–49.
61. Goldstein, "First Things First," 65–66; see also Tunsjø, *Return of Bipolarity in World Politics*, 142. On the paradox, see Glenn H. Snyder, "The Balance of Power and the Balance of Terror," in *Balance of Power*, ed. Paul Seabury (Chandler Publishing Company, 1965), 184–201.

62. See Scott Kastner and Bruno Tertrais in this volume.
63. Lind, "Geography and the Security Dilemma in Asia," 726.
64. Gholz et al., "Defensive Defense."
65. Goldstein, "First Things First," 67.
66. US Department of Defense, "2020 Defense Space Strategy Summary," 2020, https://media. defense.gov/2020/Jun/17/2002317391/-1/-1/1/2020_DEFENSE_SPACE_STRATEGY_SU MMARY.PDF, 1.
67. State Council Information Office, "新时代的中国国防" [China's national defense in a new era], 2020, http://www.gov.cn/zhengce/2019-07/24/content_5414325.htm.
68. US Department of Defense, "2020 Defense Space Strategy Summary," 3; State Council Information Office, "新时代的中国国防" [China's national defense in a new era].
69. US Department of Defense, "Military and Security Developments Involving the People's Republic of China: 2023," 99.
70. Brian Weeden and Victoria Samson, *Global Counterspace Capabilities: An Open Source Assessment* (Secure World Foundation, 2022), 1-1, https://swfound.org/media/207350/ swf_global_counterspace_capabilities_2022_rev2.pdf.
71. Ibid.
72. Xiao Tianliang, ed., 战略学 [The science of military strategy] (国防大学出版社 [National Defense University Press], 2020), 143. See also Fiona Cunningham, *Maximizing Leverage: Explaining China's Strategic Force Postures in Limited Wars* (PhD diss., Massachusetts Institute of Technology, 2018), 348.
73. Kevin L. Pollpeter, "Space, the New Domain: Space Operations and Chinese Military Reforms," *Journal of Strategic Studies* 39, no. 5–6 (2016): 725.
74. Ibid.
75. The US Space-Based Infrared System (SBIRS) is also frequently seen as relatively vulnerable, as the number of satellites is limited. However, an attack on the SBIRS would be highly escalatory, given the key role the system plays in US ballistic missile early warning.
76. Eric Heginbotham et al., *The U.S.-China Military Scorecard: Forces, Geography, and the Evolving Balance of Power, 1996–2017* (RAND Corporation, 2015), 227–57.
77. Bleddyn E. Bowen, *War in Space: Strategy, Spacepower, Geopolitics* (Edinburgh University Press, 2020), 263.
78. Jonas Vidhammer Berge and Henrik Stålhane Hiim, "Killing Them Softly: China's Counterspace Developments and Force Posture in Space," *Journal of Strategic Studies*, published online August 27, (2024).
79. 韩洪涛 and 王友利 [Han Hongtao and Wang Youli], "国外空间攻防能力现状与趋势分析" [Analysis of the current status and trends of foreign offensive and defensive space capabilities], 中国航天 [*Zhongguo Hangtian*] 9 (2015): 25; see also Huang Zhicheng, "从五克郎站成看商业航天军事价值" [Examining the military value of commercial aerospace from the Ukrainian battlefield], 国际太空 [*Guoji Taikong*] 4 (2023), 12–17.
80. Cunningham, "Maximizing Leverage."
81. Pollpeter, "Space, the New Domain," 715; see also Cunningham, "Maximizing Leverage," 348.

V

THE RUSSIA-CHINA
PARTNERSHIP

9

The Russian Invasion of Ukraine and the Sino-Russian Partnership

Elizabeth Wishnick

In a March 20, 2022, CBS News interview, former People's Republic of China (PRC) ambassador to the United States Qin Gang insisted that Russia is an asset for China, not a liability.[1] At that time Chinese officials described the Sino-Russian strategic partnership as one with "no limit, no forbidden zone and no ceiling."[2] Since the March 2023 Sino-Russian summit, however, the two sides have dropped the "no limits" formulation, contending instead that their relationship is "superior" to any Cold War alliance (although they reject this comparison altogether).[3] Chinese officials now look back to the Deng Xiaoping era's "three noes" (no alliance, no confrontation, no threatening third parties). The PRC today sees Russia supporting China in its competition with the United States and its alliances, playing a key role in ensuring China's energy security (and increasingly contributing to its food security), ensuring that China's northern border remains peaceful and secure, and buttressing the position of authoritarian states in their global ideological struggle with democracies, as well as Beijing's competition with the United States and its allies. This chapter examines the benefits Chinese officials believe their country derives from the partnership as well as its limitations in the broader context of a globalized world from which China greatly benefits economically. This is not the Cold War alliance of the 1950s—today China seeks Russian partnership to adjust the rules of the global order to accommodate the preferences and needs of authoritarian regimes as well as to buttress Chinese global economic and security positions in what Odd Arne Westad calls a "posthegemonic" world (Chapter 1). Although censorship has strictly prohibited criticism of Sino-Russian relations, some prominent retired officials have stated publicly that Russia is a liability, and a few leading scholars have criticized Russian policies. However, despite evidence of misgivings in some advisory circles, Xi Jinping is unlikely to change course as China lacks

Elizabeth Wishnick, *The Russian Invasion of Ukraine and the Sino-Russian Partnership*. In: *Not Just Another Cold War*. Edited by: Bård Nikolas Vik Steen, Oxford University Press. © Oxford University Press (2025).
DOI: 10.1093/9780197799932.003.0010

alternative partners of Russia's stature and shares a common core concern with Russian president Vladimir Putin about regime security.

Why Russia Is an Asset for China

The Sino-Russian relationship is "sturdy, complex, and deeply rooted," Fu Ying, chair of the Foreign Affairs Committee of the National People's Congress, wrote in 2016.[4] It began as a partnership of strategic cooperation in 1996, a time then Russian president Boris Yeltsin sought to rebalance his country's foreign policy away from a pro-Western tilt. In July 2001, the two countries signed an agreement outlining their strategic partnership, which was extended in June 2021. There are many enduring benefits that China has derived from this arrangement that explain why China is standing by Russia despite the reputational costs involved as a result of the Russian invasion of Ukraine. These include border security, Russia's value as a source of weapons and partner in military exercises, energy and food security, and shared views of international security and the particular concerns of authoritarian regimes.

Chinese officials often talk about "back-to-back strategic cooperation,"[5] that is, Russia's role as a strategic rear for the PRC given that their now fully demarcated border was demilitarized after Deng Xiaoping and Mikhail Gorbachev normalized relations in 1989. The tunnels Mao urged the Chinese people to dig in fear of a Soviet attack in the 1960s and 1970s are now shopping malls, and skyscrapers can be seen in Chinese border regions, long underdeveloped due to security concerns. After the dissolution of the Soviet Union, China, Russia, and their Central Asian neighbours developed a framework for confidence building and border security that would become the Shanghai Cooperation Organization (SCO).

Despite these developments, even today many in China have a long historical memory regarding Russia's territorial expansion at China's expense in the nineteenth century.[6] Chinese businesspeople continue to complain about the difficulties of doing business in eastern Russia. The long-anticipated economic integration between China's *dongbei* (northeast) and the Russian Far East has yet to occur, and the more elaborate plans have been abandoned. As PRC Russia expert and former diplomat Li Yonghui explains, "There are quite a few people in the local area [i.e., eastern Russia] who do not think that development and security can be achieved, and the economy and the environment can be guaranteed."[7] Nevertheless, despite some anxiety in the Russian border regions about the economic and population imbalance with China, Chinese military planners no longer need to focus their resources on defending against an attack from the north. This is an enormous strategic benefit, enabling the PRC to focus military spending and deployments on countering its primary competitor, the United States and its allies in Asia, as well as on its other potential adversary, India.

For many years, Russia was China's primary source of weapons. Sanctions imposed on Beijing after the Tiananmen massacre in 1989 had narrowed Beijing's options. Perceiving adverse geopolitical trends in the 1990s, Chinese officials put a new priority on military modernization, and Russian arms transfers were an important component.[8] Indeed, from 1991 to 2005 Russia accounted for 80% of PRC arms imports. Russian arms sales to China were particularly robust during the 1990s and first half of the 2000s, when Beijing purchased a wide range of systems, including Kilo-class submarines, Sovremenny-class destroyers, and Su-27/Su-30 combat aircraft.[9] For about a decade from 2006 to 2015, just after Russia's first invasion of eastern Ukraine, Chinese arms purchases from Russia plummeted due to dissatisfaction with pricing, timely delivery, and maintenance. By then China was capable of producing basic systems and sought more advanced technologies—and the know-how behind them—from Russia, which was reluctant to provide them, fearing intellectual property theft, a concern that had long plagued Sino-Russian military cooperation.

Beginning in 2015, however, new momentum developed when China signed a $5 billion deal for some of Russia's most advanced systems (that it was previously unwilling to sell to Beijing), including S-400 missile defence systems and Su-35 aircraft.[10] Since 2015, the two countries have expanded their military cooperation to include coproduction, for example, of heavy-lift helicopters.[11] The systems Russia provides support PRC policy aims in the Asia-Pacific, especially in terms of access denial to the United States and its allies.[12] On May 30, 2022, Taiwan's ministry of defence reported two PRC Su-35 aircraft crossing into its air defense identification zone (ADIZ), the first time these aircraft were used for this type of action.[13] Nevertheless, there are still limits to the types of technologies Russia will sell to China—Moscow's quietest submarines remain out of reach. A hacking attack seemingly by a PRC-linked group on the Rubin Design Bureau (involved in submarine design) provides evidence of Chinese impatience with the level of defence cooperation with Russia.[14] The ongoing Russian war in Ukraine may delay scheduled Sino-Russian defence cooperation further as Moscow prioritizes systems urgently needed on the battlefield.

Energy imports and investments have become another important driver of the Sino-Russian partnership. Chinese experts have long vaunted the economic complementarities between their country and Russia, which has the vast stores of resources that China needs to power its economy. In 2023 China imported approximately 70% of the oil it required and got 19% of it from Russia by pipeline. Gas still occupies a relatively modest position in China's energy mix, but approximately 34% of imports came from Russia (by the Power of Siberia pipeline and by liquefied natural gas [LNG] tanker) in 2023. China continues to rely on coal for more than half of its energy needs and 25% came from Russia in 2023, due to the ban the PRC imposed on Australian coal at the time and COVID-related border closures with Mongolia.[15]

In addition to concern about the security of sea lines of communication, particularly in the Strait of Malacca, through which 80% of Chinese imports pass, the deepening Sino-Russian strategic partnership increased confidence among Chinese officials regarding the stability of energy ties between the two countries. The energy risk index developed by Renmin (People's) University in Beijing includes the "China factor," measuring the nature of the relationship between resource exporters and China.[16]

For Russia, China's increased demand for energy resources—oil alone went up 24% in 2023—is a mixed blessing, enabling Russian energy companies to earn needed revenue and make up for lost markets elsewhere, but also renewing fears that Russia will become China's "resource appendage." China too has its own concerns about being too dependent on imports of Russian energy (or indeed on any single supplier) and has yet to make a final decision on a second gas pipeline from Russia, via Mongolia, to northeastern China.

For Beijing one positive consequence of the Sino-Russian partnership was that Chinese companies succeeded in investing in key upstream energy projects in the Russian Arctic—these would provide China with a new source of LNG, important for climate goals and energy security, as well as a foothold in the Arctic region, where China is eager to participate in economic development. In 2013 China's National Petroleum Corporation (CNPC) acquired a 20% stake in the first Yamal LNG project, and the Silk Road Fund followed in 2016, purchasing a 9.9% stake, in addition to providing a loan of $813 million. China's development banks (Export-Import

Bank of China and China Development Bank) provided another $11 billion in loans. In 2019, China National Petroleum Corporation (CNPC) and China National Offshore Oil Corporation (CNOOC) each bought a 10% stake in the Yamal 2 LNG project.[17] Although there is some evidence of Chinese companies taking advantage of opportunities left by Western firms exiting the Russian Arctic,[18] energy deliveries from Yamal face delays due to sanctions.

While energy was always seen as a potential area of cooperation, Russian food exports to China have developed momentum in recent years. The onset of the US-China trade war heightened Chinese concern about diversifying its sources of food imports. As of 2016, 90% of China's soybean imports came from just three countries: the United States, Brazil, and Argentina, which the Chinese Ministry of Agriculture views as a concentration risk.[19] In response to $2.4 billion in US tariffs on Chinese steel and aluminium, China imposed tariffs on imports of US agricultural and industrial products. Before China imposed 25% retaliatory tariffs on US soybeans, one-third of US soybeans went to China.[20]

With US soybean exports to China at zero in November 2018, the peak of the growing season, China scrambled to find new suppliers as well as to produce more at home. China needs to import 90% of the soy it consumes.[21] In December 2018 Russia and China signed an agreement to encourage cooperation in the Russian Far East and Trans-Baikal, involving the production of grains and the development of oil processing, animal husbandry, fisheries, and logistics. While Russia's growing interest in promoting agricultural exports of its green produce dovetails with China's food security needs, Chinese analysis notes that underlying conditions in the Russian Far East remain challenging due to demographic decline, years of neglect of the industrial base, inadequate transportation, and high electricity prices.[22]

China's demand for soybeans and other agricultural products has indeed proven a boon for Sino-Russian agricultural relations and the trade relationship overall, which has suffered from a lack of dynamism outside the energy sector. The June 2019 "Joint Statement on Developing a Comprehensive Partnership of Strategic Coordination for a New Era" highlights expanding Russian soybean exports. In August 2020 China's minster of commerce Zhong Shan called for a soybean alliance with Russia, involving all aspects of the supply chain.[23] Soybean exports have increased dramatically—90% of the Russian harvest of 800,000 tons went to China in 2018.[24] In an effort to boost Russian exports, in July 2019 the PRC Main Chinese Customs

Administration allowed exports of soybeans from all over Russia (previously only the five regions of the Russian Far East were able to do so).[25] In 2020 Sino-Russian agricultural trade reached a record $5.5 billion, involving more than $4 billion in Chinese imports, a 13.7% increase over 2019, despite the pandemic.[26] While there is talk of increasing Russian exports to China to 3.7 million tons, even such a dramatic increase in supplies from Russia would not take up the US slack, as Russian exports of soybeans currently amount to 1% of Chinese demand and it would be difficult to expand soybean production in Russia much further.[27]

To be sure, trade and resource investments have played an important role in cementing the Sino-Russian partnership, but normative factors are significant drivers as well, as Alice Ekman discusses in Chapter 10. In their March 2023 joint statement, China and Russia claim to be the true guardians of the liberal economic order, which they contend the United States and its allies are eroding with sanctions and protectionism.[28] At the same time, they have been expanding the use of the yuan in their bilateral trade, albeit for different reasons. Due to sanctions, Russia lacks alternatives, while China seeks to sanction-proof its own currency for its own financial security in the event of a future contingency.[29]

The two countries also aspire to be the guardians of a new type of international order. In their June 28, 2021, joint statement marking the twentieth anniversary of the signing of the "Sino-Russian Treaty of Good-Neighbourliness, Friendship and Cooperation," China and Russia affirmed that their relationship is "not a military-political alliance . . . but a state-to-state model that transcends this model" and creates "a new type of international relations."[30] The two countries noted they "are gravely concerned about serious international security challenges," "stand against attempts by external forces to undermine security and stability in their adjacent region," and believe "no State can or should ensure its own security separately from the security of the rest of the world."[31] These thinly veiled grievances about the role of the United States in international affairs have been regularly issued in China-Russia joint declarations since the late 1990s. The February 2022 statement went on at length about the negative impact of the US Indo-Pacific strategy, involving "the formation of closed bloc structures and opposing camps." Most notably, China formally declared for the first time in the February 2022 statement that it "oppose[s] further enlargement of NATO," though its opposition was consistent with previous criticism of a pattern of pressure by US alliances. The March 2023 joint statement highlighted the risks for strategic stability that China and Russia saw AUKUS (Australia, United Kingdom, and United States trilateral security cooperation in building nuclear submarines) posing.[32]

Although the February 4th joint statement was issued as more than one hundred thousand troops stood poised on the Russia-Ukraine border, in fact, the document reflected long-standing concerns with prior issues, including their pique with US alliance- and coalition-building activities and Washington's portrayal of both as legitimacy-deficient authoritarians. This is a partnership of ideas and principles, largely about what the two states oppose. As states that value their own sovereignty and independence[33] (though not necessarily that of other countries), the Sino-Russian agreement pushes back against President Biden's statement at the December 2021 democracy summit that "democracy knows no borders."[34] The February 4th statement decries unilateral approaches, argues against "one size fits all" templates, and contends that democracy is in the eye of the beholder; that is, states can choose their own model based on their history, traditions, and unique characteristics. Russia and China condemn "double standards" in definitions of terrorism and emphasize respect for national sovereignty in their approach to global information security. As in previous statements, the two countries state their opposition to "interference by external forces in their internal affairs."[35]

A Partnership with No Limits?

Despite areas of convergence and mutual support, the relationship has its share of limitations. China's rise is at odds with Russia's ambitions for a multipolar order and threatens to usher in a bipolar order with the United States, with Moscow excluded. In their March 2023 joint statement Russia "notes the positive significance of the Chinese ... concept of building a 'community with a common destiny for mankind,'" while China declares that it "positively evaluates the constructive and consistent efforts of the Russian side to form a fair multipolar system of international relations."[36] The latter implies a balance of power based on the participation of multiple powers, including Russia and China, while the former leaves open the possibility of a community leader, potentially China, in charge of setting common goals.[37] Since their 1997 joint declaration, China and Russia have advocated for a multipolar world, which they associate with a more equitable international system where US power would be diluted.[38] More recently, China's concept of the "community of common destiny," promoted by Xi Jinping, has found its way into Sino-Russian documents, such as the 2021 renewal of the 2001 Sino-Russian friendship treaty.[39]

This language has been a sticking point in Sino-Russian cooperation in the Arctic, for example. Some in China have labelled the Arctic a part of the "common heritage of mankind," while Russia sees it as a part of its national identity and crucial to its geopolitical and geo-economic position. In the Arctic, Russia serves as China's gatekeeper, facilitating China's access to the Northern Sea Route. Indeed, Chinese investments in the Russian Arctic are among the few successes of China's Arctic economic outreach to date. While welcoming some Chinese investment in the Russian Arctic, Russia was among those countries most sceptical about China's accession to observer status in the Arctic Council. As an Arctic state, and one with the longest Arctic coastline, Russia has resisted Chinese claims to be a near-Arctic state and build a Polar Silk Road that would compete with the Russian Northern Sea Route.[40]

In Central Asia, Russia has long been seen as the security guarantor for the region, while China has provided needed economic investment. However, prior to the Taliban's return to power in Afghanistan, China had established an unofficial base in Tajikistan, a member of the Collective Security Treaty Organization (CSTO) and where Russia has a base. China also has been developing contacts with the Taliban, which, as of this writing, Russia officially still considers to be a terrorist group. In light of the evolving situation in Afghanistan it remains to be seen in the coming months whether Russia and China will be in lockstep in their approach to regional security in Central Asia, a region that Russia has long viewed as its sphere of influence.[41] Although Russia and China are brought together by perceived geopolitical pressures, as well as their mutual need for a stable border and their stake in a world order that upholds their authoritarian values, their different regional identities serve to maintain a degree of distance between the two countries.[42]

The Russian Invasion of Ukraine and China: Where Is China's Bottom Line?

Qin Gang, when he was PRC ambassador to the United States, explained that, while the Sino-Russian partnership has no ceiling, it has a bottom line—support for the United Nations (UN) Charter.[43] By this he meant China's commitment to territorial sovereignty and integrity. These are what Chinese officials term "core interests," which justify what they see as a legitimate right to use force in the event of a move towards Taiwan independence or to defend their interests in the South China Sea. In 2014, China abstained on the UN Security Council resolution condemning Russia on March 14, 2014, and on the March 27, 2014 UN General Assembly resolution supporting Ukrainian territorial integrity.[44] Although some Chinese companies participated in investment projects in Crimea, albeit in a very low-profile manner, the Chinese government has never officially recognized the annexation and there are limits to the level of official PRC representation allowed to visit the territory.[45] Similarly, in 2008, Beijing also did not recognize the breakaway Georgian provinces of South Ossetia and Abkhazia, and Chinese opposition served to water down a Shanghai Cooperation Organization statement about the Russian annexation, that Russia likely expected (or at least hoped) would be supportive.[46]

Despite the fact that Putin's 2022 visit to China occurred as a massive Russian military presence was building up on Ukraine's borders, the February 4th Sino-Russian statement did not mention Ukraine at all. In other statements Chinese officials had voiced their general support for the principles of territorial integrity and sovereignty and had specifically upheld Ukraine's sovereignty. Ukraine had been a growing economic partner for China, mostly in agriculture and energy, but also providing some military equipment, including China's first aircraft carrier, the *Varyag*, which the Chinese repurposed as the *Liaoning*.

In the February 4th statement, China affirms that it was "sympathetic to and supports" Russia's proposals for long-term security guarantees in Europe,[47] a phrasing on European security that would have a grave impact on perceptions of China in Europe—compounding fears in European capitals that China, like Russia, rejected the post–World War II security architecture and reinforcing concerns in Europe and the North Atlantic Treaty Organization (NATO) about a "systemic" threat from China. Against this background, the investment treaty Beijing hoped to sign with Brussels on April 1, 2022, proved out of reach, put aside due to a number of concerns unrelated to the war, though aggravated by the perception of China's tacit approval of the Russian invasion of Ukraine. Xi's signature Belt and Road Initiative was another casualty—the Russian war on Ukraine also has interrupted the northern route of the Belt and Road, the new West Eurasian Landbridge, and rail traffic now has to be rerouted to the south along less developed corridors, leading to delays and economic losses.[48] Russian forces occupy or have destroyed some Ukrainian ports that Chinese firms helped expand, including Mariupol,[49] ending their hopes to use Ukrainian ports for transshipment of agricultural imports from Ukraine.

The threat of the use of nuclear weapons appears to be another red line for Xi, who warned Putin against making further nuclear threats during his visit to Moscow in March 2023.[50] Indian prime minister Narendra Modi also issued similar warnings to the Russian leader.[51] Xi and Modi became involved after US officials became increasingly concerned about Putin's potential use of tactical nuclear weapons in response to setbacks on the battlefield in late 2022 and reportedly enlisted them to discourage Putin from such a course of action.[52] The Chinese government had an added incentive to cooperate, as Beijing is on the record (thanks to a December 5, 2013, joint agreement with Kyiv) for pledging support to Ukraine in case of nuclear aggression against it.[53]

Russia's targeting Ukraine's Zaporizhzhia nuclear power plant is another source of concern for China, which may fear that an unwelcome precedent is being set at a time when the Chinese government is expanding its own nuclear power domestically. When Xi finally called Ukrainian president Volodymyr Zelenskyy—his first telephone call since the Russian full-scale invasion— the day he chose was April 26, 2023, the anniversary of the 1986 Chernobyl nuclear accident.[54]

Despite the economic costs of the Russian invasion of Ukraine, there has been little discussion about the drawbacks of Chinese support for Russia in the Chinese media. To the contrary, Chinese officials and media outlets have been echoing Russian messaging—they speak of Russia's "special military operation" rather than its invasion of Ukraine and put the blame for the conflict squarely on NATO and the United States, which they accuse of "fuelling the fire" of war. As with COVID, where US biolabs in Fort Detrick, Maryland, were accused (falsely) of being the source of the virus, the PRC has been parroting Russian conspiracy theories about the nefarious activities of such (nonexistent) labs in Ukraine.[55]

Chinese officials justify their support for Moscow by pinning the blame for the conflict in Ukraine on NATO and claiming that the United States "fuels the fire" by arming the Ukrainian military instead of seeking to end the conflict.[56] Apart from reinforcing Russian messaging, China's most obvious support for Russia has been in the UN, where China abstained on two resolutions condemning the Russian invasion of Ukraine.[57] China later supported Russia by voting against the April 7, 2022, UN resolution removing Russia from the Human Rights Council. Reportedly Russian officials had threatened countries that committed "unfriendly gestures" like supporting (or abstaining on) this resolution with unspecified changes in relations with Russia.[58]

The Chinese Foreign Ministry has angrily rejected the idea that the PRC was profiting from the war in Ukraine.[59] Nevertheless, Chinese companies have played a key role in providing dual-use items to Russia, and many have faced sanctions as a consequence. The Biden administration has called out Chinese companies for providing a wide range of technologies and products that keep the Russian war effort afloat and encouraged allies to apply pressure on Beijing to cease these activities In November 2024 the EU determined that a Xinjiang-based company is producing drones for the Russian war in Ukraine. (Reference: Finbarr Bermingham, "EU Has 'Conclusive' Proof of Armed Drones for Russia Being Made in China: Sources," *South China Morning Post*, November 15, 2024, https://www.scmp.com/news/china/diplomacy/article/3286819/eu-has-conclusive-proof-armed-drones-russia-being-made-china-sources).[60]

The Chinese government has urged state-owned companies to be cautious in investing in the Russian energy sector, and some high-profile investments were cancelled, such as Sinopec's $500 million investment in SIBUR, headed by the sanctioned oligarch Gennady Timchenko.[61] Sanctions also delayed Chinese companies who were completing work on modules for LNG extraction in Yamal, a hard-won contract that Chinese Arctic experts discussed with pride as an instance where China was providing advanced technology, not just investment capital.[62] Although China's payment system has been discussed as a potential backdoor for Russia around financial sanctions, this system accounts for a very small number of global transactions and will only make a marginal difference.[63] Nevertheless, Chinese companies are negotiating bargains in the energy sector and other areas where they do not risk countersanctions.[64] When Xi met with Putin on September 15, 2022, on the sidelines of the Shanghai Cooperation summit, he spoke of deepening cooperation and moving forward in areas such as trade, agriculture, and connectivity.[65]

Joint Sino-Russian military drills have become more complex and frequent, though these appear to be connected to their long-standing concern to push back against US alliances, not an outcome of deeper entente over Ukraine. As US president Joe Biden met with Quad leaders in Tokyo on May 24, 2022, six Chinese and Russian bombers flew over the Sea of Japan in what the PRC described as an annual joint exercise.[66] According to People's

Liberation Army (PLA) Colonel Yue Gang (retired), the PRC needed to continue to hold joint exercises with Russia both to maintain mutual trust and to counter perceived pressure by the United States and its allies.[67] PRC ambassador to Russia Zhang Hanhui also saw Sino-Russian military cooperation reflecting mutual trust between the two countries and continuing to develop steadily.[68] In September 2022, all three services of the PLA participated in a much-downsized version of Russia's Vostok military exercises in its eastern military district.

Critical Views of the Russian War in Ukraine

While PRC officials maintain an impression of normalcy in Sino-Russian relations, Chinese censors have been restricting discussion of China-Russia relations since the beginning of the invasion.[69] Despite censorship, some prominent critics, mostly retired officials, acknowledge that the Russian invasion of Ukraine has been controversial in China. Some have made scathing critiques of Russian policies and even of Chinese policy that supports them. Given the sharply restricted space for debate under Xi, it is hard to account for the persistence of critical commentary on Russia's war in Ukraine. It may be that the critics addressing the Russian war in Ukraine are very careful in the way they frame their remarks, or that they have important protectors within the system. More importantly, these criticisms may support the Chinese government's contention that it is neutral on Ukraine and serve to rebut Western criticism of the PRC's tacit support for Russia, although the Chinese experts writing the critical views may not have these goals in mind at all. The views presented here are just a small sample of some of the initial critiques by PRC experts within the first several months of Russia's war in Ukraine.[70]

Senior Colonel (retired) Zhou Bou, now a senior fellow at the Centre for International Security and Strategy at Tsinghua University, Beijing, discussed the trade-offs China faces in its strategic partnership with Russia. Unusually (for a Chinese commentator), he called attention to the steep economic costs China is bearing due to the Russian invasion. Zhou states, "Obviously, the conflict in Ukraine has done tremendous damage to Chinese interests, including its Belt and Road Initiative in Europe. But Beijing sympathises with Moscow's claim that the root cause of the conflict is NATO's inexorable expansion eastward after the fall of the Soviet Union."[71]

Another retired military officer, Colonel Gong Fangbin, who previously taught at the PRC's National Defense University, cast doubt on that explanation for the war, which he thought was based on flawed logic. In a post since removed from WeChat, Gong writes: "I still don't see how any country would have dared to invade the world's No 2 military power." According to Gong, Russia decided to invade Ukraine because it had "taken the wrong path to rejuvenation." He argued that in a globalized world economy, Russia would have done better to accumulate capital and focus on technological advancement instead of remaining obsessed with territorial control. "Countries don't have to gain power through . . . grabbing land," Gong emphasizes.[72]

Misgivings such as these beg the question of the risk China faces in its partnership with Russia. Zhou cast doubt on the likelihood that the Sino-Russian partnership was turning into a military alliance. Zhou emphasizes that "the war in Ukraine has inadvertently proved that Beijing and Moscow's rapprochement is not an alliance. China didn't provide military assistance to Russia. Instead it provided humanitarian aid and money to Ukraine twice, including food and sleeping bags, and has pledged to continue to 'play a constructive role.'"[73] Zhou further explains that a "non-alliance" is ideal because it gives each side flexibility—which they need because of the differences in their worldviews. In Zhou's view, China has a stake in preserving the existing international order, sees itself as a beneficiary of the rules-based global economy, and wants to maintain ties with the West despite many differences, while Russia considers itself to be "a victim of the existing international order."[74]

Hu Wei, vice chairman of the Public Policy Research Center of the Counselor's Office of the State Council and a professor at Shanghai's Communist Party school, urges Chinese policy makers "to cut off their country's ties to Putin as soon as possible . . . to help build China's international image and ease its relations with the U.S. and the West." For Hu, if China wants to be considered a responsible great power, "China not only cannot stand with Putin, but also should take concrete actions to prevent Putin's possible adventures."[75] Otherwise, Hu argues China will become more isolated internationally and face more pressure from the West. He predicts an even bleaker future for Russia, involving the possible fall of Putin, Russia's dismemberment, a more united West that is more reliant on US energy, further NATO expansion, and a greater ideological divide between democratic and authoritarian countries.

Published just a few days after the Chinese government abstained on the March 3, 2022, UN resolution condemning the Russian invasion of Ukraine, Hu's article initially heartened foreign observers about the possibility of daylight between Moscow and Beijing on the war. Hu had studied with Wang Huning, who went on to become an influential political advisor to the Chinese leadership, including Xi Jinping.[76] Hu's piece, published by the Carter Center's *US-China Perception Monitor [ZhongMei Yinxiang 中美印象]*, received more than 100,000 views in China—including robust pushback from Chinese nationalists, until it was deleted and the publication and its WeChat [social media] account were both blocked in China.[77]

Given the extreme sensitivity of criticizing the Sino-Russian partnership, some experts chose to downplay the closeness of the partnership. Wu Dahui, who previously worked for the PLA General Staff and now is a prominent expert on Russia at Tsinghua University, a researcher at the State Council, and a regular China Central Television commentator, agrees with Zhou Bo on the Sino-Russian non-alliance. Wu argues that China has always made its own judgments in international affairs based on its national interests. In his view, the Sino-Russian partnership cannot be an alliance because the national interests and perceptions of the two countries "cannot completely overlap. After the outbreak of the Russian-Ukrainian war, China made it clear that it respects the sovereignty and territorial integrity of all countries, including Ukraine. This also shows that China and Russia have different positions and views on certain regional and international issues, and there are differences." Regardless of such differences, Wu believes that Sino-Russian strategic cooperation will continue.[78]

For Yan Xuetong, also of Tsinghua University and one of China's most prominent experts in international relations, who also teaches at National Défense University and advises China's National Security Commission, "Beijing sees little to gain from joining the international chorus condemning Moscow."[79] Although he sees much to lose from the Russian invasion— major trade disruptions for Chinese companies, greater tensions in East Asia, deeper political divides within China—Yan believes that China has good reason to avoid further antagonizing either Russia, China's largest military-capable neighbour, or the West.

Zhu Feng, director of the China Center for Collaborative Studies of the South China Sea and of the Institute for International Relations, Nanjing University, agrees that Chinese leaders cannot just "walk away" from Russia due to China's "long-term commitment to maintaining Russia as a friendly neighbour." Zhu argues that China opposes the use of war to resolve disputes, and also has long opposed the use of sanctions [by others]. Unlike many of his colleagues, Zhu sees the conflict as an opportunity to "strengthen 'great power coordination'" on the Ukraine issue, promote peace talks, accelerate the ceasefire, and avoid the brittleness of global politics."[80]

Russia experts have focused their analysis on Russian policies, rather than on China's response. Xiao Bin, deputy secretary general of the Center of Shanghai Cooperation Organization Studies, accuses Russia of concealing information about their invasion (a point made by Thomas J. Christensen in Chapter 6) even after Xi spoke with Putin once it had already begun. Despite this apparent duplicity, Xiao points to pressure from the United States and the urgency of maintaining stable energy ties as key factors in China's interest in maintaining its partnership with Russia. This does not mean China has any say over Russian policies—"all-around strategic cooperation does not restrict Russian adventurism," Xiao concedes. Xiao argues that the "lesson of war is that hegemony can't last," and he urges his country to be more flexible and act like a responsible stakeholder.

The most scathingly critical analysis came from Gao Yusheng, a former PRC ambassador to Ukraine and deputy secretary-general of the Secretariat of the Shanghai Cooperation Organization. Gao gives a withering assessment of Russia as a state in decline since the collapse of the USSR, largely due to its own policy errors, though Western sanctions deepened its problems. Unlike many PRC observers who have held Putin in awe, despite his country's problems, Gao dismisses talk of Putin's "so-called revival" as a "false proposition" that does not exist at all. Gao sees the "Russian blitzkrieg" as unsustainable and likely to fail due to Russia's inadequate economic and financial resources that are at odds with "its so-called military superpower status."[81]

Gao views Putin's foreign policy goal as to restore the former Soviet sphere of influence relying on various integration means dominated by Russia. Like Xiao, Gao criticizes Russia for its duplicity—reneging on its promises to former Soviet states by not respecting their sovereignty or territorial integrity. Unlike most Chinese officials who pin the blame for the war on the West and NATO expansion, Gao points to Russia's disregard for the rights of its neighbours as the key factor in the ensuing confrontation between Putin and the West. Gao agrees with Hu in foreseeing many negative consequences ensuing from a possible Russian defeat, including a weakening of Russia, decreased Russian influence in former Soviet states, a greater role for Japan and Germany in world affairs, and a push for UN reform by the West.

PRC academic experts on Russia also point to Putin's policies and misjudgements leading to the invasion. Yang Cheng of Shanghai International Studies University echoes Gao's point on Russian duplicity towards neighbours. Yang emphasizes that Russia is using the same logic of unequal relations with respect to Ukraine that it finds objectionable with the West's attitude towards Russia.[82] Peking University Russia scholar Feng Yujun places the responsibility for the war squarely on Putin's quest for a buffer zone and his "impulse to avenge the collapse of the Soviet Union." While mentioning China's official line on the Russian invasion of Ukraine as a response to NATO expansion, Feng contends that, regardless of the cause of the incident, Russia's war against Ukraine violated the basic principles of the UN Charter, all bilateral relations treaties signed by Russia and Ukraine, and the 1994 Budapest Memorandum, according to which Ukraine would surrender its nuclear weapons in exchange for security guarantees.[83] In Feng's view, the Russian invasion has implications far beyond Ukraine, with potential consequences for other neighbours. Feng explains that Putin believes that he has a strategic opportunity to restore Russia's influence in the post-Soviet space. Feng writes, "If we string together this series of events and locations [referring to the annexation of Crimea and the invasion of eastern Ukraine in 2014 as well as the 2008 war with Georgia], we can see that Russia's strategy is not just in Ukraine, nor is it just in Donetsk and Luhansk, but in the entire 'post-Soviet space.'"[84]

Conclusions: China's "Neutrality" and the Future of Sino-Russian Relations

Critical remarks in China about Russia's invasion of Ukraine are few and far between, a testament to the tightened censorship on the subject. There was some speculation about Xi raising concerns in his summit meeting with Putin on September 15, 2022, on the sidelines of the Shanghai Cooperation conference in Uzbekistan, when Putin stated, "We highly appreciate the balanced position of our Chinese friends in connection with the Ukrainian crisis. We understand your questions and concerns in this regard."[85] Since the Chinese readout of their meeting failed to mention Ukraine, it remains unknown at this time of writing what questions Xi might have posed. While some observers interpreted Putin's statement as an indication of Xi's criticism, or of distance between them, it is also possible that Xi was expressing concern about the potential for the victory of democratic forces in Ukraine (or political change in Russia) in light of his subsequent speech warning against the perils of colour revolutions in Eurasia.[86] Xi's questions and concerns also came less than one week after Li Zhanshu, chairman of the Standing Committee of the National People's Congress and the third-ranking official in China, told Russian legislators that China supported Russia's Ukraine policy,[87] making it unlikely that Xi's comments were an indication of a major change in China's policy.

Generally speaking, PRC reticence, coupled with PRC support for Russian messaging on the invasion, has led to a widespread perception in the United States and Europe that China has been an implicit supporter of Russian actions. US officials have officially warned Beijing against providing overt support,[88] in terms of either dual-use equipment that could be used by the Russian military or economic aid that undermines sanctions. Chinese officials claim to be offended by such perceptions, which they reject as "disinformation,"[89] "misrepresentation," and views of those harbouring "ulterior motives."[90]

Officially, PRC officials portray their country as neutral and even as potential mediator. One year after the full-scale invasion, the PRC Foreign Ministry came out with a twelve-point peace plan highlighting the need to cease hostilities and abandon a Cold War mentality.[91] One point that this plan did not suggest, however, was the withdrawal of Russian troops from Ukraine.

Yu Bin, a scholar of Sino-Russian relations from Wittenburg University, argues that China's claim to neutrality is genuine because of its friendly relations with both countries.[92]

While Ukrainian officials have welcomed any efforts that might encourage Putin to stand down and have a history of good relations with China, they have stopped short of portraying its position as neutral. In the Ukrainian foreign minister's interview with Xinhua, for example, he called on China to act as a security guarantor in a future settlement, noting that the Russian war against Ukraine was not in China's interests and that China supported negotiation.[93] In a less than ringing endorsement of China's position, Zelensky commented on May 25, 2022, that "China has chosen the policy of staying away. At the moment, Ukraine is satisfied with this policy. It is better than helping the Russian Federation in any case."[94]

What about China? Is it satisfied with Russia as a strategic partner? Due to Russia's invasion of Ukraine, China has faced increased scrutiny of its partnership with Russia as well as reputational costs, especially in Europe, where Chinese ambitions already were facing headwinds. For Xi, the Russian invasion of Ukraine actually has heightened the value of the Sino-Russian partnership, as he has no other comparable alternatives among major countries and needs the geopolitical support at a time when China perceives heightened pressure from the United States and its allies.

Moreover, Xi is personally invested in his relationship with Putin and his policy of deepening ties with Russia. There is much hype about the "bromance" between Xi and Putin, and the two leaders have made a great show of their personal bond, celebrating birthdays and making dumplings together.[95] Xi met with the Russian leader more than forty times, a major investment of time for top leaders. To withdraw support for Russia at this juncture would raise additional questions about Chinese foreign policy choices, an area where Xi has been more directly involved than his predecessors.

Xi has an incentive to maintain the status quo in the Sino-Russian partnership. This is both to allay China's own security concerns and to forestall an even worse eventuality—the fall of Putin, which could lead to instability on China's borders and/or his replacement with a more pro-Western government. Both Xi and Putin outline a vision of a global order that safeguards and promotes the priorities of authoritarian regimes like theirs. This is a crucial area of agreement between them, despite several areas where they agree to disagree. Their partnership supports the creation of an alternative perspective of global governance, potentially fragmenting the already conflict-ridden international order. Nevertheless, China and, to a lesser extent, Russia are both integral parts of the global economy, precluding the considerable bifurcation of the world order we saw during the Cold War era when the two alternate socioeconomic and political systems squared off in two camps.

Xiao Xiang, a Chinese historian writing under a pseudonym, notes the parallel between Chinese netizens who expressed support for Ukraine and those who were critical of recent developments in China, such as the Shanghai lockdown and the widely discussed revelation of a mentally ill woman who was trafficked, forced to bear her captor several children, and then kept in chains in a shack for several years. In Xiao's view, pro-Ukraine netizens were more likely to express humanitarian concerns, make positive suggestions, and angrily criticize domestic situations, while pro-Russia netizens tend to focus only on international events. For Xiao, this is evidence of a left-right split on Ukraine, which is connected to domestic opinion. Xiao writes, "Those who support Russia are on the left, and those who support Ukraine are on the right, that is, the leftists support Russia, and the rightists support Ukraine, with a few exceptions, which is basically the case. In the final analysis, the international support for Russia and Ukraine is just the extension and reflection of domestic problems."[96]

As Xiao reveals, the Russian invasion of Ukraine has the potential to aggravate social tensions within China that have emerged as a result of the zero-COVID lockdowns and other recent instances of official callousness in the face of human suffering domestically, at a time of economic and international uncertainty. While Russia may not always be an asset for China, Xi has many incentives to stay the course with the Sino-Russian partnership, as he navigates unexpected domestic headwinds in the future.

Notes

1. "Transcript: Chinese Ambassador to the U.S. Qin Gang on 'Face the Nation,'" March 20, 2022, accessed April 18, 2022, https://www.cbsnews.com/news/qin-gang-chinese-ambassador-face-the-nation-03-20-2022/. In July 2023, Qin Gang was removed from his post, most likely for reasons unconnected to his views on Russia.
2. PRC Foreign Minister Wang Yi: "In developing China-Russia strategic cooperation, we see no limit, no forbidden zone and no ceiling to how far this cooperation can go," January 2, 2021.
3. "Совместное заявление Российской Федерации и Китайской Народной Республики об углублении отношений всеобъемлющего партнёрства и стратегического взаимодействия, вступающих в новую эпоху [Joint statement of the Russian Federation and the People's Republic of China on deepening relations of comprehensive partnership and strategic interaction entering a new era], March 21, 2023, http://kremlin.ru/supplement/5920.
4. Fu Ying, "How China Sees Russia," *Foreign Affairs*, January/February 2016, https://www.foreignaffairs.com/articles/china/2015-12-14/how-china-sees-russia.
5. "习近平同俄罗斯总统普京会谈" [Xi Jinping holds talks with Vladimir Putin], https://language.chinadaily.com.cn/a/202,202/04/WS6205fab3a310cdd39bc861ec.html;   Wang Haiyang, "王海运: 军事关系映照中俄建交70年" [Military relations reflect the 70 years since the establishment of diplomatic relations between China and Russia], *Global Times*, March 3, 2019, https://opinion.huanqiu.com/article/9CaKrnKkN1s.
6. Feng Yujun, "The Significance of Russia to China: Research Methods in Russian-Soviet Union Studies in China," in *Russia in the Indo-Pacific*, ed. Gaye Christoffersen (Routledge, 2022), 225–28.
7. Li Yonghui, "如何看贝加尔湖饮用水厂项目被叫停风波" [How to see the turmoil of the suspension of the Baikal drinking water plant project], *Shijie Zhishi*, no. 5 (2020), http://www.cnki.com.cn/Article/CJFDTotal-SJZS201910031.htm.
8. Lei Yu and Sophia Sui, "China-Russia Military Cooperation in the Context of Sino-Russian Strategic Partnership," *Asia Europe Journal* 18, no. 3 (September 1, 2020): 332–33, https://doi.org/10.1007/s10308-019-00559-x.
9. Paul Schwartz, "The Military Dimension in Sino-Russian Relations," in *Sino-Russian Relations in the 21st Century*, ed. Jo Inge Bekkevold and Bobo Lo (Palgrave MacMillan, 2019), 91.

10. Paul Schwartz, *The Changing Nature and Implications of Russian Military Arms Transfers to China*, June 2021, 2–3, https://www.csis.org/analysis/changing-nature-and-implications-russian-military-transfers-china.
11. Ibid., 4.
12. Ibid., 5–6.
13. "中華民國國防部-全球資訊網-即時軍事動態," [Ministry of National Defense of the Republic of China-Global Information Network-Real-Time Military Updates] accessed May 30, 2022, https://www.mnd.gov.tw/Publish.aspx?p=79943&title=%E5%9C%8B%E9%98%B2%E6%B6%88%E6%81%AF&SelectStyle=%E5%8D%B3%E6%99%82%E8%BB%8D%E4%BA%8B%E5%8B%95%E6%85%8B;https://twitter.com/BonnieGlaser/status/1531299606209912834?s=20&t=3_5dD9D6AADoSdRXKqD8dg.
14. Cyberreason Nocturnus, "PortDoor: New Chinese APT?," *Malicious Life*, April 30, 2021, https://www.cybereason.com/blog/research/portdoor-new-chinese-apt-backdoor-attack-targets-russian-defense-sector.
15. "Australia, Mongolia 'Gap' Sees China Coking Coal Imports Drop by a Quarter," *South China Morning Post*, January 27, 2022, https://www.scmp.com/economy/economic-indicators/article/3164807/china-coking-coal-imports-down-25-cent-due-australia.
16. Duan Fei et al., "Energy Investment Risk Assessment for Nations along China's Belt & Road Initiative," *Journal of Cleaner Production* 170 (2018): 533.
17. Elizabeth Wishnick, "Sino-Russian Partnership at a Time of Geopolitical Rivalry," *China Leadership Monitor*, March 1, 2020, https://www.prcleader.org/elizabeth-wishnick.
18. Robert Fife and Stephen Chase, "China Gains Major Arctic Foothold as Russia Turns to Beijing, Report Finds," *Globe and Mail*, February 7, 2024, https://www.cybereason.com/blog/research/portdoor-new-chinese-apt-backdoor-attack-targets-russian-defense-sector.
19. "'中国大豆产业走出去,' 现状及对策," ["'China's soybean industry goes global,' Current situation and countermeasures] http://www.fecc.agri.cn/yjzx/yjzx_yjcg/201902/t20190211_335484.html.
20. Caixin Global claims that China imports 90% of its soybeans. Huang Shulun and Liu Jiefei, "In Depth: Why China Is Still Hooked on U.S. Soybeans," Caixin Global, October 31, 2019, https://www.caixinglobal.com/2019-10-31/in-depth-why-china-is-still-hooked-on-us-soybeans-101477370.html. This section is drawn from Elizabeth Wishnick, "Sino-Russian Consolidation at a Time of Geopolitical Rivalry," *China Leadership Monitor*, March 1, 2020, https://www.prcleader.org/elizabeth-wishnick.
21. Raymond Zhong, "China's Taste for Soybeans Is a Weak Spot in the Trade War with Trump," *New York Times*, sec. Business Day, July 9, 2018, https://www.nytimes.com/2018/07/09/business/china-trade-war-soybeans.html.
22. Gao Jixiang, "Zhōng é zài èluósī yuǎndōng dìqū hézuò fāzhǎn guīhuà (2018-2024 nián)" shùpíng" [Review of "China-Russia Cooperation and Development Plan in the Russian Far East (2018-2024)," Russian Institute of Eastern Europe and Central Asia], *Eluosi xuekan* [Russian Journal] 1 (2019), accessed July 21, 2021, http://euroasia.cssn.cn/kycg/lw/201911/t20191106_5028601.shtml.
23. Wendy Wu, "China Calls for 'Soybean Industry Alliance' with Strategic Partner Russia," *South China Morning Post*, August 26, 2020, https://www.scmp.com/news/china/diplomacy/article/3098980/china-calls-soybean-industry-alliance-strategic-partner-russia.
24. Shulun and Jiefei, "In Depth: Why China Is Still Hooked on U.S. Soybeans."
25. "Kitay razreshil import soi iz vsekh regionov Rossii" [China permitted the import of soy from all Russian regions], TASS, July 28, 2019, https://tass.ru/ekonomika/6710991.
26. "China, Russia Set New Record for Agricultural Trade in 2020," TASS, accessed July 22, 2021, https://tass.com/economy/1250071.
27. Ivan Zuenko, "Can Russia's Far East Feed China with Soy?," Carnegie Moscow Center, accessed January 10, 2020, https://carnegie.ru/commentary/77443.
28. Joint Statement of the Russian Federation and the People's Republic of China on Deepening Relations of Comprehensive Partnership and Strategic Interaction Entering a New Era.
29. Zongyuan Zoe Liu, "China's Attempts to Reduce Its Strategic Vulnerabilities to Financial Sanctions," *China Leadership Monitor* 79 (March 2024), https://www.prcleader.org/post/china-s-attempts-to-reduce-its-strategic-vulnerabilities-to-financial-sanctions. On Russia's growing dependence on the yuan for its trade, see Frank Chen, "China's Yuan Replaces US Dollar, Euro as Russia's 'Primary' Foreign Currency for Overseas Economic

Activity," *South China Morning Post*, February 1, 2024, https://www.scmp.com/economy/global-economy/article/3250599/chinas-yuan-replaces-us-dollar-euro-russias-primary-foreign-currency-overseas-economic-activity.

30. Joint Statement of the People's Republic of China and the Russian Federation on the 20th Anniversary of the Signing of the Sino-Russian Treaty of Good-Neighborliness, Friendship and Cooperation, June 28, 2021, https://www.guancha.cn/internation/2021_06_28_596184.shtml.

31. Ibid.

32. Joint Statement of the Russian Federation and the People's Republic of China on Deepening Relations of Comprehensive Partnership and Strategic Interaction Entering a New Era.

33. Yu Bin, "Back to the Past: Significance of Russia and China's Joint Statement," PacNet no. 8, February 16, 2022, https://pacforum.org/publication/pacnet-8-back-to-the-past-the-significance-of-russia-and-chinas-joint-statement.

34. "The Summit for Democracy," https://www.state.gov/summit-for-democracy/.

35. "Joint Statement of the Russian Federation and the People's Republic of China on the International Relations Entering a New Era and the Global Sustainable Development," February 4, 2022, http://en.kremlin.ru/supplement/5770. For the Chinese text, see https://china.usc.edu/russia-china-joint-statement-international-relations-february-4-2022.

36. Joint Statement of the Russian Federation and the People's Republic of China on Deepening Relations of Comprehensive Partnership and Strategic Interaction Entering a New Era.

37. Aleksandr Semyonov and Anatoliy Tsvyk, "Концепция 'Общего Будущего Человечества' во Внешнеполитической Стратегии Китая" [Concept of the common future of mankind in China's foreign policy strategy], *MEiMO* 63, no. 8 (2019), https://www.imemo.ru/en/index.php?page_id=1248&file=https://www.imemo.ru/files/File/magazines/meimo/08_2019/10-Semenov.pdf.

38. Rush Doshi, "China's Grand Strategy to Displace American Order," Brookings, August 2, 2021, https://www.brookings.edu/essay/the-long-game-chinas-grand-strategy-to-displace-american-order/.

39. Joint Statement of the People's Republic of China and the Russian Federation on the 20th Anniversary of the Signing of the Sino-Russian Treaty of Good-Neighborliness, Friendship and Cooperation.

40. Elizabeth Wishnick, "Will Russia Put China's Arctic Ambitions on Ice?," *The Diplomat*, June 5, 2021, https://thediplomat.com/2021/06/will-russia-put-chinas-arctic-ambitions-on-ice/.

41. Elizabeth Wishnick, "Prospects for Sino-Russian Coordination in Afghanistan," *War on the Rocks*, November 8, 2021, https://warontherocks.com/2021/11/prospects-for-sino-russian-coordination-in-afghanistan/.

42. Ying Liu, "Strategic Partnership or Alliance?," in *Russia in the Indo-Pacific*, ed. Gaye Christoffersen (Routledge, 2022), 107.

43. "China Says UN Charter Is the 'Bottom Line' in Relationship with Russia," *South China Morning Post*, March 24, 2022, https://www.scmp.com/news/china/diplomacy/article/3171765/china-says-un-charter-bottom-line-relationship-russia.

44. "UN General Assembly Adopts Resolution on Ukraine," March 4, 2022, http://www.china.org.cn/world/2014-03/28/content_31927319.htm.

45. Ivan Safranchuk and Igor Denisov, "China and Russia in the Black Sea: Between Global Convergence and Regional Divergence," Frontier Europe Initiative, November 2020, https://mei.edu/sites/default/files/2020-11/A%20Sea%20Change%3F-China%27s%20Role%20in%20the%20Black%20Sea.pdf; Fu, "How China Sees Russia."

46. Elizabeth Wishnick, "China's Challenges in Central Asia," PONARS Eurasia Policy Memo no. 73, September 2009, https://www.ponarseurasia.org/wp-content/uploads/attachments/pepm_073-6.pdf.

47. http://en.kremlin.ru/supplement/5770. Also see "Joint Statement of the Russian Federation and the People's Republic of China on Strengthening Global Strategic Stability in the Modern Era," June 5, 2019, http://kremlin.ru/supplement/5412 and http://en.kremlin.ru/supplement/5770.

48. Elizabeth Wishnick, "China's Belt and Road Loses a Notch and Gains a Bump: Ukraine and the BRI," May 10, 2022, https://www.chinasresourcerisks.com/post/china-s-belt-and-road-loses-a-notch-and-gains-a-bump-ukraine-and-the-bri.

49. Elizabeth Wishnick, "Ukraine: China's Burning Bridge to Europe?," *The Diplomat*, February 2, 2022, https://thediplomat.com/2022/02/ukraine-chinas-burning-bridge-to-europe/.

50. Max Seddon et al., "Xi Jinping Warned Vladimir Putin against Nuclear Attack in Ukraine," *Financial Times*, July 5, 2023, https://www.ft.com/content/c5ce76df-9b1b-4dfc-a619-07da1d40cbd3.

51. Pia Krishnankutty and Keshav Padmanabhan, "Post CNN Report, Ukraine Diplomat Says Modi Statement on Nukes Helped, Russia Slams US 'Propaganda,'" *The Print*, March 11, 2024, https://theprint.in/diplomacy/post-cnn-report-ukraine-diplomat-says-modi-statement-on-nukes-helped-russia-slams-us-propaganda/1996106/.

52. Jim Sciutto, "Exclusive: US Prepared 'Rigorously' for Potential Russian Nuclear Strike in Ukraine in Late 2022, Officials Say," CNN, March 9, 2024, https://edition.cnn.com/2024/03/09/politics/us-prepared-rigorously-potential-russian-nuclear-strike-ukraine/index.html.

53. China Central Government, "中国和乌克兰关于进一步深化战略伙伴关系的联合声明" [Joint Statement between China and Ukraine on Further Deepening Strategic Partnership], December 5, 2013, http://www.gov.cn/jrzg/2013-12/05/content_2543057.htm.

54. "President of Ukraine had a phone call with the President of the People's Republic of China, "President of Ukraine Official Website, April 26, 2023, https://www.president.gov.ua/en/news/vidbulasya-telefonna-rozmova-prezidenta-ukrayini-z-golovoyu-82489.

55. Elizabeth Wishnick and Josiah Case, "China's Aid to Russia: Lip Service?," CEPA, March 21, 2022, https://cepa.org/chinas-aid-to-russia-lip-service/.

56. "US Adding Fuel to Fire to Benefit from Ukraine Crisis," Chinadaily.com.cn, accessed May 27, 2022, https://global.chinadaily.com.cn/a/202204/02/WS624785a1a310fd2b29e54c15.html.

57. Julian Borger, "UN Votes to Condemn Russia's Invasion of Ukraine and Calls for Withdrawal," *The Guardian*, sec. World news, March 2, 2022, https://www.theguardian.com/world/2022/mar/02/united-nations-russia-ukraine-vote; "UNEP Combats Pollution, Restores Ozone and Protects Seas, UN Chief Tells 50th Anniversary Session," UN News, February 25, 2022, https://news.un.org/en/story/2022/02/1112802.

58. Matthew Impelli, "China Votes with Russia at U.N. after Kremlin Issues Threat," *Newsweek*, April 7, 2022, https://www.newsweek.com/china-votes-russia-un-human-rights-counicl-1696080.

59. "China Says It Will Not Seek to Gain from War in Ukraine," *Straits Times (Singapore)*, April 8, 2024, https://www.straitstimes.com/asia/east-asia/china-says-it-will-not-seek-to-gain-from-war-in-ukraine.

60. "US Warns China Is Providing China with Drone, Missile Components," *Business Insider (Singapore)*, April 14, 2024, https://www.businesstimes.com.sg/international/us-warns-china-providing-russia-drone-missile-components.

61. Chen Aizhu et al., "EXCLUSIVE China's Sinopec Pauses Russia Projects, Beijing Wary of Sanctions—Sources," Reuters, March 28, 2022, https://www.reuters.com/business/energy/exclusive-chinas-sinopec-pauses-russia-projects-beijing-wary-sanctions-sources-2022-03-25/.

62. Laura Zhou, "Chinese Firms 'Told to Stop Work on Russian Arctic LNG 2 Project' Due to EU Sanctions," *South China Morning Post*, May 20, 2022, https://www.scmp.com/news/china/diplomacy/article/3178572/chinese-firms-told-stop-work-russian-arctic-lng-2-project-due.

63. Nathan Handwerker, "Can China's SWIFT Alternative Give Russia a Lifeline?," *The Diplomat*, March 10, 2022, https://thediplomat.com/2022/03/can-chinas-swift-alternative-give-russia-a-lifeline/.

64. Francesca Regalado, "Shell Exits Russia's Sakhalin-2: Five Things to Know," Nikkei Asia, March 1, 2022, https://asia.nikkei.com/Politics/Ukraine-war/Shell-exits-Russia-s-Sakhalin-2-Five-things-to-know.

65. "President Xi Jinping Meets with Russian President Vladimir Putin," accessed September 17, 2022, https://www.fmprc.gov.cn/mfa_eng/zxxx_662805/202209/t20220915_10766678.html.

66. "China and Russia Hold First Military Exercise since Ukraine Invasion," Reuters, May 24, 2022, https://www.reuters.com/world/asia-pacific/china-russia-hold-first-military-exercise-since-ukraine-invasion-2022-05-24/.

67. Teddy Ng and Amber Wang, "China-Russia Pacific Patrol Shows a Willingness to Step Up Military Ties," *South China Morning Post*, May 26, 2022, https://www.scmp.com/news/china/military/article/3179115/strong-china-russia-ties-show-pacific-patrol-despite-beijings.

68. Friendship between Russian, Chinese leaders boosts relations between countries — envoy," TASS, October 3, 2024, https://tass.com/politics/1851477

69. "A Chinese News Outlet Accidentally Leaked Its Own Censorship Instructions on Russia-Ukraine Coverage: Report," Business Insider India, accessed May 27, 2022, https://www.businessinsider.in/politics/world/news/a-chinese-news-outlet-accidentally-leaked-its-own-censorship-instructions-on-russia-ukraine-coverage-report/articleshow/89758963.cms.

70. Experts continue to publish critical views of Russia in Ukraine. For a recent view see Feng Yujun, "Russia Will Lose in Ukraine, Reckons a Chinese Expert on Russia," *The Economist*, April 11, 2024, https://www.economist.com/by-invitation/2024/04/11/russia-is-sure-to-lose-in-ukraine-reckons-a-chinese-expert-on-russia.

71. "Senior Colonel Zhou Bo Says the War in Ukraine Will Accelerate the Geopolitical Shift from West to East," *The Economist*, May 14, 2022, https://www.economist.com/by-invitation/2022/05/14/senior-colonel-zhou-bo-says-the-war-in-ukraine-will-accelerate-the-geopolitical-shift-from-west-to-east.

72. "Russia 'Obsessed with Owning Land': Chinese Scholar Calls Out Flawed War Logic," *South China Morning Post*, May 21, 2022, https://www.scmp.com/news/china/diplomacy/article/3178631/russias-war-ukraine-based-flawed-logic-chinese-military.

73. "Senior Colonel Zhou Bo Says the War in Ukraine Will Accelerate the Geopolitical Shift from West to East."

74. Ibid.

75. Philip Cunningham, "It's Time to Reinvigorate the Historic Friendship of the U.S. and China," China-US Focus, accessed May 26, 2022, https://www.chinausfocus.com/society-culture/its-time-to-reinvigorate-the-historic-friendship-of-the-us-and-china.

76. Ibid.

77. Mimi Lau, "China Risks Isolation 'If It Doesn't Distance Itself from Russia,'" *South China Morning Post*, March 14, 2022, https://www.scmp.com/news/china/politics/article/3170421/ukraine-war-china-must-cut-ties-russia-within-weeks-or-become.

78. "吴大辉: 中俄互信是全球稳定的正资产" [Wu Dahui: mutual trust between China and Russia is a positive asset for global stability], Huanqiu [Global Times] March 23, 2022, https://opinion.huanqiu.com/article/47JbesfUpJG.

79. Yan Xuetong, "China's Ukraine Conundrum," *Foreign Affairs*, May 18, 2022, https://www.foreignaffairs.com/articles/china/2022-05-02/chinas-ukraine-conundrum.

80. "朱锋: 平息乌克兰危机需要中美协调" [Zhu Feng: China and the US are needed to quell the Ukrainian crisis], originally published in Huanqiu [Global Times], March 26, 2022, now available at https://www.igcu.pku.edu.cn/info/2355/3615.htm.

81. Originally published in news.ifeng.com and archived from the Google cache https://archive.ph/5yeZp. Also see David Cowhig's *Translation* blog, May 10, 2022, https://gaodawei.wordpress.com/2022/05/10/fmr-prc-amb-to-ukraine-on-russias-impending-defeat-and-international-relations/.

82. Cheng Yang, "杨成 | 认知偏差、平等声索与乌克兰危机的深层原因" [Cognitive bias, equality claims, and the deep causes of the Ukraine crisis], February 27, 2022, http://mp.weixin.qq.com/s?__biz=MzA4MjcxMDEwNQ==&mid=2686308912&idx=2&sn=15091a40ed0a6e188920cf52da3b74e7&chksm=ba68e9068d1f60104a15841c7039f5dd72c9b6eadc9c3cbfeea8149a256ac82f6268342e065c#rd.

83. "Feng Yujun: The Origin, Prospect and Strategic Impact of the Russian-Ukrainian War," accessed May 24, 2022, http://www.aisixiang.com/data/133907.html.

84. "Feng Yujun on the Situation in Ukraine: Today's International Relations Are Not 'Romance of the Three Kingdoms,'" *Southern China Weekly*, February 26, 2022, https://xw.qq.com/cmsid/20220226A03OE200.

85. "Встреча с Председателем КНР Си Цзиньпином," [Meeting with the PRC President Xi Jinping] Президент России [President of Russia], accessed September 15, 2022, http://kremlin.ru/events/president/news/69356.

86. "Full Text of Xi's Speech at SCO Samarkand Summit-Xinhua," accessed September 16, 2022, https://english.news.cn/20220916/bccf28f3bcd9442f9d501a8a07f067a7/c.html.

87. "Leaders of the State Duma Factions Met with Chairman of the Standing Committee of the National People's Congress," State Duma, accessed September 12, 2022, http://duma.gov.ru/en/news/55208/.

88. "Ukraine Crisis: US Warns China," March 14, 2022, https://www.bbc.com/news/world-asia-china-60732486.
89. "Foreign Ministry Spokesperson Wang Wenbin's Regular Press Conference on March 4, 2022," accessed May 29, 2022, https://www.fmprc.gov.cn/mfa_eng/xwfw_665399/s2510_665401/2511_665403/202203/t20220304_10648111.htm.
90. "Foreign Ministry Spokesperson Hua Chunying Hosted a Regular Press Conference on February 24, 2022," accessed February 24, 2022, https://www.sohu.com/a/525273977_120849665?editor=%E9%BD%90%E6%B1%9D%E9%92%B0%20UN970&scm=1104.0.0.0&spm=smpc.home.top-news2.1.1645727973638RLaOopU&_f=index_news_0.
91. Ministry of Foreign Affairs of the People's Republic of China, "China's Position on the Settlement of the Ukraine Crisis," February 24, 2023, https://www.fmprc.gov.cn/mfa_eng/zxxx_662805/202302/t20230224_11030713.html. For more on the peace plan, see Elizabeth Wishnick, "What China's Peace Plan Tells Us," InDepth, March 17, 2023, https://www.cna.org/our-media/indepth/2023/03/what-chinas-ukraine-position-paper-tells-us.
92. Yu Bin, "China's Neutrality in a Grave New World," Russia in Global Affairs (blog), accessed May 25, 2022, https://eng.globalaffairs.ru/articles/chinas-neutrality/.
93. "Ukrainian Foreign Minister Dmitry Kuleba Gives Exclusive Interview to Xinhua News Agency," Xinhua, accessed May 29, 2022, http://www.news.cn/world/2022-04/30/c_1128610853.htm.
94. "Zelensky: Ukraine Is Fine with China's Position on War with Russia," accessed May 29, 2022, https://www.ukrinform.net/rubric-polytics/3491830-zelensky-ukraine-is-fine-with-chinas-position-on-war-with-russia.html.
95. Elizabeth Wishnick, "Putin and Xi: Ice Cream Buddies and Tandem Strongmen," October 25, 2019, https://www.ponarseurasia.org/putin-and-xi-ice-cream-buddies-and-tandem-strongmen/
96. Li Yuan, "Seeking Truth and Justice, Chinese See Themselves in a Chained Woman," New York Times, March 1, 2022, https://www.nytimes.com/2022/03/01/business/china-chained-woman-social-media.html.

10

China-Russia Rapprochement

Beyond Rationality, the Strength of Ideology

Alice Ekman

Sino-Russian rapprochement has been accelerating since the annexation of Crimea in 2014 and has not been put into question since the beginning of Russia's invasion of Ukraine on February 24, 2022. For both leaders, the consolidation of the Sino-Russian partnership appeared to be a natural strategic move in the context of prolonged tensions with the United States and, more recently, to counter the coalition-building efforts promoted by Washington and its allies since 2021.

China, in particular, officially rejects the adoption and consolidation of Indo-Pacific strategies and shares a similarly jaundiced view of the trilateral security partnership between Australia, the United Kingdom, and the United States (AUKUS); the Quadrilateral Security Dialogue (Quad); and other security arrangements in the greater Indo-Pacific region. This chapter looks at the political and geostrategic drivers of the Sino-Russia rapprochement. In particular, the analysis takes into account China's coalition-building strategy under Xi Jinping[1] and the role of Russia within this strategy. It argues that, even if significant imbalances remain between the two countries, the Sino-Russian partnership is likely to continue to consolidate at a rapid pace in the coming years, as China considers Russia as a core pillar of its coalition-building strategy in a context of deep and multilayered rivalry with the United States.

Russia at the Core of China's Coalition-Building Strategy

China conceives its opposition with the United States not as a mere bilateral rivalry but also as part of a larger rivalry between groups of states, that is, between China and its friends on one side and between the "United

Alice Ekman, *China-Russia Rapprochement*. In: *Not Just Another Cold War*. Edited by: Bård Nikolas Vik Steen, Oxford University Press. © Oxford University Press (2025). DOI: 10.1093/9780197799932.003.0011

States and its allies" on the other side. Indeed, the "United States and its allies," an expression used four times in the February 2022 joint statement between China and Russia, are depicted as the main troublemakers in the world according to the discourse of the Chinese and Russian authorities.[2] Anti–North Atlantic Treaty Organization (NATO) rhetoric is increasingly frequent and explicit.[3] In addition, China and Russia jointly and openly criticize the AUKUS trilateral security partnership.[4]

More than ever, China aims to compete with the United States and its allies by developing an alternative security partnership in which China-Russia security cooperation constitutes a solid core. For both Beijing and Moscow, the objective is to push the military presence and umbrella of the United States away from their neighbourhood as far as possible, and they have publicly expressed, in early 2022, their readiness to coordinate efforts in this vein in their respective regions.[5] Over the last ten years, Beijing and Moscow have progressively reinforced military cooperation—regularly conducting joint military exercises and starting to jointly develop defence systems. For instance, on the margins of the Xiangshan forum, and later the Valdai Discussion Club in October 2019, China and Russia announced that they were cooperating in the joint development of a ballistic missile early warning system. Although China and Russia are not allies by treaty, both countries emphasize that "the new inter-State relations between Russia and China are superior to political and military alliances of the Cold War era." The February 2022 joint statements and following joint communications de facto formalize the China-Russia security partnership and "their mutual support for the protection of their core interests,"[6] including Taiwan,[7] which marks a new step in the bilateral relationship.

At the same time, China and Russia continue to formally reject the use of the term "Indo-Pacific"—which they consider illegitimate and not politically neutral—and continue to use instead the term "Asia-Pacific."[8] Over the last four years, Chinese and Russian official media and researchers have been quick to publicly underline divergences of definitions and approaches existing among countries who have adopted an Indo-Pacific strategy,[9] for instance, between Japan and India, between the United States and the European Union (EU), or among EU member states. They have also been keen, since early 2022, to underline that India, a Quad member and country that is considered a pillar of the Indo-Pacific strategy, is not aligned with its partners on the issue of Russia's invasion of Ukraine, after Delhi abstained from condemning Russia's action at the United Nations (UN).[10]

China is also aware that historical and political divergences remain strong between Washington's two core allies in Northeast Asia, Japan and South Korea; that both countries have trouble coordinating their geostrategic and security approaches; and that Seoul had not, under the Moon administration, officially and fully endorsed an "Indo-Pacific" strategy[11]. This has certainly changed under the Yoon administration, marked by the adoption of such a strategy and fast-paced consolidation of existing security ties with Washington—which Beijing openly rejects. Overall, China and Russia oppose any reinforcement of security ties with the United States from countries in their neighbourhood. In August 2023, as a form of signalling of their opposition, Chinese and Russian warships sailed in the East China Sea, close to several Japanese islands, on the eve of a trilateral summit between the United States, South Korean, and Japan.

From a purely security perspective, China's ambition to compete with the US-led alliance system in the region and promote a post-alliance regional order appears unrealistic at this time given the asymmetric military capabilities (naval capabilities in particular) and the structural role that the US alliance system continues to play in Asia. But the diverse array of China's partnerships in the region, including economic and technological partnerships, tends to blur the lines. Most countries with strong security relations with the United States, including Japan and South Korea, continue to maintain strong economic ties with China. And several Association of Southeast Asian countries that are US partners remain relatively open to China's technological investments. The flexible and multilayered nature of China's coalition-building architecture (no alliance treaty, no official endorsement of a fixed concept such as the "Indo-Pacific," initiatives tentatively proposed to a vast range of countries including US allies and partners) makes it difficult for countries to establish a clear-cut and consistent position towards it.

China's coalition-building strategy, launched after the Nineteenth Party Congress held in 2017, is still in the first stage of implementation, and it is too early to say if China will be able to "win by numbers." But observations of voting patterns at the UN Human Rights Council underline that in some instances China is able to mobilize a majority of countries around its own agenda and positions. For instance, in early October 2022, the UN Human Rights Council voted against holding a debate on alleged widespread abuses in China's Xinjiang region after intense lobbying by Beijing. Within the UN and some of its agencies, two different sets of like-minded actors are currently emerging. Just as democratic "like-minded" partners exist, as exemplified by the United States and the EU, there also exists a like-minded group of autocracies. China and Russia took part in the establishment and revival of the "Like-Minded Group" (LMG). The coordination of the group has been undertaken by Russia, China, and then Egypt since 2013.[12] By 2016, the LMG was a cross-regional group of more than fifty-two states, including Cuba and Venezuela among other countries, and became particularly active at the UN Human Rights Council in the following years. Beyond this specific group, China increasingly refers to like-mindedness in its official communications. In July 2021, a senior Chinese diplomat on behalf of a group of "like-minded countries" expressed concerns over what he perceived as disinformation on multilateral human rights work.[13]

Among the like-minded countries, Russia has been described as the "best friend of China" by Xi Jinping.[14] Both countries have clearly reinforced coordination at the UN and other multilateral institutions to promote their positions on various international security issues.[15] In many of the UN's specialized agencies, China is working not only to reinforce its influence but also to change their governance rules and procedures. This is the case, for instance, within the International Telecommunications Union, where China, along with Russia, is very proactively deploying a set of initiatives with the aim to reform internet governance.[16]

Although Chinese officials are much more proactive today and have developed professional lobbying and negotiation skills and practices, the general positioning is not radically different from four decades ago: China had always positioned itself on the side of the "nonaligned" South. At the UN it has always been close to the Group of 77 (G77), the coalition of developing countries. The G77 is still a rather solid coalition at the UN today.[17] Many of the countries that support China's positions are members of the G77—not all, however. Recently, a group of countries self-designated the "Group of Friends in Defense of the Charter of the United Nations" has emerged: established in March 2021, it includes seventeen UN member states, among them China, Russia, Algeria, Iran, Belarus, and Syria. China also pushed for the creation of another "group of friends" in April 2021: the "Group of Friends on the Safety and Security of United Nations Peacekeepers," gathering forty-nine countries and regional organizations, including Russia, Brazil, Indonesia, and Rwanda—according to Chinese official media.[18] This has been facilitated by the fact that China has been the second-largest financial contributor to the UN peacekeeping operations budget in recent years.[19] It is too early to assess the impact of these groups on voting dynamics at the UN, but it already confirms China's activism in building country groupings of various forms, with the ultimate aim to promote its positions and interests.

The signing on February 4, 2022, on the margins of the Winter Olympics opening ceremony, of the China-Russia joint statement[20] confirms such a convergence of outlooks between the two countries and shows that the bilateral rapprochement has been planned by the authorities in a strategic and detailed manner. The level of ambition expressed in the document, as well as the frequent exchanges between the two presidents since then (Xi's visit to Moscow in March 2023, Putin's visits to Beijing in October 2023 and May 2024) clearly indicate a strong political willingness to rapidly consolidate the bilateral relationship, which is based on a shared post-Western view of the world order. China is certainly not alone in its efforts to restructure global governance. Among the "profound transformations" the world is going through, the Chinese and Russian authorities jointly identify the "transformation of the global governance architecture and world order." They consider that "a trend has emerged towards redistribution of power in the world."[21]

Shared Normative Ambitions and Emphasis on the "Decline" of the West

China and Russia both aspire to bolster their position within international institutions but also to reshape the functioning and alter the norms, values, and principles that underpin them. Chinese diplomacy has, for instance, been very active over the last ten years in advocating for an alternative definition of "human rights," "democracy," or the "rule of law" at the multilateral level as well as in promoting its own foreign policy concepts and innovations, such as the "Community of a shared future for humankind" or the Belt and Road Initiative.[22] This trend can also be detected in the Sino-Russian joint statement signed on the margins of the Beijing Winter Olympics, in which many Chinese official concepts feature prominently, and which articulates a lengthy alternative conceptualization of "human rights," giving priority to economic rights.[23]

At the same time, Beijing does not hesitate to present its governance system to officials of developing countries as an example to emulate and learn from—for instance, during delegation visits to China or during the various training sessions that the Chinese government periodically offers to them.[24]

At the same time, China's official communication—conveyed in the Chinese language on national television but also in foreign languages on social networks, such as X (formerly Twitter)—does not hesitate to emphasize the perceived weaknesses of other governance systems, and first and foremost Western democracies. This is not a new trend: in previous years, in its official statements China has sought to draw attention to, for instance, Europe's perceived economic decline, or the anticipated political demise of the EU following Brexit. But this discourse became more pronounced in 2020–2021: Chinese diplomacy has been particularly keen to underline the tensions existing between part of the community and the police in the United States, with explicit reference to the Black Lives Matter movement, for instance,[25] or to state on a regular basis that Western countries are not managing the COVID-19 crisis as well as China is.[26] Chinese and Russian official communication and disinformation campaigns on the so-called decline of the West are increasingly converging.

Both countries also consider that "colour revolutions" are illegitimately orchestrated by Western powers to promote their own interests. Only a few weeks before the start of the war in Ukraine, the February 4, 2022, joint document stated that "Russia and China stand against attempts by external forces to undermine security and stability in their common adjacent regions, intend to counter interference by outside forces in the internal affairs of sovereign countries under any pretext, oppose colour revolutions, and will increase cooperation in the aforementioned areas."[27]

China is also opposed to numerous international security concepts and practices. In particular, it has strong misgivings about the notion of regime change, whether in Syria, North Korea, or Venezuela, and wishes to articulate this opposition in more systematic terms at the UN and other multilateral frameworks. Top officials in China publicly state that regime changes and the "colour revolutions" that may lead to them are orchestrated by the West—and first and foremost the United States—to promote its own interests.[28] China's position on the matter is supported by Russia, and both denounce the West's "interference in the internal affairs of others" and promote alternative security concepts in their multilateral and bilateral communications.[29]

This perception, and China's strong opposition to what it calls "foreign interference in internal affairs of other nations," is fuelled by deep concerns that at some point China itself might become the target of such interference—as expressed by a senior representative from China's Ministry of Foreign Affairs in an interview in August 2022: "Some people in the United States have been spreading rumors and making slanderous attacks on China. If we always stay silent and do nothing about it, the international community will be easily misled by these lies. We should not forget that Iraq was destroyed because the United States displayed a little test tube containing washing powder, and Syria suffered military strikes because of a few staged photos of alleged chemical weapons attacks. We will never allow such tragedies to happen to China."[30]

Regarding Hong Kong more specifically, Chinese official media and communication do not hesitate to accuse "Western media" of seeking to foment a colour revolution on the territory.[31] While these claims are highly questionable, such distrust of the West is deeply embedded in China's foreign policy mindset and shapes China's normative activism. Ultimately, they underpin China's strong political ambition to form a coalition that would be able to block any form of "Western interventionism." No matter who the incumbent in the White House, this deep-rooted and widespread perception prevails across the Chinese policy-making community. For instance, China's perception of the United States under the Biden presidency is still highly negative and based on the assumption that the United States is bent on waging war across the world, even after the effective withdrawal of American troops from Afghanistan and a framing of US-China relations in rather less offensive terms than under the Trump administration. In general terms, China's diplomacy considers that all Western actions in foreign countries are illegitimate and frequently lists what are perceived as illegitimate and negative interferences by the West in the internal affairs of others.[32] It has a different view of actions conducted by non-Western countries, such as Russia's invasion of Ukraine, for which Chinese diplomacy has been keen to accuse the West as being primarily responsible,[33] and reiterates that it understands "Russia's legitimate security concerns."[34] The definition and perception of "interventionism" or "interferences" are certainly relative. But more than ever, political stability is the top priority for Beijing, which is now facing in November 2022 a rise of protests against its zero-COVID policy in various cities, and in some instances against the leadership of Xi Jinping.

Looking Forward: China's Coalition-Building Strategy and Likely Consolidation of the Sino-Russian Partnership

Russia's war against Ukraine is inevitably having an impact on the coalition-building dynamics analysed above. The most likely scenario is that it will accelerate pre-existing coalition trends. There is already a clear divide between two groups of countries: countries that have condemned Russia's behaviour and countries that have not, or not clearly. More specifically, there exists a divide between countries that have taken sanctions against Russia and countries that have not. Chinese diplomacy has repeatedly positioned itself against sanctions towards Russia, and the Ministry of Foreign Affairs has stated that both countries "will continue to conduct normal trade cooperation."[35] So far, China has kept its words on this, and bilateral trade has increased sharply and continuously since Russia's invasion of Ukraine.

The world order is likely to polarize further during the coming years. Two blurred groups of countries are opposing each other more frontally: on one side, the "Western coalition," and on the other, an alternative coalition where China and Russia play prominent roles. These two groups of countries have diverging positions not only on Ukraine but also on the Israel-Hamas war and overall tensions in the Middle East. China and Russia have converging positions on the issue: both did not explicitly condemn Hamas's terrorist attack on Israel on October 7, 2023, nor Iran's attack on the country in April 2024.

Beyond convergence of position on these issues, Beijing knows that there is convergence on issues closer to home. Under Xi Jinping, China's over-arching, long-term ambition has remained to "reunify" Taiwan. Beijing is fully aware that under the presidency of Vladimir Putin, Russia would not oppose China's reunification moves, especially given that China had not opposed Russia's war on Ukraine. The Chinese authorities, having closely watched how the war in Ukraine unfolded, seem more than ever convinced that a traditional military invasion would not be the best option. But China has other tools at its disposal to promote its interests. In addition to economic warfare, China resorted to lawfare, as well as cyberattacks and disinformation campaigns, to destabilize the democratic functioning of Taiwan, especially during the presidential election campaign of 2024, which did not prevent the Democratic Progressive Party candidate from emerging as the winner. The US administration has repeatedly reaffirmed its commitment to Taiwan throughout the years, including through various official declarations and high-level visits to the island. For this reason, as well as many others—ranging from human rights issues to China's support to Russia's war efforts—Sino-American tensions have become even more acute, and trade and tech sanctions between the two countries are likely not only to remain in place but also to become larger in scope, as Chinese companies are now directly targeted by sanctions for their exports of dual-use components to Russia.

Still, Beijing continues to strongly oppose any sanction targeting national entities or individuals. In the short term, China may be cautiously handling these sanctions, but in the long term, it is likely that China and Russia will reinforce cooperation in developing tools and connections enabling both countries to limit the impact of these sanctions and bypass them as much as possible.

China and Russia are also likely to reinforce their bilateral cooperation in the field of technology, as prolonged sanctions and retaliatory measures have led to the acceleration of digital and telecommunications network decoupling (5/6G mobile networks, undersea cables, satellite systems, etc.). But they may also strongly promote their technology to third countries that formed part of their network of "friendly" countries. In parallel, they may step up offensive capabilities and actions to attack/weaken the "Western" networks: undersea cables are being cut by Russian or Chinese boats on a more frequent basis, satellites are being incapacitated or destroyed by anti-satellite weapons, and the number and range of cyberattacks may increase sharply. At the user end, strong incompatibility between technologies (hardware as well as software) may lead to the emergence of two types of distinct online communities (those using Huawei, WeChat, Baidu, and other compatible devices and apps vs. those using Apple, WhatsApp, Google, Twitter, and other compatible devices and technology). The strict censorship existing in some countries (in particular in China but also in Russia, where censorship had been intensified since the invasion of Ukraine)[36] may reinforce the growing digital divide and the construct of two very different types of media ecosystems and news coverage of both domestic and international issues.

Diverging coverage on Russia's action in Ukraine clearly amounted to diverging views on the war itself. They revealed a deeper gulf in perceptions. On one side, a group of countries including Russia, Iran, North Korea, and Venezuela argued in the same vein as the Chinese Ministry of Foreign

Affairs that the United States was responsible for the escalation of tensions, that it had "started the fire and fanned the flames," and on the other side, a Western coalition, formed by the United States, EU member states, and NATO allies primarily, was of the view that Russia was responsible and that supporting Ukraine was also part of a broader endeavour of support to democracies against authoritarian countries. The ideological dimension of coalition building may become more pronounced over the years, in part due to a hardening of the domestic political climate in both Russia and China (President Putin had intensified censorship of the media and a crackdown on dissent since the beginning of the invasion of Ukraine, and later on restored the death penalty in Russia—about 30 years after it was de facto abolished for most offences, after a moratorium was placed on the issue in 1996), and also in part due to the strong political will of both countries to destabilize or weaken Western democracies in various ways (via disinformation campaigns, cyberattacks, or kidnapping of foreign citizens in their national territory).

In the coming years, China, Russia, and their partners will probably not hesitate to continue to proclaim that the West is in terminal decline and to portray themselves, in particular to authoritarian governments, as a successful alternative. On the other side, the protection and promotion of democracy will become more than ever a common objective of the Western alliance. It is likely that both sides will be more than ever on constant alert to fight foreign influence/interference: China fears that what it calls "foreign hostile forces" might destabilize the monopoly of the Chinese Communist Party and has applied a strict policy of censorship towards Western media, nongovernmental organizations, and individuals on topics it considers sensitive (Taiwan, Hong Kong, Xinjiang, South China Sea, etc.). On the other side, democracies in Europe and beyond will be more than ever fearful of Russia, China, and other countries conducting interference and disinformation operations in their domestic affairs, especially during electoral campaigns. In this context, many countries will create or consolidate institutions and cyber agencies dedicated to the identification and prevention of these threats to democracy.[37]

In the coming years, it is likely that China and Russia will step up their coordination within the UN and some of its agencies[38] to promote their positions and block UN missions, investigations, or military interventions in most countries—which they consider illegitimate interference in the internal affairs of other states. This coordination has intensified following Russia's invasion of Ukraine, which China never condemned in the UN or other settings. The fact that forty countries abstained or refused to demand that Russia end its military operations in Ukraine in March 2022 did not go unnoticed by Russia and China, which thereafter invested more heavily in the consolidation of the bilateral relationship with these countries at various levels, proposing concrete cooperation opportunities (in the trade, technology, and military domains) and anticipating that this loyal group of countries would continue to support their position on core interests in multilateral gatherings. China and Russia are also likely to step up their coordination within the Shanghai Cooperation Organization as well as within the BRICS+ (an intergovernmental organisation initially comprising Brazil, Russia, India, China, South Africa + joined to date by Iran, Egypt, Ethiopia and the United Arab Emirates), for which they have jointly, and successfully, pushed for its enlargement in 2023.

Conclusion

Significant rational limits exist to the Sino-Russian partnership since the beginning of the war in Ukraine: many Chinese companies risk very damaging secondary sanctions if they continue to conduct business with Russia; China's diplomatic relations with key trade partners, including the EU, risk further deterioration due to strong divergences on the Ukraine issue (a deterioration that was already visible at the EU-China Summit of April 1, 2022); and Russia has become more economically dependent on China over the last three years. Significant imbalances exist between the two countries not only economically but also, and increasingly, diplomatically, technologically, and militarily.

At the same time, the current global divide over sanctions towards Russia may lead to the consolidation of normative rapprochement between China, Russia, and members of their "circle of friends": norms for financial and payment systems, norms for an internet governance regime, and norms regulating blockchain and digital currency and other tools that may facilitate the circumvention of sanctions. And the Chinese authorities are likely to continue to seek more autonomy from the West regarding technological hardware and software, in line with the objectives stated in China's Fourteenth Five-Year Plan (2021–2025) of self-reliance and promotion of domestic consumption ("dual circulation").

All in all, the Sino-Russian rapprochement is likely to continue to consolidate in the coming years, as it is driven by shared and strong resentment against the West as well as strong geopolitical ambitions to restructure global governance and norms towards a post-Western order. The coalition-building efforts on both sides—"Western led" or "China-Russia led"—are likely to remain diametrically opposed because they wish to convene countries around radically different types of political systems, development models, and ideals.

Notes

1. This analysis builds upon recent work on China's coalition-building strategy. It has been initially written in spring 2022 and last updated in May 2024. A preliminary analysis has been published here: A. Ekman, "China and the Battle of Coalitions. The 'Circle of Friends' versus the Indo-Pacific Strategy," Chaillot Paper 174 (EUISS, May 6, 2022), https://www.iss.europa.eu/content/china-and-battle-coalitions.
2. Joint Statement of the Russian Federation and the People's Republic of China on the International Relations Entering a New Era and the Global Sustainable Development, Official website of the President of Russia, February 4, 2022.
3. See, for instance: "The sides believe that certain States, military and political alliances and coalitions seek to obtain, directly or indirectly, unilateral military advantages to the detriment of the security of others, including by employing unfair competition practices, intensify geopolitical rivalry, fuel antagonism and confrontation, and seriously undermine the international security order and global strategic stability. The sides oppose further enlargement of NATO and call on the North Atlantic Alliance to abandon its ideologized cold war approaches, to respect the sovereignty, security and interests of other countries, the diversity of their civilizational, cultural and historical backgrounds, and to exercise a fair and objective attitude towards the peaceful development of other States." Ibid.
4. "The sides are seriously concerned about the trilateral security partnership between Australia, the United States, and the United Kingdom (AUKUS), which provides for deeper cooperation between its members in areas involving strategic stability, in particular their decision to initiate cooperation in the field of nuclear-powered submarines. Russia and China believe that such actions are contrary to the objectives of security and sustainable development of the Asia-Pacific region, increase the danger of an arms race in the region, and pose serious risks of nuclear proliferation. The sides strongly condemn such moves and call on AUKUS participants to fulfil their nuclear and missile non-proliferation commitments in good faith and to work together to safeguard peace, stability, and development in the region." Ibid.
5. "The sides call on the United States to respond positively to the Russian initiative and abandon its plans to deploy intermediate-range and shorter-range ground-based missiles in the Asia-Pacific region and Europe. The sides will continue to maintain contacts and strengthen coordination on this issue." Ibid.
6. "The sides reaffirm their strong mutual support for the protection of their core interests, state sovereignty and territorial integrity, and oppose interference by external forces in their internal affairs." Ibid.
7. "The Russian side reaffirms its support for the One-China principle, confirms that Taiwan is an inalienable part of China, and opposes any forms of independence of Taiwan." Ibid.
8. "The Chinese and Russian sides stand against the formation of closed bloc structures and opposing camps in the Asia-Pacific region and remain highly vigilant about the negative impact of the United States' Indo-Pacific strategy on peace and stability in the region. Russia and China have made consistent efforts to build an equitable, open and inclusive security system in the Asia-Pacific Region (APR) that is not directed against third countries and that promotes peace, stability and prosperity." Ibid.

9. Author's interviews and think tanks exchanges with Chinese researchers and diplomats.
10. See, for instance, Chinese media on this: "US Ropes in Quad Allies to Fight 'Two-Front Wars' with China and Russia despite Spent Force," *Global Times*, February 11, 2022, https://www.globaltimes.cn/page/202202/1252049.shtml; "The US Tries Hard to Hijack World's View on Russia, but More Countries Not Buying It," *Global Times*, March 3, 2022, https://www.globaltimes.cn/page/202203/1253786.shtml.
11. But this is likely to change under the new administration following the election of Yoon Suk-yeol as president of the Republic of Korea in March 2022.
12. A. Essam, "The Like Minded Group (LMG): Speaking Truth to Power," *Universal Rights Group* (blog), May 10, 2016, https://www.universal-rights.org/blog/like-minded-group-lmg-speaking-truth-power/.
13. "China, Like-Minded Countries Voice Concern over Disinformation on Multilateral Human Rights Work," Xinhua, July 2, 2021, http://www.xinhuanet.com/english/2021-07/02/c_1310040247.htm.
14. CGTN, "Xi and Putin, the Helmsmen of China-Russia Friend 'Ship,'" June 5, 2019, https://news.cgtn.com/news/3d3d514e3545444d35457a6333566d54/index.html.
15. A. Ekman et al., "Stand by Me! The Sino-Russian Normative Partnership in Action," Brief No. 18 (EUISS, August 2020), https://www.iss.europa.eu/sites/default/files/EUISSFiles/Brief%2018%20China%20Russia_0.pdf.
16. "The sides support the internationalization of Internet governance, advocate equal rights to its governance, believe that any attempts to limit their sovereign right to regulate national segments of the Internet and ensure their security are unacceptable, are interested in greater participation of the International Telecommunication Union in addressing these issues." Joint Statement of the Russian Federation and the People's Republic of China on the International Relations Entering a New Era and the Global Sustainable Development.
17. According to Richard Gowan, United Nations Director for the International Crisis Group, interviewed by the author in 2022.
18. United Nations, press release, "Issuing Presidential Statement, Security Council Expresses Grave Concern about Threats, Attacks against Peacekeepers around Globe," May 24, 2021, https://www.un.org/press/en/2021/sc14528.doc.htm; "China, 40 Plus Countries Launch Group of Friends on Safety and Security of UN Peacekeepers," Xinhua, April 28, 2021, http://www.xinhuanet.com/english/2021-04/28/c_139911891.htm.
19. R. Gowan, "China's Pragmatic Approach to UN Peacekeeping," Brookings, September 14, 2020, https://www.brookings.edu/articles/chinas-pragmatic-approach-to-un-peacekeeping/.
20. Joint Statement of the Russian Federation and the People's Republic of China on the International Relations Entering a New Era and the Global Sustainable Development.
21. Ibid.
22. On this, see A. Ekman, "What If . . . We Avoided Wordplay with China?," in "What If . . . ? 14 Futures for 2024," Chaillot Paper No. 157, ed. F. Gaub (EUISS, January 2020), https://www.iss.europa.eu/sites/default/files/EUISSFiles/CP_157.pdf; A. Ekman, "China and the 'Definition Gap': Shaping Global Governance in Words," Asan Forum, November 2017, https://theasanforum.org/china-and-the-definition-gap-shaping-global-governance-in-words/.
23. "The Russian side notes the significance of the concept of constructing a 'community of common destiny for mankind' proposed by the Chinese side to ensure greater solidarity of the international community and consolidation of efforts in responding to common challenges. The Chinese side notes the significance of the efforts taken by the Russian side to establish a just multipolar system of international relations. All States must have equal access to the right to development." Joint Statement of the Russian Federation and the People's Republic of China on the International Relations Entering a New Era and the Global Sustainable Development.
24. Author's analysis of the syllabus of the training courses and seminars offered by the Chinese government for the year 2019. See, for instance, the syllabus of the seminar "China's Experience, China's Social System and Public Policy," provided in 2019 by the Chinese government to "government officials and administrators of public areas in developing countries," posted by the Ministry of Public Administration of the Government of the Republic of Trinidad and Tobago, Summer 2019, https://mpa.gov.tt/Seminar%20on%20China%27s%20Experience%2C%20China%27s%20Social%20System%20and%20Public%20Policy.

25. For instance, the Chinese delegation explicitly referred to it during the first (and tense) high-level meeting between the United States and China held during the Biden administration, in Anchorage, Alaska, in March 2021. US Department of State, "Remarks—Secretary Antony J. Blinken, National Security Advisor Jake Sullivan, Director Yang and State Councilor Wang at the Top of Their Meeting," March 18, 2021, https://www.state.gov/secretary-antony-j-blinken-national-security-advisor-jake-sullivan-chinese-director-of-the-office-of-the-central-commission-for-foreign-affairs-yang-jiechi-and-chinese-state-councilor-wang-yi-at-th/.

26. According to the Chinese embassy in Paris, for instance, which posted texts on its website pointing at the perceived weaknesses of the local crisis management efforts.

27. Joint Statement of the Russian Federation and the People's Republic of China on the International Relations Entering a New Era and the Global Sustainable Development, Official website of the President of Russia, February 4, 2022.

28. Ministry of Foreign Affairs of the People's Republic of China, "Reviving the Cold War Is Anachronistic—Vice Foreign Minister Le Yucheng's Exclusive Interview with Guan-cha.cn," August 12, 2020, https://www.fmprc.gov.cn/eng/wjdt_665385/zyjh_665391/202008/t20200812_678881.html. See, for instance, this extract: "Over the years, the United States has been acting with absolutely no respect for the law and justice when it goes around the world to incite color revolution here and there, grossly interfere in others' internal affairs, arbitrarily enforce long-arm jurisdiction, threaten use of force, and even carry out decapitation operations."

29. "Some actors representing but the minority on the international scale continue to advocate unilateral approaches to addressing international issues and resort to force; they interfere in the internal affairs of other states, infringing their legitimate rights and interests, and incite contradictions, differences and confrontation, thus hampering the development and progress of mankind, against the opposition from the international community." Joint Statement of the Russian Federation and the People's Republic of China on the International Relations Entering a New Era and the Global Sustainable Development.

30. Ministry of Foreign Affairs of the People's Republic of China, "Reviving the Cold War Is Anachronistic."

31. See, for instance, Y. Shen, "How Western Media Promotes Color Revolution: A Case Study of Hong Kong," *Global Times*, September 9, 2019, https://www.globaltimes.cn/content/1164100.shtml.

32. See, for instance, the message by Ministry of Foreign Affairs spokesperson Zhao Lijian on Twitter on February 23, 2022: "Never forget who's the real threat to the world," accompanied by a graphic entitled "USA Bombing List: The Democracy World Tour" listing over thirty countries bombed by the United States in the last sixty-five years. https://twitter.com/zlj517/status/1496486130698813441?lang=fr.

33. See, for instance, this answer from Ministry of Foreign Affairs spokesperson Hua Chunying during a press conference covering Russian-Ukrainian tensions: "Many people are asking the US: Did the US respect the sovereignty and territorial integrity of the Federal Republic of Yugoslavia when US-led NATO bombed Belgrade? Did the US respect the sovereignty and territorial integrity of Iraq when it launched military strikes on Baghdad on unwarranted charges? Did the US respect the sovereignty and territorial integrity of Afghanistan when US drones wantonly killed innocent people in Kabul and other places? Did the US respect the sovereignty and territorial integrity of other countries when it instigated color revolutions and meddled in their internal affairs all around the world? It is hoped that the US take these questions seriously and abandon double standards." "Foreign Ministry Spokesperson Hua Chunying's Regular Press Conference on February 23, 2022," Official Website of the Ministry of Foreign Affairs of the People's Republic of China, February 23, 2022.

34. See the official summary of Foreign Minister Wang Yi's remarks during a telephone conversation with Russian foreign minister Sergei Lavrov on February 25, 2022: "Noting there is a complex and special historical context of the Ukraine issue, Chinese State Councilor and Foreign Minister Wang Yi on Thursday told his Russian counterpart that the Chinese side understands Russia's legitimate security concerns": 'China Understands Russia's Legitimate Security Concerns,' *People's Daily*, February 25, 2022, http://en.people.cn/n3/2022/0225/c90000-9963062.html.

35. Ministry of Foreign Affairs of the People's Republic of China, "Foreign Ministry Spokesperson Wang Wenbin's Regular Press Conference on February 28, 2022," February 28, 2022, https://

www.fmprc.gov.cn/mfa_eng/xwfw_665399/s2510_665401/202202/t20220228_10646378.
html.

36. "Russia Bans Facebook and Restricts Twitter as It Tightens Grip on Information," *Financial Times*, March 4, 2022, https://www.ft.com/content/b2bc707c-70bb-4b7a-bfca-93ae19125588.

37. For instance, France created the technical and operational service, Viginum, in July 2021: Secrétariat Général de la Défense et de la Sécurité Nationale, "Viginum, vigilance et protection contre les ingérences numériques étrangères," http://www.sgdsn.gouv.fr/le-sgdsn/fonctionnement/le-service-de-vigilance-et-de-protection-contre-les-ingerences-numeriques-etrangeres-viginum/.

38. As they had planned in 2022: "The sides will strengthen cooperation within multilateral mechanisms, including the United Nations, and encourage the international community to prioritize development issues in the global macro-policy coordination." Joint Statement of the Russian Federation and the People's Republic of China on the International Relations Entering a New Era and the Global Sustainable Development.

VI
THE GEOPOLITICAL
CONSEQUENCES

11

The Geography of Rimland and Heartland

Why the US-China Rivalry Differs from the Cold War

Jo Inge Bekkevold

The era of US-China rivalry resembles the Cold War in terms of distribution of power, with two superpowers dominating the system.[1] In any international system, power is the most important and defining factor shaping interstate relations.[2] Thus, when the distribution of power among the great powers in the international system shifts, between unipolar, bipolar, and multipolar systems, we can expect the system to change accordingly. This is why the Cold War is a natural point of reference for the contemporary era of US-China rivalry. The Cold War bipolar system was characterized by an intense and all-encompassing rivalry between the United States and the Soviet Union, and sensitivity towards mutual gains created a distinct two-bloc international order centered around the two superpowers and their respective allies, with a low degree of economic and institutional interdependency across this two-bloc divide.[3] Nonetheless, two bipolar systems may not share all the same features.

One obvious difference between the current US-China bipolar system and the previous Cold War bipolar rivalry is the origin of two systems. The US-Soviet bipolar system came about in a rather abrupt manner as the result of World War II, whereas the current shift in polarity has been gradual and peaceful. This variation in origin has arguably created a lesser sense of urgency in containing China than what was the case vis-à-vis the Soviet Union. More than a decade after the Obama administration launched its "pivot to Asia" strategy in 2011, the United States has yet to formulate a clear-cut China strategy, whereas during the Cold War, the main elements of the US containment strategy of the Soviet Union was largely in place already by 1949–1950.[4] Another important difference is the level of interdependence at the starting point of the two bipolar systems. The US–Soviet Union rivalry

Jo Inge Bekkevold, *The Geography of Rimland and Heartland*. In: *Not Just Another Cold War*. Edited by: Bård Nikolas Vik Steen, Oxford University Press. © Oxford University Press (2025).
DOI: 10.1093/9780197799932.003.0012

was from the very beginning highly polarized, with a very low degree of economic interaction and institutional linkages across the East-West two-bloc system.[5] China, on the other hand, has risen within the US-led international order for five decades since the United States engaged China in the early 1970s. As discussed in the chapters by Tunsjø and Fravel in this volume, the gravity of bipolarity is already having an effect, driving the United States and China to de-risk their dependencies on each other. Yet, China's high level of interdependence with the global economy, including with the United States and allies, slows down the effect bipolarity has on the polarization of the US-China system. A third difference, pointed to by Westad, Christensen, and others in this volume, is the lighter ideological footprint in the US-China rivalry.

Nevertheless, the aim of this chapter is to draw the reader's attention to the role of geography and geopolitics shaping international systems. Geopolitics in its classical version is how the interplay of power, geography, and technology informs state strategy. In the post–Cold War era of globalization, geopolitics was often referred to as obsolete and an illusion.[6] Nevertheless, the notion of geopolitics being irrelevant is a misconception, with economic globalization and the absence of great power rivalry under US unipolarity blurring its importance. Geography is still inescapable in shaping strategy and policy,[7] even with new technologies and domains in cyber and space.[8] This chapter emphasizes the continued importance of geography and explains how the geopolitical logic of the US-China bipolar system differs from the Cold War. The difference between these two bipolar systems is best explained by revisiting the heartland and rimland thesis developed by Halford J. Mackinder and Nicholas J. Spykman. The argument put forward in this chapter is that China's geographic position in the East Asian rimland molds a distinct bipolar system and an international order that differs from the US Cold War rivalry with heartland Soviet Union.

The chapter consists of five parts. The first part outlines how geography molds international systems. The next part examines how the geographical position of China as a rimland power compels the United States to develop a different balancing strategy against its current peer competitor than the one developed against heartland Soviet Union. It explains why the United States has to balance China through an offshore strongpoint strategy based on India, Japan, and Australia, in contrast to the onshore perimeter defense strategy it pursued against the Soviet Union. The third part emphasizes the geopolitics of Sino-Russian ties. It posits that the US rivalry with rimland

China enhances the Sino-Russian partnership, whereas the heartland position of the Soviet Union contributed to undermine the Sino-Soviet alliance. The fourth part explains why Europe has a more peripheral role in the US-China bipolar system than during the Cold War, and how this challenges transatlantic relations. The fifth part of the chapter examines how China's rimland position shapes an economic order that differs from during the Cold War.

The Geography of International Systems

States balance power, not geography, but geography informs the effect of power, creating an interplay of power and geography that shapes balancing, state strategy, and the international order at large. In fact, it is commonly accepted that balance-of-power theories are bound by certain scope conditions. As emphasized by Jack Levy: "Unless one specifies who balances against whom, in response to what levels of concentration of what kinds of power or what kinds of threats in what kinds of systems, it is impossible to construct an empirical test of balancing propositions."[9] In other words, a clearly defined international system based on its power structure, its key actors, and the geographical scope of the system increases the possibility to make predictions about state behavior and international outcome.

Geography, understood as a country's location in relation to trade routes, natural resources, oceans, mountains and rivers, and centers of power, has always been a conditional factor on national strategy.[10] Geography can exacerbate or mitigate the ability to project military power, and thus the fear associated with power, through distance and barriers like mountains, rivers, and oceans, or in the form of buffer states located between rival states.[11]

Geography is the most enduring factor in international systems, but shifts in the balance of power alter the advantages and disadvantages of geography and strategic location. The balance of power informs whether a state has weak or strong neighbors, the number of frontiers it has to defend, and whether it can easily project power or faces the possibility of encirclement.[12] This is why Spykman contends that all descriptions of the power position of a state must begin with an analysis of its geography: "It is the geographic location of a country and its relation to centers of military power that define its problem of security."[13] Geoffrey Sloan and Colin Gray state that "one of the aims of geopolitics is to emphasise that political predominance is a question not just of having power in the sense of human or material resources, but also of the geographical context within which that power is exercised."[14] It follows from this that great powers might pursue different strategies depending on the geopolitical theatre.[15]

With regard to the US-China rivalry, it matters that the United States has a more favorable geographic location than China. Bordering two relatively weak neighbors, Canada and Mexico, the United States is largely free from any threats on its land borders. In contrast, China has a large number of contiguous neighbors, including several major powers (e.g., Japan, Russia, and India) and several secondary powers (including South Korea and Vietnam). Research informs us that a high number of contiguous neighbors increases the likelihood of a state being dragged into militarized disputes and wars.[16] Moreover, whereas the United States has direct unhindered access to both the Atlantic and Pacific Oceans, China borders the Pacific Ocean only, and the Chinese navy has to navigate through the US forward posture along the first island chain to access the high seas.

However, the United States also had a more favorable geographic location than the Soviet Union. Like China, the Soviet Union bordered a high number of countries, in Europe, in the Middle East, in South Asia, and in East Asia. In addition, two of the Soviet Union's four naval fleets, the Baltic Fleet and the Black Sea Fleet, faced severe geographic restraints accessing the high seas, while the two other fleets, the Northern Fleet based in the Arctic Ocean and the Pacific Fleet based in the Sea of Okhotsk, were largely unable to assist each other due to geographic distance.

Thus, the main purpose here is not to analyze whether the United States or China is in a better position for competition and rivalry, but to understand how geography shapes the US-China rivalry differently from the US-Soviet rivalry. To do so, it is necessary to compare more specifically how the variation in geography between China and the Soviet Union shapes two distinct geopolitical logics. The best tool available to do so is the heartland-rimland thesis developed by Mackinder and Spykman.

Halford J. Mackinder and Nicholas J. Spykman are two of the most important contributors to classical geopolitics. Building on Mackinder, Spykman divided the world into four geographic areas: the Eurasian heartland; the Eurasian rimland, which is the area between the heartland and the ocean; offshore islands (the British Isles and the Asian first island chain) and continents (Africa and Oceania); and, finally, the Americas.[17] The British geographer Mackinder feared the threat to Britain from a hegemon based in the Eurasian heartland. In an article submitted to the British Royal Geographical Society in 1904, Mackinder outlined how a Eurasian hegemonic power or alliance could exploit the material advantages of the continent for the purpose of assembling a world-conquering sea power to complement the advantages in land power it already enjoyed.[18] A few decades later, the US-based international relations scholar Spykman developed Mackinder's thinking further. In contrast to Mackinder, Spykman argued that the Eurasian littoral in Europe and Asia, which he called the rimland, was the critical zone. Spykman's concern was American security, and he contended that a great power in control of any of the two rimlands would be able to challenge the United States. He pointed to the easier access from the rimlands to the sea and eventually to the United States via the Atlantic and Pacific Oceans.[19]

During the Cold War, the United States faced a heartland power, while today it faces a rimland power. This distinction makes for two very different geopolitical configurations. China's rimland position is unique from the Soviet Union in three main ways. First, China is a one-flank challenge only for the United States, whereas the Soviet Union was a two-flank challenge. Second, from its rimland position, China has more limited geographic reach into the Eurasian continent than the Soviet Union had from its heartland position. Third, while the Soviet Union remained a continental power until the later stages of the Cold War, China is a hybrid land and sea power from the outset of the new bipolar system. I will discuss these variations in geopolitical features in further detail in the remaining parts of this chapter, starting with how it shapes the US defense strategy.

Rimland China and US Strongpoint Defence

The chief security concern for the United States is to prevent the rise of a regional hegemon on the Eurasian continent. A long-standing goal of US grand strategy has thus been to ensure a balance of power in its two transoceanic flanking regions, preventing the rise of a regional hegemon in Europe and East Asia that would consider expansion into the Western Hemisphere.[20] With a multipolar distribution of power among the major states in Europe and Asia, the United States can rely on these states to balance each other. However, during the Cold War, due to the Soviet Union's dominant position on the Eurasian continent, the United States had to balance the Soviet Union through a forward posture across its two transoceanic flanks.

According to Spykman, to balance power in Eurasia, it is essential for the United States to balance "onshore," meaning that the United States should be present in the rimlands. This is how the United States balanced the Soviet Union, with a perimeter defence in the Eurasian rimlands. The Sino-Soviet friendship treaty in early 1950, and the Korean War a few months later, left no doubt that the Soviet Union represented a threat to all Eurasian rimlands, and thus a two-flank threat to US security. As part of its perimeter defence strategy, the United States intervened militarily in Korea and Vietnam, it established a military presence in Thailand, and in the early 1970s, it aligned with China. It intervened in the Middle East and Afghanistan, and it created the North Atlantic Treaty Organization (NATO) in Europe to balance the Soviet Union in the rimlands across its transatlantic flank.

Today, if the United States still wants to keep its flanks divided, it has to balance China through a forward posture. China's gross domestic product (GDP) is now larger than the combined GDP of China's three major neighbors, India, Japan, and Russia, and China's defence expenditure is also larger than the combined expenditures of its three major neighbors. In addition, Russia is aligning with China. Unable to rely on regional powers, the United States has to balance China through a forward military posture in Asia. Yet, balancing China requires another type of strategy than balancing the Soviet Union, because China's dominant rimland position rules out onshore perimeter defence as a strategy in East Asia.

The US forward posture along the first island chain, which runs from the Kurile Islands through the main islands of Japan, the Ryukyu Archipelago, Taiwan, and the Philippines to Borneo, is often referred to as the US "maritime defense perimeter" in the Pacific. Cold War historian John L. Gaddis rightly argued that this is misleading. He contends that this is not the defence of a perimeter at all, but rather the safeguarding of selected island strongpoints.[21] As the dominant land power in Asia, China controls the East Asian rimland in a way the Soviet Union never achieved, leaving the United States with no other option but to balance China through a strategy of offshore strongpoint defence. This strategy is centered on alignments with Japan, Australia, and India, as well as smaller islands and movable naval platforms in the wider Indo-Pacific naval theater.

In addition to controlling the rimland, China's growing sea power capabilities shape the content of US strongpoint defence. Since the collapse of the Soviet Union, China has been the dominant land power in East Asia, enabling it to give priority to the sea. The main purpose of Chinese sea power is to enhance China's growing anti-access/area-denial capabilities. The combined power of China's navy, air force, missile, and space capabilities has now turned the three "near seas" in China's periphery—the South China Sea, East China Sea, and Yellow Sea—into a contested zone, meaning that China now has the capabilities to challenge the traditional US command of the commons in the area.[22] For instance, in the East China Sea, China responded to the 2012 Senkaku/Diaoyu Islands crisis by escalating its military activity in the area, and it has since kept the Japanese navy and air force on high alert. In recent years, China has also strengthened its military presence on several disputed islands, atolls, and shoals of the South China Sea, and in 2022, China used US Speaker Nancy Pelosi's visit to Taiwan as an opportunity to establish a "new normal" in the Taiwan Strait. Moreover, China's missile capabilities represent a significant threat to US forward bases along the first island chain, and increasingly so to US naval surface vessels operating within the second island chain that extends from Japan, east of the Philippine Sea, to the Marianas and Palau Islands, as well as to assets located at Guam.

On top of this, China is building a growing number of blue-water platforms that operate beyond the first island chain with increasing frequency, sailing into the Indian Ocean and the Northern Pacific. In this volume, Robert S. Ross correctly points out that China's navy only has regional reach, in contrast to the global reach of the US Navy. Still, China's growing sea power is widening the geographic scope of the US rivalry with China, from China's near seas to the wider Indo-Pacific theatre. Responding to this development, the United States has changed its Pacific Command at Hawaii into the Indo-Pacific Command, and it is writing Indo-Pacific strategies.

Thus, in contrast to the land-based US-Soviet rivalry, the US-China rivalry mainly takes place in a maritime theatre. An important debate in the era of US-China bipolar rivalry is therefore if a naval theatre is more or less conflict prone than a land-based theatre.[23] Balancing at sea in the Indo-Pacific is potentially less static and predictable than balancing on land in Europe during the Cold War, and it entails a higher degree of uncertainty with regard to horizontal (geographic scope) and vertical (weapon platforms) escalation. Indeed, in this volume, Tunsjø argues that the risk of a limited war is higher in the US-China naval rivalry than it was during the US rivalry with the Soviet Union.

The Indo-Pacific Strongpoints

The United States has a vast network of allies and military facilities in East Asia and the wider Indo-Pacific region. It includes a footprint on the Asian mainland through its alliance with South Korea; a strong presence along the first and second island chains, including in Japan, the Philippines, and Guam; and military facilities in the Indian Ocean region, such as the Naval Support Facility Diego Garcia. A withdrawal from one or more of these forward positions would arguably weaken the US position vis-à-vis China and upset the current balance in Asia. For instance, a US military withdrawal from the Korean Peninsula would have a direct impact on Japan's security, with the Korean Peninsula becoming the primary vector for possible attacks on Japan from the Asian mainland. Furthermore, it would signal a weakened US commitment to Asia and potentially embolden China to pursue a more forward-leaning policy in the region.[24] Nonetheless, not all positions in Asia are equally important for US strategy. If the United States remains committed to balance China through a strongpoint defence posture, the strategy would ultimately rest on strong alignment with three countries: Japan, India, and Australia.

In September 2021, US president Biden hosted Prime Minister Scott Morrison of Australia, Prime Minister Narendra Modi of India, and Prime Minister Yoshihide Suga of Japan at the White House for the first-ever in-person Leaders' Summit of the Quadrilateral Security Dialogue, also known as the Quad. Official statements from the Quad often refer to a shared vision for the free and open Indo-Pacific anchored in democratic values. Nevertheless, there is also a geopolitical logic to the Quad.

From a US perspective, Japan, Australia, and India serve three specific purposes in a strongpoint defence strategy in the Indo-Pacific. Japan is arguably the only nation along the first island chain that in partnership with US forces can withstand a Chinese invasion. During World War II, US forces had to withdraw from the Philippines, and today, the US ability to defend Taiwan from a future Chinese invasion is increasingly uncertain. A US military withdrawal from Japan would not only diminish the US ability to patrol East Asian waters but also open East Asia up for Chinese regional hegemony. India is potentially the only secure access point for the United States to the Eurasian rimland in Asia. The United States currently has troops based in South Korea, but the experience from the Korean War informs us that it may be challenging to hold the Korean Peninsula. In addition, India would also be an important partner in naval operations in the Indian Ocean region. Australia is both an important staging area and the natural pivot point between the Pacific and Indian Oceans.

The geopolitical logic of US-China rivalry also explains why India, Japan, and Australia are aligning with the United States, including why they do so at a different pace and depth.

Japan's geographic position is similar to Britain, both being offshore islands facing a large continent. Still, their geopolitical positions are very different. Historically, Britain could always align with one or more great powers on the European continent powerful enough to counter the rise of a potential hegemon, hence its role as the "holder of the balance" in European balance-of-power politics.[25] In contrast, Japan faces a rising China that occupies an almost all-dominant position on the Asian mainland, with no Asian mainland power in China's vicinity that can assist it balancing China's power. Tokyo is particularly susceptible to a potential coordinated two-flank pressure from the growing ties between China and Russia. The Sea of Japan and the East China Sea provide Japan more protection against Chinese pressure and a possible invasion than if they shared a common land border. However, unlike the British, who as the dominant sea power could always rely on possessing the strongest navy when faced with a potential hegemon on the European continent, Japan's navy is now inferior to the Chinese navy. Japan is currently facing the threat that Mackinder and Spykman feared the most: a dominant land power with superior sea power. Japan has therefore responded to China's rise by gradually reforming its own defence posture and by deepening its alliance with the United States.[26] Due to its location in the geographic center of the US-China rivalry, Japan is relatively certain of US alliance commitment.

India has four frontiers, and it faces China on all four fronts, although in various form and strength.[27] In the north, India shares a land border with China. Even though China is located across the Himalayas, with the world's highest mountain chain mitigating the effect of China's growing power, China has gradually strengthened its posture, and the border is disputed, with a number of serious incidents in recent years that threaten stability between the two countries. To the west, India faces Pakistan, which is the closest Beijing has to an ally, and to the east, India shares a border with Bangladesh and Myanmar, another two countries with relatively close ties to Beijing. Pakistan, Bangladesh, and Myanmar all cultivate relations with China as a counterweight to India's dominant position in South Asia, whereas China finds these relationships useful as means to hem in India and to secure alternative transit/access routes to the Indian Ocean. India's fourth frontier is the Indian Ocean, and China is increasingly projecting sea power and military capabilities into the Indian Ocean region.[28]

Despite China's growing footprint in India's neighborhood, India's geopolitical position is different from that of Japan. The US-China rivalry keeps China preoccupied in a naval theatre directed away from India, and this mitigates the effect of China's rise on India. Furthermore, due to India's more peripheral position in the US-China rivalry, there is a certain degree of skepticism in New Delhi concerning US commitments safeguarding Indian interests. India is now managing China's rise by moving away from its traditional nonalignment policy towards an alignment with the United States, but it is still a relatively moderate form of alignment.[29] India has joined an increasing number of US military exercises in the region, on a bilateral basis as well as in the context of the Quad. The most important development, however, is India signing defence cooperation agreements with the United States that facilitate Indian access to a wide range of US military and dual-use technologies, although India will need time to shift from Russian technology and defence systems to US-based imports. Nevertheless, in tandem with China's growing blue-water capabilities and the expansion of the US-China strategic theatre from East Asian maritime waters to the Indo-Pacific, India's strategic relevance for the United States will increase, and vice versa.

As an offshore continent, Australia is beholden to the Eurasian power structure, even though it is not located in the immediate vicinity of China. The distance from the city of Darwin in the Australian Northern Territory to China's Hainan Island is approximately 4,000 kilometers. Measured from Urumqi, the provincial capital of Xinjiang in Western China, travelling a similar distance would take you to places like Sri Lanka and Ukraine, and the Kola Peninsula in the Russian Arctic. Nevertheless, in terms of security, Australia's relative geographic isolation is both a blessing and a curse. The notion that Australia's isolation strengthens its security has been called a "beguiling fallacy."[30] Australia's main security concern is the danger of isolation, and the emergence of a potentially hostile Pacific power with a strong navy that can dominate the seas around it. This could strangulate Australia's economy and threaten its independence.

The first time the rise of an Asian power triggered such concerns in Australia was in the 1920s, when they looked at the steady accretion of Japanese military capabilities with mounting unease. Following the Pacific

War, Australia turned to the United States for strategic defence, signing the Australia, New Zealand, and United States (ANZUS) treaty in 1951, and this alliance agreement has now been in place for more than seventy years. During the last decade, the emerging US-China rivalry has strengthened Australia's geostrategic value in the US military strategy, and its value will only increase as the US-China strategic theatre expands from East Asian waters to the larger Indo-Pacific. In fact, the Chinese navy is now occasionally sailing closer to Australia, and Chinese military facilities in Australia's neighborhood could indeed be a realistic scenario in the future. The Australia, United Kingdom, and United States (AUKUS) agreement signed in 2021, strengthening the strategic defence cooperation between these three countries, was a strong signal of Australia's alliance commitment working together with the United States in the Indo-Pacific region.

The Geopolitical Foundation of the Sino-Russian Partnership

While India, Japan, and Australia are responding to China's rise by strengthening their respective alignments with the United States, Russia is moving in the opposite direction, accommodating China's rise. The rapid development of the Sino-Russian partnership over the last decade is often explained as being the result of ideology, identity, and leadership, with Xi Jinping and Vladimir Putin working closely together and both states moving in the direction of more authoritarian regimes.[31] Moreover, as discussed by Ekman and Wishnick in their respective contributions to this volume, the Russia annexation of Crimea in 2014 and its full-scale invasion of Ukraine in 2022 has strengthened the Sino-Russian relationship. Nonetheless, I will here highlight how the geopolitical logic of the US-China rivalry contributes to enhance the Sino-Russian partnership, which differs from the rather weak geopolitical platform of the Sino-Soviet Cold War alliance, and explain its implications for the United States and the security order in Asia and Europe. The bipolar rivalry between the United States and rimland China favors Sino-Russian alignment for three main reasons.

First, despite China's military rise in recent years, both China and Russia face an even larger power gap vis-à-vis the United States and its allies then vis-à-vis each other. Seen from Beijing, Russia is a secondary power only, with a military posture that is significantly weaker in Asia than in Europe. Seen from Moscow, the combined military expenditures of European NATO member states have not yet surpassed China's defence expenditure, and when US military capabilities devoted to the transatlantic theatre are added on top of NATO Europe, the power gap Russia faces on its European flank is wider than the one it faces on its China flank.

Second, in a bipolar power structure, China's main security concern is the United States, and as outlined above, the Sino-US rivalry is mainly a maritime theatre. China's naval rivalry with the United States means that Beijing's military buildup is directed away from Russia, towards the Indo-Pacific strategic theatre, mitigating the effect of China's rise on Russian security concerns.

Third, rimland China is less threatening as the preponderant power in a Sino-Russian alignment than heartland Soviet Union was as the dominant part in the Sino-Soviet Cold War alliance. During the Cold War, due to the vast geographic reach of heartland Soviet Union, it represented a potential threat along a substantial part of the Chinese border, from Xinjiang in the western part of China to the Heilongjiang province in China's northeast. Today, China represents a direct threat to Russia only in the Far East, and to some extent in Central Asia. Given China's more limited geographic reach from its rimland position in East Asia, China has no ability to encircle Russia in a similar fashion to how the Soviet Union exercised influence on the Chinese frontier during the Cold War.

The strong geopolitical foundation of the current Sino-Russian partnership has at least three important consequences. First, it allows Russia to channel most of its resources to its European frontier. If Russia had a strained relationship with China and faced a large Chinese military buildup on its border in the Russian Far East region, Moscow would probably not have been in a position to launch a full-scale invasion of Ukraine, much less to engage in a protracted war in Europe. Second, it allows Beijing to give priority to its naval rivalry with the United States. Third, it will be difficult for the United States to play Russia off against China in a similar fashion to how it played the "China card" against the Soviet Union during the Cold War.

Today, with China as its peer competitor and rival, the United States may, at some point down the road, find it tempting to consider playing the Russia card against China. In fact, this policy option was a subject of debate within the American strategic community prior to Russia's invasion of Ukraine. The Sino-US rapprochement in the early 1970s was indeed one of the main events during the Cold War. Through aligning with China, the United States was able to strengthen its position in the East Asian rimlands, to "box in" the Soviet Union, and to force Moscow into a costly two-flank military posture. Yet, the United States was able to play the China card against Moscow only because of the Sino-Soviet split a few years earlier and the rather shaky geopolitical foundation of the Cold War Sino-Soviet alliance. As alluded to above, contemporary geopolitics inform us that playing Russia off against China will be more difficult. As long as China is preoccupied in a naval rivalry with the United States, Moscow has a much stronger geopolitical position to bargain with Washington than was the case for Beijing in the early 1970s. In fact, in the context of strongpoint defence in the Indo-Pacific, it may be that the United States will find greater value in the India card than the Russia card.

Rimland China and European Security

China's rimland position versus the heartland position of the Soviet Union also shapes European security and the transatlantic alliance in two unique ways. During the Cold War, the Soviet Union represented a threat to all Eurasian rimlands, in Europe and in East Asia, and it embodied a challenge for the United States across both its transpacific and transatlantic flanks. This forged converging views of the Soviet Union within the Western bloc. China, on the other hand, due to its rimland position, represents a one-flank challenge only for the United States, and US balancing of China will thus to a larger degree be regional, in the Indo-Pacific. As elaborated on by Vik Steen in this volume, China's rise may enforce US retrenchment from other regions as well, and not only from Europe, potentially causing instability in the various regions. With the Indo-Pacific as the new nexus of international security affairs, Europe has moved from being in the center of the previous bipolar system to occupying a more peripheral role in the new US-China bipolar rivalry. This shift has three important consequences for European security and transatlantic relations.

First, the United States has moved from a two-flank posture during the Cold War to a thick Asia and thin Europe posture today. In fact, the US military rebalance to Asia had been underway long before the Obama administration announced its "pivot to Asia" policy in 2011, although the latter caused the alarm bells to ring across Europe. At the time, a resurgent Russia and its annexation of the Crimea in 2014 soon contributed to the United States strengthening its military commitment to Europe. The Russian invasion of Ukraine in February 2022 has forced the United States to further enhance its presence in Europe. Nonetheless, even though Russia remains a serious security challenge for Europe, the war in Ukraine has, more than anything else, demonstrated Russia's weaknesses. Long term, it is China, not Russia, that constitutes the number one competitor and challenge for the United States. This message was clearly conveyed in the US National Defense Strategy issued after Russia's invasion of Ukraine,[32] and if this was not proof enough, the growing risk of a conflict in the Taiwan Strait definitely is.[33]

Second, bordering a smaller part of the Eurasian continent than the Soviet Union, China does not constitute a direct military threat to Europe, leading to diverging threat perceptions of China between the United States and its European allies. Europe's view of China started to change already a few years ago, moving from engagement towards ambivalence and skepticism, with the European Union declaring China as a systemic rival in 2019 and NATO including China in its agenda soon after. Furthermore, the joint statement issued by China and Russia in Beijing on February 4, 2022, declaring a "no limits" partnership while Russia was preparing an offensive against Ukraine, and China's ongoing support to Russia during the war, has been met with unease in Europe.[34] Even though China's role in the war is highly indirect, its position on Russia's warfare has significant symbolic value for its relationship with Europe, because this is the first time China has played a role in European security. New technologies like cyber, 5G, and space capabilities are also bringing China closer to Europe. Nevertheless, notwithstanding a more realpolitik-driven European view of China, geography still creates two different threat perceptions of China in Europe and in the United States, leading to more reservation among European allies to support a US containment policy of China compared to containing the Soviet Union.

Finally, due to geopolitics, the overarching challenge for the transatlantic alliance in the era of US-China rivalry is the question of division of labor between the European and Indo-Pacific theatres, how distinct the division of labor should be, and the risk of strategic drift and disagreements that this arrangement entails.[35] A complete and total division of labor, with the United States engaging in the Indo-Pacific theatre only, while Europe and NATO remain focused on deterring Russia and safeguarding Europe's immediate neighborhood, could undermine NATO and endanger transatlantic relations. In fact, a full US withdrawal from Europe will leave behind a more unstable multipolar regional power structure in Europe that in the long term could diminish Europe's military and economic value to the United States. The opposite strategy, with Europe and the United States fully engaged in both theatres, is not a realistic alternative either. NATO may have strengthened its dialogue with partner countries in Asia, but there is a distinct difference between NATO having a global outlook versus a global posture. Indeed, most European nations lack the relevant military capabilities to engage in a naval theatre in the Far East. Thus, the way forward has to be somewhere in between, with the United States implementing a "thick Asia and thin Europe" posture, and Europe pursuing a "thick Europe and thin Asia" strategy. In this volume, both Heisbourg and Walt expand on the future of transatlantic relations.

Rimland China and International Economic Order

The variation between China's rimland position and the heartland position of the Soviet Union also informs two distinct international economic orders. More specifically, while the Soviet Union's heartland position contributed to strengthen the Cold War polarization, China's rimland position will slow down the economic polarization of the US-China bipolar system. In other words, both China's high level of economic interdependence with the world economy and China's rimland position both contribute to a less polarized economic order than during the previous US-Soviet bipolar system. China's rimland position informs the economic order in three ways.

First, while the continent-sized Soviet Union was self-sufficient on natural resources, rimland China is to a larger degree dependent on imports. This difference shapes two opposite approaches to power projection, sea power, and the international economic order. Due to its increasing demand for energy, metals, and minerals, China has faced a serious natural resources constraint for a number of years already, and it has consequently developed a global resource acquisition strategy and strengthened its commercial relationship with resource-rich countries.[36] China's consumption and global purchase of natural resources should be expected to change as China's economic model is rebalanced from an industry-driven model towards a more consumption-, services-, and green technology–driven model. However, this transition period will take several years, and China's economy will remain more dependent on imports of natural resources than the Soviet Union.

Second, the rimland favors trade and a global strategy. The Cold War pre-dominantly remained a rivalry between the Soviet Union as a continental power and the United States as a sea power. It was only towards the second half of the Cold War that the Soviet Union managed to put to sea a sizeable fleet. This distinct land-sea power divide consolidated the difference between Moscow's natural resource–based and relatively closed economy versus the more open and trade-based economic order within the US-led block. Throughout the Cold War era, the value of Soviet exports of goods accounted for 25% to 30% of US exports, and the Soviet Union mainly traded with its Eastern European neighbors. In contrast, China operates the world's second-largest merchant fleet (in terms of tonnage), the world's largest ocean-going fishing fleet, and the world's largest coast guard fleet, and China is the largest shipbuilder in the world. China's maritime prowess is reflected in its foreign trade. In 2020, the value of China's exports of goods and services exceeded that of the United States', and China's two most impor-tant export markets today are the United States and the European Union.

The third impact of China's rimland position on the international eco-nomic order relates to its limited geographic reach into the Eurasian con-tinent and the diverging threat perceptions across the Atlantic. Due to geopolitics, European countries are thus more reluctant to decouple from the Chinese economy and less willing to support US economic containment than when they faced the Soviet Union during the Cold War. US alliance partners in Europe and Asia have largely adhered to US policy with regard to restricting Huawei's market access, but they may be less willing to do so in other business sectors, with less obvious dual-use technologies. It was no coincidence that the shift in China policy, from decoupling to derisking, was a European initiative.[37]

Conclusion

This chapter has outlined how geography molds the era of US-China rivalry in a distinct fashion that differs from the Cold War on four important accounts. First, it posits that geography forces the United States to balance China at sea and from strongpoints in the Indo-Pacific. Balancing at sea is different from balancing on land, and the Indo-Pacific may be a more unstable theatre than the land-based Cold War theatre in Europe. Second, it argues that geography enhances the endurance of the Sino-Russian partnership. Third, it explains how geography challenges European security and transatlantic cooperation in unprecedented ways. Fourth, it claims that China's geographic position in the rimlands informs the international economic order, slowing down the effect bipolarity has on polarization.

International relations scholar Kenneth Waltz stressed that his structural realist theory on polarity never was intended to explain all we want to know about state behavior and international order. Instead, its main contribution, according to Waltz, was to "tell us a small number of big and important things."[38] In similar fashion, geography does not determine strategy and policy, and states may or may not act and behave according to their geopolitical context.[39]

For instance, there is no guarantee that China will stay interconnected with the global economy. China has throughout history shifted between phases of inward-looking and outward-looking policies. The most dramatic shift from global outlook to an inward-oriented policy was the decision in the early fifteenth-century Ming Dynasty to shut down its trade and shipbuilding capacity. During the Qing Dynasty, China was reluctant to engage in foreign trade with Western powers. Another example is China closing a large part of its foreign economic relationships after the Communist takeover in 1949. In fact, like many imperial dynasties before them, China's communist leaders have been uncomfortable with the concept of interdependence, because it challenges their core values of independence, sovereignty, and self-reliance, the opposed concept of dependence.

Furthermore, even though geopolitics tell us that the United States will remain committed to balancing China through a forward position in Asia, Trumpian isolationist trends in US policy could set in motion policies that in the end cause US retrenchment and home-shoring of its military. Nonetheless, even though states may defy the logic of geopolitics, geography continues to provide us with valuable information about state strategy, including in the era of US-China rivalry. And, if states indeed defy the logic of geopolitics, it will cost them, in the form of diminished security and prosperity.

Notes

1. Øystein Tunsjø, *The Return of Bipolarity in World Politics: China, the United States, and Geostructural Realism* (Columbia University Press, 2018).
2. Robert Gilpin, *War and Change in World Politics* (Cambridge University Press, 1981), 25–39, 186–87.

3. On bipolar and multipolar international systems, see Kenneth N. Waltz, *Theory of International Politics* (Waveland Press, 1979); and Kenneth N. Waltz, "Realist Thought and Neorealist Theory," *Journal of International Affairs* 44, no. 1, Theory, Values and Practice in International Relations: Essays in Honor of William T. R. Fox (1990): 32–37. On unipolar systems, see William C. Wohlforth, "The Stability of a Unipolar World," *International Security* 24, no. 1 (1999): 5–41.

4. The US containment strategy against the Soviet Union evolved throughout the Cold War over time, but the main content of it was in place by 1950. See John L. Gaddis, *Strategies of Containment: A Critical Appraisal of American National Security Policy during the Cold War* (Oxford University Press, 1982). On the debate about the contemporary US China strategy, see, for instance, Elbridge A. Colby, *The Strategy of Denial: American Defense in an Age of Great Power Conflict* (Yale University Press, 2021); Michael Beckley and Hal Brands, *Danger Zone: The Coming Conflict with China* (W. W. Norton, 2023); Thomas J. Christensen, "Mutually Assured Disruption: Globalization, Security, and the Dangers of Decoupling," *World Politics* 75, no. 5 (2023): 1–18, https://www.doi.org/10.1353/wp.0.a918726; and White House, *Indo-Pacific Strategy of the United States*, February 2022, https://www.whitehouse.gov/wp-content/uploads/2022/02/U.S.-Indo-Pacific-Strategy.pdf

5. Paul Kennedy, *The Rise and Fall of the Great Powers* (Vintage Books, 1987).

6. G. John Ikenberry, "The Illusion of Geopolitics: The Enduring Power of the Liberal Order," *Foreign Affairs*, May/June 2014; Christopher Fettweis, "Revisiting Mackinder and Angell: The Obsolescence of Great Power Geopolitics," *Comparative Strategy* 22, no. 2 (2003): 109–29, https://doi.org/10.1080/01495930390202580.

7. Colin S. Gray, "Inescapable Geography," *Journal of Strategic Studies* 22, no. 2–3 (1999): 161–77.

8. Nicolas Miailhe, "The Geopolitics of Artificial Intelligence: The Return of Empires?," *Politique étrangère*, no. 3 (2018): 105–17; Everett C. Dolman, "Geostrategy in the Space Age: An Astropolitical Analysis," *Journal of Strategic Studies* 22, no. 2–3 (1999): 83–106.

9. Jack S. Levy, "Balances and Balancing: Concepts, Propositions, and Research Design," in *Realism and the Balancing of Power: A New Debate*, ed. John A. Vasquez and Colin Elman (Prentice Hall, 2003), 128–53.

10. Nicholas J. Spykman, "Geography and Foreign Policy, II," *American Political Science Review* 32, no. 2 (1938): 213–36; Mackubin Thomas Owens, "In Defense of Classical Geopolitics," *Naval War College Review* 52, no. 4 (1999): Article 5; Kennedy, *The Rise and Fall of the Great Powers*, 86–100.

11. See Robert Jervis, "Cooperation under the Security Dilemma," *World Politics* 30, no. 2 (1978): 167–214; and Kenneth E. Boulding, *Conflict and Defense: A General Theory* (Harper and Row, 1963), 230–32.

12. Nicholas J. Spykman, "Geography and Foreign Policy, I," *American Political Science Review* 32, no. 1 (1938): 28–50; Spykman, "Geography and Foreign Policy, II."

13. Nicholas J. Spykman, *America's Strategy in World Politics: The United States and the Balance of Power* (Harcourt, Brace & Co., 1942), 11–26, 41–42, 446–47.

14. Geoffrey Sloan and Colin S. Gray, "Why Geopolitics?," *Journal of Strategic Studies* 22, no. 2–3 (1999): 2. See also Harold Sprout, "Geopolitical Theories Compared," *Naval War College Review* 6, no. 5 (1954): 19–36.

15. Jack S. Levy and William R. Thompson, "Balancing on Land and at Sea: Do States Ally against the Leading Global Power?," *International Security* 35, no. 1 (2010): 7–43.

16. John A. Vasquez, "Why Do Neighbors Fight? Proximity, Interaction, or Territoriality," *Journal of Peace Research* 32, no. 3 (1995): 277–93.

17. Nicholas J. Spykman, *The Geography of the Peace*, ed. Helen R. Nicholl (Harcourt, Brace & Co., 1944).

18. Halford J. Mackinder, "The Geographical Pivot of History," *Geographical Journal* 23, no. 4 (1904): 421–37.

19. Spykman, *America's Strategy in World Politics*.

20. Mearsheimer, *The Tragedy of Great Power Politics*, 237; Robert S. Ross, "US Grand Strategy, the Rise of China, and US National Security Strategy for East Asia," *Strategic Studies Quarterly* 7, no. 2 (2013): 20–40; Spykman, *America's Strategy in World Politics*.

21. Gaddis, *Strategies of Containment*.

22. Barry R. Posen, "Command of the Commons: The Military Foundation of U.S. Hegemony," *International Security* 28, no. 1 (2003): 5–46.

23. See, for instance, Øystein Tunsjø, "Another Long Peace?," *National Interest* 158 (November/December 2018): 34–43; Ian Bowers, "Escalation at Sea: Stability and Instability in Maritime East Asia," *Naval War College Review* 71, no. 4 (2018): Article 5.

24. Scott A. Snyder, *The United States–South Korea Alliance: Why It May Fail and Why It Must Not* (Columbia University Press, 2023).

25. Paul M. Kennedy, "The First World War and the International Power System," *International Security* 9, no. 1 (1984): 7–40.

26. Watanabe Tsuneo, "What's New in Japan's Three Strategic Documents," Commentary, Center for Strategic and International Studies, February 13, 2023, https://www.csis.org; Eric Heginbotham and Richard J. Samuels, "Active Denial: Redesigning Japan's Response to China's Military Challenge," *International Security* 42, no. 4 (2018): 128–69; Bjørn Elias Mikalsen Grønning, "Japan's Shifting Military Priorities: Counterbalancing China's Rise," *Asian Security* 10, no. 1 (2014): 1–21.

27. On India's response to China's rise, see Jo Inge Bekkevold and S. Kalyanaraman, eds., *India's Great Power Politics: Managing China's Rise* (Routledge, 2021).

28. Darshana M. Baruah, "Maritime Competition in the Indian Ocean," Testimony before the U.S.-China Economic and Security Review Commission, Carnegie Endowment for International Peace, May 12, 2022.

29. Bekkevold and Kalyanaraman, *India's Great Power Politics: Managing China's Rise*.

30. A. D. McLennan, "Australia's Security Dilemma," *Policy* 18, no. 2 (2002): 23.

31. On the development of China-Russia relations during the last ten to fifteen years, see, for instance, Jo Inge Bekkevold and Bobo Lo, eds., *Sino-Russian Relations in the 21st Century* (Palgrave Macmillan, 2019); Sarah Kirchberger et al., eds., *Russia-China Relations Emerging Alliance or Eternal Rivals?* (Springer, 2022).

32. US Department of Defense, "Fact Sheet: 2022 National Defense Strategy," https://www.businessdefense.gov/docs/ndis/NDIS-Fact-Sheet_JAN24.pdf

33. Christopher P. Twomey, "The Fourth Taiwan Strait Crisis Is just Starting," *War on the Rocks*, August 22, 2022, https://warontherocks.com/2022/08/the-fourth-taiwan-strait-crisis-is-just-starting/.

34. Ian Johnson, "Has China Lost Europe? How Beijing's Economic Missteps and Support for Russia Soured European Leaders," *Foreign Affairs*, June 10, 2022; Jo Inge Bekkevold, "China's 'Peace Plan' for Ukraine Isn't about Peace," *Foreign Policy*, April 4, 2023,.

35. Jo Inge Bekkevold, "NATO's New Division of Labor on Russia and China Won't Be Easy," *Foreign Policy*, July 11, 2022, foreignpolicy.com.

36. Jo Inge Bekkevold and Øystein Tunsjø, "Sustaining Growth: Energy and Natural Resources," in *The Sage Handbook of Contemporary China*, ed. W. Wu and M. Frazier (Sage Publications, 2018), 262–80.

37. Emily Benson and Gloria Sicilia, "A Closer Look at De-risking," Commentary, Center for Strategic and International Studies, December 20, 2023, https://www.csis.org/analysis/closer-look-de-risking

38. Kenneth N. Waltz, "Reflections on *Theory of International Politics*: A Response to My Critics," in *Neorealism and Its Critics*, ed. Robert O. Keohane (Columbia University Press, 1986), 329.

39. Jakub J. Grygiel, *Great Powers and Geopolitical Change* (Johns Hopkins University Press, 2006).

12

Geotransition and the Future of Global Stability

Bård Nikolas Vik Steen

One of the most important characteristics distinguishing the US-China rivalry from the Cold War is that it necessitates a fundamental shift in the geographical distribution of global military power. Whereas the Cold War began where the front lines of the Second World War ended, China's rise requires a shift of US military resources from one geostrategic centre of gravity to another. As a result of this shift, we are likely entering a period of increased global instability and Russia's invasion of Ukraine may only mark the beginning.

The invasion of Ukraine, the West's coordinated response, and Russia's heavy losses prompted a degree of triumphalism across the Western world in 2022 and 2023. Leaders and commentators alike suggested that the war would lead to the dissipation of key security concerns. Francis Fukuyama even foresaw "a new birth of freedom" that will "get us out of our funk about the declining state of global democracy."[1]

Such triumphalist pronouncements are premature. Not only do they fail to account for the continuing attempts to undermine Western democracy and the uncertain long-term consequences of a war whose outcome has become far more uncertain after the failure of the Ukrainian counteroffensive in 2023,[2] but also they do not account for the destabilizing effect of the changing geographical distribution of power. A distribution that has reached a tipping point and suggests that the war may only mark the beginning of a period of increased global instability.

This chapter demonstrates that the power shift away from the Euro-Atlantic epicentre of the Cold War to a new epicentre in Pacific Asia is likely to create destabilizing power vacuums in the areas left behind. While the North Atlantic Treaty Organization's (NATO's) European members should

Bård Nikolas Vik Steen, *Geotransition and the Future of Global Stability*. In: *Not Just Another Cold War*.
Edited by: Bård Nikolas Vik Steen, Oxford University Press. © Oxford University Press (2025).
DOI: 10.1093/9780197799932.003.0013

have the incentives and finances to maintain their security for as long as U.S. extended nuclear deterrence is guaranteed, they are unlikely to pick up the slack in the Middle East, North Africa, the Caucasus, and other areas not covered by US security guarantees. As unsatisfied states and armed non-state actors take advantage of this, the destabilizing effects of the US-China rivalry could ripple around the world.

This chapter begins by showing that America's role as a geopolitical pivot is forcing an escalating shift of US military resources from the Euro-Atlantic and Mediterranean to Pacific Asia. It goes on to argue that Europe appears unlikely to fill the vacuum the United States leaves behind, resulting in increased instability as revisionist actors capitalize by attempting to shape the regions that the United States deprioritizes. It concludes that although the Western response to Russia's invasion offers some promise, the United States' geotransition to Asia is likely to have a destabilizing effect on regions that have traditionally relied on US engagement but are not formally allied to the United States.

The Many Threats to Bipolar Stability

Over the past thirty years, scholars have highlighted the conflict potential in the United States and China's competition for dominion in East Asia. Structural realists like John Mearsheimer have pointed to states' ever-expanding lust for security to argue that the United States and China would eventually come to blows.[3] Hegemonic war theorists like Robert Gilpin have discussed how hegemonic transition may lead to war.[4] Power transition theorists like Jacek Kugler and Ronald Tammen have argued that the rise of China and the relative decline of the United States would incentivize both sides to strike against the other.[5] Andrew Krepinevich Jr. has argued that China's emergence as a nuclear superpower might challenge nuclear stability.[6]

Some have also noted that the geopolitical context of the crisis may contribute to increased instability. In Chapter 2, Øystein Tunsjø convincingly argues that the international system has already returned to bipolarity. The gap between the American and Chinese economies, and other great powers, is now so large that we again live in a system dominated by two superpowers.[7]

Tunsjø goes on to defy structural realist convention when he argues that bipolarity will not decrease the risk of war. According to Kenneth Waltz, the emergence of a bipolar international system should lead to increased stability.[8] But Tunsjø argues that geography indicates that bipolar relations between China and the United States are more likely to result in conflict than the rivalry between the United States and the Soviet Union. Unlike the Cold War, the Sino-American rivalry takes place in the seascape of Pacific Asia, reducing the threat to state survival and the need to use nuclear weapons, but also increasing the risk that either party might risk conventional war.

What appears to be missed, however, is how the geographical context of the Sino-American rivalry is also likely to lead to increased instability in other parts of the world. That is the topic here.

The US Pivot of History

As a continent-sized power divided from—and at the same time connected to—the world by its two greatest oceans, the United States occupies a unique geographical and geopolitical position. Its combination of relative isolation, vast natural and human resources, and unobstructed access to the global commons gives it a geographical position uniquely favourable to global power and influence. However, as Nicholas J. Spykman observed during World War II, America's position also dictates a particular geopolitical strategy: that of a geostrategic pivot.

The key to America's power is to ensure a favourable balance of power in Europe and Asia. If such a balance can be maintained, the United States can ensure that no other power can threaten its control of the world's oceans, which is essential to US hegemony. As Spykman put it: "who controls the Rimland rules Eurasia, who rules Eurasia controls the world's destinies."[9] With Pearl Harbor serving as a vivid reminder of the potential consequences of failure, the United States has therefore laboured to "prevent the domination of [Europe and Asia] by hegemonic powers whose principles and ideals are opposed to . . . Western civilisation."[10] The foremost US national security interest in the twenty-first century is therefore likely to remain what it has been since 1776, namely, "to ensure a balance of power in its two transoceanic flanking regions that keeps them internally divided."[11]

This grand strategy also means that US geostrategic priorities are likely to change with variations in the balance of power in Asia and Europe. Maintaining balances of power favourable to America's interests necessarily means that active measures will be taken to keep them so. In the present strategic environment, and as underscored by pretty much every US strategic document over the last few years, this means that a considerable shift of military power to Pacific Asia will have to be undertaken. With the massive growth of Chinese power in the past thirty years, a considerable shift in the distribution of US military resources is required. With China's economy catching up and US allies too weak to oppose Beijing alone, it is Asia and the Pacific, rather than Europe and the Atlantic, that are in the greatest need of America's stabilising hand. But that does not mean that the need to reinforce the Pacific flank will not have serious consequences for those theatres whose priority will be decreased as a result.

The Geotransition from the Euro-Atlantic to the Pacific

Starting with the Obama administration's "pivot to Asia" in 2011, the United States has begun the transfer of power from the Euro-Atlantic to the Pacific. China has replaced the Soviet Union not only as the world's leading authoritarian superpower but also as the United States' main strategic rival. Albeit interrupted by various crises, the United States diverts more and more of its power and attention to balancing China, and the urgency is felt at every level of government. President Joe Biden has noted how the withdrawal from Afghanistan resulted from the need to rebalance in preparation for "extreme competition between Washington and Beijing."[12] Secretary of State Antony Blinken described balancing China as "the biggest geopolitical test of the twenty-first century."[13] Secretary of Defence Lloyd Austin has described China as wanting to become "a dominant world power" that requires a "whole of government approach."[14] Former vice chairman of the Joint Chiefs of Staff General John Hyten has described China's military advances as "stunning" and noted that "the pace they are moving and the trajectory they're on will surpass Russia and the United States if we do not do something to change it."[15]

Despite impressive initial support for Ukraine, the Biden administration also continued to increase its focus on China. The administration's interim national security guidance, and its subsequent National Security Strategy, considered China "the only competitor potentially capable of combining its economic, military, and technological power to mount a sustained challenge to a stable and open international system."[16] And the administration's 2022 National Defense Strategy clearly prioritized China over Russia as America's "most consequential strategic competitor and pacing challenge." It further noted that "the growing multi-domain threat posed by the PRC" is now the United States' number one priority.[17]

But the US need to refocus its resources to the Pacific has also started to have consequences for America's global presence. Although Washington's political class remains strongly supportive of NATO, and the invasion of Ukraine has brought US troop numbers in Europe back up again, there is deep bipartisan agreement that China's rise must have consequences for the United States' global force posture. The present administration has made it no secret that its attempts to withdraw from the Middle East are moti- vated largely by China. President Biden pointed out how "our true strategic competitors—China and Russia—would love nothing more than the United States to continue to funnel billions of dollars in resources and attention into stabilising Afghanistan indefinitely." Secretary of State Antony Blinken has stated that America would do "less, not more" in the Middle East—stressing the need to refocus on China.[18]

The focus on Asia is also having consequences for America's presence in Europe. To avoid drastic cuts for as long as possible, Washington has tried to find creative ways to release more resources. For example, the 2018 National Defense Strategy set out to prop up America's "eroding military advantage" by relying more on allied deterrence and using US capabilities more unpredictably to achieve the same effect with less permanent pres- ence.[19] As explained by a Center for Strategic and International Studies report: "With a limited pool of capabilities and forces ... [and] to maximise the strategic impact of the existing U.S. force structure, the 2018 National Defense Strategy introduced the concept of 'dynamic force employment', aiming to deter adversaries globally by being strategically predictable, but operationally unpredictable."[20] In practice, this means that US forces will seek to "pop up" in strategically important areas with little or no warning to imitate the pressure generated by a permanent US presence while avoiding its costs. The US prioritization of Asia has also been felt at the diplomatic level. The Australia, United Kingdom, and United States (AUKUS) agree- ment to sell nuclear submarines and strengthen strategic relations at the expense of a formerly agreed-upon submarine deal between France and Australia is another demonstration of how the US shift to Asia is coming at the expense of European interests. Botched diplomatic craftsmanship played a role in provoking French ire, but at its heart, it was a clear prioritization of Asia over Europe.

Nor has Russia's attack on Ukraine made balancing US global interests any easier. The United States has increased its presence in Europe to one hundred thousand troops for the first time since 2005 and sent two of the destroyers urgently needed in Asia to Rota in Spain. With Russia having made a direct challenge to the European security architecture, Tod D. Wolters, commander of US European Command, testified that an increased presence in Europe would be needed.[21] At the same time, Chairman of the Joint Chiefs Mark Milley was quick to add that the increased force numbers will have to join in a rotational capacity, reflecting the need to "keep a sharp focus on the Pacific."[22]

It is not developments so far that are of greatest concern to US military planners. Rather, the primary concern is what will happen as China realizes an even greater share of the military potential allowed by its economy. China's gross domestic product (GDP) is equivalent to about 70% of the US GDP. A fact that is even more extraordinary considering that the economy of the Soviet Union was never larger than a maximum of 58% of US GDP at its relative peak in 1975.[23] In other words, China already has nearly twice as many resources available to it as the Soviet Union had at the height of its competition with the United States. China, in other words, represents the greatest challenge to US hegemony ever.

To be sure, China is facing a number of economic and societal challenges. Its COVID-19 strategy resulted in severe economic headwinds; a housing bubble threatens market stability; isolationism and decoupling on both sides of the Pacific may limit growth; demographic challenges loom; and the Communist Party's authoritarian intransigence is leading to poor decision-making. In Chapter 4 of this book, Arthur Kroeber demonstrates that Chinese growth is likely to slow. However, as David Dollar shows in Chapter 3, China's economic miracle is in many ways already complete.[24] Regardless of the slowdown, at almost twice the size the Soviet economy ever reached relative to the United States, China's economy is already more than large enough to present an unparalleled challenge to the United States. Whether growth flattens out at 70%, 90%, 150%, or 200% of the US GDP,

China already represents the most potent challenge the United States has ever faced.

This is even clearer when considering China's productive capacity. For the same reason that the Soviet Union managed to present a formidable challenge despite its shortcomings, China is an even more formidable challenger than its nominal GDP suggests. The International Monetary Fund projects that China's purchasing power–adjusted GDP will be 15% larger than the United States' by 2026.[25] Considering the raw numbers, it is clear that China has taken on the role that used to form the foundation of US military domination: it has become the factory of the world. China now produces more than 50% of the world's ships, more than 50% of the world's steel, and close to 90% of drones. In 2023, China was responsible for about 30% of global car manufacturing, with production of thirty million vehicles, compared to the United States' ten million.[26] A leaked Pentagon document has also revealed that China maintains a manufacturing capacity for military vessels that is about two hundred times larger than the United States.[27] While the United States can rely on friends and allies to make up for some of this deficit and it is not all about numbers in modern warfare, this enormous manufacturing capacity means that China has a lot more resources that it could rapidly direct towards increasing its military capacity than the United States does. In the words of Lee Kwan Yew: "This is not just another player—this is the biggest player in the history of the world."[28]

China having become the world's largest manufacturing power is also demonstrated by what China has been able to do with only relatively moderate military spending so far. As Robert Ross demonstrates in Chapter 5, China has already built the largest and one of the most advanced navies in the world. Thousands of precision-guided missiles look out across the oceans, and the Chinese air force is undergoing rapid improvements. Much like the run-up to World War I, when the Royal Navy was spread out across the world, allowing Germany to threaten Britain's hegemony in Europe, Beijing's ability to leverage geographical proximity presents a major challenge to US military dominance in the Western Pacific. With a superior number of surface vessels and submarines, highly advanced area denial capabilities, and the ability to station its military resources in its home region, China is threatening to push the United States out of East Asia. As noted by former Pentagon official and RAND analyst David Ochmanek in 2019, the United States routinely "gets its ass handed to it" in wargames with China.[29]

Unlike the United States, China also has considerable military potential in reserve. So far, Beijing has relied on just the annual growth of its economy to increase its defence budgets. China spends only about 2% of its GDP on the military compared to the United States' 3.5%.[30] Current budget levels have nevertheless allowed China to accumulate the world's largest navy, modernize and expand its nuclear forces, and threaten core US strategic interests. Its relatively low defence spending as a share of GDP indicates that China could probably spend considerably more on its military than it is doing today. Xi Jinping's confrontational rhetoric and the historical willingness of authoritarian regimes to spend disproportionate resources on security mean that this does not seem an unlikely prospect.

For Pentagon planners, China's enormous human, financial, and productive resources are perhaps the greatest cause for alarm. In 2021, Admiral Philip Davidson, head of the US Indo-Pacific Command, said China could achieve "overmatch"—the ability to force the United States out of the region through sheer weight of force—within five years.[31] He added that "we are accumulating risk that may embolden China to unilaterally change the status quo before our forces may be able to deliver an effective response."[32] China's productive capacity is no longer just numbers on a piece of paper, but starting to put the US position in Asia in real danger.

Geotransition as a Strategic Imperative

Keeping China at bay as it transforms more of its unrivalled productive capacity into military power will force the United States to reduce its commitment in other areas. The United States has already had to adjust its global military posture in the face of Chinese defence spending of only 2% of GDP. As China's productive capacity leaves the United States further behind, this will put the United States' global commitments under greater strain. As strategic competition between the United States and China grows more intense, China also has room to increase its military spending. Beijing's recent push to expand its space-based capabilities and rapidly grow its nuclear arsenal to over one thousand warheads by 2030 appears to be the beginning of a broader challenge to the United States. China's ambition to field a "world-class military" by 2049 stands firm. And as the first state to rival US productive capacity, it may also rival its military power.[33]

America's friends and allies have started to notice that China is taking up a disproportionate share of America's attention. But these trade-offs are only likely to increase as the intensity of the rivalry grows. Despite Russia's invasion of Ukraine, the simple mechanics of economic scarcity is likely to force the United States to use fewer resources in the rest of the world than it does to counter China—its main strategic rival. One of the 2018 National Defense Strategy's principal architects, and the Trump administration's nominee for Under Secretary of Defense for Policy Elbridge Colby, has noted how the United States must prioritize balancing China over more "peripheral theatres" like the Middle East and Europe because the United States simply:

> [does] not have a military large or capable enough to fight major wars against Russia and China in even roughly concurrent timelines. The military scarcity we now face is most acute and consequential in our ability to fight major wars with China and Russia in anything like concurrent timeframes. As a practical matter, we lack enough of the key capabilities—such as penetrating bombers, attack submarines, advanced munitions, and the right reconnaissance platforms.[34]

Up to a point, the United States might find creative solutions to take off the pressure with operational concepts like "dynamic force employment" and "integrated deterrence." However, the cracks can only be hidden for so long. Over time, Washington will be unable to maintain a favourable balance of power against an economic peer if it spreads its resources too thin across the globe. Whether suddenly or gradually, it will be necessary to prioritize Pacific Asia over other regions—forcing the United States to reduce its presence in theatres more peripheral to US interests or more capable of upholding a favourable balance of power.

Nor can the need to prioritize Asia just be spirited away with more money. Kori Schake's suggestion that the United States should simply increase defence spending to meet the growing security concerns seems unrealistic in the present political climate.[35] While the extraordinary price increases on military equipment after the beginning of the war in Ukraine mean more money will be needed just to maintain today's force structure, US budgets are also coming under significant pressure. With much of US military industrial capacity having been shut down since the Cold War, a fundamental shift in the priorities of American society would be needed to take on

China while maintaining today's global presence. That seems unlikely short of war. As the 2024 election cycle clearly indicated, American voters are not ready to finance a stronger global presence in exchange for reduced social programmes or higher taxes.

Furthermore, in the face of China's immense productive capacity, these would be short-lived solutions.[36] China can match US defence production step by step. As Robert Ross notes in Chapter 5, China has a considerable and growing advantage in terms of shipbuilding capacity.[37] Increased military spending can therefore only delay the fundamental problem the United States is faced with: the emergence of a rival with equal military potential cannot easily be dealt with if a substantial share of the nation's military capabilities is tied up elsewhere.

The result is that the United States will need to shift an increasing share of its resources away from other regions. As competition with China grows more intense, this dynamic is also likely to be amplified by the need to concentrate naval forces. As Alfred Mahan notes, "Victory at sea is only possible through fleet concentration, and a fleet should never be strategically subdivided into detachments weaker than the enemy forces they are likely to encounter."[38] While much has changed since Mahan wrote and there are now several technologies available that moderate this point, it is still true that the United States will have to keep more forces in theatre and ready if a fight becomes likely. If the United States is to prevent the emergence of a threat on either side of the Eurasian landmass, it is becoming unrealistic to "size, shape, or posture its military to deal simultaneously with any other scenario alongside a war with China."[39] Simple mechanics of scarcity mean that America will increasingly have to spend its resources balancing China in the Pacific. That of course does not mean that the United States will necessarily leave other parts of the world immediately or entirely. The US grand strategy still puts a premium on maintaining a favourable balance of power in Europe, and Russian nuclear weapons remain a serious threat. However, as security competition in Pacific Asia demands an increasing share of US military resources, America's presence in other parts of the world will decrease. Without a replacement to fill the void, increased instability is likely.

Filling the Void

No such replacement is likely to be found. At least not one that will be able to fill the full range of capabilities the U.S. currently provides. To be sure, Europe's response to Russia's attack on Ukraine gives some grounds for optimism. European nations have provided significant military support for Ukraine, trained soldiers, and increased ammunition production. They have also imposed economic sanctions that have hurt Russia's economy, even if these have been less effective than planned. Several thousand pieces of military equipment have also been destroyed, and hundreds of thousands of Russian soldiers have been killed or wounded. The invasion has also prompted a shift in Europe's military posture. Finland and Sweden have joined NATO,[40] and European states have pledged significant increases in military expenditure, with the majority of member states now on track to reach NATO's 2% spending target.

Nevertheless, Europe is unlikely to fill the gap that the United States leaves behind. To be clear, self-interest probably dictates that European nations will make the necessary investments to defend their own borders. At least as long as U.S. extended nuclear deterrence persists. Even if it will take longer to have an effect than some might have hoped, Europe's increase in military spending and military production capacity will be significant. However, that task will be challenging enough following the massive cuts made to European militaries over the past 30 years.

To truly fill the gap that the United States leaves behind would require Europe to build strategic autonomy, that is, the capacity to independently plan and conduct military operations across the full spectrum of conflict, not only for territorial deterrence and defence but also for expeditionary warfare.[41] Creating an independent alternative to American capabilities and a military industry that enables NATO not just to function but to maintain superiority throughout the Euro-Atlantic, Mediterranean, Middle East, and Africa would require vast, coordinated, and sustained investment over many years. And although Europe has the money to do it, thirty different nations with different priorities, often with large social services with differing priorities, are unlikely to muster the extraordinary unity of purpose to make such a project possible. Especially at a time when Europe is marred by polarization and the tensions resulting from persistently weak growth.

Today, the United States is responsible for about 70% of total NATO defence spending. It is the very spine of the alliance: It provides the capabilities and political unifying force necessary to make thirty-three highly diverse countries function as one. It provides the nuclear umbrella that keeps NATO countries insulated from nuclear extortion. It provides NATO with the logistics, ammunition, aerial refuelling, surveillance capabilities, and many of the standing forces that allow the alliance to maintain its credibility. It is also the only country capable of providing the military-bureaucratic machine necessary to plan, organize, and execute large or complex missions. And perhaps most importantly, it is the dominance of US power that keeps bickering over smaller issues from turning into political disunity.

The United States also contributes nearly all the intelligence, communications, surveillance, and reconnaissance capabilities that are the keystone of NATO's military superiority. These same American capabilities warned Ukraine of Russia's invasion plans and provided critical intelligence to fend off the Russian onslaught. The network of intelligence platforms that allow NATO to detect and target threats is overwhelmingly US owned and operated. For example, the fleet of seventeen E-8 Joint Stars ground surveillance radar aircraft that has reportedly provided Ukraine with real-time information on Russian movements in and around Ukraine are exclusively operated by the United States. Almost all of the Rivet Joint signals surveillance aircraft and the RQ-4 Global Hawk drones that can survey an area the size of South Korea in a single day are American. Open-source flight tracking data show that these aircraft have been circling Ukraine night and day since the beginning of the invasion. The same goes for the long-range missile systems and the ammunition that have proved critical in targeting Russian military infrastructure and ammunition depots, as well as most of the artillery and air defence ammunition that Ukrainian independence depends on.

America is also by far the largest provider of the satellites and logistics NATO relies upon to reach out across the world. For example, the F-35 fighters that will soon make up the core of NATO's military punch disproportionately rely on US systems and communications. The importance of US space dominance has also been demonstrated in Ukraine, with SpaceX providing Ukrainian battlefield communications as standard forms of communication degraded. The evacuation from Afghanistan in 2021 also demonstrated how the United States is almost solely responsible for NATO's strategic airlift capacity. The US fleet of 222 C-17 Globemaster transport planes evacuated 100,000 people from Kabul in a week and 21,600 people in a single twenty-four-hour period. No European country has anything close to such a capability. If these capabilities are busy or taken out in a conflict with China, Europe could lose the very capabilities that ensure NATO's military superiority.

Nevertheless, it is true that the war in Ukraine creates both an opportunity and a strong incentive for Europe to acquire some of these capabilities, become more independent, and fill some of the gaps that the United States is likely to leave behind. As Stephen Walt, Barry Posen, and others have pointed out, Europe's economy is more than large enough to acquire the capabilities necessary to achieve strategic autonomy.[42] Even if large overheads and high prices mean that they get little for their money compared to Russia's militarized society, NATO's European members spend nearly six times more on defence than Russia does. Europe's will to defend itself has also been strengthened by Russia's attack on Ukraine; European countries are increasing their defence budgets, and NATO has pledged that it will increase its rapid response force from forty thousand to three hundred thousand.

Yet, Europe is also grappling with a stagnant economy that appears likely to remain so as European nations are faced with a deepening demographic crisis and weak productivity growth. Lest we forget, Europe remains a highly heterogeneous collection of states that often harbour fundamentally different interests. Sharing responsibility for the military last resort between thirty different and neighbouring countries is a very different collective action problem than letting the United States take care of most of it. Despite the European Union's impressive track record, one does not have to go much further than Brexit, Germany's Alternative Für Deutchland, Marine Le Pen's polling numbers, or Victor Orban's brinkmanship to see that serious differences remain beneath the surface. Getting a continent where each country has its own defence industry, regional interests, and pet projects to divide responsibility for each other's critical security interests will not only be difficult, but also challenge European conceptions of sovereignty and security at a time when the continent will have to grapple with the populism resulting from economic difficulties.

Moreover, the US security guarantee provides a lasting disincentive for Europe to pay more than the minimum required to guarantee club-membership. As long as the United States is willing and able to defend Europe with European assistance, unrestricted US support will remain a fundamental assumption of European defence planning. The fact that NATO is a transatlantic rather than global alliance means that NATO continues to assume that the US capabilities required for the defence of Europe will be available—even though the capabilities Europe relies upon would also have to be used in a conflict with China. When taking the full support of the United States for granted, it makes little sense for other countries to acquire the capabilities the United States already possesses. As a result, much of Europe's increased defence spending is likely to end up being spent on further integration with US systems and support structures, rather than on redundancy that would increase European strategic autonomy.

Indeed, there has so far been little to suggest that Europe's pledge to spend more on defence translates into increased independence. The first thing Germany did with its 100-billion-euro post-Ukraine "Zeitenwende-fund" was to order more F-35 fighters—one of the main selling points of which is closer US integration. Decades of defence cuts also mean that many of the promised funds will be needed just to get Europe's armed forces back to an acceptable level of readiness.[43] Most of Germany's "Zeitenwende-fund" will fill deep holes left by years of underinvestment. In 2018, the Bundestag's commissioner for the armed forces concluded that "the readiness of the Bundeswehr and its major weapons systems are dramatically low in many areas."[44] A considerable share of the money allocated will have to be spent replacing Germany's military aircraft, submarines, and combat vehicles—only about half of which are currently operational.[45]

As long as the transatlantic bond between Europe and the United States survives, self-interest probably dictates that European NATO members will be able to do what is necessary to maintain their security. However, little seems to indicate that European nations will replace the capability to conduct expeditionary operations as the United States shifts capabilities elsewhere.

In 2018, a joint study by the International Institute for Strategic Studies and the German Council on Foreign Relations found that "Europe's capability shortfalls are so significant, Europeans would struggle to autonomously undertake operations even at the low end of the spectrum of conflict."[46] In terms of expeditionary capability the situation is even more dire. Today, Britain and France are the only European countries in possession of any expeditionary capability at all. And even those have been fading rapidly. Britain's new aircraft carriers do not have the support ships necessary to operate a carrier group without allied support. Lack of funding has also meant that the original order of 138 F-35s has been cut to 74 and that the British army is set to shrink to 72,500 personnel by 2025—smaller than at any point since the 1700s.[47] French expeditionary capability is in even worse shape. A parliamentary report from February 2022 described the French army as a bonsai tree. Exquisite, but tiny. As a RAND report pointed out in 2021, the French military has a number of excellent capabilities, but they are very few in number, and not at all prepared for high-intensity conflict. The once *grande armée* has cut equipment stocks significantly and suffers a serious lack of ammunition in almost every category.[48] And even though the French military budget of 2024–2030 was increased by 40% in 2023, these issues will take a long time and a considerable effort to fix, especially as most of the recent budget hike was needed just to make up for inflation.[49] To be sure, these are no longer the military organizations that were able to provide substantial, if supplementary, support to the United States back in the 1990s or even the early 2000's.

With 1,300 kilometres of new NATO borders and an increasingly difficult economic situation, Europe seems unlikely to muster the support necessary to significantly decrease dependence on US enablers or build capacity for direct military involvement outside the territory of NATO members. Finding the money to deter an aggressive, militarized, and revisionist Russia will be challenging enough. Finding the common ground necessary to fund the capability to do much outside Europe seems improbable.

Expected Turbulence

With Europe unlikely to fill the gaps the United States leaves behind, increased global instability is likely to result, particularly in areas not already protected by US security guarantees. If the United States cannot be relied upon to intervene out of concern for its commitments elsewhere and Europe does not have the ability to do so independently, power vacuums will emerge, and revisionist actors will be emboldened.

Indeed, mounting Russian aggression and escalating war's in the Middle East may be early symptoms. As demonstrated by Robert Gilpin, power shifts like the one created by the rise of China "weakens the foundations of the existing system, because those gaining power see increasing benefits and decreasing cost of changing the system. The result is that actors seek to alter the system through territorial, political, or economic expansion."[50] With US power and attention fixed on Asia, other actors will seek to alter the regions where the United States is perceived as less likely to intervene.

The consequences this is likely to have on global stability are already apparent. Statements leading up to Russia's full-scale invasion of Ukraine in 2022 suggest that the decision to invade was at least partly based on US retrenchment and a perceived unwillingness to intervene. Having witnessed the United States' unwillingness to intervene directly in Syria, Washington's withdrawal from Afghanistan, and what US officials like to refer to as their "laser focus" on China, the Kremlin's decision seems in part to have been based on the view that the United States cannot maintain the full breadth of its interests in Asia and Europe at the same time. As Vladimir Putin stated during the St. Petersburg economic forum in June 2022:

> After declaring victory in the Cold War, the United States proclaimed itself to be God's messenger on Earth. . . . They seem to ignore the fact that in the past decades, new powerful and increasingly assertive centres have been formed. . . . These are objective processes and genuinely revolutionary tectonic shifts in geopolitics.[51]

As long as the United States does not retract its security guarantee or become overburdened with a war in Asia, economic and technological superiority should allow European NATO members to make the adjustments necessary to keep Russia at bay. If properly and promptly executed, the expansion of NATO's force structure announced during the alliance's 2022 Madrid summit, combined with an impressive set of budgetary commitments leading up to the Washington summit in 2024, should fill the most important gaps in NATO's force structure. Russia's severe losses in in Ukraine have also provided Europe some time to get their militaries and industrial complexes ready for the needs of deterrence and defence.

Nevertheless, and almost regardless of the outcome of the war in Ukraine, the challenge Russia presents to global stability shows little sign of abating. As of 2024, Russia has weathered the storm of Western sanctions. Although it is true that Russia's massive increase in defence spending is likely to have negative long-term consequences, Russia's shift to a war economy has been far more successful than expected.[52] With China replacing most of the European trade Moscow used to be dependent on, and supercharged by military spending, the Russian economy outgrew all G7 economies in 2023[53]—a very stark contrast to predictions of double-digit recession when the war begun. After large initial losses, Russia has also scaled up military production to levels far beyond what has been possible in Western countries. With vast numbers of missiles and artillery shells produced per year and substantial support from China, Iran, and North Korea, Russia has been able to consistently regenerate forces while adapting to Western weapons and tactics. Most importantly, this happened in parallel with a period of delayed U.S. aid in 2023, which led Russia to regain the battlefield initiative. With the United States and Europe renewing aid for Ukraine, and Donald Trump embarking on a second term in office, the end result of the war remained very much undecided when this chapter was finalized.

However, few of the possible outcomes suggest that its termination will introduce a period of tranquillity. Vladimir Putin's age and the Wagner Group's mutiny in 2023 are reminders that personalized totalitarian regimes are stable until they are not. But neither of these scenarios seems likely to contribute to stability in the present context. Should Western efforts be redoubled in ways that result in a regime-threatening collapse of the Russian military, it is not impossible that the Russian regime might consider its nuclear options. Nor are the candidates who take over the reins after Putin's death likely to divert from Russia's present course of imperialistic revisionism. And should the transfer of power prove unsuccessful, that could result in widespread internal conflict, possibly even thousands of nuclear weapons out of control. Even though a peaceful transition à la the collapse of the Soviet Union is theoretically possible, there are few indications of such a development in the present context.

While highly contingent, the most likely scenario currently seems to be that Russia will remain a revisionist, militarized, and vindictive great power that continues to occupy parts of Ukraine.[54] With a leadership that considers itself to be in an existential conflict with the United States, Russia could also become a more destabilizing force than it already is. Russia's war economy and adaption to modern warfare, combined with considerable industrial and military support from China, Iran, and North Korea, could also lead to a more effective military organization than before.[55] As pointed out by the head of the British army, General Sir Patrick Sanders, in the summer of 2022:

It's also worth remembering that historically, Russia often starts wars badly. And because Russia wages war at the strategic, not the tactical level—its depth and resilience means it can suffer any number of campaigns, battles and engagements lost, regenerate and still ultimately prevail. History has also shown us that armies that have tasted defeat learn more quickly. We don't yet know how the war in Ukraine will end, but in most scenarios, Russia will be an even greater threat to European security after Ukraine than it was before.[56]

Nor is Russia the only actor seeking to profit from a changing global distribution of power. The instability resulting from US geotransition is also starting to be felt in North Africa and the Middle East, with the collapse of the Afghan government as an early example. After President Joe Biden made it clear that his decision to leave Afghanistan was final and that it was motivated by the need to focus resources and attention on China, European nations had no capacity to pick up the baton—despite their strong opposition to leaving. With no one to fill the vacuum, it took only days from when Washington made its intentions clear until the Taliban had regained control over the country. As the United States makes it increasingly clear that its Middle Eastern footprint is being reduced, varieties of this dynamic are being replicated across the region. Without the United States or Europe, others are attempting to fill the gap and instability is the result.

Indeed, since the first draft of this chapter was written, state and non-state actors have been testing the limits of their power in a regional security architecture that is about to be redrawn. Israel's indiscriminate bombing campaign in response to Hamas' repulsive October 7th attacks, may indicate that Israel feels less bound by the United States than before. The same may be said for its bombing campaign and invasion of parts of Syria, as well as Turkey's support for the rebellion that led to the collapse of the Assad-regime in late 2024. Proxy conflicts like the war in Yemen and Iran's attempts to gain influence over the remains of Syria and Iraq have provided other early examples of regional actors seeing an opportunity to test where the new limits are. The same goes for Iran's missile and drone attack's on Israel and Israel's attack on Lebanon in September and October 2024. The likelihood of a broader regional conflict seems greater than it has in decades, and finding a new equilibrium as the United States withdraws from the region is unlikely without a period of turbulence.[57]

The destabilizing effect of the power shift to Pacific Asia is also likely to be amplified by the decreasing cost and increasing availability of advanced weapons technology, particularly advanced surveillance and precision attack capabilities. Since the end of the Cold War until recently access to precision-guided weapons was the privilege of the United States and those it sold them to. As increasingly powerful microchips, cameras, batteries and avionics have become available at lower and lower prices, the weapons such technology enable's have become far easier to access.[58] Not just states but an increasing number of non-state and terrorist organizations now have the ability to strike at range with millimetre precision, be it via drone, missile, or precision-guided bombs and artillery. With the proliferation of small commercial satellites and surveillance drones, it has also become much easier to find targets and much harder to hide or stay protected.

The widespread availability of such powerful force multipliers effectively means that a much larger number of state and non-state actors are positioned to take advantage of strained US resources and attention. One example is the war in Nagorno-Karabakh, where Azerbaijan took advantage of drone strikes and loitering munitions to decimate Armenian forces and evict them from the enclave. Another is Iran's access, sale, and use of increasingly capable missiles and drones. However, the most telling example of the destabilizing power of such technology-enabled exploitation of the global power shift was when Houthi rebels held global trade hostage with low-cost drones and missiles in early 2024. With considerable costs to the global economy and a large naval and air operation needed to counter the threat, it was an example of how costly and challenging it will be to deal with even minor revisionist actors armed with the right tools. With US power stretched thin and Europe unprepared to fill the gap, even smaller actors can cause real damage and consume considerable resources.

The United States' increasing focus on Asia and perceived unwillingness to get directly involved in regional conflicts could also increase the risk of nuclear proliferation. Iran's nuclear ambitions are well known, and with the United States increasingly preoccupied, the risks associated with crossing the atomic threshold could decrease over time. With the United States' lack of capacity to effectively combat nuclear proliferation, as well as the decreasing credibility of its demands as its power becomes stretched, more countries may find the temptation to acquire nuclear weapons greater than the risks. In the event of Iranian nukes, Saudi Arabia would probably also consider acquiring nuclear weapons. Rapidly growing Chinese and North Korean arsenals mean that South Korea and Japan are reportedly already considering their options. And if the sanctity of America's extended deterrence is to be questioned again, the nuclear question might even be revisited by European NATO members. With Russia's sabre rattling, China's large-scale construction of nuclear weapons, and concerns about US isolationism bringing back questions about the reliability of the US nuclear umbrella, the non-proliferation regime may be difficult to uphold.[59]

While it is difficult to predict exactly what the next shock to the system will be, the transition of US power to Asia probably means that the war in Ukraine marks the beginning, rather than the end, of a period of increased global instability. Weak states may no longer have the same confidence that US power can be relied upon, while revisionist states and non-state actors may have less to fear from Washington's zeal. The world also faces the same exacerbating crises as before—and then some. Supply chain crises continue to rock global markets, and the disruption of global energy markets are coming at a cost. The increased impact of climate change will challenge national economies and livelihoods and change how and where militaries operate. The technological revolution that is underway will bring dramatic changes and lead to destabilizing military asymmetries. Recent history also demonstrates how unity and philanthropic spirits are quick to falter as crises drag on and economic consequences start hitting closer to home. This could create new threats and will be more difficult to manage as China occupies US attention.

Conclusion

The geographical transition of US power from the Atlantic to the Pacific represents a serious challenge to global stability. China's continued rise is forcing the United States to divert an increasing share of its military resources and attention to the Pacific. With Europe a long way from strategic autonomy, this is likely to generate power vacuums in areas that have traditionally relied on US power and attention. While NATO will probably insulate members from the most serious consequences, these are already being felt in parts of the world not covered by the US security guarantee. And with few prospects that Europe will replace US expeditionary capabilities, increased instability is already becoming apparent. The geotransition of US power from Europe to Asia will not happen without significant turbulence.

Notes

1. Francis Fukuyama, "Preparing for Defeat," *American Purpose Magazine*, March 10, 2022, https://www.americanpurpose.com/blog/fukuyama/preparing-for-defeat/.
2. Charles Kupchan, "Western Unity Starts at Home," Project Syndicate, March 30, 2022, https://www.project-syndicate.org/commentary/america-europe-must-oppose-both-russia-and-domestic-illiberalism-by-charles-a-kupchan-2022-03.
3. J. J. Mearsheimer, *The Tragedy of Great Power Politics*, updated ed. (W. W. Norton, 2014).
4. R. Gilpin, *War and Change in World Politics* (Cambridge University Press, 1981).
5. J. Kugler and R. Tammen, "Regional Challenge, China's Rise to Power," in *The Asia-Pacific: A Region in Transition* (Asia-Pacific Center for Security Studies, 2004), 33–53.
6. Andrew Krepinevich, "The New Nuclear Age: How China's Growing Nuclear Arsenal Threatens Deterrence," *Foreign Affairs*, April 19. 2022, https://www.foreignaffairs.com/articles/china/2022-04-19/new-nuclear-age.
7. Øystein Tunsjø, *The Return of Bipolarity in World Politics* (Columbia University Press, 2019).
8. Kenneth N. Waltz, "The Stability of a Bipolar World," *Daedalus* 93, no. 3 (1964): 881–909, http://www.jstor.org/stable/20026863; Kenneth N. Waltz, *Theory of International Politics* (Addison-Wesley Publishing Company, 1979).
9. Nicholas J. Spykman, *America's Strategy in World Politics: The United States and the Balance of Power* (Transaction Publishers, 1942), 27.
10. Nicholas J. Spykman, *The Geography of the Peace* (Harcourt Brace and Company, 1944), 45.
11. Robert S. Ross, "US Grand Strategy, the Rise of China, and US National Security Strategy for East Asia," *Strategic Studies Quarterly* 7, no. 2 (2013): 20–40, http://www.jstor.org/stable/26270764.
12. Joe Biden, "Remarks by President Biden on Afghanistan," White House, 2022, https://www.whitehouse.gov/briefing-room/speeches-remarks/2021/08/16/remarks-by-president-biden-on-afghanistan/.
13. Simon Lewis and Humeyra Pamuk, "Blinken Singles Out China as 'Biggest Geopolitical Test' for U.S.," Reuters, March 3, 2021, https://www.reuters.com/world/china/blinken-singles-out-china-biggest-geopolitical-test-us-2021-03-03/.
14. Jim Garamone, "Official Talks DOD Policy Role in Chinese Pacing Threat, Integrated Deterrence," US Department of Defense, June 2, 2021, https://www.defense.gov/News/News-Stories/Article/Article/2641068/official-talks-dod-policy-role-in-chinese-pacing-threat-integrated-deterrence/.
15. Alex Marquardt and Oren Liebermann, "Senior US General Warns China's Military Progress Is 'Stunning' as US Is Hampered by 'Brutal' Bureaucracy," CNN, October 28, 2021, https://edition.cnn.com/2021/10/28/politics/hyten-stunning-china-military-progress/index.html.
16. Joe Biden, "Interim National Security Strategic Guidance," White House, March 2021, https://www.whitehouse.gov/wp-content/uploads/2021/03/NSC-1v2.pdf.
17. US Department of Defense, "Fact Sheet: 2022 National Defense Strategy," March 28, 2022, https://media.defense.gov/2022/Mar/28/2002964702/-1/-1/1/NDS-FACT-SHEET.PDF.
18. Dalia Dassa Kaye, "America Is Not Withdrawing from the Middle East: Washington Needs a New Strategy but Not an Exit Strategy," *Foreign Affairs*, December 1, 2021, https://www.foreignaffairs.com/articles/united-states/2021-12-01/america-not-withdrawing-middle-east.
19. Jim Mattis, "Summary of the 2018 National Defense Strategy" (US Department of Defense, 2018), https://dod.defense.gov/Portals/1/Documents/pubs/2018-National-Defense-Strategy-Summary.pdf.
20. Rachel Ellehuus et al., "Surprise and Stability in the High North," Center for Strategic and International Studies, December 14, 2020, https://www.csis.org/analysis/surprise-and-stability-high-north.
21. Greg Hadley, "Eucom Boss: 'My Suspicion Is We're Going to Need More' US Troops in Europe Long-Term," *Air Force Magazine*, March 30, 2022, https://www.airforcemag.com/eucom-boss-my-suspicion-is-were-going-to-need-more-us-troops-in-europe-long-term/#:~:text=%E2%80%9CWe'll%20have%20to%20continue,Kevin%20Cramer%20(R%2DN.
22. Ellie Kaufman and Barbara Starr, "US Likely to Keep 100,000 Troops in Europe for Foreseeable Future in Face of Russian Threat, US Officials Say," CNN, May 20, 2022, https://edition.cnn.com/2022/05/20/politics/us-troops-in-europe/index.html.

23. Mark Trachtenberg, "Assessing Soviet Economic Performance during the Cold War: A Failure of Intelligence?," *Texas National Security Review* 1, no. 2 (2018), p. 83 https://repositories.lib.utexas.edu/bitstream/handle/2152/63942/Trachtenberg-TNSR-Vol-1-Issue-2-.pdf?sequence=2&isAllowed=y

24. Danny Rosen, "The Age of Slow Growth in China," *Foreign Affairs*, April 15, 2022, https://www.foreignaffairs.com/articles/china/2022-04-15/age-slow-growth-china.

25. "World Economic Outlook: War Sets Back the Global Recovery" (International Monetary Fund, 2022).

26. Linda Lew, "China Produces a Record 30 Million Cars and Exports Soar," Bloomberg, January 11, 2024, accessed April 18, 2024, https://www.bloomberg.com/news/articles/2024-01-11/china-produced-a-record-30-million-autos-in-2023-on-russian-exports.

27. Justin Katz, "'It's Not about Numbers' in Shipbuilding Race with China: US Navy Chief," *Breaking Defense*, 2024, accessed April 18, 2024, https://breakingdefense.com/2024/02/its-not-about-numbers-in-shipbuilding-race-with-china-us-navy-chief/.

28. Graham Allison, *Lee Kuan Yew* (MIT Press, 2013).

29. Sydney Freedberg Jr., "The U.S. Gets Its Ass Handed to It in War Games: Here's a $24 Million Fix," *Breaking Defense*, March 7, 2019, https://breakingdefense.com/2019/03/us-gets-its-ass-handed-to-it-in-wargames-heres-a-24-billion-fix/.

30. Information from the Stockholm International Peace Research Institute (SIPRI), 2022, https://milex.sipri.org/sipri.

31. Michael Beckley, "America Is Not Ready for a War with China," *Foreign Affairs*, 2021, https://www.foreignaffairs.com/articles/united-states/2021-06-10/america-not-ready-war-china.

32. Helen Davidson, "China Could Invade Taiwan in Next Six Years, Top US Admiral Warns," *The Guardian*, March 10, 2021, https://www.theguardian.com/world/2021/mar/10/china-could-invade-taiwan-in-next-six-years-top-us-admiral-warns.

33. "Military and Security Developments Involving the People's Republic of China 2020 Annual Report to Congress" (US Department of Defense, 2020), https://media.defense.gov/2020/Sep/01/2002488689/-1/-1/1/2020-dod-china-military-power-report-final.pdf.

34. Elbridge A. Colby, "More Spending Alone Won't Fix the Pentagon's Biggest Problem," *Time*, March 28, 2022, https://time.com/6161573/us-defense-budget-strategy/.

35. Kori Schake, "America Must Spend More on Defense," *Foreign Affairs*, May 12, 2022, https://www.foreignaffairs.com/articles/united-states/2022-04-05/america-must-spend-more-defense.

36. Robert S. Ross, "The End of U.S. Naval Dominance in Asia," *Lawfare* (blog), November 18, 2018, https://www.lawfareblog.com/end-us-naval-dominance-asia.

37. Robert S. Ross, "Keeping Up with China's Plan," *National Interest*, April 15, 2018. https://nationalinterest.org/feature/keeping-chinas-plan-2538.

38. Barry M. Gough, "Maritime Strategy: The Legacies of Mahan and Corbett as Philosophers of Sea Power," *RUSI Journal*, Winter 1988, 56.

39. Andrew F. Krepinevich, "The U.S. Military and the Coming Great-Power Challenge," *Foreign Affairs*, November 17, 2021, https://www.foreignaffairs.com/reviews/review-essay/2021-11-17/us-military-and-coming-great-power-challenge.

40. Carl Bildt, "NATO's Nordic Expansion," *Foreign Affairs*, April 28, 2022, https://www.foreignaffairs.com/articles/europe/2022-04-26/natos-nordic-expansion.

41. Hugo Meijer and Stephen G. Brooks, "Illusions of Autonomy: Why Europe Cannot Provide for Its Security If the United States Pulls Back," *International Security* 45, no. 4 (2021): 7–43, https://doi.org/10.1162/isec_a_00405. This article also uses Hugo Meijer and Stephen G. Brooks's definition of strategic autonomy: "the institutional capacity to independently plan and conduct military operations across the full spectrum of conflict, including in high-intensity military operations such as expeditionary warfare or territorial defence missions."

42. Stephen M. Walt, "Exactly How Helpless Is Europe?," *Foreign Policy*, May 21, 2021, https://foreignpolicy.com/2021/05/21/exactly-how-helpless-is-europe/.

43. Sven Biscop, "European Defence: Give PESCO a Chance," *Survival* 60, no. 3 (2018): 173, https://doi.org/10.1080/00396338.2018.1470771.

44. "Annual Report 2017 (59th Report)" (German Parliamentary Commissioner for the Armed Forces, February 20, 2018), 41.

45. Peter Hille and Nina Werkhäuser, "Germany's Army: Will €100 Billion Make It Strong? DW: 03.03.2022," *Deutsche Welle*, March 3, 2022, https://www.dw.com/en/germanys-army-will-100-billion-make-it-strong/a-60996891.
46. Meijer and Brooks, "Illusions of Autonomy."
47. "Britain's Armed Forces Are Stretched Perilously Thin," *The Economist*, January 29, 2024, accessed April 15, 2024, https://www.economist.com/britain/2024/01/29/britains-armed-forces-are-stretched-perilously-thin.
48. Stephanie Pezard et al., "A Strong Ally Stretched Thin". June 16, 2021 (RAND), accessed April 15, 2024, https://www.rand.org/pubs/research_reports/RRA231-1.html.
49. Leila Abboud, "Macrons 'Bonsai Army' Needs More Money to Grow," *Financial Times*, July 17, 2023, accessed April 15, 2024, https://www.ft.com/content/9d72e855-3a60-4efc-95f6-c3132e76a6f8.
50. Gilpin, *War and Change in World Politics*, quote from the abstract.
51. Vladimir Putin, "St Petersburg International Economic Forum Plenary Session," President of Russia, June 17, 2022, http://en.kremlin.ru/events/president/news/68669.
52. Alexandra Prokopenko, "Is the Kremlin Overconfident about Russia's Economic Stability?," Carnegie Endowment for International Peace, April 10, 2024, accessed April 17, 2024, https://carnegieendowment.org/2024/04/10/is-kremlin-overconfident-about-russia-s-economic-stability-pub-92174.
53. Anastasia Stognei, "The Surprising Resilience of the Russian Economy," *Financial Times*, February 2, 2024, accessed April 17, 2024, https://www.ft.com/content/d304a182-997d-4dae-98a1-aa7c691526db.
54. Stephen Kotkin, "The Five Futures of Russia: And How America Can Prepare for Whatever Comes Next," *Foreign Affairs*, April 18, 2024, https://www.foreignaffairs.com/russian-federation/five-futures-russia-stephen-kotkin?utm_medium=promo_email&utm_source=fa_edit&utm_campaign=pre_release_kotkin_prospects&utm_content=20240418&utm_term=promo-email-prospects.
55. Demetri Sevastopulo and Sam Jones, "US Says China is Supplying Missile and Drone Engines to Russia," *Financial Times*, April 12, 2024, accessed April 18, 2024, https://www.ft.com/content/ecd934b6-8a91-4b78-a360-9111f771f9b1.
56. General Sir Patrick Sanders, "UK Ministry of Defence," accessed September 10, 2022, https://www.Army.Mod.Uk/News-And-Events/News/2022/06/Rusi-Land-Warfare-Conference-Cgs-Speech/. June 28, 2022.
57. Seth Cropsey, and Gary Roughead, "A U.S. Withdrawal Will Cause a Power Struggle in the Middle East," *Foreign Policy*, December 17, 2019, https://foreignpolicy.com/2019/12/17/us-withdrawal-power-struggle-middle-east-china-russia-iran/.
58. Chris Miller, *Chip War: The Fight for the World's Most Critical Technology* (Scribner, 2022).
59. US Department of Defense, "Military and Security Developments Involving the People's Republic of China," 2021, https://media.defense.gov/2021/Nov/03/2002885874/-1/-1/0/2021-CMPR-FINAL.PDF.

VII

THE FUTURE OF NATO

13

Can NATO Survive the Geostrategic Pivot to Asia?

François Heisbourg

The global shift of power from the Euro-Atlantic theatre that defined the Cold War to the Asia Pacific epicentre of the present rivalry also presents a considerable challenge to the North Atlantic Treaty Organization (NATO). In addressing the prospects of NATO's survival as a result of the geostrategic pivot to Asia, also known by its briefer British name "the Tilt," several assumptions will be made.[1]

The first one involves the notion of "NATO's survival." Because NATO is the organisational expression of the Atlantic Alliance, its survival will be meant here to consist of the continued commitment of its members to its article 5, which is at the core of the mutual defence guarantee created by the Washington Treaty signed on April 4, 1949.[2] Other articles matter greatly, such as article 6, which concerns the implementation of article 5, or article 4, about security consultation.[3] But without article 5 there would be and can be no Atlantic Alliance and, by extension, no NATO. Therefore, it is the survival of the article 5 commitment that lies at the heart of alliance's survival, rather than merely that of the specific enabling organisation known as NATO.

It is worth noting that article 5 existed from the day the treaty entered into force on August 24, 1949, well before NATO as such emerged as an organisation by virtue of the Ottawa Agreement of September 20, 1951. These were concluded after the beginning of the Korean War, a triggering event that itself occurred in the Pacific region, a fact that reminds us of the power of the long-standing de facto strategic links between the Atlantic and Pacific theatres.

Before the creation of NATO as an organisation, a common allied military staff was headquartered in Fontainebleau since April 1948 between the five signatories—the Benelux countries, Britain, and France—of the Brussels

François Heisbourg, *Can NATO Survive the Geostrategic Pivot to Asia?*. In: *Not Just Another Cold War*. Edited by: Bård Nikolas Vik Steen, Oxford University Press. © Oxford University Press (2025).
DOI: 10.1093/9780197799932.003.0014

treaty (March 17, 1948). Field Marshal Montgomery was the commander of this Western Union Defence Organisation.[4]

Over the decades, NATO has proven to be a resilient organisation capable of weathering shocks such as the Suez crisis, the Algerian war, the French withdrawal from much of NATO's command structure (1966–2009), the divergent options vis-à-vis the role of nuclear deterrence in NATO strategy, and the deep splits resulting from American expeditionary wars in Vietnam and Iraq.[5] It also adapted to the shift from intratheatre deterrence and defence during the Cold War to post–Cold War shooting wars of an offensive (Kosovo, Libya) or counteroffensive nature (Afghanistan). It went out of area without going out of business, before refocussing its defence tasks on the European theatre from 2014 onwards, as a result of the first Russo-Ukrainian war.

In view of this history, it may be argued that the Atlantic Alliance could survive as a binding mutual defence pact as long as article 5 remains in place de jure and de facto even if NATO as an organisation embracing the parties to the Washington Treaty were to cease to exist, as was the case during the first two years. The point isn't purely academic since this is one of several possible outcomes in the long run.

A second assumption involves timeframes, with mid-2030s as the basic horizon. The revised Russian Constitution makes it legally possible for the current leader to serve until 2036. Similarly, the Chinese president refers to the mid-2030s as an operational horizon.[6] Both men will be in their early eighties during the mid-2030s.[7] This circa-fifteen-year horizon has the advantage of considering the issue at hand with a reasonably high probability that today's people, institutions, and indeed defence dispositions and weapon systems will still be in place or emerging at the time of writing.

Therefore, a third assumption is that during this period, the United States will remain a constitutional democracy, the European Union will not have become a single state, Russia will not have become a satisfied status quo power, the Chinese Communist party will still be in power in Beijing, India will pursue variations of its strategic *Sonderweg* as a federal state, and Britain will not have returned to the European Union (EU). However, some wild cards may occur during the current decade: they will be briefly discussed in conclusion.

Finally, the words "Europe" and "European" will be used in a geographical manner; they designate neither the EU as such nor the European members of NATO: in each of these cases, the words "EU" or "NATO" will be used.

The "Tilt" and Transatlantic Interests

The pivot to Asia affects the American and European interest on different timelines. For the United States, the Indo-Pacific and its Chinese challenger are a here-and-now problem, no less so than the problems created inter alia by Russia's role in the European and Mediterranean theatres. Although the invasion of Ukraine has predated a possible Chinese grab for Taiwan, both belong to the 2020s strategic map, and in Washington, talk about one readily leads to the other.

Furthermore, China already carries more weight than Russia in nearly all measures of power: three times Russia's defence expenditure, five times its nominal gross domestic product (GDP), ten times its population, and seven times its foreign trade.[8] Russia's primacy as an energy producer remains but it's a wasting asset as the world moves to carbon neutrality, independently of the West's attempts to restrict Russia's access to the global market for hydro-carbons. Russia's ranking as the sole nuclear strategic superpower alongside the United States is also eroding as China's nuclear holdings are surging from less than 300 warheads at the beginning of this decade—a minimal deter-rent rather like that of France–to a possible 1,000 by 2030, within reach of the New Strategic Arms Reduction Treaty (New START) ceiling of 1,550 operational strategic nuclear warheads for Russia as for the United States: the nuclear duopoly will be no more, which in itself will downgrade Rus-sia's status as the other nuclear giant in America's eyes.[9] All of the above justify the American pivot to Asia and will reinforce it with the passing of time.

For Europe, space and time function differently. Geographically and mil-itarily Russia is next door: its attempts to roll back the post–Cold War European security order, its empire-rebuilding policy, and the wars of inva-sion against its neighbours are acutely present. By the same measures, China is far away. Even as its commercial prowess, its technological progress and plundering, and its assaults on the rules-based international order affect Europe, China remains an alien rather than a live-in threat of the Russian variety. It is difficult to imagine that the Europeans would have, of their own volition, treated the 5G issue primarily as a strategic issue in the absence of American pressure: indeed, the United Kingdom decided to cut a deal with Huawei in December 2019; it was only after American intimations that this could have consequences for the future of the Five Eyes Agreement that this accord was jettisoned. For the United States, the fate of 5G was an immediate strategic concern; for the Europeans it was less obviously so. They eventually converged, but this was through deliberate efforts, not as a result of default settings.

In a nutshell, seen from Europe, Russia is today's storm, whereas China is like climate change: the latter is something to be taken seriously but as different in policy-making terms as deciding which weapons to deliver to Ukraine next week is to the setting of EU aims for carbon neutrality.

Even if there were a full and fundamental identity of interest between the United States and Europe on strategic goals vis-à-vis the Indo-Pacific region, this difference of temporalities will call for careful and deliberate management, with the Australia, United Kingdom, and United States (AUKUS) affair being a case in point of what can happen when this requirement is ignored (details below).

Furthermore, interests are not all spontaneously convergent. The United States has the dollar and remains the pivot of the global financial system set up at the end of World War II. The EU's euro isn't the full equivalent of the dollar. While the euro has carved a big niche as a reserve currency at some 21% in 2020, the EU can, and sometimes is, as much a victim of the dollar's seignorage and US monetary preponderance as any third-rate dictatorship, notably through secondary sanctions.[10] This need not be a strategic showstopper as we have seen vis-à-vis Iran in 2012–2015 or Russia today: but here again, efforts are called for. When China set up the Asian Infrastructure Investment Bank in 2016, the United Kingdom and the continental Europeans were quicker to pick up Beijing's offer than to heed America's admonitions.

The United States and the EU are also competitors in terms of trade with China. The United States tends to underscore the EU's heavy dependence on the Chinese market. China is Germany's second-largest non-EU export market, narrowly outranked only by the United States.[11] Given the export-driven nature of the German economy, this is not without potential political consequences. Chancellor Merkel's visits to Beijing emphasised trade more than they highlighted human rights issues. Nor were economic issues forgotten during Chancellor Scholz's visit to China in November 2022, against the backdrop of the war in Ukraine.

Although the EU imports more from China than the United States does, this was a difference of degree, not of nature, with $626 billion and $523 billion, respectively; furthermore, during the previous year, the United States imported more than the EU. A similar situation applies to EU and US exports to China, with $230 billion and $196 billion, respectively, in 2022. The contrasts between the United States and the EU vis-à-vis the Chinese market are not as stark as they are sometimes made to be, and they share the same complaints vis-à-vis China's limited respect for the rule of law and predatory approach to foreign investment in China. When it comes to China, trade issues can, and sometimes do, federate the United States and the EU.

The same applies to information technology, albeit with a twist. Europe, like the United States, has substantial complaints vis-à-vis China's techno-looting and scant respect for intellectual property rights. But the EU has been no less, and often even more, upset by the lax attitude of US tech titans vis-à-vis privacy rights in the EU's single market, prompting the EU to issue the general directive on privacy rights. Attitudes can and do change, as is evidenced by the creation in 2021 of the EU-US Trade and Technology Council (with China), but it takes hard, uphill work.

These difficulties and others are made harder to deal with not simply because of the differing temporal horizons, but also by the differences of political and organisational culture. Many of the key "battlefields" of the rivalry or confrontation with China lie in areas that in most of Europe are handled by the EU's institutions, such as external trade broadly defined, data standards, intellectual property rights rules, and legal and technical norms, and the trend over time is to broaden the scope of issues thus covered, including financial compliance issues for instance. Norm setting and monitoring of implementation are long-term and managerial tasks, not operational ones. This lies in some contrast with US executive agencies, such as the Department of Treasury. The US familiarity and use of the logic of power stand in some contrast to the slow deliberations of the European normative empire.

These differences should not be overstated: the European Central Bank can be very quick on its feet, and the European Commission has begun to acquire experience and a taste for operational tasks, notably when it was charged with devising and implementing an EU-wide COVID vaccine strategy. The EU may be moving from the habits of influence to the requirements of power.

What is clear, however, above and beyond these contrasts, is that the main arenas for dealing in a US-European mode with the Tilt aren't currently handled by NATO. This is the case for the EU-dominated areas just mentioned, but it also applies to politico-strategic affairs. For the United States, United States Indo-Pacific Command (USINDOPACOM) is the relevant theatre command, not United States European Command (USEUCOM), and by extension therefore not NATO. Military interoperability between the United States and its European and Canadian allies is produced in the NATO framework, not via INDOPACOM (nor Central Command (CENTCOM)): indeed, this has posed some problems in non-EUCOM/ United States Africa Command (AFRICOM) war zones such as Afghanistan, with US forces under EUCOM sharing more interoperability with their European colleagues than with their CENTCOM compatriots.

More generally, political and strategic consultation between the United States and the Europeans with matters relating to Indo-pacific (INDOPAC) is not just, nor even principally, channelled by NATO: "minilats" or bilats are much in favour in Washington and Honolulu.

Those European states that are directly engaged in military terms in the Indo-Pacific naturally favour those formats that are used by the countries of the regions, such as bilaterals (France-India, France-Japan, United Kingdom–Japan, United Kingdom–Republic of Korea), as well as those involving the United States (the Asian Quad, AUKUS). NATO isn't absent, with its links with Australia (a so-called NATO equal opportunity partner). It has been building links with INDOPACOM, and the North Atlantic Council does discuss China-related issues. But it would be wrong today to state that NATO has become pivotal to INDOPACOM or vice versa.

Avenues for change are being cleared, both by external events, as China looms larger and closer as a menace to the European set of interests, and through deliberate efforts by the Europeans to craft Indo-Pacific strategies (or policies vying to be seen as strategies). France (in 2018), the United Kingdom through its 2021 "Integrated Review," and Germany (in 2020) have done so, as has the EU with its 2021 "EU Strategy for Cooperation in the Indo-Pacific."[12] It remains to be seen where these avenues will lead. None of them have posited a substantial role for NATO as part of the corresponding visions and policy recommendations. However, there is also no obvious incompatibility with NATO's current tasks or potential future endeavours.

Policy Options

Five possible policy paths will be outlined here, with varying impacts on the future of NATO and its article 5 commitments. These options are presented in their starkest form: for instance, "division of labour" is meant to mean in strategic terms that the United States moves out of Europe and the Europeans keep out of the Indo-Pacific, not merely "fewer GIs in Europe." Although these options are sometimes quite different or even opposed, there are also areas of overlap: reality, as is most often the case, usually doesn't stick to one chosen scenario.

Equidistance

Until the last years of the last decade, Europe was largely following a de facto policy of not choosing between the United States and China. The United States since President Obama's speech in Canberra in 2011 was viewing China primarily as a rising strategic peer competitor, while Europe over-all tended to consider China mainly as a larger version of Japan, albeit one freighted with some unpleasant human rights problems. This "not choos-ing" policy was most clearly the case for the Central and Southeast European members of the China-centric sixteen plus one (subsequently seventeen plus one) format set up in 2012 in Budapest: fourteen members of this body also belong to NATO.[13] Initially, they had no difficulty in working *pari passu* with China and the United States, albeit on different agendas—or so it was until the United States began to press them to choose, notably on 5G. Germany, until the last months of the Merkel era (2006–2021), emphasised *Wandel durch Handel* and saw no reason to have a strategic view of China, even as the latter began attempting to plunder local high-tech firms of strategic value. The same went, and to some extent still goes, for Italy. Even countries such as Britain and France that saw China as a strategically problematic actor, in the South China Sea or in the United Nations Security Council, did not connect this reality to the broader relationship with China: while British and French warships would exercise their navigational rights in the South China Sea, London struck its first 5G deal with Huawei in 2019.

This equidistance has waned because of increasingly arrogant and strate-gically charged Chinese misbehaviour, fuelled by China's handling or rather mishandling of the COVID pandemic, presented by Beijing as competition between decadent and inefficient democracies and a victorious communist-led Chinese system. China's political support of Russia in the preparation and the conduct of the invasion of Ukraine was even more important: it made clear to many Europeans that there was a direct link between the Rus-sian threat and the Chinese challenge. China's cause wasn't helped by its unceasing refusal to provide adequate data on the origins of the pandemic and by Beijing's disorderly exit from its anti-COVID measures, with serious human and still-extant economic damage.

In parallel, American pressure during and after the G5 decisions has led many European countries to take America's side versus China, forgoing potential Chinese investments or trading opportunities. Lithuania dropped out of the G17 format in 2021; after the Russian invasion of Ukraine, Estonia and Latvia also left the forum, followed by Italy, the most recent and the most consequential partner. Those European countries that feel particularly threatened by Russian revisionism have drawn the conclusion that links with China could not take equal status with relations with the American strategic guarantor. The United Kingdom and France, given their interests in the Indo-Pacific region, are subjected to the direct and growing threat posed by China and no longer need reminders that these challenges cannot be met without tighter cooperation with the United States.

The shift in European attitudes has not or not yet produced the same strategic consensus on China as the one that has emerged on a cross-party basis in the United States, but the general trend is for the time being going in that direction. The German coalition that came to power in December 2021 was a setback for the Merkelian approach, all the more so since it was looking more and more as if *Handel* was causing more *Wandel* in Germany than in China.

However, equidistance can regain vigour as a result of political change in Europe. Populist parties such as those prevailing in Hungary or Serbia are keen on playing both sides against the middle: China's vaccine strategy in both countries played on this temptation, and it met with some success until it became clear that Chinese vaccines were not quite as effective as the Western ones and were widely mistrusted by the Chinese population. Populism coming to power in larger countries would create massive disruption vis-à-vis the establishment of a US-compatible European consensus regarding China. If the United States were to assume that Europe were a spoiler rather than a partner with regard to China, there would necessarily be a negative impact on the level and content of America's NATO commitment.

Division of Labour

Managing a multilateral defence alliance is by definition a more complex task than acting alone. To establish something resembling a global NATO would be more complex still. During the Second World War, the European and the Pacific theatres of war were run essentially as two distinct ventures. This was most stark between the aggressor states: Germany and Italy and Japan had established a line of separation along the 70-degree longitude east line (roughly running near Karachi) with limited exchanges of intelligence and precious goods between the two theatres, plus a German U-Boot base in Malaya. Even the Western allies, who were militarily active in both the Atlantic and the Indo-Pacific, only shared efforts between the theatres at their margins, once the basic decision to beat Germany first had been made and fleshed in. A joint strategic and operational approach was all the more difficult in that the Soviet Union was a belligerent in Europe but not in the Pacific until the last week of the war. It was only in 1945 at the Yalta (February) and Potsdam (July) conferences that the main leaders coordinated strategic options covering the two theatres.

As we are now facing the Euro-centric challenge of Russian revisionism and the rise of the Indo-Pacific Chinese superpower, it is no less tempting to play it simple rather than complicated. In this regard, few things would appear to be simpler than decreeing that the United States will focus on the Indo-Pacific while the Europeans will be the prime mover in the Euro-Atlantic theatre. The temptation is all the stronger in that it already corresponds to the present reality in the Indo-Pacific, in which the Europeans have much less skin in the strategic game than the United States. For US force planners, such a division would concentrate on USINDOPACOM the ever-greater resources required to deal with the Chinese threat. Even under the Biden administration, this isn't an abstract consideration: when questioned in 2021, the US secretary of defence Lloyd Austin made it clear at the International Institute for Strategic Studies Fullerton Lecture that the United States wasn't calling for more European military involvement in the Indo-Pacific and would be more comfortable with a greater effort in the Euro-Atlantic area.[14]

The flip side is that this would also satisfy those Europeans who would be relieved at not being pressed into taking sides against China: in this respect, division of labour is compatible with equidistance. Although disturbing for those Europeans who feel the most immediately at risk from Russia, this division of labour could be politically tempting for those Europeans who consider strategic autonomy as an alternative to NATO rather than as companion to the United States' and NATO's lead role in Europe.

The Russian invasion of Ukraine has dealt a body blow to the division of labour option. It has made abundantly clear that the risk of war with Russia as a nuclear superpower cannot be met by the Europeans alone: only the United States can extend deterrence at that level of threat. It also made clear that America's prospects of deterring China from an invasion of Taiwan or other areas would be badly weakened if the United States was unable to successfully deal with the invasion of Ukraine by Russia, a country with a GDP smaller than Italy's.

This reality test also highlights the structural flaws of the division of labour approach. One is that it is incompatible with America's post–Pearl Harbor position as a global power: by opting out of its lead role in the Euro-Atlantic theatre, the United States would be reduced to the status of a regional power—no doubt still the world's most powerful country but no longer a global superpower. Harbingers of what this may mean have been present for about a decade in the Mediterranean–Middle Eastern theatre. By backing down from its self-ordained red-line commitment to use force in Syria in case of a chemical attack against the civilian population, the United States created a strategic vacuum from 2013 onwards. This was eventually filled by Russia and local powers. Presidents Trump and Biden confirmed the trend by refusing to take the lead against Iran and by acting to end "forever wars," culminating in the disorderly withdrawal from Kabul. These points are not meant to be critical (staying in Kabul would probably not have been a wise policy) but simply to display that the United States can cede the prime-mover role at its own convenience and has indeed done so in the broader Middle East.

The companion drawback of division of labour is that it leads the United States to approach the Chinese priority from a regional rather than a global vantage point. That this risk is real was spectacularly demonstrated by the manner in which the minilat known as AUKUS was sprung as a surprise to the EU in general and France in particular in September 2021. Here again, the point is not made critically: the creation of AUKUS is not in itself a bad idea, as is made clear by the positive reaction of America's Asian partners, such as Japan. Nor is it intrinsically wrong for Australia to gain greater access to key defence technologies: nuclear attack submarines, hypersonic missiles, and so forth.

The problem is that all of the above were discussed and decided without a proper interagency review on the US side, and therefore with little or no factoring in of their global rather than purely Indo-Pacific dimension. NATO as a body was not in the loop. Nor was France brought into the confidence of the AUKUS partners, despite having a vested interest in Australia's ongoing submarine procurement; more importantly, it also happens to have substantial interests in both the Indian and Pacific Oceans, with more than 9 million square kilometres of exclusive economic zone, 1.6 million inhabitants, and 8,300 military personnel.[15]

The lack of any prior consultation, compounded by egregious Australian diplomatic malpractice, created a severe crisis that came close to derailing the new EU-US Trade and Technology Council (see above), which had been scheduled to hold its first meeting within days of the AUKUS affair breaking out. Through prompt recognition by President Biden of the stakes involved—a recognition that came as close to a formal apology as can be expected of a superpower—and President Macron's wise decision to give the green light to the EU-US Trade and Technology Council's meeting, the crisis was brought under control. Although the breakdown in trust between France and Australia remains at the expense of their previously strong cooperation as Indo-Pacific partners, US-French and US-EU relations were repaired.

The episode remains an object lesson of what can and does occur when Asia is put in one box and Europe, in both its NATO and EU incarnations, is put in a separate one.

Division of labour doesn't pass the reality test.

It could nonetheless come back in a new form if political change in the United States were to lead to a return of Trumpian transnationalism, which in its extreme forms could mean a de facto withdrawal from NATO as a commitment and/or as an organisation. Another extreme form would be a pseudo-realpolitik US attempt to cut a deal with Russia at Europe's expense as a quid pro quo for Russia curtailing its strategic partnership with China. Academic versions of this approach have been put forward in recent years.[16] Here again, the invasion of Ukraine presumably shuts the conceptual and therefore the political door to this last contingency, at least under the current American administration.

Risk Sharing

Another approach is to organise Europe's cooperation with the United States on the Indo-Pacific region essentially around the notion of risk sharing, that is, by having the Europeans participate directly in the defence and the security of the region within and with the region itself. This would reinforce and put at the centre of Europe's Indo-Pacific strategy policies that are already implemented, either by nation-states individually or on an ad hoc coalition basis or via set-piece partnerships, both militarily and politically.

France and the United Kingdom have been engaging in freedom-of-navigation missions in the tension-ridden South China sea since at least 2016, sometimes joined by others such as Germany or exercising with local partners such as Australia. In the broader Indo-Pacific, France and Britain have their own bases, notably in Djibouti and in the United Arab Emirates for the former and Bahrein for the latter, with a more or less continuous naval or joint military presence, sometimes joined by other European navies. In addition, France has bases in its Indian Ocean and Pacific departments and territories, notably La Réunion, Nouméa, and Papeete. France and India have recurring set-piece as well as ad hoc exercises involving their respective territories and entertain a substantial strategic dialogue.

In effect, if conflict were to break out between China and the United States, America's allies could be readily drawn in, even if, as a share of Europe's defence effort, these assets represent a modest share of its manpower, equipment, and military budget. Until recently, in strategic terms, the protection of Europe's stake in the Indo-Pacific has been largely dependent on America's role as a strategic guarantor in the region and until recently on China's relatively low profile in both the Indian Ocean and the Pacific east of the first island chain extending along the East Asian coast from the Kuriles in the north to the Borneo by way of Japan, Taiwan, and the Philippines. In particular, Australia, New Zealand, and France didn't really need to worry about external threats to the South Pacific—an area that covers one-sixth of the world's surface.

With the rise of China and the growing overall importance of the Indo-Pacific, such a posture is being put in question. China is rapidly ramping up its presence in the region as elsewhere, from submarine cables across the Pacific to mining ambitions in New Caledonia to the New Silk Road infrastructure far and wide. China is even set to open a base in the Solomon Islands, at the risk of inviting parallels with the imperial Japanese invasion in 1942.

To maintain the same level of security as in the recent past, the Europeans have good reason to militarily and politically increase their strategic investment in the Indo-Pacific. Yet, on their own the Europeans are not up to the task of meeting the Chinese challenge, in a manner in which here too is reminiscent of the situation that prevailed with the rise of Japan in the late 1930s.

The United States was then and is today the only credible guarantor. To benefit fully from that guarantee, the Europeans have cause to display readiness to help defend the general interest, notably in the region's global commons—hence British or French ships including aircraft carriers or nuclear attack submarines sailing in the contested waters of the South and East China Seas. Such risk sharing may also be helpful in securing influence vis-à-vis American choices inside and outside of the region.

However, there are narrow limits to how far this may go.

The bottom line is that Europe cannot play a lead role in the Indo-Pacific, even as a number of European countries want to jack up their defence and political investment in the region. Europe's military priority will remain overdetermined by proximity, notably that of Russia; this doesn't include the Indo-Pacific as such. The United Kingdom's Integrated Review may spend more time discussing the Tilt than the EU, but the fact of the matter is that translating that into reality is as unlikely as it was on the eve of World War II, in the heyday of the British Empire.

Tomorrow, like today and yesterday, risk sharing leaves NATO on the sidelines, insofar as the geographical parameters of the Washington Treaty are abided by. It is indirectly that NATO may get involved, as partners may wish to consult about the impact that burden sharing in the Indo-Pacific may have on the article 5 allies to fulfil their commitments as a result of force drawdowns to Asia.

Euro-Atlantic Integration

The Russian invasion of Ukraine powerfully highlighted the actual and potential connections between the Euro-Atlantic and Indo-Pacific theatres and the impact of the Russian-Chinese strategic partnership that has evolved over the last twenty years or so.

This was the case during the march to war. Russia secured China's endorsement of a "friendship which has no limit" in a joint statement signed by Presidents Putin and Xi on the occasion of the Beijing Olympic Games on February 4, 2022. It is not yet clear that Russia had fully apprised China of the imminence and ambition of Russia's "special military operation," launched on February 24 and, if so, whether China simply took at face value the then-current expectation that the war would be decided within a matter of days, thus relieving China of the need to do more than acknowledging a fait accompli calling for few if any difficult choices for China. Nor is it apparent that China expressed worry about the recessive and inflationary consequences that the widely announced Western sanctions would have on the global economy in general and on Chinese growth and corporations by ricochet.

When war came, it didn't end in a few days. As it ground on, China was faced with hard-to-meet requests from the Kremlin: in a remarkable role reversal, Beijing was asked by Moscow to transfer weaponry to Russia, while the United States threatened Beijing with direct or third-party sanctions as Western measures against the Russian economy were put in place. Nor could China ignore the war's impact on the rise of commodity prices.

It became immediately apparent that the Russian invasion of Ukraine and Moscow's attempt to roll back the post–Cold War security order of more than a quarter of a century were not only a binary Russia-versus-the-Euro-Atlantic affair but also one involving China. Conversely, the Indo-Pacific pivot became an integral part of the Euro-Atlantic picture. For all concerned, the United States and Europe, Russia and China, a degree of de facto integration of strategies and policies became mandatory.

For the Euro-Atlantic West, this involves two basic dimensions. One is military-strategic and consists of treating the response to Russia's invasion of Ukraine as a contingency that isn't competing for priority status with the Tilt but as operating in synergy with the Indo-Pacific: the success or failure in beating back Russia is seen in Washington as elsewhere as having a bearing on America's ability to credibly deter or repel a Chinese offensive in the Indo-Pacific, notably against Taiwan.

The other dimension is geo-economic: the West's economic sanctions against Russia's ability to wage war against Ukraine and possibly others can hardly succeed if China is in a position to replace the West in terms of trade and technology transfers with Russia. The threat of secondary sanctions broadly defined against China thus became part and parcel of the US-led response against Russia's war of invasion.

In practice, this scenario has moved from the realm of the possible to the field of practical implementation. That this has been the case came as a strategic surprise for many, given the reasonably good progress made at the Geneva Summit in June 2021 between Biden and Putin on important issues such as strategic arms control. However, the reality is that within a few months, President Putin was overseeing the military buildup around Ukraine and planning the Russian draft treaties aiming to revise the European security order. Nor is it clear that China was expecting to find itself deeply drawn into the subsequent drama, having to choose between sustaining its partnership with Russia at the expense of its economic ties with the West or vice versa. All of this is happening at a time and under circumstances not of its own choosing, on the eve of a crucially important Communist Party Congress, and while the struggle against the COVID pandemic is locking down key swathes of Chinese society.

This unexpected interaction of the Russian war, the West's riposte, and China's conundrum was clearly not prepared ahead of time. In the West, it came about in an ad hoc but decisive manner, in the form of US leadership acting in systematic concert with its allies, first and primarily European, but eventually more broadly. What appeared to trigger it was initially less the eventual plight of Ukraine than Russian's bid in December 2021 to revise Europe's security order via a quasi-ultimatum. This generated a unanimous rejection by every single member of NATO and the EU—even Orban's Hungary—cemented by astute US leadership using every institution at hand: since massive sanctions were crafted to deter a Russian invasion of Ukraine, the Asian allies were inevitably drawn in. When deterrence failed and Russia began an all-out invasion of Ukraine, thus triggering the corresponding sanctions packages, the United States engaged in vigorous diplomacy with China.

All of this was done on the hoof, with little forethought about future management, if only because there was and still is little visibility of how Russia's imperial rampage in Ukraine will evolve and eventually end.

What is clear, however, is that the heavy lifting of sanctions is done via the United States acting bilaterally with its Asian allies and most portentously by the United States operating multilaterally via the EU, and the G7, whereas in this arena, NATO is for the time being involved in political and symbolic. terms.

Conversely, NATO is the prime mover when it comes to military matters, both in terms of adapting collective defence dispositions to the new circumstances and organising consultations between its members as well as the EU and in terms of arms transfer policies to Ukraine.

This de facto institutional configuration should be relatively easy to sustain in the longer run, which may last for a number of years, with a secure role for NATO, at least in the absence of an isolationist shift in the United States. What is still missing, and which could be set up, is a more systematic association of the Europeans, notably with the Asian Quad (United States, India, Australia, Japan), as the primary forum for consultations on security issues, broadly defined, in the Indo-Pacific. The Quad isn't a defence organisation but nor is it an all-purpose body such as the Association of Southeast Nations (ASEAN) or the EU. Nor is the Quad geostrategically neutral like ASEAN—the Quad is clearly positioned against China—but unlike AUKUS (both as it is today and as it may become if Japan were to join), it isn't beholden to the United States, as is demonstrated by India's presence and role in the Quad.

Therefore, a symmetry of forms should be found in terms of the association between the Europeans and the strategically like-minded countries of the Indo-Pacific. This can be done on the one hand by inviting Indo-Pacific powers to NATO meetings: this was done at the April 2022 meeting of NATO foreign ministers, with the participation of Japan, South Korea, Australia, and New Zealand, and may be repeated at a higher level at NATO's June 2022 Summit in Madrid, which will focus on China-related issues. From an exceptional event, this could become a recurring fixture. Symmetrically, select NATO members could either join the Quad or, barring full membership, participate in a number of its working groups, a formula sometimes referred to as Quad-X.

Such a choice would be fully compatible with the existence of assorted minilats (e.g., AUKUS) and "bilats," while also being compatible with existing EU-ASEAN consultative machinery, notably the Asia-Europe Meeting.

This flexible and non-provocative approach would also have the virtue of not attempting to deal with the Russian-China partnership as a set-piece alliance forming a single theatre. However, there are high-level suggestions that they should be viewed as such, and hence follows a brief examination of that option.[17]

Global NATO

The strategic partnership between Russia and China began to develop at the beginning of the century, with the creation of the Shanghai Cooperation Organization as its symbolic starting point. It has deepened over the years notwithstanding Russia's forceful support of what China terms "splittist" policies during the Russian wars against Georgia (2008) and Ukraine (2014 onwards). The secession of Abkhazia, South Ossetia, and the so-called People's Republics of Donetsk and Luhansk was all too reminiscent of what China is trying to prevent Taiwan from doing. Yet this has not prevented the steady progress of the Moscow-Beijing partnership, culminating in February 2022 with the joint statement affirming the limitless nature of the friendship between China and Russia.

This has not, or not yet, led to the establishment of a joint defence alliance: a war between Russia and Ukraine does not commit China to co-belligerence; thus, border clashes between China and India do not imply that Russia take sides with China. Indeed, India is one of Russia's closest diplomatic and defence-industrial partners.

In many ways, the situation is reminiscent of the Molotov-Ribbentrop pact between the Third Reich and the USSR between August 1939 and June 1941: a deep strategic partnership involving military cooperation, and division of labour in carving up territory from Finland to Romania, up to and including battlefield cooperation in the partition Poland. However, it stopped just short of forming a mutual defence pact.

Then as now, it was tempting for the Western allies to view these closely bound strategic partners as forming a single operational theatre. For instance, in early 1940, Britain and France came close to bombing the Soviet oilfields of Baku as a means to hamper Germany's oil imports. The Western allies also viewed the planned deployment of troops to Finland during the Winter War as part and parcel of preventive operations against German access to Swedish iron ore.

Cooler heads (to a limited extent) and, more decisively, events, in the form of Finland's suing for peace with the USSR in March 1940 and the German invasion of Western Europe in May 1940, prevented the emergence of a situation in which the West would have been at war simultaneously with both the Third Reich and the USSR.

This should serve as a warning against considering Russia and China as allies in a single theatre: adopting an integrated approach to the partnership, as discussed above, is one thing; treating it as a single strategic challenge would be quite another. Setting aside the lessons of World War II, strategic history more broadly is there to remind us that good strategy is about dividing one's actual or potential foes rather than about uniting them.

The "what if Russia and China conclude a defence pact?" question remains. A global NATO, folding into a single organisation the

Euro-Atlantic's multilateral NATO and the US-centric hub-and-spokes allies of the Pacific, could then become a strategically rational option. But rational doesn't mean reasonable. As the course of World War II after Pearl Harbor indicates (see above), the dictates of geography would suggest that different organisations for two regional theatres would make more sense. Arbitrage in terms of general priorities (e.g., the decision in 1941 to "do" Germany first) and policy guidelines (unconditional surrender, war crimes prosecution) went up to the top leadership level but did not mean the setting up of a global organisation to run the war.

Another global approach, that of organising an ideological-political coalition of democracies, has been put forward by President Biden. As a generic framework, this harkens back to both World War II and the Cold War: the Atlantic Charter and its translation in the form of FDR's "Four Freedoms" in 1941, and the "Free World" of the Cold War era.[18] These were politically important mobilising devices, but they didn't and couldn't serve as receptacles for strategic or operational purposes.

A Provisional Conclusion and Three Wild Cards

The invasion of Ukraine by Russia is shaping the answer to the question posed in this chapter. The war has reaffirmed the key role of NATO in the European and transatlantic security order, in a manner that is more than superficially akin to the Cold War era. We have had to resurrect the vocabulary of that period and relearn the grammar of escalation control. But its impact is not simply of a *Back to the Future* nature, to use the title of a Reagan-era movie. This conflict differs greatly from the Cold War era in which there was a sharp distinction between what belonged to the realm of kinetic warfare and what belonged to the long haul of containment by all other means. The current war is hot, it is multidimensional, and it calls on tools, such as massive sanctions and institutions such as the EU, which are wielded in close concert with those belonging to NATO's sphere of competence. The transatlantic operating system is being transformed as a consequence.

The war has also brought to the fore the strategic interaction between the Euro-Atlantic and the Indo-Pacific theatres in an active and practical manner, not simply as a gradually emerging concern to be managed politically. We actually have a real-world if still preliminary answer to the question posed: yes, NATO can survive the pivot to Asia. Not only is the West's success in Ukraine critical to survival of the post–Cold War security order in Europe, but also it is seen—and managed—as being of great relevance to the preservation of the post–Vietnam War security order in Asia-Pacific, and NATO plays a key role in this context.

We also have found out that this entails in practice a degree of integration between strategies and policies in the Atlantic and Indo-Pacific realms, rather than equidistance of Europe between the United States and China, strict geographical division of labour, or something resembling a "global NATO." This discovery is provisional and ad hoc, but the arguments in favour of it developing into a durable modus operandi are powerful.

But the war also reminds us that massive strategic disruption can and does happen suddenly, particularly when powerful underlying trends are at work, notably the rise of China and the unravelling of the post-1945 rules-based international order, processes sharpened by the traumatic consequences of the COVID pandemic. Therefore, our preliminary findings may well have to contend with what investors call "tail-risks": high-consequence nonlinear events. Three "wild cards" of this sort can be cited.

One is the return to power of an isolationist and transactionalist executive and legislative in the United States: this could lead to an outcome resembling an extreme form of our division of labour scenario, possibly morphing into an "equidistance" scenario. The existence of NATO as a transatlantic alliance including the extension of article 5 by US power would be open to question. Such a process could begin as early as January 2025 with the inauguration of Trump as president and the convening of the Congress elected in November 2022. Of course, such a process may not eventuate.

Another process could originate in Russia, as a result of a change in the Russian vertical of power. Speculation on the timing, form, and content of such an event is not a fruitful exercise at this stage: suffice it to say that change, which is both epochal and benign, of the sort that characterised the end of the Soviet empire is historically highly abnormal in human affairs generally, and in Russian governance in particular. Therefore, there is no preordained outcome to such turmoil, during which NATO would presumably serve as a prudent hedge.

Finally, and this has been an often-mentioned contingency during the Russian invasion, there is the possibility of an attempted seizure of Taiwan by China. Both US and Taiwanese defence planning institutions appear to consider that the mid-2020s would constitute the threshold beyond which such a challenge would become militarily feasible. In such a situation, the United States and some of its allies, such as Australia and Japan, may threaten and execute a forceful response. This would presumably mobilise the bulk of US warmaking potential, in which case a labour-sharing scenario vis-à-vis Europe could kick in; but this could well be one that would occur by common consent, with the United States continuing to be a full article 5 member of NATO if Russia were still a revisionist power operating in partnership with China. For Europe, common prudence is therefore to continue to increase its defence spending.

This also happens to be a recommendation suggested by all of the scenarios examined here, with or without wild cards, and the strategically logical course.

Notes

1. "Global Britain in a Competitive Age—The Integrated Review of Security, Defence, Development and Foreign Policy," in *The Indo-Pacific Tilt*, chap. 2.3, https://assets.publishing.service.gov.uk/media/60644e4bd3bf7f0c91eababd/Global_Britain_in_a_Competitive_Age-_the_Integrated_Review_of_Security__Defence__Development_and_Foreign_Policy.pdf.
2. ". . . an attack against one or more . . . shall be considered an attack against . . . all [and the Parties] will assist the Party . . . so attacked by taking forwith . . . such action as it deems necessary including the use of armed forces." https://www.nato.int.
3. Ibid., referring to the definition and scope of armed attack and consultation.
4. See https://www.cvce.eu on the origins of the Western European Union. https://www.cvce.eu/en/education/unit-content/-/unit/803b2430-7d1c-4e7b-9101-47415702fc8e/6d9db05c-1e8c-487a-a6bc-ff25cf1681e0
5. Ibid. The then-Algerian départements of France were covered by article 6 and by extension article 5.
6. Xi Jinping's report at the 19th Chinese Communist Party National Congress, October 17, 2017, https://www.chinadaily.com.cn/china/19thcpcnationalcongress/2017-11/04/content_34115212.htm.
7. Vladimir Putin's eighty-fifth birthday would fall on October 7, 2037, Xi Jinping's on June 15, 2038.
8. Author's estimates.
9. See New START entry, https://www.state.gov/new-start/.
10. See "Here's How Reserve Currencies Have Evolved," December 8 2021, https://www.visualcapitalist.com/cp/how-reserve-currencies-evolved-over-120-years/
11. German exports of goods in 2021 to the United States were $144.7 billion and to China were $123.7 billion. See "German Exports by Country," https://tradingeconomics.com/germany/exports-by-country.
12. Council conclusions on an EU Strategy for cooperation in the Indo-Pacific, Council of the European Union, 16. April, 2021. https://data.consilium.europa.eu.-doc/ST-7914-2021-INIT/en/pdf.
13. See Wikipedia entry "Cooperation between China and Central and Eastern European Countries." https://en.wikipedia.org/wiki/Cooperation_between_China_and_Central_and_Eastern_European_Countries
14. "Britain 'More Helpful' Close to Home than in Asia, Says US Defence Chief," July 27. 2021, https://www.ft.com/content/7fb26630-a96a-4dfd-935c-9a7acb074304 The content of the piece is less categorical than the title.

15. See "Zone économique exclusive française," https://www.geostrategia.fr; "Indopacifique," December 3, 2021, https://www.marianne.net.

16. Inter alia and to varying degrees: Graham T. Allison and Dmitri K. Simes, "A Sino-Russian Entente Again Threatens America," *Wall Street Journal*, January 29, 2019, https://www.wsj; Charles A. Kupchan, "The Right Way to Split China and Russia," *Foreign Affairs*, August 4, 2021, https://foreignaffairs.com; John J. Mearsheimer, "Bound to Fail," *International Security* 43, no. 4. 7–50 (Spring 2019).

17. Notably in "Transcript—'China Is Coming Closer to Us,' Jens Stoltenberg, NATO's Secretary-General," *Financial Times*, October 18, 2021, https://www.ft.com/content/cf8c6d06-ff81-42d5-a81e-c56f2b3533c2.

18. See FDR and the Four Freedoms speech, State of the Union address of January 6, 1941, https://www.archives.gov/milestone-documents/president-franklin-roosevelts-annual-message-to-congress

14

Will Europe Balance China?

Transatlantic Security Cooperation in an Era of Sino-American Rivalry

Stephen M. Walt

The United States and China will be intense competitors for many years to come. As several chapters in this volume make clear, these two states will be the most powerful actors in the international system by a considerable margin. As such, each will regard the other as its principal long-term rival and keep a watchful eye on what the other is doing. China and the United States also espouse fundamentally different political and economic models, and their views on digital governance, human rights, and the institutions that presently regulate global economics and politics are increasingly at odds. Moreover, their broad strategic goals are incompatible: China hopes to reduce or eliminate the US military presence in Asia, while the United States seeks to strengthen that presence and prevent China from becoming a "regional hegemon."[1]

The Biden administration has made no secret of its desire to enlist America's principal allies—and especially its fellow democracies—as active partners in this competition. But will Europe make a meaningful contribution to this effort? Can institutions originally created to defend the "North Atlantic area" adapt to a new strategic competition, one whose principal arena lies on the other side of the world? America's allies in Asia have for the most part welcomed US efforts to do more in the region and are increasing their own defence capabilities, but Europe's likely role in this emerging rivalry is far less clear.[2]

European attitudes toward China have hardened of late, but this chapter will argue that prospects for significant transatlantic security cooperation against China are modest. Although North Atlantic Treaty Organization (NATO) Secretary-General Jens Stoltenberg recently declared that "strengthening our collective defence . . . [is] also about how to address

Stephen M. Walt, *Will Europe Balance China?*. In: *Not Just Another Cold War*. Edited by: Bård Nikolas Vik Steen, Oxford University Press. © Oxford University Press (2025). DOI: 10.1093/9780197799932.003.0015 the rise of China," Europe is unlikely to develop the hard power needed to counter China, even in partnership with the United States.[3] Europe will not opt for strict neutrality (let alone align with Beijing), but neither will it make a direct and significant military contribution to a US-led effort to balance China's rising power in the Indo-Pacific region.

Europe will limit its direct role for several reasons. Some European states will be reluctant to jeopardize their economic ties to China, which has become a valuable economic partner in recent decades. Despite clear and important differences on human rights and growing concerns about China's long-term ambitions, most Europeans still do not see China as a major threat to their own security, especially compared to more pressing dangers. Moreover, Europe lacks the military capabilities needed to balance China and is unlikely to acquire them, especially given renewed concerns about Russia in the wake of the war in Ukraine. Europe's reluctance to actively balance China need not place undue strain on transatlantic relations, however, provided Europe facilitates US efforts to pivot to Asia by taking greater responsibility for its own defence. As Jo Inge Bekkevold suggests in his own chapter in this volume, the key is to negotiate a division of labour that ends Europe's current dependence on US protection but does not entail complete US disengagement.[4]

The remainder of this chapter is organized as follows. Because past behavior is an unreliable guide when balances of power are shifting, forecasting the future of transatlantic security cooperation requires us to rely on general theories of international politics.[5] Accordingly, I begin by briefly summarizing existing theories of alliance formation and security cooperation, drawing primarily on realist "balance-of-threat theory." Next, I apply the theory to Europe's security situation vis-à-vis China and argue that the level of threat that China poses will be insufficient to provoke a significant European response, either individually or collectively. Here I emphasize several obstacles: Europe's geographic distance from China (and the Indo-Pacific theatre), the evolving state of European public opinion, and the current state of European defence preparations. I also consider the other threats that Europe now faces—including the impact of the war in Ukraine—and conclude that these concerns will take precedence over any desire to balance China. I then examine several possible objections to my argument and identify developments that might lead to either more or less transatlantic cooperation than I expect. I conclude by sketching how the United States and Europe should address these new strategic circumstances. In addition to sharing intelligence and limiting the transfer of sensitive technology, the United States and its NATO allies should negotiate a new division of labour, one where Europe gradually takes more responsibility for its own security, thereby allowing the United States to focus more resources on maintaining a favourable balance of power in Asia.

Why Do States Form Alliances?

In a world with no central authority that can protect states from each other, states pay close attention to the distribution of power and adjust their own positions and alignments in response to major shifts. According to traditional balance-of-power theory, states will mobilize their own resources (internal balancing) or form alliances with others (external balancing) to prevent stronger powers from dominating them. In this view, states ally and coordinate their security polices to protect themselves from rivals or coalitions whose superior resources appear dangerous.

For structural realists, balancing behaviour is solely a response to a stronger state's capabilities. If states cannot "pass the buck" and get someone else to contain a rising challenger, then balancing is the preferred response. It might appear tempting to "bandwagon" with a more powerful state—either to avoid a clash or to profit from its largesse—but this approach is risky because it requires trusting in the stronger power's continued benevolence. The safer course is to join with states that cannot dominate their partners, to avoid being dominated by states that can.[6]

Balance-of-power theory is clear and parsimonious, but it does not tell the whole story. Logically, powerful states might join forces against a weaker rival if the latter seems more dangerous for other reasons. Empirically, balance-of-*power* theory cannot explain why America's Cold War alliances were always significantly stronger than the coalition led by the Soviet Union (and became even more so over time), eventually exceeding the latter by comfortable margins in population, gross domestic product (GDP), size of armed forces, and annual defence spending.[7] Similarly, the ad hoc coalition that drove Iraq from Kuwait in the 1991 Gulf War outmatched Iraq by wide margins on every conceivable dimension of power. Nor can structural balance-of-power theory explain why balancing behaviour was limited at the beginning of the unipolar era, when the United States was vastly stronger than any other country.[8]

These anomalies can be resolved if we recognize that states ally against the foreign power that poses the greatest *threat* to their security or well-being, and that aggregate power is only one factor in their calculations. The level of threat is a function of power, offensive capabilities, geographic proximity, and perceived intentions. *Ceteris paribus*, powerful states with large, offensively oriented militaries are more threatening than states that have modest military capabilities or armed forces designed more for territorial defence than for power projection or conquest. Other things being equal, nearby states with lots of economic and military power are more threatening than those that are far away and thus more likely to prompt states in their neighbourhood to ally against them. A weaker state judged to have especially malign intentions might be seen as more threatening than a powerful state that appears to be strongly committed to the status quo; the former is more likely to trigger balancing behaviour than the latter.[9]

Several other features can also affect the propensity to ally and the ability to cooperate effectively to meet common dangers. States facing an internal challenge (an insurgency, military coup, nonviolent protests, etc.) may seek external support to deal with the problem, and governments in poor or weak states can sometimes be "bribed" into alignment by promises of economic or military assistance.[10] States with similar ideologies or domestic political systems are sometimes seen as more likely to ally with one another, although certain ideologies (such as Marxism-Leninism and pan-Arabism) proved to be more divisive than unifying.[11] States may also enter or remain within an alliance in order to influence or manage their alliance partners.[12]

Finally, alliances appear to be more effective and long-lived when they are made up of liberal states and highly institutionalized, where explicit norms or rules regulate alliance decision-making.[13]

China, the Balance of Threat, and Europe's Response

Although Chinese officials constantly stress their commitment to peaceful cooperation, it is not hard to understand why many countries now regard the country as a growing threat. China's aggregate power has risen dramatically over the past four decades, and it is translating its growing wealth into increasingly potent military capabilities. China's military forces are no longer designed primarily to defend mainland China from direct attack and can now be used to project power against some of its neighbours and eventually even farther afield. China has publicly abandoned its stated goal of "rising peacefully" and adopted a more nationalistic and confrontational approach to foreign affairs. Its revisionist actions in the South and East China Seas and along the Indo-Chinese border and President Xi Jinping's repeated declarations that China aims to become a (and possibly *the*) leading power of the twenty-first century have heightened concerns about China's long-term ambitions, especially among China's immediate neighbours.[14]

From the perspective of balance-of-threat theory, therefore, it is easy to explain why states in Asia are rearming, moving closer together, and seeking additional support from the United States, whose grand strategy has long emphasized containing potential regional hegemons. As Bård Steen correctly observes in his own contribution to this volume, "With China's economy catching up and US allies too weak to oppose Beijing alone, it is Asia and the Pacific, rather than Europe and the Atlantic, that are in the greatest need of America's stabilising hand."[15] But what about Europe? How are the different components of threat likely to affect Europe's response to China's emergence as a major global power?

Power

There is no question that European nations are increasingly aware of China's growing power. As the European Commission noted in 2019, in a memorandum highlighting the growing tensions in relations with Beijing: "China's economic power and political influence have grown with unprecedented scale and speed. . . . China can no longer be regarded as a developing country. It is a key global actor and leading technological power." For this reason, the European Union (EU) for the first time labelled China a "systemic rival promoting alternative models of governance."[16]

Yet China's rising power has also been a powerful source of attraction, primarily in the economic sphere. China is now the EU's largest trading partner and a vital export market: its share of Germany's total exports increased from a mere 1.6% in 2000 to more than 7% by 2018, and exports plus imports between the two countries totalled more than 253 billion euros in 2023.[17] Several European countries received Chinese investment as part of its signature Belt and Road Initiative, and an ambitious investment agreement was nearly completed before being suspended over European concerns over human rights conditions.[18]

By itself, in short, the growth of Chinese power has not provoked a powerful balancing impulse on the part of most (if not all) European powers. Until very recently, there was no European analogue to the Obama administration's efforts to "pivot" to Asia; indeed, European concerns that this move implied a pivot *away* from Europe eventually led the United States to replace this label with the more anodyne term "rebalancing." Despite concerns about Chinese trade practices, European states were wary of Donald Trump's trade war with China, although several eventually bowed to US pressure and agreed not to employ Huawei 5G technology in their domestic digital systems.[19] More recently, however, EU countries have begun to "derisk" their economies by reducing their dependence on China and moving to impose tariffs on heavily subsidized Chinese electric vehicles.[20]

Offensive Capabilities

States are more threatening when they acquire specific capabilities that can be used to threaten another country's territorial integrity or political stability. The Chinese military modernization program has increased its ability to threaten Taiwan, Japan, India, South Korea, and other countries in the Indo-Pacific region, and it poses a long-term challenge to US naval supremacy in the Pacific.[21] But as discussed in more detail below, these capabilities (including its expanding nuclear arsenal) do not present an immediate threat to Europe.

States also appear more threatening if they embody an ideology or political order that might be contagious, and whose spread would undermine the political stability of other countries, including those who may be some distance away. The possibility of political contagion made revolutionary France, Bolshevik Russia, and the Islamic Republic of Iran seem more dangerous to others, for example, and the resulting fears of contagion eventually led others to join forces to try to contain them.[22]

If China were actively promoting its model of state-led one-party capitalism in other countries and finding receptive audiences in Europe, European governments would almost certainly take steps to counter it. At present, however, this possibility seems remote. Although some European governments have drifted in authoritarian directions over the past decade or more, these impulses reflect a marriage of local nationalist and religious affinities and neither resemble the Chinese model nor exhibit much sympathy for it. We may safely conclude that this form of offensive power has not increased the threat Europeans perceive from China or inclined them to respond more vigorously to it.

Proximity

The most obvious obstacle to a major European effort to balance against China is geography. Historically, balancing coalitions among European states have formed to stop a single *European* power from dominating the others and establishing itself as a continental hegemon. The coalitions that defeated Napoleonic France and Wilhelmine and Nazi Germany, and the NATO alliance that eventually outlasted the Warsaw Pact illustrate this tendency perfectly. There is no threat of a European hegemon at present, however, and Chinese hegemony over Europe is even harder to imagine.

It is worth remembering that NATO's past efforts to address out-of-area contingencies have always been somewhat fraught. From the beginning, the alliance's raison d'être has always been to deter direct attacks on its members. Despite sometimes-intense disagreements over strategy, doctrine, or burden sharing, NATO has been remarkably successful in this mission.[23]

NATO's record outside the North Atlantic area is much less impressive, however. Some NATO members contributed forces to the United Nations–authorized "peace action" in Korea in 1950, but others did not. Most NATO members opposed the long US war in Indochina, and none of them sent troops to fight there. The United States actively worked to thwart the Anglo-French-Israeli attack on Egypt during the Suez Crisis in 1956, and the United States and its European allies disagreed frequently over other aspects of Middle East policy in subsequent years. NATO was bitterly divided during the Balkan Wars and nearly came unglued during the Kosovo War in 1999, and the NATO-led International Security Assistance Force in Afghanistan (and its successor, Operation Resolute Freedom) failed to achieve its stated mission. Great Britain and several Eastern European states backed the US invasion of Iraq in 2003, but France and Germany were openly opposed. The lesson is clear: once the focus shifts beyond the direct defence of Europe or North America, Washington and Brussels (or Paris, London, Berlin, Rome, etc.) do not always see eye to eye and are often unwilling to help each other.

Although China is becoming richer and more capable militarily—developments that are ringing loud alarm bells in Asia—it poses no threat whatsoever to the territorial integrity of any European state. China is not going to invade Europe, attack it with nuclear weapons, or sponsor terrorist attacks there. China's navy may be expanding rapidly, but it is not going to sail halfway around the world and blockade European shipping. From a purely military point of view, there is little for Europe to balance against.

These factors suggest that it would not be in Europe's interest to participate directly in a military confrontation with China. As French finance minister Bruno Le Maire said in 2021, "The United States wants to confront China. The European Union wants to engage China." French president Emmanuel Macron echoed this view, declaring that a "situation to join all together against China" would be "counterproductive." In the same spirit, former German chancellor Angela Merkel explicitly warned against the "building of blocs."[24]

Even today, most European countries remain reluctant to jeopardize their economic ties with China, creating a further disincentive to balance China militarily. As Sven Biscop observed in 2021, "Russia's annexation of Crimea and China's de facto annexation of much of the South China Sea are cases where real pushback is needed. But whereas the former has led to sanctions, the latter has been met with only a weakly worded EU declaration."[25] German chancellor Olaf Scholz and French president Emmanuel Macron visited China in 2022 and 2023, respectively (accompanied by trade delegations), and neither has echoed EU president Ursula von der Leyen's warning that "the Chinese Communist Party's clear goal is a systemic change of the international order with China at its centre."[26] European publics appear to agree; according to a 2023 survey by the European Council on Foreign Relations, 43% of Europeans see China as "a necessary partner—with which we must strategically cooperate," and only 11% see it as "an adversary—with which we are in conflict."[27]

Some European countries have significant interests in Asia: France has extensive maritime possessions, and more than a million citizens in the Pacific and the United Kingdom retain close ties with Commonwealth members Australia and New Zealand. Among other things, such ties help explain the British decision to participate in the so-called Australia, United Kingdom, and United States (AUKUS) agreement to provide Australia with advanced nuclear power submarines. Yet this agreement does not involve a commitment of British forces to Asia and will not affect the maritime balance of power for a decade or more.[28]

A careful reading of the EU's 2021 "Strategic Compass" also reveals a limited interest in the Asian balance of power. The report describes China as "a partner for cooperation, an economic competitor, and a strategic rival"; devotes less space to the Indo-Pacific than to other regions; does not even mention China when discussing the area; and recommends working more closely with the Association of Southeast Nations but says nothing about military cooperation with the United States in this context.[29] Bekkevold's chapter in this volume puts it well: "With the Indo-Pacific being the new nexus in international security affairs, Europe has moved from being in the centre of the previous bipolar system to occupy a more peripheral role in the new US-China bipolar rivalry."[30] Or as a distinguished group of European and American experts noted in 2021: "With regard to security, there is a high degree of asymmetry between the U.S., Canada, and European nations in terms of their security exposure in the Indo-Pacific and their respective capabilities."[31]

Equally important, Europe lacks the military capacity to affect the balance of power in Asia in any significant way. Even if the war in Ukraine and doubts about US reliability eventually lead to a substantial increase in European defence efforts, Europe's ground forces are irrelevant to any conflict involving China. Meanwhile, Europe's naval power has eroded, while the Chinese navy has expanded. European navies now devote their activities primarily to low-end missions (search and rescue, counterpiracy, disaster relief, halting human trafficking, etc.), and years of defence cuts have left them ill-prepared for high-intensity warfare. According to Pierre Morcos and Colin Wall, "As the prospect for high-intensity wars is growing amid the mounting strategic competition with China and Russia, European navies are under-equipped and under-prepared."[32] To date, European participation in Asian military exercises—including occasional participation in US-led FONOPS patrols in the South China Sea or the participation of six *Luftwaffe* Eurofighters and supporting aircraft in Australia's Pitch Black military exercises in September 2022—have been more symbolic than substantive. Germany sent the frigate *Bayern* on a six-month deployment to the Indo-Pacific in 2021 as a signal of its commitment to freedom of navigation in the region, but it is unlikely that Chinese officials were much daunted by the presence of a small (3,600-ton displacement), thirty-year-old, and lightly armed warship.[33] The EU's "Strategic Compass" highlights the proposed construction of a new European Patrol Class surface ship, but even a dozen of these small three-thousand-ton corvettes are not going to tip the maritime balance in Asia.

Most important of all, Europe faces more serious security challenges closer to home. The Russian invasion of Ukraine has galvanized Europe opinion and triggered a broad commitment to rearmament, reflecting the need to upgrade NATO's defensive and deterrent strength in its immediate vicinity. Assuming European rearmament efforts are sustained over the longer term, they will inevitably focus on strengthening the ground and air capabilities needed to deter Russia and not on creating the capacity to intervene in distant theatres of lesser strategic importance to Europe. As Bård Steen lays out clearly in his own contribution to this volume, it will be hard enough for Europe to translate its considerable economic and industrial potential into the military assets needed to defend Europe itself.[34] Sweden's and Finland's entry into NATO will help, but both states will undoubtedly concentrate on their neighbour to the east and not on the more populous and powerful country on the other side of Eurasia. Even robust rearmament efforts will leave few resources for distant theatres.

Europe will also be forced to devote considerable resources to the problem of migration. European states may have opened their borders to refugees from Ukraine, but they continue to limit migration from trouble spots in the Middle East, Central Asia, and Africa. Given demographic, economic, and climate-related trends in some of these regions, this problem will loom even larger in European calculations in the years ahead and will almost certainly take priority over dangers arising on the other side of the world.[35]

Intentions

China's rising power has gradually heightened European perceptions of threat, but changing assessments of Chinese intentions have had an even greater impact. The Chinese economy expanded very rapidly from 1980 to 2010, but Beijing's consistent emphasis on the need to "rise peacefully" and its efforts to resolve several outstanding territorial disputes dampened concerns about its growing economic strength. The widespread belief that a wealthier China would eventually embrace democracy and become a "responsible stakeholder" in the so-called liberal economic order diminished perceptions of threat even more.

Under Xi Jinping, however, China has abandoned its strategy of a "peaceful rise" and become far more assertive. It has pursued a more confrontational approach toward Taiwan (including various forms of military pressure), placed military forces on reclaimed islands in the South China Sea and made unilateral claims of sovereignty there, engaged in low-level military clashes with India along their Himalayan border, and adopted a highly confrontational approach (known as "wolf warrior" diplomacy) in many of its diplomatic exchanges. Beijing has also reacted harshly to even the slightest hint of foreign criticism, launching economic boycotts against key trading partners for very minor offenses.[36]

These actions have affected European perceptions of China dramatically. Twenty years ago, European attitudes toward China were mostly positive; however, the share of the population with an "unfavourable" view of China reached 73% in Spain, 85% in Sweden, 70% in France, and 71% in Germany in 2020.[37] China's mishandling of the initial coronavirus outbreak contributed to this worsening image as well.[38]

Similarly, Chinese threats against Taiwan prompted the European Parliament to back a resolution calling for stronger ties with the island nation, which it identified as "a partner and a democratic ally." A formal EU delegation visited Taiwan shortly thereafter and the head of the delegation told Taiwanese president Tsai Ing-Wen that "we are standing with you."[39] Well-documented reports of Chinese human rights abuses—and especially efforts to eradicate Uighur culture through mass "re-education" camps—triggered a sharp response in Europe and led the EU to suspend a major investment agreement in May 2021.[40]

Until the invasion of Ukraine, however, there was little sign that these deteriorating perceptions would lead Europe to join the United States in an active effort to balance Chinese power. A 2019 European Council on Foreign Relations survey found that "in conflicts between the US and either China or Russia, [European voters] have a clear preference for the EU to remain neutral, pursuing a middle way between competing great powers."[41] A 2021 poll conducted by the European Council on Foreign Relations found that two-thirds of Europeans believed a new cold war was underway between the United States and China (with a simple majority including Russia as well), but solid majorities rejected the idea that a new cold war was underway between their own country and either China or Russia.[42] As Fredric Grare and Manisha Reuter observe in their own survey of European attitudes: "When asked which partners in the [Indo-Pacific] region the EU should work with, [citizens of] only five countries name the U.S—the same numbers as those that select India."[43]

Although several European states have signalled a desire to play a more active military role in the Indo-Pacific region, the EU as a whole has not. In June 2021, for example, the European Commission sent the European Parliament and Council a new report outlining a "strategy for cooperation in the Indo-Pacific." Although the report begins by declaring that the region "is increasingly strategically significant for Europe," its recommendations focus almost entirely on promoting cooperation, defending the rule of law, preserving trade and investment opportunities, addressing climate change, and so forth. It devotes only two of its seventeen pages to issues of "security and defence," does not advocate increasing the EU's ability to act militarily in the region, and says only that it will "explore ways to ensure enhanced naval deployments . . . in the region."[44]

Germany's official report on its *Strategy on China* (2023) strikes a similar tone. While emphasizing the need to "change our approach to China" because "elements of rivalry and competition in our relations have increased," the report insists that cooperation remains "a fundamental element of Federal Government's Strategy on China," declares that Germany "is not seeking to decouple from China," and devotes a mere one and half pages to a discussion of "security policy" that contains no new policy initiatives. Such pronouncements hardly constitute a vigorous response.[45]

To be sure, the war in Ukraine has introduced new frictions into Sino-European relations. EU leaders were deeply disappointed by China's response during the EU-China summit meeting in April 2022, which featured sharp exchanges over Ukraine between European and Chinese officials and ended with no formal communique. Even so, the economic consequences of the war—and especially the costs of the sanctions imposed on Russia and the effort to reduce European reliance on Russian energy supplies—may inhibit Europe from taking overtly anti-Chinese positions. If European economies are struggling, jeopardizing relations with their largest trading partner will be even less appealing. European leaders are clearly troubled by China's refusal to condemn the Russian invasion, but whether they take tangible steps in response remains to be seen.

Summary

Taken as a whole, balance-of-threat theory suggests that transatlantic security cooperation vis-à-vis China will be modest. China's rising power and growing assertiveness is a direct challenge to US primacy and threatens the security of many countries in Asia. There is every reason to expect vigorous balancing behaviour within the region and growing cooperation between many Asian countries and the United States. But an ambitious and increasingly powerful China does not pose a severe or imminent threat to any European state, especially when compared to the dangers they face closer to home. Even if Europeans are willing to play a slightly more active role in the Indo-Pacific region—if only to keep Uncle Sam happy—they will remain reluctant to participate directly in a US-led effort to preserve its own hegemony in the region.[46]

Counterarguments

What developments might lead to greater transatlantic cooperation vis-à-vis China than I expect? One possibility is that a future US administration succeeds in rebuilding a powerful global alliance of democracies, and the shared desire to reverse the spread of authoritarianism unites both sides of the Atlantic in a common global crusade. In this scenario, common democratic values drive major strategic decisions and security commitments. If the main threat to liberal democracy is the rising power of China and the main arena of competition is in the Indo-Pacific region, then one could imagine a reinvigorated NATO and the EU focusing on these distant spheres and committing real resources to an effort to roll back an authoritarian tide. A division along ideological lines becomes somewhat more likely if the war in Ukraine solidifies the existing bonds between Moscow and Beijing.

Yet this possibility still seems remote. Shared values can solidify alliances formed to address a common threat, but states rarely make costly sacrifices for ideological reasons alone. In this regard, it is worth noting that democratic India, South Africa, and Brazil did not condemn Russia's invasion of Ukraine, and democratic Israel did not impose sanctions on Moscow. The illiberal trends in Poland, Hungary, Turkey, and elsewhere remind us that some members of the current transatlantic security community are only loosely committed to liberal values, and democratic institutions are under significant pressure in the United States itself. Moreover, an effective balancing coalition against China will by necessity include some states (e.g., India, Vietnam) whose commitment to liberal values is weak to non-existent. And if Donald Trump returns to the presidency in 2025, he is more likely to undermine democratic solidarity than to enhance it. For these reasons, pinning one's hopes for transatlantic solidarity against China on a resurgence of democratic solidarity seems overly optimistic.

A second possibility is that China continues to act in ways that lead more states to view it as a global threat.[47] If Beijing were to back Russia strongly over Ukraine, continue to exploit its market power to punish states that do business with Taiwan or offend other Chinese sensibilities, remain stubbornly insensitive to concerns about its treatment of minority populations, and use its growing military strength to press for significant changes in the territorial status quo in its own region (e.g., by attacking Taiwan), then one can imagine European states doing more to decouple their economies from China and directing more of their military efforts toward the China challenge. In this scenario, disagreements over digital standards and wariness toward dependence on Chinese technology (e.g., Huawei) will divide the internet and related digital spheres into distinct China-centric and Western-centric architectures. Globalization will continue to slow or possibly reverse, democracies and autocracies will line up primarily with like-minded partners, and the United States and its traditional European partners will focus their efforts on China because it is now seen as an aggressive superpower posing a fundamental threat to all.

Such a development cannot be ruled out, but it assumes that (1) China continues to rise economically and militarily, (2) China remains committed to an overly confrontational approach to diplomacy, (3) China makes little effort to exploit potential rifts within Europe and between Europe and the United States, and (4) illiberal forces in the West (such as Marine Le Pen's National Rally in France) are held in check. China has many ways to undermine a transatlantic coalition against it, and such efforts are more likely to succeed if the United States pressures its European allies to do more than they want. If China succeeds in uniting the West against it—and convincing Europeans to commit real resources to balancing China directly—Beijing will have only itself to blame.

A third possibility—by far the most likely—is that Europe will contribute to US efforts to contain China indirectly, primarily by limiting the transfer of advanced technology in peacetime and (possibly) imposing economic sanctions in the event of war. The Netherlands barred ASML from exporting its most sophisticated chip lithography machines to China in 2023, as part of a US-led effort to slow Chinese acquisition of advanced semiconductors, and the EU has recently adopted new regulations intended to "keep sensitive technology from falling into the hands of geopolitical rivals."[48] Whether Europe would sanction China in the event of a clash over Taiwan would in all likelihood depend on whether the attack was clearly unprovoked, and the disappointing impact of economic sanctions on Russia following its invasion of Ukraine is a reminder that this tool is rarely decisive. But even if Europe does not take on an active military role in countering China, it can aid US efforts in the economic realm.

Prescriptions

European views of China are hardening and there are signs of greater interest in the Indo-Pacific region, but neither the EU nor the European members of NATO are likely to make balancing China the central focus of their foreign or security policy. The United States is already focusing more effort and attention on countering China, but the European contribution to this effort will be comparatively modest. Balance-of-threat theory predicts that Europeans will focus primarily on dangers arising closer to home and will be reluctant to put their citizens' lives or future prosperity at risk by helping maintain the regional balance of power in Asia.[49] Europe cannot remain neutral as Sino-America rivalry heats up, however, because Americans will not continue to underwrite Europe's defence if it tries to sit on the sidelines. Europe will have to align with Washington—at least to some extent—or go it alone.

The ideal outcome would be a new transatlantic division of labour, where Europe gradually assumes much greater responsibility for its own security, thereby allowing the United States to shift resources and attention toward Asia.[50] Instead of being Europe's "first responder," the United States would be its "ally of last resort." Over a period of years (say, a decade), US forces committed to and/or deployed in Europe would gradually decline and European states would ramp up their own capabilities, including some of the areas (e.g., satellite reconnaissance or long-range transport aircraft) where they are almost totally dependent on the United States. The main focus, however, would be on developing the ground and air capabilities required to deter (and, if necessary, defeat) a future Russian invasion.

Such a shift would be facilitated if Washington abandoned its long-standing opposition to greater European "strategic autonomy" and actively encouraged such a development. As long-time Atlanticists Hans Binnendijk and Alexander Vershbow wrote in 2021, "The United States should drop its objections [to strategic autonomy], agree with its European allies on how to ensure that strategic autonomy results in greater European strategic responsibility, and then embed that agreement in both NATO's new strategic concept and the European Union's new strategic compass." They note further that a central goal "should be to reduce excessive European reliance on the United States to defend the European continent against Russia or any other peer competitor."[51] Or as a transatlantic "Reflection Group" convened by the Aspen Strategy Group concluded that same year, "With regard to defence [vis-à-vis China], a key role for European allies will be to backfill for US forces in Europe and adjacent areas."[52]

Contrary to François Heisbourg's claims in the previous chapter, the war in Ukraine strengthens the case for a new division of labour.[53] The war has been a wakeup call for Europeans who once believed that international norms, global institutions, economic interdependence, and US protection made large-scale war there impossible. Russia's actions have reminded them that hard power is still vitally important and that close economic ties create vulnerabilities along with benefits. President Biden's refusal to send US forces to fight in Ukraine or to impose a no-fly zone is also a subtle reminder that there are limits to how far the United States will go to defend European states, and the possibility that Donald Trump will win the US presidential election in 2024 suggests that US protection cannot be taken for granted. The lesson: if the nations of Europe do not want to be forever dependent on US security guarantees, they need to do more themselves.

The war has also exposed the limitations of Russian military power. Before the war, threat inflators in the West had issued dark warnings about Russia's supposed mastery of "hybrid warfare" and its ability to use a modernized military, sophisticated cyber-weapons, and "little green men" with stealth, speed, and effectiveness. Despite having months to plan and prepare, its initial invasion of a far weaker Ukraine was an embarrassing debacle. Russia's armed forces have shown themselves to be especially poor at conducting the type of high-mobility combined arms operations needed for a major offensive operation elsewhere in Europe.[54] Its battlefield performance improved significantly in 2023, but its recent territorial gains have been slow and extremely costly.[55] The obvious conclusion is that Russia is still much too weak to restore its former empire, let alone pose a strategic threat that the rest of Europe cannot possibly handle without a lot of American assistance.[56]

Some Western defence officials have recently warned that Russia's ability to recover and adapt should not be underestimated, suggesting that
"Russia will be an even greater threat to European security after Ukraine
than it was before."[57] Complacency is never advisable, of course, but such
views are overly pessimistic. Even if Moscow is eventually able to eke
out a pyrrhic "victory" in Ukraine, it will face formidable and mounting obstacles to a future effort to menace the rest of Europe. In addition to unfavourable demography, Russia has lost a sizeable percentage of
its most sophisticated military equipment and best-trained military manpower. Its economy has been damaged by Western sanctions and is likely
to shrink further over time. Educated Russian professionals have fled the
country in the wake of the invasion, and neither Europe nor the United
States will return to "business as usual" so long as Vladimir Putin rules in
Moscow. Isolating Russia economically will make it harder for its defence
industries to acquire the advanced semiconductors and other technologies that cutting-edge weaponry requires, crippling the Russian military
still further.[58] Over time, European efforts to reduce their dependence
on Russian oil and gas will deprive Moscow of future revenues and constrain its ability to rebuild its military forces once the fighting in Ukraine
is over.

Given time to prepare and the will to do so, Europe can handle a possible Russian threat on its own, with the United States standing in reserve.
NATO's European members have always had far greater power potential
than Russia: at least three times the population and more than ten times
the combined GDP. These same states also spend nearly four times more on
defence every year than Russia does. These funds could and should be spent
more efficiently, but now that Russia's true capabilities have been revealed,
confidence in Europe's capacity to handle its own security problems should
increase. The entry of a rearmed Sweden and Finland into NATO tips the
balance even more heavily in Europe's favour, even if the United States
gradually begins to play a smaller role.

In addition to negotiating a new transatlantic division of labour, Europe
and America should continue to share intelligence and coordinate their
diplomatic stances on climate, human rights, norms of territorial integrity,
weapons proliferation, digital standards, and the management of trade and
investment. They should also coordinate efforts to counter cyberthreats
from any source, to limit certain forms of technology transfer (and especially
those with direct military applications). Even if the United States is no longer

directly responsible for defending Europe, there are still many areas where the two sides of the Atlantic can and should strive for common ground.[59]

Conclusion

The war in Ukraine will not last forever. In the years ahead, powerful structural forces will inevitably lead the United States to devote greater attention to balancing China. In a world of finite resources, this shift will inevitably divert American attention (and effort) from NATO and Europe. Such a development could damage transatlantic security ties and maybe even trigger a decisive rupture, but this outcome is far from inevitable. To avoid it, the United States and its European partners should negotiate a new division of labour, with European states doing more to defend themselves and the United States doing more to balance China in the Indo-Pacific.

The new transatlantic bargain proposed here recognizes that the world has changed since NATO was founded, and that earlier visions do not apply to a world where America's principal rival is an Asian power and a major player in the global economy. That is as it should be. Alliances form in response to threats; as the level or source of threat changes, so should they. As I wrote a quarter-century ago, "Wise statecraft anticipates and exploits the tides of history, instead of engaging in a fruitless struggle against them."[60]

Notes

1. The logic of this tension is spelled out clearly in John J. Mearsheimer, *The Tragedy of Great Power Politics*, 2nd ed. (W. W. Norton & Co., 2014), chap. 10.
2. The emergence of the so-called Quad (United States, India, Japan, and Australia) is one manifestation of this trend, as is Japanese defense minister Nobuo Kishi's statement in June 2021 that the security of Taiwan was directly linked to Japan. See "Japan Sees China-Taiwan Friction as Threat to Its Security," *Japan Times*, June 21, 2001, https://www.japantimes.co.jp/news/2021/06/25/national/japan-taiwan-kishi/.
3. Quoted in Roula Khalaf and Henry Foy, "NATO to Expand Focus to Counter Rising China," *Financial Times*, October 21, 2021.
4. See Jo-Inge Bekkehold, "The Geography of Rimland and Heartland: Why the U.S.-China Rivalry Differs from the Cold War," this volume, pp. 237.
5. On the value of theory for analyzing the past and predicting the future, see John J. Mearsheimer and Stephen M. Walt, "Leaving Theory Behind: Why Simplistic Hypothesis Testing Is Bad for IR," *European Journal of International Relations*, 19(3), 427–57.
6. As Kenneth Waltz explains, "Secondary states, if they are free to choose, flock to the weaker side, for it is the stronger side that threatens them. On the weaker side, they are both more appreciated and safer, provided, of course, that the coalition they form achieves enough defensive or deterrent strength to dissuade adversaries from attacking." *Theory of International Politics* (Addison-Wesley, 1979), 127.
7. See Stephen M. Walt, *The Origins of Alliances* (Cornell University Press, 1987), chap. 9.

8. See Stephen M. Walt, "Keeping the World 'Off-Balance': Self-Restraint and U.S. Foreign Policy," in *America Unrivaled: The Future of the Balance of Power*, 121–54 ed. G. John Ikenberry (Cornell University Press, 2002); and Stephen M. Walt, "Alliances in a Unipolar World," *World Politics* 61, no. 1, 86–120 (January 2009).

9. See Walt, *The Origins of Alliances*, especially chaps. 2 and 5.

10. See Steven David, *Choosing Sides: Alignment and Realignment in the Third World* (John Hopkins University Press, 1991).

11. See Walt, *Origins of Alliances*, chaps. 6 and 7.

12. As Paul Schroeder points out, alliances are both "weapons of power" and "tools of great power management." See Paul W. Schroeder, "Alliances, 1815–1945: Weapons of Power and Tools of Management," in *Historical Dimensions of National Security Problems*, ed. Klaus Knorr (University of Kansas Press, 1976), 230–31. Robert Osgood argues that "next to accretion [of power], the most prominent function of alliances has been to restrain and control allies." See Robert Osgood, *Alliances in American Foreign Policy* (Johns Hopkins University Press, 1968), 22; see also Patricia Weitsman, *Dangerous Alliances: Proponents of Peace, Weapons of War* (Stanford University Press, 2004); and Jeremy Pressman, *Warring Friends: Alliance Restraint in International Politics* (Cornell University Press, 2008).

13. See Haftendorn et al., *Imperfect Unions: Security Institutions Over Time and Space*, Oxford University Press, 1999, 1st edition.; Thomas Risse-Kappen, *Cooperation among Democracies: The European Influence on U.S. Foreign Policy* (Princeton University Press, 1997); Robert B. McCalla, "NATO's Persistence after the Cold War," *International Organization* 50, no. 3. (1996): 445–75; and G. John Ikenberry, *After Victory: Institutions, Strategic Restraint, and the Rebuilding of Order after Major Wars* (Princeton University Press, 2000).

14. See Britta Petersen, "What Asia Thinks . . . about China's Rise," *Internationale Politik Quarterly*, September 30, 2021, https://ip-quarterly.com/en/what-asia-thinks-about-chinas-rise; and Joshua Kurlantzick, "Why China's Global Image Is Getting Worse," *In Brief*, Council on Foreign Relations, January 24, 2022, https://www.cfr.org/in-brief/why-chinas-global-image-getting-worse.

15. See Bård Nikolas Vik Steen, "Geotransition to the Pacific and Global Stability," this volume, p. 259.

16. See High Representative to the Commission for Foreign and Security Policy, "EU-China: A Strategic Outlook," Joint Communication to the European Parliament, European Council, and the Council, Strasbourg, March 12, 2019.

17. German exports to China declined in 2023, but it remained Germany's largest trading partner and slightly ahead of the United States. See Statistisches Bundesamt, "China Still Germany's Most Important Trading Partner in 2023, but by a Small Margin," press release no. 56, February 14, 2024, https://www.destatis.de/EN/Press/2024/02/PE24_056_51.html. German direct investment in China reached an all-time high that same year, however; see Tom Hancock, "German Direct Investment in China Rose to Record in 2023," Bloomberg News, February 16, 2024, https://www.bloomberg.com/news/articles/2024-02-16/german-direct-investment-in-china-rose-to-record-in-2023.

18. For example, the Chinese state-owned firm COSCO purchased a 67% ownership stake in the Greek port of Piraeus, and Hungary received $7.6 billion in Belt and Road Initiative investments in 2022. See Shin Watanabe, "China's COSCO Raises Stake to 67% in Top Greek Port Piraeus," Nikkei Asia, October 26, 2021, https://asia.nikkei.com/Business/Transportation/China-s-COSCO-raises-stake-in-top-Greek-port-Piraeus-to-67; and Christoph Nedopil Wang, "China Belt and Road Initiative Investment Report 2022" (Fudan University, Green Finance and Development Center, January 2023), https://greenfdc.org/china-belt-and-road-initiative-bri-investment-report-2022/. In a setback for the Belt and Road Initiative, in December 2023 Italy announced it would withdraw from the Belt and Road Initiative when the 2019 memorandum of understanding expired. See Ilaria Mazzocco and Andrea Leonard Palazzi, "Italy Withdraws from China's Belt and Road Initiative," Center for Strategic and International Studies, December 14, 2023, https://www.csis.org/analysis/italy-withdraws-chinas-belt-and-road-initiative.

19. See Anabel Gonzalez and Nicholas Veron, "EU Trade Policy amid the US-China Clash: Caught in the Crossfire?," Working Paper (Bruegel Institute, September 10, 2019), https://www.bruegel.org/wp-content/uploads/2019/09/WP-2019-07.pdf.

20. See Jorge Valero and Alberto Nardelli, "EU Moves toward Hitting China with Tariffs on EV Vehicles," *Bloomberg News*, March 6, 2024, https://www.bloomberg.com/news/articles/2024-03-06/eu-moves-toward-hitting-china-with-tariffs-on-electric-vehicles?embedded-checkout=true.

21. Chinese naval expansion has increased its ability to exert sea control in the South China and East China Seas, and its large short-, medium-, and intermediate-range missile force poses a growing threat to Japan, South Korea, India, and US military bases in Asia. See Missile Defense Project, "Missiles of China," Missile Threat, Center for Strategic and International Studies, June 14, 2018, https://missilethreat.csis.org/country/china/.

22. On the role of contagion fears in these cases, see Stephen M. Walt, *Revolution and War* (Cornell University Press, 1996).

23. Intra-alliance wrangling within NATO was sometimes intense, as debates of the proposed Multilateral Force, the doctrine of "flexible response," the Euromissile deployment, and burden sharing all attest.

24. Quoted in Liz Alderman and Roger Cohen, "Clear Differences Remain between France and U.S., French Minister Says," *New York Times*, October 11, 2021; Rym Momtaz, "Macron: EU Shouldn't Gang Up on China with US," *Politico*, February 4, 2021, https://perma.cc/TJ3Z-UDLV; and Stuart Lau and Laurenz Gehrke, "Merkel Sides with Xi on Avoiding Cold War Blocs," *Politico*, January 26, 2021, https://perma.cc/5K4U-2QHK.

25. Sven Biscop, "EU Strategy: Resolutely Moderate," in *The Future of European Strategy in a Changing Geopolitical Environment: Challenges and Prospects*, ed. Michiel Foulon and Jack Thompson (Hague Centre for Strategic Studies, 2021), 45.

26. "Speech by EU President Von der Leyen on EU-Chinese Relations," March 30, 2023, https://ec.europa.eu/commission/presscorner/detail/en/speech_23_2063.

27. See Jana Puglierin and Pawel Zerka, "Keeping America Close, Russia Down, and China Far Away: How Europeans Navigate a Competitive World," Policy Brief, European Council on Foreign Relations, June 2023, https://ecfr.eu/wp-content/uploads/2023/06/Keeping-America-close-Russia-down-and-China-far-away-How-Europeans-navigate-a-competitive-world-published.pdf.

28. See Chris Buckley, "Nuclear-Power Submarines for Australia? Maybe Not So Fast," *New York Times*, October 29, 2021, https://www.nytimes.com/2021/10/29/world/australia/nuclear-powered-submarines.html.

29. See Council of the European Union, "A Strategic Compass for Security and Defense," March 21, 2022, https://www.consilium.europa.eu/en/press/press-releases/2022/03/21/a-strategic-compass-for-a-stronger-eu-security-and-defence-in-the-next-decade/.

30. Bekkevold, "Geography of Heartland and Rimland," this volume, pp. 249.

31. *Mind the Gap: Report of the Distinguished Reflection Group on Transatlantic China Policy* (Aspen Strategy Group, July 2021), 10, https://www.aspeninstitute.org/wp-content/uploads/2021/07/210706_ReflectionGroupTransatlanticChinaPolicy_Report_Digital.pdf.

32. See Pierre Morcos and Colin Wall, "Are European Navies Ready for High Intensity Warfare?," *War on the Rocks*, January 31, 2022, https://warontherocks.com/2022/01/are-european-navies-ready-for-high-intensity-warfare/.

33. The *Bayern* deployed to the Indo-Pacific region for approximately six months. According to the German Ministry of Defense, "This voyage was also about demonstrating that Germany will stand by its international partners when it comes to securing the freedom of the sea routes and upholding international law in the region." See "Indo-Pacific Deployment 2021," https://www.bundeswehr.de/en/organization/navy/news/indo-pacific-deployment-2021.

34. See Steen, "Geotransition to the Pacific and Global Stability," this volume, pp. 256.

35. The twenty countries with the highest population growth rates are all located in sub-Saharan Africa, and their combined population is projected to increase by nearly 750 million people over the next thirty years. *Ecological Threat Register 2020* (Institute for Economics and Peace, 2020), 27, https://www.visionofhumanity.org/wp-content/uploads/2020/10/ETR_2020_web-1.pdf.

36. For example, when Australia called for an independent inquiry into the origins of the coronavirus, China banned imports of a variety of Australian products. It later published a doctored photograph of an Australian soldier supposedly holding a knife to the throat of an Afghan child and refused to apologize when its deception was exposed.

37. See "Unfavorable Views of China Reach Historic Highs in Many Countries," *Pew Global Attitudes Survey*, October 6, 2020, at https://www.pewresearch.org/global/2020/10/06/unfavorable-views-of-china-reach-historic-highs-in-many-countries/. See also Richard Q. Turcsanyi et al., "European Public Opinion on China in the Age of Covid 19," Real Institute El Cano, December 3, 2020, https://www.realinstitutoelcano.org/en/monographs/european-public-opinion-on-china-in-the-age-of-covid-19-differences-and-common-ground-across-the-continent/.

38. See Steven Lee Myers, "China, Seeking a Friend in Europe, Finds Rising Anger and Frustration," *New York Times*, September 17, 2020.

39. See Amy Qin and Steven Erlanger, "As Distrust with China Grows, Europe May Inch Closer to Taiwan," *New York Times*, November 10, 2021.

40. The deal had been negotiated for over seven years and was concluded with strong German backing during its presidency of the Council of the EU. It broke down after the EU Parliament sanctioned four Chinese officials and one entity over human rights issues in Xinjiang province, which led China to sanction ten EU officials (including four members of the EU Parliament) and four entities. See Euronews, "EU Suspends Efforts to Ratify Investment Deal with China," May 19, 2021, https://www.euronews.com/my-europe/2021/05/04/eu-suspends-efforts-to-ratify-controversial-investment-deal-with-china.

41. Susi Dennison, "Give the People What They Want: Popular Demand for a Strong European Foreign Policy," Policy Brief, European Council on Foreign Relations, September 10, 2019.

42. See Ivan Krastev and Mark Leonard, "What Europeans Think about the US-China Cold War," Policy Brief, European Council on Foreign Relations, September 2021, and Ivan Krastev and Mark Leonard, "Europeans Want to Stay Out of the New Cold War," *Foreign Policy*, September 22, 2021, https://foreignpolicy.com/2021/09/22/europeans-want-to-stay-out-of-the-new-cold-war/.

43. See Frederic Grare and Manisha Reuter, "Moving Closer: European Views of the Indo-Pacific," European Council on Foreign Relations, September 2021, 7–8, https://ecfr.eu/special/moving-closer-european-views-of-the-indo-pacific/.

44. European Commission, "The EU Strategy for Cooperation in the Indo Pacific," Joint Communication to the European Parliament and the Council, September 16, 2021, https://www.eeas.europa.eu/eeas/joint-communication-indo-pacific_en.

45. *Strategy on China of the Federal Republic of Germany* (Federal Foreign Office, 2023), https://www.auswaertiges-amt.de/blob/2608580/49d50fecc479304c3da2e2079c55e106/china-strategie-en-data.pdf.

46. Two European analysts who favor more active European efforts to balance China nonetheless caution that "no official in Paris or Berlin would publicly support the view that the goal of Indo-Pacific strategies is to build a 'balance of influence in the world that is maximally favorable to the United States, our allies and partners, and the interests and values we share,' as outlined by the White House in the newly released US Indo-Pacific Strategy." See Mathieu Duchatel and Roderick Kefferputz, "Balancing China in the Indo-Pacific: The Role of France and Germany," MERICS Brief, February 12, 2022, https://merics.org/de/kurzanalyse/balancing-china-indo-pacific-role-france-and-germany.

47. For evidence that this development is now occurring, see Chris Buckley and Keith Bradsher, "Faced with a Changed Europe, China Sticks to an Old Script," *New York Times*, April 15, 2002.

48. See Chemaine Lee, "Analysts See New EU Rules Hurting China Exports, Further Straining Ties," Voice of America, January 26, 2024, https://www.voanews.com/a/analysts-see-new-eu-rules-hurting-china-exports-further-straining-ties-/7459300.html.

49. It is revealing that a 2020 report advocating greater EU support for a "Free and Open Indo-Pacific" (FOIP) confined its proposals to economic measures and acknowledged the "structural constraints on the full military institutionalization of FOIP." See Paul Bacon, "Competition, Cooperation, and Connectivity: How the Indo-Pacific Can Shape Transatlantic Relations," in *Turning the Tide: How to Preserve Transatlantic Relations*, ed. Simona R. Soare (EU Institute of Security Studies, 2020), especially 101–2.

50. US secretary of defense Lloyd Austin made a similar suggestion during a visit to Singapore in July 2021, saying that Great Britain could best help the United States in Asia by doing more closer to home. In his words, "If for example, we focus a bit more here [in Asia], are there areas that the UK can be more helpful in other parts of the world?" Or as Eric Sayers, an advisor to the US Indo-Pacific Command, put it, "The best contribution European countries can make

to a global alliance strategy for deterring great powers is to prioritise their finite resources for Russia." See Kathrin Hille et al., "Britain 'More Helpful' Closer to Home than in Asia, says U.S. Defence Chief," *Financial Times*, July 27, 2021.

51. See Hans Binnendijk and Alexander Vershbow, "Needed: A Trans-Atlantic Agreement on European Strategic Autonomy," Defense News, October 10, 2021, https://www.defensenews.com/global/europe/2021/10/10/needed-a-transatlantic-agreement-on-european-strategic-autonomy/.

52. See *Mind the Gap*, 51, 55.

53. See François Heisbourg, "Can NATO Survive the Geostrategic Pivot to Asia?," this volume, pp. 290-291. The gap between Heisbourg's views and my own is not as great as it might appear, insofar as his version of the "division of labour" model assumes the United States abandons Europe and focuses entirely on Asia, whereas mine calls for NATO's members to negotiate and implement a distribution of burdens that would reduce the US role but not eliminate it completely.

54. See Michael Kofman and Rob Lee, "Not Built for Purpose: The Russian Military's Ill-Fated Force Design," *War on the Rocks*, June 2, 2022, https://warontherocks.com/2022/06/not-built-for-purpose-the-russian-militarys-ill-fated-force-design/.

55. Russia presently controls slightly less than 20% of Ukraine, but it has lost between 66,000 and 120,000 soldiers killed, more than 8,000 armored vehicles, and twenty naval vessels in the Black Sea since the war began in February 2022. Its army repelled a Ukrainian counteroffensive in the summer of 2023 and successfully seized Bakhmut and Avdika in early 2024, but these territorial gains came at a very high cost. See Mary Glantz, "Ukraine War Takes Toll on Russia," US Institute of Peace, March 11, 2024, https://www.usip.org/publications/2024/03/ukraine-war-takes-toll-russia.

56. On this point, see Stephen M. Walt, "Exactly How Helpless Is Europe?," *Foreign Policy*, May 21, 2021, https://foreignpolicy.com/2021/05/21/exactly-how-helpless-is-europe/; and Barry R. Posen, "Europe Can Defend Itself," *Survival* 62, no. 6, 7–34 (December 2020–January 2021).

57. See, for example, "Chief of the General Staff Speech at RUSI Land Warfare Conference," June 28, 2022, https://www.gov.uk/government/speeches/chief-the-general-staff-speech-at-rusi-land-warfare-conference.

58. See James Byrne et al., *Silicon Lifeline: Western Electronics at the Heart of Russia's War Machine* (Royal United Services Institute, August 2022), https://rusi.org/explore-our-research/publications/special-resources/silicon-lifeline-western-electronics-heart-russias-war-machine. Even if Russia continues to obtain some of these technologies clandestinely, to do so is inherently less efficient and its ability to field cutting-edge military capabilities will be reduced.

59. *Mind the Gap* contains an extensive list of diplomatic issues where transatlantic cooperation should be encouraged.

60. Stephen M. Walt, "The Ties That Fray: Why America and Europe Are Drifting Apart," *National Interest* 54, 3–11 (Winter 1998/1999).

VIII

THE HOT WAR

15

Assessing the Prospects for Armed Conflict in the Taiwan Strait

Scott L. Kastner

In March 2021 testimony to the US Senate Armed Services Committee, Commander of US Indo-Pacific Command Philip Davidson suggested that a Chinese attack against Taiwan was a danger that is "manifest during this decade, in fact in the next six years."[1] Davidson's assessment reflects what has become almost conventional wisdom in Washington: that the risk of war in the Taiwan Strait is increasing, and that Taiwan represents the most danger-ous potential flashpoint in the increasingly confrontational Sino-American relationship. Outside of Washington, some in the academic community like-wise argue that the chances of a cross-strait military conflict are rising.[2] China's harsh reaction to recent events, such as the 2022 Taiwan visit by then Speaker of the US House of Representatives Nancy Pelosi (which included extensive military exercises directed at the island), appears to confirm this general sentiment.

A war in the Taiwan Strait would be a catastrophe for both China and Tai-wan. Taiwan and its people are highly vulnerable to missile strikes from the People's Republic of China (PRC), and Taiwan's vibrant democracy would likely end were the island to suffer defeat and occupation. Even if Taiwan were to prevail, the economic toll would be enormous, in no small part because Taiwan's economy is heavily intertwined with mainland China's. A war could also impose tremendous costs on the PRC. Many PRC sol-diers would likely lose their lives, particularly if Beijing were to attempt a risky gambit to invade and occupy the island. Because the PRC's economy is highly integrated into global markets, a war would likely entail high eco-nomic costs, especially if it led to international sanctions against China. And, not least, a war risks escalating to a broader conflict with the United States.

Although these costs make a cross-strait war seem almost unimagin-able, the disastrous wars in Ukraine and Gaza serve as a reminder that the

Scott L. Kastner, *Assessing the Prospects for Armed Conflict in the Taiwan Strait*. In: *Not Just Another Cold War*. Edited by: Bård Nikolas Vik Steen, Oxford University Press. © Oxford University Press (2025).
DOI: 10.1093/9780197799932.003.0016

horrific costs of modern war do not make it obsolete—even among industrialized states. In the Taiwan Strait, the underlying sovereignty dispute is both intractable and highly salient in both Beijing and Taipei, and a host of structural and domestic political factors make it virtually impossible for either side to make credible long-term promises relating to that dispute. In turn, the Taiwan Strait will almost certainly remain a potential flashpoint, and the most volatile issue in what has become an increasingly adversarial US-China relationship. Yet war is not inevitable, and there are concrete things that leaders in Washington, Taipei, and Beijing can do to foster stability without walking away from their key interests in the dispute.

The remainder of this chapter proceeds as follows. The following section elaborates on the nature—and fundamental intractability—of the cross-strait sovereignty dispute. I then outline several stabilizing factors in the cross-strait relationship, focusing in particular on the high costs a conflict would entail. However, I next observe that wars nevertheless occur periodically despite being costly, and following existing literature I show how conflict might occur even in cases where war seems unimaginably costly. I then consider in greater detail how a Taiwan Strait conflict could occur. Finally, I discuss some implications arising from my analysis, emphasizing in particular that war is not an inevitable outcome. I also offer some specific policy recommendations that could help lower the risk of a cross-strait conflict.

The Persistent Intractability of the Cross-Strait Sovereignty Dispute

At issue in the Taiwan Strait is a sovereignty dispute that has persisted since the end of the Chinese Civil War. In the years after the 1949 Nationalist retreat to Taiwan, the dispute concerned which government—the newly formed PRC on the mainland or the Republic of China (ROC) on Taiwan—was the rightful government of China. Both governments viewed Taiwan as a part of China: the PRC viewed the island as Chinese territory that must be reunified with the rest of China, while the Nationalists saw the PRC government as illegitimate and hoped, ultimately, to re-establish ROC authority on the mainland.

The fundamentals of Beijing's position regarding Taiwan have remained largely unchanged over the past seven decades. The PRC continues to view itself as the sole legal government of China, to view Taiwan as a part of China, and to view formal unification as an important goal. Although Beijing has since the 1970s embraced a policy of "peaceful reunification" and has promised that Taiwan would retain a high level of autonomy if it agreed to reunify, the PRC still refuses to renounce the use of force against Taiwan. Indeed, Beijing explicitly threatens to go to war if Taiwan were to formally declare its independence from China, if it were to be occupied by foreign forces, or if it were to delay—indefinitely—negotiations over formal unification.

Taipei's approach to the sovereignty issue, on the other hand, has changed dramatically since 1949—changes that reflect the ROC's growing marginalization on the international stage, rapid economic development, and seismic domestic political shifts in Taiwan. The ROC faced several major diplomatic setbacks in the 1970s, including the loss of representation in the United Nations and the decision by Washington to recognize the PRC and sever formal ties with Taipei. Although the Nationalist government remained committed in principle to the goal of re-establishing ROC governance on mainland China, the goal was becoming increasingly (and obviously) unrealistic. Meanwhile, after decades of authoritarian rule and martial law, Taiwan in the 1980s and 1990s transitioned to an open, high-income, and democratic polity. In this new environment, the nature of the island's relationship with China—and, indeed, whether Taiwan should even be considered Chinese—became increasingly contested and the subject of open debate. By the 1990s, a major political party—the Democratic Progressive Party (DPP)—had embraced Taiwan independence as a goal (although the party later downplayed any need to formally declare independence), and ROC president Lee Teng-hui openly contested the idea of a "one China" principle, framing relations across the strait as "state-to-state, or at least special state-to-state." The cross-strait dispute, in short, increasingly centered not on which government is the rightful government of China, but on whether Taiwan should be considered a part of China in principle, and whether it should be formally unified with mainland China in the future.

The cross-strait relationship experienced a period of détente after Ma Ying-jeou of the Nationalist Party was elected Taiwan's president in 2008. Paving the way for improved relations was Ma's embrace of the "1992 consensus" concept, referring to an understanding that helped to serve as a basis for cross-strait dialogue in the early 1990s. Ma interpreted the concept to mean that each side of the Taiwan Strait has its own interpretation as to the meaning of "one China," which for Ma meant the ROC (even though its current geographical proximity covered only Taiwan, along with several smaller islands).[3] Ma's willingness to endorse a version of a one-China principle was enough to jump-start extensive cross-strait dialogue, resulting in numerous agreements that helped to normalize the bilateral economic relationship and improve cooperation in other functional areas. Yet bilateral dialogue skirted sensitive political issues, and by Ma's second term in office (2012–2016) the limits of détente became increasingly apparent: some of the economic agreements negotiated with Beijing were triggering backlash in Taiwan even as the PRC appeared to be growing frustrated with the lack of progress in the political arena. Relations worsened sharply after the DPP won the 2016 presidential election in a landslide. Although newly elected president Tsai Ing-wen signaled moderation in her approach to Beijing, she refused to endorse any version of a one-China principle. The PRC, in turn, ended cross-strait dialogue.

The divergence between Beijing and Taipei has continued to widen in recent years. Chinese president and Communist Party chief Xi Jinping has signaled repeatedly that he wishes to make progress on unification with Taiwan. Xi argued even during the Ma administration that the Taiwan issue could not be passed down "from generation to generation," and he reiterated this view in a 2019 speech.[4] He has also argued that national unification is a necessary part of what he terms the Chinese dream of national rejuvenation,[5] a dream that should be realized by 2049.[6] In Taiwan, on the other hand, support for unification with mainland China has continued to wane. Tracking polls suggest that fewer respondents than ever view unification, even over the long term, as a desirable outcome, while support for independence is at an all-time high. Meanwhile, a large majority of Taiwan's citizens have self-identified as solely Taiwanese—rather than as Chinese or both Chinese and Taiwanese—in recent years.[7] And although the Nationalist Party—which remains committed to the 1992 consensus—performed better in the 2024 presidential election than other recent national elections, it nevertheless has now lost three presidential races in a row. Meanwhile, PRC military activities near Taiwan, including military flights into Taiwan's air defense identification zone, have increased sharply over the past several years—especially since the Pelosi visit.[8]

In sum, at the root of recent tensions in the Taiwan Strait is a complex and dynamic dispute over Taiwan's sovereign status. It is today in some sense a territorial dispute, whether the PRC can rightfully claim Taiwan as part of its territory. But the dispute also revolves more fundamentally around Taiwan's political identity—the degree to which Taiwan's people and its leaders consider Taiwan to be Chinese and a part of China.[9] The underlying dispute has been intractable, with the PRC government remaining committed to unification even as a dwindling minority of Taiwanese citizens view unification with the PRC as an acceptable outcome. That intractability—combined with China's growing military power and Beijing's belief that military force is, in principle, a justifiable means to accomplish unification—makes the Taiwan Strait a potentially volatile flashpoint for armed conflict.

Stabilizing Factors

To be certain, several stabilizing factors remain in place that combine to help reduce the risk of war in the Taiwan Strait. Perhaps most important are the enormous costs that a cross-strait war would potentially generate. The war between Russia and Ukraine reminds us that wars—particularly in today's interconnected world—can impose large costs on all parties, and that the outcomes of wars are almost always clouded in uncertainty.

For Taiwan, the likely costs of a cross-strait war are obvious. Simply put, a war would be disastrous for the island. As one prominent analyst put it more than a decade ago, "Every citizen of Taiwan lives within seven minutes of destruction, and they know that."[10] Taiwan's vulnerability to PRC air and missile strikes has only grown since then.[11] In turn, although analysts disagree over whether the PRC has the capacity—or will soon possess the capacity—to invade and occupy Taiwan,[12] even a more limited coercive conflict meant to either punish Taiwan moves toward independence or compel moves toward unification would have the potential to have devastating consequences for Taiwan. Those costs, of course, would be much greater in the event of an actual invasion. Based on the PRC's willingness to crush opposition in other regions under its control, a successful occupation would, at a minimum, likely lead to the loss of Taiwan's democracy. Finally, Taiwan is highly dependent on economic ties with the PRC and is highly integrated into global markets; a war in the Taiwan Strait would certainly have a large effect on these ties and would likely be devastating to the Taiwan economy.[13]

For Beijing, the possible costs of a cross-strait war are more uncertain, but the downside risks are also very high. At a minimum, the PRC would face major economic disruptions in even a limited, coercive war where Beijing stops short of a full-scale invasion of Taiwan.[14] A war would likely disrupt the supply of critical components including most importantly microchips,[15] and the Ukraine conflict demonstrates the possibility of extensive multilateral sanctions directed against China should it attack Taiwan. A war in the Taiwan Strait would almost certainly add to a growing list of economic challenges for China.[16] Any attempt to invade and occupy Taiwan, moreover, would entail substantial risks for the PRC. Perhaps most important in this regard, the United States has taken a range of steps in recent years to signal stronger commitment to the island's security.[17] US intervention in a cross-strait war would greatly increase the likelihood that China would suffer considerable casualties and the destruction of military equipment, and would also make it more likely that any effort to invade Taiwan would fail. US intervention also raises the risk of escalation to a more general war against a nuclear-armed superpower. And the possibility of catastrophic failure in a war of unification carries its own secondary risks, including to the hold on power of any leader making the decision to launch such a war.

That a cross-strait war would entail considerable costs for both Taiwan and the PRC implies that both sides continue to have strong incentives to avoid such an outcome. And, indeed, both sides have continued to demonstrate a degree of pragmatism in their interactions. In Beijing, although policy toward Taiwan has hardened under Xi Jinping, the PRC nevertheless emphasizes a continued commitment in principle to peaceful unification, and Beijing has likewise avoided hard ultimatums on unification (such as demanding resolution by some certain date). PRC leaders also continue to view economic development as a central goal, which in turn likely remains an important deterrent to launching a war over Taiwan. In Taiwan, although the Tsai government has pursued a range of policies that have angered Beijing—including seeking improved security ties with the United States—the fact remains that Tsai has been much more cautious in her approach to cross-strait relations than her DPP predecessor, Chen Shui-bian. Tsai's newly elected successor, Lai Ching-te, appears likely to pursue a similar approach. And Taiwan's public also remains quite pragmatic on sovereignty issues. Although support for independence has grown in recent years, and although most Taiwan citizens no longer identify as Chinese, most Taiwanese continue to support the status quo, and a large majority of respondents typically say they oppose independence if it would lead to a cross-strait war.[18]

Wars Are Always Costly and Inefficient Outcomes

Although a war in the Taiwan Strait would entail enormous costs, and risks, for all parties involved, the same can unfortunately be said of most wars. As James Fearon puts it, the "central puzzle about war, and also the main reason we study it, is that wars are costly but nonetheless wars recur."[19] Fearon and other scholars working in the rationalist war literature have highlighted two broad causal mechanisms that sometimes lead to war despite war's inefficiency as a means to resolve disputes. First, information problems can lead to armed conflict under certain conditions; leaders might underestimate, for instance, the resolve of their adversaries, and those adversaries might have a difficult time making threats credible. Second, credible commitment problems can give rise to conflict. Simply put, leaders might not trust their adversaries to uphold bargains that all might in principle prefer to fighting a war.[20]

Consider, for instance, the current war in Ukraine. Vladimir Putin's 2022 decision to invade Ukraine has been—by all accounts—a disaster for both Russia and Ukraine. Ukraine, of course, has paid dearly for Putin's aggression. Tens of thousands of Ukrainian soldiers lost their lives in the first two years of the war, as have thousands of civilians. Some Ukrainian cities have been reduced to rubble, and estimates of the costs to rebuild Ukraine range from the hundreds of billions to over a trillion US dollars.[21] But the costs to Russia have also been staggering. One recent estimate suggests that more than three hundred thousand Russian soldiers have been killed or injured, and that direct costs of the war exceed US$200 billion. The overall damage to the Russian economy through the mid-2020s likely exceeds US$1 trillion.[22] Although factors outside the rationalist framework likely contributed to war in this case—including, for instance, Putin's personal isolation and grievances—it also appears that both information and credible commitment issues were major contributing factors. Russian leaders clearly underestimated Ukraine's resolve and ability to fight, overestimated the capabilities of Russia's own military, and appear to have underestimated the reaction the invasion would provoke in the West.[23] And a democratizing and modernizing Ukraine cannot credibly promise not to move ever closer to the West, even as Russia has almost no ability to make credible security assurances to neighboring countries for obvious reasons relating to Moscow's past behavior. In short, a set of serious information and credible commitment problems likely contributed to an inability of Ukraine and

Russia to resolve their differences peacefully and, ultimately, to a decision to invade that appears catastrophically bad in retrospect.

Information and credible commitment problems also loom large in the Taiwan Strait. In turn, because Taiwan is a high-stakes issue for Beijing, Taipei, and Washington, armed conflict remains a real possibility despite the stabilizing factors outlined in the previous section. To see how information and credible commitment problems potentially manifest in this case, it is important first to differentiate between two discrete conflict scenarios.

Taiwan Strait Conflict Scenarios

Earlier I described the underlying dispute in the Taiwan Strait as a disagreement over Taiwan's sovereign status: whether Taiwan is, or should be, a part of China. Further complicating matters, both Taiwan and the PRC hold a mix of status quo and revisionist goals with respect to Taiwan's sovereignty. In Taiwan, there is agreement across the political spectrum that unification with mainland China in the near term should be avoided (a status quo goal). But both major political parties also advocate for more international space for Taiwan (which can be interpreted as revisionist),[24] and some in Taiwan hold more expansive revisionist preferences—such as those advocating that Taiwan formalize its independence from China. Beijing, meanwhile, seeks to prevent movement toward Taiwan independence (a status quo goal) while also seeking unification with Taiwan (a clear revisionist goal). A Taiwan conflict, in turn, can arise in the context of either side pursuing its revisionist goals, which conflict with the status quo goals of the other side.[25]

In the first conflict scenario, a Taiwan government pursues goals that depart from the current status quo of a Taiwan that is diplomatically isolated, is blocked from participating in most international intergovernmental organizations, and enjoys de facto independence but has not tried to formalize this independence. A future Taiwan government might do so via dramatic policy choices, such as changing the official name of the country to omit "China," or formally declaring Taiwan to be an independent republic. But Taiwan's leaders sometimes pursue revisionist goals via more incremental, and often mostly symbolic, shifts in policy, rhetoric, and behavior. Past examples include Lee Teng-hui's 1999 description of cross-strait relations as "special state-to-state," which represented a clearer break from a one-China principle than prior statements had. Likewise, President Chen Shui-bian pursued what he termed a "rectification of names" campaign—which included renaming state entities with "China" in their names—to highlight Taiwan's distinctness from China. Chen also promoted a national referendum that advocated for Taiwan to apply for membership in international organizations under the name Taiwan (rather than the ROC or other pragmatic names used in the past such as Chinese Taipei). Taiwanese presidents have also taken high-profile trips abroad, as when Lee traveled to Cornell University in 1995 to give a speech that demanded a greater role in the world for Taiwan, or when Tsai Ing-wen traveled to the United States in 2018 and gave a speech—while technically on stopover to visit diplomatic allies in Central and South America—at the Reagan Library outside Los Angeles.

As noted earlier, the PRC views Taiwan independence as cause for war, and in 2005 the National People's Congress passed an anti-secession law warning that "major incidents entailing Taiwan's secession from China" would be met with "non-peaceful means and other necessary measures."[26] One plausible pathway to conflict, then, involves a Taiwan government that pursues independence or "major incidents" of independence, thereby triggering a PRC military response. Such a scenario would represent a deterrence failure by Beijing: war occurs in response to (or possibly in anticipation of, as I elaborate on below) Taiwanese actions that appear to be redefining the cross-strait status quo despite Beijing's warnings that such behavior could provoke a military response.

A second conflict scenario involves a PRC that acts to achieve its own highly revisionist preference of formal unification with Taiwan. Key PRC documents—including the 2000 white paper on Taiwan and the 2005 anti-secession law—describe indefinite delay on unification as a legitimate reason for the PRC to go to war, and Xi Jinping has (as noted earlier) indicated some impatience on the matter, for instance, in describing the Taiwan issue as something that should not be passed down from generation to generation. Although the PRC has long viewed unification with Taiwan as an important national goal, military analysts in the past tended to downplay the feasibility of a PRC military operation designed to compel Taiwan's unification (such as via invasion and occupation of the island). However, such a scenario is becoming more plausible as PRC military capabilities continue to improve rapidly, and some US analysts believe that the PRC might soon be able to win—at least with some reasonable probability—a war of unification with Taiwan.[27] In this second scenario, war occurs as a result of deterrence failure by Taipei and Washington, an inability to convince Beijing that the potential costs and risk of losing a war outweigh the possible gain of national unification.

Evaluating the Risks

Both conflict scenarios should in principle be avoidable, particularly in light of the stabilizing factors outlined earlier. Taiwanese leaders should have strong incentives to avoid crossing Beijing's bottom lines on sovereignty issues—the trigger for the first war scenario—because war, regardless of the ultimate outcome, would impose tremendous costs on Taiwan. Simply put, it is hard to imagine that a cross-strait war would leave Taiwan better off than the current status quo of de facto independence, even if Taiwan were ultimately to prevail in such a contest. Meanwhile, China's rapidly improving military capabilities would seem, on the surface at least, to make the second scenario more likely as Beijing becomes more confident in its ability to prevail in a war to unify Taiwan with the mainland. Yet, if China is likely to prevail in a war of unification, then it is reasonable to ask: why wouldn't Taiwan be willing to bargain with China? Shouldn't Taipei prefer to accommodate the PRC just enough that Beijing prefers peace over war? As with the war in Ukraine, however, both information and credible commitment problems complicate the search for peaceful solutions.

Taiwan Revisionism as a Source of Conflict

Consider first the conflict scenario involving revisionist behavior by Taiwan. During the 1990s and 2000s, analysts who worried about a cross–Taiwan Strait military conflict typically had this scenario in mind, particularly considering the policy and rhetoric—outlined earlier—of the Lee Teng-hui and Chen Shui-bian administrations. War seemed possible not because either president might deliberately provoke a military response from Beijing, but rather because they might underestimate PRC resolve to respond forcefully to their envelope pushing on sovereignty-related issues. Lee, for instance, was openly dismissive of PRC resolve—suggesting at one point that China's economy is "so unstable . . . where is the means to willy-nilly take action against Taiwan"—even as Chinese officials warned that he was "playing with fire" with his behavior and rhetoric.[28] Simply put, it was hard for external observers to discern where China's bottom lines on sovereignty issues actually resided: short, perhaps, of an actual declaration of independence, it wasn't clear what sorts of policies would be sufficiently revisionist to trigger a military response. And Beijing could not easily communicate this information credibly, since it had obvious incentives to overstate its resolve.

More recently, a conflict triggered by Taiwanese efforts to revise the cross-strait status quo has almost certainly become less likely. The PRC's rapidly improving military capabilities (including, in particular, its growing capacity to launch a devastating strike campaign against Taiwan), combined with Taiwan's extensive economic dependence on the mainland Chinese market, imply that Taiwan faces substantial and growing downside risks when it tests China's bottom lines on sovereignty issues. These risks were likely reflected in Tsai Ing-wen's relatively pragmatic approach to cross-strait relations.

Nevertheless, numerous trends in Taiwan and Taiwan-US relations remain quite worrisome from Beijing's perspective. These trends include the growth in Taiwan-centric identity and declining interest in unification among Taiwan's citizens noted earlier, recent poor performance of the Kuomintang in national elections, and deepening US-Taiwan security cooperation.[29] During the Chen Shui-bian administration, Thomas Christensen warned about the dangers of pessimism in Beijing regarding long-term trends in the Taiwan Strait: such pessimism could lead even a defensively minded PRC government to initiate military force, particularly if Beijing perceived a "closing window of opportunity" to prevent Taiwan independence.[30] In essence, armed conflict occurs because Chinese leaders fear future Taiwan revisionist behavior and believe that it is important to act sooner rather than later to stop it. At root of such a dynamic is a commitment problem: if Chinese leaders are pessimistic about long-term political trends in Taiwan, it can be difficult to assuage these concerns today since current leaders in Taiwan have limited influence over the future direction of public opinion in Taiwan and cannot commit future governments to pursue policies that are at odds with the wishes of the average Taiwan voter.

There are at least two reasons to think that a conflict rooted in the possibility of future Taiwan revisionist behavior remains relatively unlikely. First, it is unclear that the use of military force would alter the long-term trends that Beijing finds worrisome. While military displays short of war could serve as a signaling device, as a warning to the United States about the risks of ever-strengthening commitments to Taiwan and a warning to the Taiwan people about the dangers of rejecting cross-strait political integration, the actual use of force risks reinforcing the very trends Beijing finds concerning. Military conflict would likely strengthen Taiwanese nationalism (witness the Ukraine example) while reinforcing views in Washington that China poses a grave threat to US national security. The upshot would likely be increased—not decreased—US-Taiwan security cooperation. Second, although Beijing is clearly concerned about some trends in the Taiwan Strait, other factors—such as, most importantly, China's continued rise as a military power—give PRC leaders reason to think that time remains on China's side. Because use of military force in the near term risks undercutting these more favorable long-term trends—by, for instance, putting China's continued economic modernization at risk if conflict escalates—Beijing retains considerable incentive to remain cautious despite the presence of some, from Beijing's perspective, unfavorable trends in cross-strait relations.

Still, as Thomas Christensen's chapter in this volume makes clear, conflict rooted in Taiwan revisionism cannot be ruled out—particularly in light of an increasingly adversarial US-China relationship and a US domestic political environment that rewards hawkishness toward China. If, for instance, a future US administration were to dramatically upgrade the US-Taiwan relationship, as some prominent Republican politicians have advocated, it would likely lead to an even stronger PRC response than was seen in the aftermath of Nancy Pelosi's visit to Taiwan.

PRC Revisionism as a Source of Conflict

Whereas in the 1990s and 2000s analysts tended to have the revisionist Taiwan scenario in mind when thinking about the risks of cross-strait conflict, more recently the second scenario—of a revisionist PRC seeking to realize its goal of unification with Taiwan—has come to dominate thinking in this regard. At root of this change in thinking has been China's dramatic rise as a military power; in turn, many analysts believe that the PRC could have the capability sometime within the next decade to win a war of unification, a war that would most likely require the successful invasion and occupation of Taiwan. As someone who is not a military expert, I take an agnostic view concerning whether China is in fact likely to have such capability in the next several years, noting simply that strong arguments have been advanced on both sides of this debate.[31] The key point I wish to make in this section, rather, is that if we do reach a point where Chinese leaders believe that the PRC can win a war of unification at acceptable cost, daunting information and credible commitment problems would make it quite challenging to avoid such a war.

As noted earlier, war should be avoidable in principle even if PRC leaders are confident that China would prevail in a war of unification: both Taiwan and the PRC would presumably be better off from a peaceful bargain that involved some Taiwanese accommodation on sovereignty issues and that spared both sides the heavy costs of actually fighting a war. To get this accommodation, however, Beijing would need to convince Taiwan that it really is prepared to fight a war of unification if Taiwan were to demur. Doing so is likely to prove difficult, since Beijing has until now been willing to live in peace with the status quo of de facto Taiwan independence. In short, it is hard for Taiwan to discern whether Beijing really is prepared to fight a war of unification, and even a highly resolved Beijing—one that in fact is willing to launch such a war—is likely to find it challenging to communicate this resolve to Taiwan credibly.

Perhaps more fundamentally, even if this information problem is overcome and Taipei recognizes that China is in fact prepared to fight a war to unify Taiwan, two intertwined commitment problems would almost certainly complicate efforts to find a peaceful resolution. First, accommodating PRC demands by offering some sovereignty-related concessions (such as accepting a loose "one country, two systems" arrangement that left the island with extensive autonomy) would further undermine Taipei's future bargaining power vis-à-vis Beijing. Most importantly, US security commitments to Taiwan would weaken if the island appeared to be moving into Beijing's orbit. Washington, for instance, would likely end weapons sales to Taiwan if it appeared that Taipei was moving toward peaceful unification with the PRC. Taiwan, in turn, will likely remain reluctant to start down a path of accommodation, as such a path—by weakening Taipei's bargaining power— risks opening the door to ever greater PRC demands on the island.[32] Second, it is hard for Beijing to make credible promises concerning Taiwan's autonomy, because it has obvious motive to intervene in Taiwan domestic affairs if given the opportunity to do so. Just as PRC leaders view dissent elsewhere in China as a threat to Chinese Communist Party rule, they will likely view dissent in a postunification Taiwan as a threat.[33] Furthermore, there are no credible legal constraints that prevent PRC leaders from intervening in Taiwan domestic affairs if given the opportunity to do so. Indeed, Beijing has a long record of ignoring past promises of regional autonomy elsewhere in China.

Implications

In sum, the cross–Taiwan Strait relationship is characterized by a series of thorny information and credible commitment problems that could contribute to armed conflict. I have argued that, despite these problems, a war triggered by Taiwan revisionist behavior is relatively unlikely in today's world. For Taiwan, the downside risks of testing Beijing's bottom lines on sovereignty issues have become catastrophic; these risks, in turn, have led to increased caution in Taipei. For Beijing, even though there are reasons to be pessimistic about some long-term trends in the Taiwan Strait, it is unclear that military force would arrest those trends. Moreover, Beijing still has some reason to think that time remains on its side in any event. I have also suggested, however, that war scenarios grounded in PRC revisionism are becoming more worrisome. Simply put, due to difficult-to-resolve information and credible commitment problems, if we ever get to a point where PRC leaders believe a war of unification could be won at acceptable cost, it will be difficult to find peaceful bargains to avoid the war outcome.

This does not mean, though, that war is becoming inevitable. To the contrary, so long as PRC leaders believe that a war of unification could fail and that the probable costs of a conflict would be very high, they will likely remain deterred from pursuing such a course of action. Several policy implications follow from this basic point.

For the United States and Taiwan, successful deterrence will require a continued balancing act that aims to accomplish three things: raising the likely costs of conflict for China, increasing the benefits that the PRC reaps from peace, and reassuring Beijing that the maintenance of the status quo will not erode the prospects of long-term unification, thereby assuaging PRC concerns that time might not be on China's side in the dispute.[34] Concretely, this means taking steps to increase the credibility that the United States can intervene effectively in a cross-strait conflict—such as hardening Taiwan's self-defense capabilities (especially encouraging what some refer to as a "porcupine" strategy of relatively inexpensive capabilities that greatly increase the costs the PRC would face if it were to invade Taiwan), increasing and dispersing US forward deployments in the region, and increasing coordination with regional allies like Japan and the Philippines—while avoiding mostly symbolic actions that do little to improve deterrence but that harm US-China relations and that play into PRC fears about creeping Taiwan independence. For instance, a 2022 decision to delete from the US State Department webpage language drawn from the three joint US-China communiques (where the United States "acknowledges" the Chinese position that Taiwan is a part of China) and language that the United States "does not support" Taiwan independence (which has been US policy for decades) did little to enhance deterrence in the Taiwan Strait. But this change led to a strong reaction from the Chinese government and likely exacerbated fears in Beijing about the long-term implications of US-Taiwan security cooperation.[35] These sorts of policies should be avoided. Likewise, the White House should resist efforts to pursue widescale economic "decoupling" from China, as doing so both reduces the benefits that the PRC gains from the current peaceful status quo and reduces the likely costs that could be imposed on China ex post in the event of conflict.[36]

To be clear, finding the right balance between credible threats and credible assurances will always be difficult for the United States. Finding a balance between threats and assurances is inevitably fraught because strong assurances can undercut the credibility of threats and vice versa. Putting US troops on Taiwan, for instance, might dramatically increase the likelihood that the United States would intervene in a cross-strait conflict, but it would also undermine assurances that the United States could accept a future peaceful unification bargain. Rather than enhance deterrence, such a step might undercut it by convincing Beijing that it needs to act immediately to prevent Taiwan's permanent separation from China. Moreover, future US resolve to intervene in a Taiwan conflict, and to remain engaged in a protracted conflict, will always be clouded in some uncertainty, no matter the strength of stated US commitments. This reality is seen in past and present conflicts—Vietnam, Iraq, Afghanistan, and now Ukraine—where stated US resolve at the outset proved exaggerated as the costs of conflict, and domestic political opposition to continued US involvement, grew. The United States simply cannot make ironclad promises to Taiwan's defense, as any promises made today can be reconsidered by a future administration facing different circumstances. What Washington can do, however, is to make clear the logic of why it is in US interests that Taiwan not be forced—through coercion or brute force—into unification with the PRC, to maintain the capacity to intervene if the PRC does attempt such an outcome, but also to signal a willingness to accept a future unified China that occurs with the consent of the Taiwan people (even if such assurances themselves can never be ironclad).[37]

For Beijing, successful deterrence will also require a careful balance between threats to use military force in the event of efforts to formalize Taiwan's separation from China and reassurances that Beijing can live with Taiwan governments that are pragmatic and do not push the envelope on sovereignty issues. Yet Beijing pursued a more coercive approach—with more frequent and explicit brandishing of military capabilities—toward the Tsai Ing-wen government than it did toward the much more revisionist Chen Shui-bian administration. Doing so is potentially counterproductive, since Tsai is a relative moderate in a DPP that will likely remain a key—if not the key—party in Taiwan politics in the years ahead. Beijing's policies suggest to prospective DPP leaders that moderation in cross-strait policies doesn't pay, which could pave the way for more clearly revisionist politicians to lead the party in the future. Meanwhile, Beijing's coercive diplomacy could undercut even the Nationalist Party in Taiwan politics by underscoring the threat that the PRC poses to Taiwan—which in turn risks making a platform that emphasizes détente and accommodation appear dangerously naïve.

Conclusion

The Taiwan Strait remains a serious potential flashpoint for conflict, and the intractability of the sovereignty dispute means it is unlikely to be resolved anytime soon. As such, the goals of all three key parties—Washington, Beijing, and Taipei—should be pragmatic: avoiding armed conflict without sacrificing core interests at stake. In turn, all should come to an implicit understanding that any final resolution of the dispute will likely need to sit on the backburner for the foreseeable future.

Notes

1. "China Building Offensive, Aggressive Military, Top US Pacific Commander Says," CNN, March 10, 2021, https://www.cnn.com/2021/03/10/asia/us-pacific-commander-china-threat-intl-hnk-ml/index.html.

2. See, for instance, Oriana Skylar Mastro, "The Taiwan Temptation: Why Beijing Might Resort to Force," *Foreign Affairs* 100, no. 4 (2021): 58–67.
3. For a discussion of Ma's approach to one China and the 1992 consensus, see Richard C. Bush, *Uncharted Strait: The Future of China-Taiwan Relations* (Brookings, 2013), 21–22.
4. Richard C. Bush, "8 Key Things to Notice from Xi Jinping's New Year Speech on Taiwan," Brookings Institution, 2019, https://www.brookings.edu/articles/8-key-things-to-notice-from-xi-jinpings-new-year-speech-on-taiwan/.
5. Ibid.; Qiang Xin, "Having Much in Common? Changes and Continuity in China's Taiwan Policy," *Pacific Review* 34, no. 6 (2021): 926–45.
6. See, for example, Xi's 2017 speech to the Chinese Communist Party National Congress, available at http://www.xinhuanet.com/english/download/Xi_Jinping's_report_at_19th_CPC_National_Congress.pdf. Note that Xi, even in his 2019 speech noted above, has not publicized any explicit unification deadlines.
7. See polling data from the National Chengchi University Election Study Center, available at https://esc.nccu.edu.tw/eng/PageDoc?fid=7424.
8. See, for instance, "PLA Aircraft Again Surround Taiwan with US Intervention on Mind," *Global Times*, March 30, 2021, https://www.globaltimes.cn/page/202103/1219869.shtml.
9. On this point, see Thomas J. Christensen, "The Contemporary Security Dilemma," *Washington Quarterly* 25, no. 4 (2002): 7–21.
10. Mark Stokes, Testimony before the U.S.-China Economic and Security Review Commission, March 18, 2010.
11. Michael A. Hunzeker et al., *A Question of Time: Enhancing Taiwan's Conventional Deterrence Posture* (Schar School of Policy and Government, George Mason University, 2018), 51.
12. On the continued challenges the PRC would face in attempting an invasion of Taiwan, see Office of the Secretary of Defense, *Annual Report to Congress: Military and Security Developments Involving the People's Republic of China* (US Department of Defense, 2020), 114, https://media.defense.gov/2020/Sep/01/2002488689/-1/-1/1/2020-DOD-CHINA-MILITARY-POWER-REPORT-FINAL.PDF. On the PRC's growing capacity to launch an invasion and occupation, see, for example, Mastro, "Taiwan Temptation." For a systematic discussion of the People's Liberation Army's military threat toward Taiwan, see also Joel Wuthnow et al., eds., *Crossing the Strait: China's Military Prepares for War with Taiwan* (National Defense University Press, 2022).
13. According to Taiwan's statistics, cross-strait trade hit an all-time record high in 2021, exceeding US$200 billion. See *Liang'an Jingji Tongji Yuebao* [Cross-Strait Economic Statistics Monthly], no. 348, available at https://ws.mac.gov.tw/Download.ashx?u=LzAwMS9VcGxvYWQvMjk1L2NrZmlsZS8xYTQyNzMyMyYi1jNmM3LTRjOWUtYmMyZi01YTllNDljM2Y2ZTYTYucGRm&n=MzQ45pyf5YWo5paHLnBkZg%3d%3d.
14. For a good discussion of the distinction between PRC coercive use of force versus an actual invasion of Taiwan, with implications for US involvement, see Owen R. Cote Jr., "One If by Invasion, Two If by Coercion: US Military Capacity to Protect Taiwan from China," *Bulletin of the Atomic Scientists* 78, no. 2 (2022): 65–72.
15. See, for example, Jon Stokes, "Why a Chinese Invasion of Taiwan Would Be a Catastrophe for China and the World," *Doxa*, April 13, 2021, https://doxa.substack.com/p/why-a-chinese-invasion-of-taiwan.
16. On China's growing economic challenges, see Daniel H. Rosen, "The Age of Slow Growth in China," *Foreign Affairs*, April 15, 2022, https://www.foreignaffairs.com/articles/china/2022-04-15/age-slow-growth-china.
17. On signs of strengthening US-Taiwan security relations, see Scott L. Kastner, "Stronger than Ever? US-Taiwan Relations during the First Tsai Administration," in *Taiwan during the First Administration of Tsai Ing-wen: Navigating in Stormy Waters*, ed. Gunter Schubert and Chun-yi Lee (Routledge, 2021), 303–27.
18. See data posted on the National Chengchi University Election Study Center webpage. On conditional preferences on independence, see the 2020 National Security Survey, conducted by the Election Study Center of the National Chengchi University, Taipei, Taiwan, under the auspices of the Program in Asian Security Studies at Duke University: http://sites.duke.edu/pass/.
19. James D. Fearon, "Rationalist Explanations for War," *International Organization* 49, no. 3 (1995): 379.

20. Key works in the rationalist study of war literature include Fearon, "Rationalist Explanations"; Robert Powell, "War as a Commitment Problem," *International Organization* 60, no. 1 (2006): 169–203; Erik Gartzke, "War Is in the Error Term," *International Organization* 53, no. 3 (1999): 567–87; Alex Weisiger, *Logics of War: Explanations for Limited and Unlimited Conflicts* (Cornell University Press, 2013); among others.

21. On Ukraine's war costs, see "What Has Two Years of War Cost Ukraine and Russia?," *Christian Science Monitor*, February 23, 2024, https://www.csmonitor.com/World/Europe/2024/0223/What-has-two-years-of-war-cost-Ukraine-and-Russia; and "Even as the War Persists, Ukraine Is Rebuilding—Here's How," *World Economic Forum*, February 6, 2024, https://www.weforum.org/agenda/2024/02/even-as-the-war-persists-ukraine-is-rebuilding-heres-how/.

22. "Russia Operations in Ukraine Have Probably Cost Up to $211 Billion—US Official," Reuters, February 16, 2024, https://www.reuters.com/world/europe/russia-operations-ukraine-have-probably-cost-up-211-billion-us-official-2024-02-16/.

23. For a discussion of Russian miscalculations, see "As Russia Stalls in Ukraine, Dissent Brews over Putin's Leadership," *New York Times*, March 22, 2022, https://www.nytimes.com/2022/03/22/world/europe/putin-russia-military-planning.html.

24. For instance, both parties have advocated for participation in international organizations such as the World Health Organization.

25. For a more detailed consideration of the microfoundations of possible conflict scenarios in the Taiwan Strait, see Scott L. Kastner, *War and Peace in the Taiwan Strait* (Columbia University Press, 2022).

26. The full text of the law is available from the PRC's mission to the EU at http://eu.china-mission.gov.cn/eng/more/gs/200503/t20050314_8303591.htm

27. See, for example, Mastro, "Taiwan Temptation."

28. "China's New Demands 'Unfounded,'" *Taipei Times*, September 10, 1999, https://www.taipeitimes.com/News/front/archives/1999/09/10/0000001547.

29. See Xin, "Having Much in Common."

30. See, for example, Thomas J. Christensen, "Beijing's Views of Taiwan and the United States in Early 2002: The Renaissance of Pessimism," *China Leadership Monitor* 3 (2002), https://www.hoover.org/sites/default/files/uploads/documents/clm3_TC.pdf; and Thomas J. Christensen, "Windows and War: Trend Analysis and Beijing's Use of Force," in *New Directions in the Study of China's Foreign Policy*, ed. Alastair Iain Johnston and Robert S. Ross (Stanford University Press, 2006), 50–85.

31. See the roundtable "Strait of Emergency: Debating Beijing's Threat to Taiwan," in the September/October 2021 issue of *Foreign Affairs*. See also Wuthnow et al., eds., *Crossing the Strait*.

32. This line of argument is further developed in Scott L. Kastner and Chad Rector, "National Unification and Mistrust: Bargaining Power and the Prospects for a PRC/Taiwan Agreement," *Security Studies* 17, no. 1 (2008): 39–71. On commitment problems that can arise when bargaining over strategic goods, see Fearon, "Rationalist Explanations."

33. Consider, for instance, recent comments from China's ambassador to France, who has warned that Taiwan's people would need to be "re-educated" after unification with the PRC. See "Chinese Envoy to France Lu Shaye Doubles Down on Taiwan 'Re-Education' Aims," *South China Morning Post*, August 8, 2022, https://www.scmp.com/news/china/diplomacy/article/3188192/chinese-envoy-france-lu-shaye-doubles-down-taiwan-re-education.

34. On the importance of combining credible threats and assurances in the crafting of US Taiwan policy, see Christensen, "Contemporary Security Dilemma."

35. "China Rebukes U.S. for Changing Taiwan Wording on State Department Website," Reuters, May 10, 2022, https://www.reuters.com/world/china-slams-us-changing-taiwan-wording-state-department-website-2022-05-10/.

36. For an elaboration of this point, see Thomas J. Christensen, "Mutually Assured Disruption: Globalization, Security, and the Dangers of Decoupling," *World Politics* 75, no. 5 (2023): 1–18.

37. For a thorough recent statement on the importance of balancing threats and assurances in US policy toward the Taiwan Strait, along with policy recommendations, see Bonnie S. Glaser et al., "Taiwan and the True Source of Deterrence: Why American Must Reassure, Not Just Threaten, China," *Foreign Affairs* 103, no. 1 (2024): 88–100.

16

What a Conflict over Taiwan Would Look Like

Bruno Tertrais

This chapter will detail the possible unfolding of a conflict over Taiwan, focusing on the canonical scenario of a Chinese invasion of the island. It will emphasize the uncertainties over the outcome of such a war, as well as the real possibilities of escalation to the nuclear level. After outlining the context (correlation of forces, timeframe, and probability) of the conflict, it will assess its probability and describe the variables that would come into play. It will then describe the military scenario itself as well as the possible US reactions. It will finally emphasize the high risk of escalation to the extremes (the use of nuclear weapons by one party or another).

It is difficult to predict the shape, scope, and magnitude of a US-China conflict over Taiwan. The range of scenarios goes from a US abstention to fight Beijing to a nuclear worldwide war. It would all depend, of course, on the circumstances. First, the political circumstances: Would Taiwan have declared its independence? In such a case, Washington, especially under a neo-isolationist president, might very well decline to engage US armed forces. Second, the temporal circumstances: Does the conflict happen in the early 2020s or in the late 2040s? It is reasonable to assume that the more time passes, the more difficult it would be for the United States to defeat a China fighting for a vital interest in its own neighborhood. And does the scenario assume that China and the United States have already fought one another, for instance, in the South China Sea, or that they have never done so? Third, the strategic circumstances: Would a Chinese offensive happen against the background of a relatively calm period in international relations? Or would it happen while Washington is already busy fighting a major conventional war elsewhere, in Europe or in the Middle East? Even though the United States is aware of the risk of strategic opportunism by Beijing, it is hard to

Bruno Tertrais, *What a Conflict over Taiwan Would Look Like*. In: *Not Just Another Cold War*. Edited by: Bård Nikolas Vik Steen, Oxford University Press. © Oxford University Press (2025). DOI: 10.1093/9780197799932.003.0017 imagine that this would not have any consequences on the US willingness and ability to fight.

Then there are the many ways in which Beijing could decide to break the stalemate and embark on the reunification of the motherland. The ideal scenario for the People's Republic of China (PRC) would be to subjugate the island without any use of kinetic force. Two scenarios would be likely to trigger a US-China war. The first relies on patient salami tactics. Beijing could gradually encroach on Taipei's de facto sovereignty on distant islands, before attacking the main island. The second scenario is a tactical surprise: not a completely out-of-the-blue surprise attack, which would be difficult to organize, but a cold-start decision to invade without any triggering decision. The political and economic repercussions of any US-China open military engagement could be immense. A key question is how various friends and allies of both parties would react—by siding with or opposing one side, of course, but also perhaps by seizing a perceived opportunity to advance their own agendas.

Whatever the outcome, it would be likely to determine the future of the PRC and the future of the US alliances—and perhaps much, much more given that the risk of nuclear escalation once war had begun would be significant.

Context

A possible inspiration for how a US-China war would unfold is the number of "techno-thrillers" that narrate such a conflict. Three recent best-sellers are among those.[1] None of them directly relate to Taiwan, though. In addition, techno-thrillers have historically proven pretty poor guides to strategic forecasting.[2] Even though the scenario of a US-China war over Taiwan is a decades-old one, planning for it is constantly changing according to political, strategic, military, and technological circumstances.

The consequences of the Ukraine war are the latest example. Both sides are watching carefully the events in Europe and will adjust their planning accordingly.[3] China may have been surprised at the breadth of Western sanctions and the speed with which they were decided. Surely it was disappointed and perhaps shocked by the scope of Russian losses, despite massive firepower, in the first weeks of the offensive. But it may also have concluded that the United States would hesitate before getting directly involved on the battlefield to protect a friendly but not formally allied country. Taiwan, for its part, watched with interest but also concern the ability of the Ukrainian population to resist, aware of its shortcomings regarding civil defense and air defense.[4]

Correlation of Forces

At this time, the balance of military forces is clearly in favor of China. To be sure, both Beijing and Taipei have common strengths (a conflict would be existential for both of them) and weaknesses (neither of the two countries has any experience of large-scale combat).

But the PRC has the advantage of both mass and technology. It has made extraordinary progress in recent decades, especially since the advent to power of Xi Jinping in 2012, who has presided over "the most ambitious restructuring of the People's Liberation Army (PLA) since its founding."[5] In a decade, the Chinese budget grew by 76%, reaching $252 billion in 2020 according to the Stockholm International Peace Research Institute (SIPRI).[6] A comparison using purchasing power parity reveals that the Chinese defense budget is now more than 50% of the US one and may be on a path to parity.[7]

China's Eastern Theater Command includes three group armies, a naval fleet, two marine brigades, two air force bases, and one missile base. Chinese anti-access/area denial encompasses the first island chain "from Hokkaido to Borneo" (the Kuril Islands, the Japan mainland, the Ryukyu Islands, Taiwan, the Philippines), and its reach might include the second island chain. The second island chain is generally understood as comprising the Japanese Bonin and Iwo Islands (Volcano Islands), the Marianas Islands (including Guam), the Western Caroline Islands (Yap, Palau), and Western New Guinea. China may dominate the battlespace as early as 2025.[8] By that time, the PLA Navy (PLAN) is expected to have four hundred battleships. Today, the PLA Rocket Force's (PLARF) conventional ballistic and cruise missiles positioned against Taiwan alone number around a thousand. Beijing has developed the ability to conduct "integrated joint operations." Most importantly, Xi Jinping has recognized that technology alone cannot solve the PLA's deficiencies and focused reforms on organizational and personnel issues (for instance, recruiting more noncommissioned officers to be less reliant on conscripts and officers). Joint large-scale exercises are increasingly impressive.[9] A new "Joint Integrated Operations" doctrine was published in 2020. And against the United States, China would be "playing home" at less than 130 kilometers (the narrowest coast-to-coast distance) from its main target.

China does have weaknesses, though. First, while the motivation of troops called upon to participate in the republic's most important mission since its inception cannot be questioned, nationalistic fever can turn into hubris and nondemocratic armed forces are historically not well placed and trained to adapt and adjust quickly to unforeseen military developments. Second, China cannot afford to destroy Taiwan: it would seek to subjugate an entity governed by "separatists" and the narrative of reunification would hardly fit with a complete destruction of the island's infrastructure and its people (not to mention its economy).

The Republic of China (ROC) is not without strengths. It has been preparing itself for decades for the possibility of having to defend the island against the PRC. The mountainous terrain with only a dozen landing sites is honeycombed with tunnels. Taipei has had decades to ensure the physical and electronic resilience of the state and its infrastructures and to prepare for guerilla warfare and defensive capabilities to inflict what it hopes to be "unacceptable consequences" to Beijing.[10] With some 330 combat aircraft and 30 major combat ships, it is not a minor military power.

But there is only so much that a small island populated with nearly twenty-four million inhabitants and 215,000 soldiers with no strategic depth (although the country numbers nearly a hundred islands and islets) can do against a military giant that spends twenty-five times what it does on defense. Moreover, its defense manpower has degraded along with the gradual shortening of conscription in the 2000s, which now is reduced to four months.[11] The country has struggled to assemble a volunteer force (only some four-fifths of professional soldier billets are filled). Reserve forces are badly trained and separated from the rest of the military (as "reserve battalions") even though they could augment the country's potential to five hundred thousand soldiers. Taipei now envisions reversing the gradual reduction of military service and the creation of a defense mobilization agency.

Probability

The likelihood of a deliberate decision by Beijing to engage in a decisive operation against Taipei in the coming years is clearly growing, for several reasons. First—not, it should be noted, unlike Ukraine as seen from Russia—culturally and politically speaking, Taiwan is increasingly moving away from the motherland and toward the liberal West. Conversely, support for unification is dwindling, a trend accelerated by the fate of Hong Kong. Second, a deliberate operation to militarily subjugate the island is increasingly reportedly considered feasible by the Chinese leadership.[12] Third, China probably interpreted Western attitudes vis-à-vis Hong Kong, as well as the withdrawal from Kabul (and perhaps the unwillingness to fight for Kyiv), as weaknesses. A prolonged instability in Eastern Europe and/or the election of a neo-isolationist US president in November 2024 would also be incentives for Beijing to go forward. Fourth, Beijing may think we could not bear the cost of sanctions and countersanctions that would result from an attack on Taiwan. (Recall that China is winning the diplomatic battle and that Taipei was recognized by only fourteen countries in 2022.) Last but not least, many analysts now believe that "Xi wants unification with Taiwan to be part of his personal legacy."[13]

Hence the prognosis of some observers that Xi may believe he can regain control of Taiwan without jeopardizing his "Chinese dream" and that it could happen, depending on estimates, between 2025 and 2035.[14] The Taiwanese defense minister said that China would be able to launch a full-scale attack on the island with minimal losses by 2025.[15] Xi's target date for the completion of the Chinese dream is now widely considered to have been moved forward to 2035.

Variables

For the sake of the scenario, let us suppose the attack on Taiwan is a deliberate decision even though a US-China war could also happen as a result of escalation after an incident—either in the vicinity (say, for instance, if a Chinese plane was downed by the Taiwanese air force after having penetrated its airspace) or in the East China Sea (at the occasion of a conflict over the disputed Senkaku/Diaoyu Islands) or the South China Sea given the close interconnection of the three theaters.

Analysts believe that it would still be very risky for China to embark on such a venture in the current decade. The PLA still needs to refine its ability to conduct massive and rapid joint operations (including its command and control abilities). By the 2030s, China would be better prepared in every way, including because the decoupling of its economy with the West and its insulation to sanctions would have been at least partially achieved (as opposed to the period from 1995 to 2020, during which it seems to have acted as a brake against bilateral military disputes).[16]

For the sake of argument—including because a realistic forecasting of what the military balance would look like in 2035 is difficult—let us pretend that it happens around 2025.

Scenario

Certainly Beijing would not benefit from the effect of strategic surprise. But could it get away with tactical surprise? One possible scenario would have the PLA transitioning from a large-scale exercise to an actual invasion. Given the increasing number of exercises specifically designed to prepare Chinese armed forces for an actual attack on Taiwan, outside observers might not be able to say in advance that this could be "the real thing."

Another scenario would forego any element of surprise and see Beijing gradually encroach on Taipei's de facto sovereignty on distant islands: Taiping (Itu Aba) in the Spratleys, then the Dongshas (Pratas), then Kinmen (Quemoy), and finally the Penghu (Pescadores), close to the main island. This would be a risky scenario given that all these territories are Taiwanese military strongholds.

The nominal PLA scenario for a Chinese contingency reportedly involves four distinct campaigns.[17]

The first three campaigns are designed to coerce—and possibly to make a full-scale invasion unneeded. A massive kinetic and nonkinetic campaign (with cyber and electromagnetic assets) would aim at disarming Taiwan and crippling its infrastructures. A barrage of several hundreds of ballistic and cruise missiles would seek to saturate the island's defense bubble and render most Taiwanese ports, air bases, and unprotected communication centers unusable. Underwater cables would be cut. This phase might include cyber and space attacks against the United States to prevent immediate assistance (early warning in particular). A blockade—or at the very least a harassment of Taiwanese ships—would ensue. Separately, the PLA envisions preventive (or preemptive) strikes against US bases in the region.

The fourth campaign would be the occupation. To secure beachheads on the flat west coast and landing sides, a first echelon of forces would involve thousands of paratroopers and airborne troops. A series of numerous landings would ensue, with the goal of bringing ultimately at least five hundred thousand, perhaps up to two million (including police and militia), men to the island. Given that the PLAN would probably not have—recall that the year is 2025—enough of its modern Type 071 and Type 075 amphibious assault ships operational at that time for a massive and sudden landing, it is likely that all available maritime assets, including civilian ships, would be mobilized.

A key early goal of the operation would be decapitation. It is unlikely that Beijing would want to flatten Taipei (including because the National Palace Museum, which hosted the most precious artifacts of China and had been transferred hastily to the island in 1949, is located in its immediate vicinity). The full-scale replica of the Presidential Palace built in Outer Mongolia suggests that it could attempt to capture it with land forces—even though it is likely that at the first warning of a PRC attack the Taiwanese government would have taken refuge in one of the many subterranean bunkers that exist in the rocky and mountainous island.

The operation would present Beijing with three dilemmas. First, should it favor a slow-motion, "salami tactics–like" strategy of gradual encroachment (see above) or a "shock and awe" operation? The former would test Taiwan's defenses and give a chance to an ROC surrendering, and would perhaps be less likely to trigger immediate and massive international sanctions, but it would also give time to Taipei—including to mobilize and to train its reserve force—and to the United States. Second, should it strike US forces based in Japan and Guam from the onset to maximize its chances of early success, at the risk of immediately dragging Washington (and Tokyo) into the conflict? Third, should it make a massive use of kinetic force against Taiwanese cities at the risk of losing political legitimacy in the eyes of the non-Western or nonaligned world?

US Involvement

A key variable would of course be the nature and scope of US military involvement. It is important to bear in mind that this involvement would not be a given—not only because there is no US treaty–based defense commitment toward Taiwan, but also because nobody knows what the domestic political situation will be in the United States at the time of the invasion. What if, for instance, the United States was just fighting a conflict in Europe or the Middle East at the same time? Or if, as suggested above, a neo-isolationist president had been elected in November 2024?

It would be very difficult, however, for the United States to refrain from any military involvement in the conflict.

The main stake for Washington would be no less than its ability and reputation for defending an Asian ally—and perhaps its global reputation as a security guarantor. US deterrence would have failed: it would have to restore it. The fall of Taiwan would make the defense of Japan and the second island chain almost impossible. Japan's offshore Shakishima Islands (which are part of the Ryukyu archipelago) connect the mainland with Taiwan and would be highly vulnerable: Yonaguni Island, which is part of the Shakishima, is closer to Taiwan (about 100 kilometers) than Taiwan to China. Taiwan-controlled Pengiayu Island is less than 150 kilometers from the disputed Senkaku Islands. The capture of Taiwan would also give Beijing an additional foothold in the South China Sea given that the ROC controls Taiping (Itu Aba), the biggest natural island of the Spratly archipelago.

The increasingly mature character of Taiwanese democracy has made it easier for Washington to marshal domestic support for its defense of Taipei. Simply put, it shows that a "democratic China" is not a contradiction in terms. This may have contributed to the growing US public opinion support for the defense of the ROC, which is now at an all-time high: a majority of Americans (52%) now support using US troops if China were to invade Taiwan.[18] Finally—and irrespective of the economic consequences of any US-China war—Taipei has gained a new economic importance given its leadership role in chip making, not only as a US provider but also as a global good. Taiwan Semiconductor Manufacturing Company (TSMC) currently holds more than 50% of the global market share of semiconductor fabrication and has a near-monopoly on chips less than 10 nanometers. Taiwan holds an even more important place in semiconductor assembly, notably through its Advanced Semiconductor Engineering (ASE) Group. It will have lost some of its dominance by 2025 but will remain a key player in this strategic industry. All things equal, this dimension of a Taiwan contingency could be compared to that of 1991, when the US involvement in the Iraq War was partly justified by the need to avoid rupturing the oil market.

The Biden administration has clearly confirmed that it would defend Taiwan against Beijing, rhetorically putting the island on a par with countries protected by treaty-based obligations.[19] The timing of active US involvement, however, is difficult to predict—not only in the "salami tactics" scenario but also in the "shock and awe" contingency. Of course, any preventive PLA strike on US bases in Asia and the Pacific—notably the US strongholds of Okinawa (where most of the III Marine Expeditionary Force is still based) and Guam—or other actions such as massive cyber-attacks or actions against US satellites, for instance, would force Washington to react. But what if Beijing initially and deliberately refrained from overtly provocative actions? The United States would then have the choice of being actively involved either to break a blockade of Taiwan or, if it came to that, in the final and most important phase of the operation, to prevent the full-scale invasion of the island.

Whatever the US decision, the direct and indirect economic and financial consequences of the war would already be enormous. The Chinese financial market would almost certainly be closed at the onset of the operation, Asian markets would almost certainly tumble, and European markets would take a significant dip.

What about other US allies? Beyond geography (see above), any US involvement would mean a de facto Japanese involvement from the onset because of the importance of US bases on the archipelago (whether they are struck or merely used). Japanese officials made it clearer that their countries would support the United States in a conflict over Taiwan.[20] Australia has stated that it would support the United States in a conflict over Taiwan.[21] South Korea is a different matter; while recent statements indicate that it tilts toward the United States, it is unlikely that it would get involved.[22] As per European countries, they would be unlikely to get involved save for assisting in maintaining freedom of navigation in the Southeast Asian straits.

Phase One: War Begins

What happens then is almost anybody's guess. Over the past twenty years—and as forecasted by many experts—the US perspective on the outcome of a US-China war has become much more pessimistic than was the case before. Wargames conducted by the RAND Corporation indicate a high probability of a US defeat and a successful invasion in a matter of days and weeks.

In the 2010s, those conducted by the US Department of Defense reportedly showed a US defeat in eighteen out of eighteen such exercises.[23]

But while Ukraine is not a template for Taiwan, the surprise most observers experienced at the poor performance of Russian armed forces in 2022 should give pause to any firm judgment about the possible unfolding of a US-China war over Taiwan. Wasn't Russia "playing home" as much as Beijing would? In fact, "China's untested military could be a force—or a flop."[24] Many operational uncertainties remain regarding the actual capabilities of PLA systems in war. These include the ability of Chinese land-based missiles such as the DF-21D and DF-26 (and perhaps the DF-17 with a hypersonic glide vehicle) to effectively sink US carriers, or of the (not yet deployed) Russia-made S-400 air defense systems to shoot down F-22 or F-35 fighter aircraft. Some of the best experts believe that the PLA "cannot safeguard a properly sized, seaborne invasion force and the follow-on shipping necessary to support it during multiple transits across the 100-plus mile-wide Taiwan Straits."[25] It does not have the command of the air or the sea, and would certainly be vulnerable to US attack submarines and bombers operating from the first island chain, at least as long as they operate "as a team." Furthermore, some US analysts are convinced that "Chinese submarines will not play a major role in preventing American submarines from operating against Chinese invasion shipping."[26] The new US air-launched long-range anti-ship missile could be a key instrument in implementing the "strategy of denial" promoted inter alia by prominent Republican experts.[27]

Then again, would the United States be able to "sink 300 Chinese ships in about 48 hours"?[28] According to some calculations, it may need some twenty to twenty-five attack submarines (thus nearly half of the current US fleet) on site to do so.[29] Simply put, we do not know what a full-scale invasion of Taiwan would result in, because "nothing even remotely similar has occurred in history." Comparisons with D-Day landings in Normandy are inappropriate.[30] The PLA would have command neither of the air nor of the seas. The Taiwan Strait is known for treacherous seas and winds, limiting the safe timeframe for an invasion to the spring and summer. The western beaches' terrain would make landings difficult for environmental (mudflats, salt marshes) reasons, forcing the PLAN to use hydrofoils, to say nothing of large-scale mining.

Would it be a splendid little war or "limited war," as optimistic experts believe it would be? Perhaps, but it would be unwise to bank on it. It might very well become a true "hegemonic war"—and these tend to last long. It is quite possible that both China and the United States end up mobilizing for the prospect of total war.[31]

Phase Two: Escalation

To be sure, there would be brakes on escalation, starting of course with economic and financial interdependence. By 2025, the West will probably still be dependent on China for critical imports such as health and pharmaceutical products, processed rare earths, and so forth. Likewise, the stock of US (and Japanese) government bonds held by the PRC, as well as Western investments in China, would still bind the two economies in ways that did not exist during hegemonic wars of the past. Also recall that there are several hundreds of thousands of foreigners living in Taiwan. (They numbered 765,000 in September 2021.[32])

But the stakes at play would also be a powerful engine for climbing up the escalation ladder. For the PRC, it would be more than a hegemonic war: it would be an existential one in the political sense of the term. Adding fuel to the fire would be Beijing's intense paranoia vis-à-vis US designs: recall that in October 2019, it believed that Washington was ready to attack the country.[33] On the US side, how would the public react if a *Nimitz*-class aircraft carrier, with some five thousand on board, was sunk by the PLAN? Pressure for operations on the Chinese mainland would certainly be strong. But if the United States were to cross that threshold, it would certainly want to have decisive results. To give a sense of the scale of such operations, it has been estimated that an offensive counterair campaign against land-based Chinese air forces with an ability to reach Taiwan unrefueled would need to target nearly a thousand aim points.[34] As per destroying Chinese conventional (regional) missile launchers on the mainland: this would require control of the airspace over significant areas of the mainland, or—at least until hundreds of land attack missiles would be available on the theater— "to accept sortie attrition rates not seen since the Christmas bombings in Vietnam or even the battles over Europe to defeat the German night fighter force in 1944."[35]

In addition, war in the cyber and outer spaces would be an inevitable dimension of any US-China conflict. Actions in such spaces would have a high probability to affect the normal functioning of domestic institutions and infrastructures, as well as the daily lives of ordinary citizens.

Phase Three: Going Nuclear

Any US-China war would have a nuclear dimension from the onset. Recall that China's nuclear deterrence force was primarily designed to avoid Beijing being subjected to what it calls "US nuclear blackmail," or simply to neutralize the US nuclear deterrent. At a very early stage of the conflict, the PRC would almost certainly issue thinly veiled warnings to that effect. One remembers that in March 1996, a senior Chinese military official told a US ambassador: "In the 1950s, you three times threatened nuclear strikes on China, and you could do that because we couldn't hit back. Now we can. So you are not going to threaten us again because, in the end, you care a lot more about Los Angeles than Taipei."[36] A perceived hardening of the US stance in the late 2010s reportedly led to a shift in Chinese nuclear policy. Beijing leaders saw the US administration increasingly interested in "regime change" in the PRC.[37] More than ever, "Chinese leaders see a stronger nuclear arsenal as a way to deter the US from getting directly involved in a potential conflict over Taiwan."[38]

China could also undertake an indirect nuclear threat. It could warn North Atlantic Treaty Organization (NATO) allies to "stay out" by reminding them of their vulnerability to missile strikes, which in turn would force Paris or London—which both have sea-based ballistic missiles that can reach East Asia—to counter Chinese threats through nuclear deterrence. Absent a strong European reaction, Beijing could decide that threatening US allies as the "soft underbelly" of the West is a good way to threaten Washington. Additionally, a missile threat against the continental United States could compel NATO allies to express their solidarity with Washington (only the continental United States is included in the NATO Treaty area) and get involved.

Some US analysts are tempted to set aside nuclear use scenarios when discussing the possibility of a US-China war, arguing that "mutual deterrence prevails in the Sino-US strategic-nuclear relationship."[39] This is also, surprisingly, the case for well-informed experts such as former Pacific Command (PACOM, since then morphed into Indo-Pacific Command, INDOPACOM) commander Admiral Dennis Blair, who judges the possibility of US-China nuclear escalation to be "somewhere between zero and nil," as well as for a number of Chinese experts.[40]

This reflects a degree of confidence that is unwise. There are two main possible pathways to Chinese nuclear use during a US-China conflict over Taiwan.

The first pathway would be a misreading of US intentions. This could happen if Washington engaged in conventional strikes on the Chinese mainland (to degrade PLA forces or its command and control structure) or—in a less probable hypothesis—if, say, it accidentally sunk a Chinese ballistic missile submarine (SSBN) while hunting for PLAN ships. Beijing could see it as the beginning of a "disarming" strike.[41] A decision to then cross the nuclear threshold would not be inconsistent with a loose interpretation of Beijing's stated "no first use" doctrine.[42] A recent wargame has shown that both sides would come close to the nuclear threshold, and maybe cross it, if China engaged in massive conventional strikes against US territories (Guam) or the United States struck Chinese coastal installations.

The second pathway would be a deliberate decision to coerce the United States through nuclear escalation in case the Taiwan campaign did not go as well as Beijing expected. This would run contrary to Beijing's stated nuclear doctrine, but basic doctrinal principles can easily be jettisoned in wartime provided that the force posture is agile enough. China's likely options would range from a simple signal (a demonstration shot at sea in the Pacific Ocean) to the use of medium-range nuclear-armed missiles against a carrier naval group or task force (the PLARF is not reported to have theater nuclear weapons designed to use at sea against naval targets) to a series of strikes on US bases in Asia and the Pacific, from Okinawa to Guam to Hawaii.[43]

Even though, contrary to China, it does not have a no-first-use doctrine, the United States would be less likely to use nuclear weapons even in the face of severe military difficulties. As stated above, although extremely important for Washington, the stakes would not be "existential" as they would be for the PRC. In addition to its well-entrenched tradition of nonuse, Washington would pause before being once again the country using nuclear weapons against an Asian adversary (to say nothing, in some circumstances, of possible fallout over allied territory), especially if it was to be "first" in the war. And while the dual capability of Chinese missiles may be grounds for suggesting that inadvertent escalation could also happen on the US side, it is very hard to imagine that Washington would resort to nuclear arms without the certainty that a nuclear strike is on the way. A Chinese nuclear strike against a US territory (Guam) or, especially, a US state (Hawaii) would, however, alter the picture. In the first case, a possible US nuclear retaliation might be limited to Chinese island bases (including the submarine stronghold of Hainan, near the mainland). The second hypothesis—a nuclear Pearl Harbor in the real sense of the term—would generate immense pressure on a US president to retaliate with nuclear weapons on the Chinese mainland.

As is often said in the US think-tank community, "nobody knows how a China-US war would end." Once bilateral conflict would have begun in earnest, however, it is hard to imagine the circumstances under which the Chinese Communist Party would accept defeat or even an unfavorable compromise.

Conclusion

The Taiwan Strait may be the most dangerous place in the world and become the crucible of international security for the twenty-first century whatever its outcome of a Chinese invasion. A US abstention would affect the reputation of Washington to the point that it could be a death blow for the credibility of American security commitments and defense guarantees around the world. A Chinese victory would have equally dire consequences, given that it would psychologically and geographically consolidate Chinese power in the region to the point that the United States would have to completely revamp its defense of Asia—or, alternatively, accept Beijing's primacy in the region. Conversely, a US victory would put a halt to Chinese expansionism and perhaps endanger the very legitimacy of the Communist regime. Finally, the crossing of the nuclear threshold would in itself be an event of momentous proportions whatever the outcome.

According to most experts, the probability of a deliberate, massive Chinese attack on Taiwan remains, at this point, relatively low for the coming years, though growing through the decade. Nevertheless, given that this scenario would have massive repercussions and extraordinary consequences for the global balance of power—even more than the Ukraine war—it is critical to think through its possible unfolding, and to do so with an open mind.

Notes

1. Recent best-sellers narrating a US-China war include P. W. Singer and August Cole, *Ghost Fleet: A Novel of the Next World War* (Houghton Mifflin Harcourt, 2015); Elliot Ackerman and Admiral James Stavridis, *2034: A Novel of the Next World War* (Penguin Press, 2021); and Ken Follett, *Never* (Penguin Press, 2022).
2. "Technothrillers that seem prophetic on publication often don't age well. World War III never broke out in Europe as the Soviet Union disintegrated, as British general John Hackett's 1978 novel *The Third World War* posits. Nor, for that matter, did an energy crisis spark the same kind of conflict, as occurs in Tom Clancy's *Red Storm Rising* from 1986. The late Clancy, arguably

the modern master of the military technothriller, rarely had any success in predicting real-world conflicts. One of the most important events in his series of novels about spy Jack Ryan is a 9/11-style terror attack on the United States that's inspired by . . . ultra-nationalist Japanese industrialists." David Axe, "Don't Let 'War with China' Thrillers Scare You," *National Interest*, December 11, 2018.

3. See, for instance, Jeffrey W. Hornung, "Ukraine's Lessons for Taiwan," *War on the Rocks*, March 17, 2022.
4. Harry Halem and Eyck Freymann, "Ukraine Shows Why Taiwan Needs More Air Defense," *War on the Rocks*, April 7, 2022.
5. Oriana Skylar Mastro, "The Taiwan Temptation: Why Beijing Might Resort to Force," *Foreign Affairs*, July–August 2021, 58–67.
6. Chris Buckley and Steven Lee Myers, "'Starting a Fire': US and China Enter Dangerous Territory over Taiwan," *New York Times*, October 9, 2021.
7. Graham Allison and Jonah Glick-Unterman, *The Great Military Rivalry: China vs. the US* (Belfer Center for Science and International Affairs, Harvard Kennedy School, December 2021), 5.
8. Demetri Sevastopulo, "Admiral Warns US Military Losing Its Edge in Indo-Pacific," *Financial Times*, March 9, 2021.
9. Orlana Skylar Mastro and Derek Scissors, "Beijing Is Used to Learning from Russian Failures," *Foreign Policy*, April 18, 2022.
10. Quoted in Sheryn Lee, "Towards Instability: The Shifting Nuclear-Conventional Dynamics in the Taiwan Strait," *Journal for Peace and Nuclear Disarmament* 5, March 31, 2022, 8.
11. Paul Huang, "Taiwan's Army Is a Hollow Shell," *Foreign Policy*, February 15, 2020.
12. Mastro, "The Taiwan Temptation."
13. Ibid.
14. Ibid.; Allison and Glick-Unterman, *The Great Military Rivalry*, 4.
15. Gordon Lubold, "US Troops Have Been Deployed in Taiwan for at Least a Year," *Wall Street Journal*, October 7, 2021.
16. Mina E. Tanious, "The Impact of Economic Interdependence on the Probability of Conflict between States: The Case of American–Chinese Relationship on Taiwan since 1995," *Review of Economics and Political Science* 4, no. 1 (2019): 38–53.
17. Mastro, "The Taiwan Temptation."
18. Dina Smeltz et al., *A Foreign Policy for the Middle Class—What Americans Think, Results of the 2020 Council Survey of American Public Opinion and US Foreign Policy* (Chicago Council on Foreign Relations, 2021).
19. David Brunnstrom, "US Position on Taiwan Unchanged despite Biden Comment—Official," *Reuters*, August 20, 2021.
20. "Japan Deputy PM Comment on Defending Taiwan If Invaded Angers China," *Reuters*, July 6, 2021; Jeffrey W. Hornung, "Taiwan and Six Potential New Year's Resolutions for the US-Japanese Alliance," *War on the Rocks*, January 5, 2022.
21. "'Inconceivable' Australia Would Not Join US to Defend Taiwan—Australian Defence Minister," *Reuters*, November 13, 2021.
22. Seong-Hyon Lee, *South Korea Angle on the Taiwan Strait: Familiar Issue, Unfamiliar Option* (Henry L. Stimson Center, February 23, 2022).
23. Allison and Glick-Unterman, *The Great Military Rivalry*, 4.
24. Timothy R. Heath, "China's Untested Military Could Be a Force—or a Flop," *Foreign Policy*, November 27, 2018.
25. Owen R. Cote Jr., "One If by Invasion, Two If by Coercion: US Military Capacity to Protect Taiwan from China," *Bulletin of the Atomic Scientists* 78, no. 2, March 2022: 65.
26. Ibid., 67.
27. Elbridge A. Colby, *The Strategy of Denial: American Defense in an Age of Great Power Conflict* (Yale University Press, 2021).
28. Richard Bernstein, "The Scary War Game over Taiwan That the US Loses Again and Again," Real Clear Investigations, August 17, 2020.
29. Ibid.
30. Ian Easton, "Why a Taiwan Invasion Would Look Nothing Like D-Day," *The Diplomat*, May 26, 2021.

31. Hal Brands and Michael Beckley, "Washington Is Preparing for the Wrong War with China. A Conflict Would be Long and Messy," *Foreign Affairs*, December 16, 2021.
32. Ministry of the Interior, National Immigration Agency, Republic of China (Taiwan), October 25, 2021, accessed April 25, 2022.
33. Bob Woodward and Robert Costa, *Peril* (Simon and Schuster, 2021), 128–29.
34. Cote, "One If by Invasion, Two If by Coercion," 70.
35. Caitlin Talmadge, "Would China Go Nuclear? Assessing the Risk of Chinese Nuclear Escalation in a Conventional War with the United States," *International Security* 41, no. 4 Spring 2017: 72.
36. Quoted in Barton Gellman, "US and China Nearly Came to Blows in '96," *Washington Post*, June 21, 1998.
37. Alaister Gale, "China Is Accelerating Its Nuclear Buildup over Rising Fears of US Conflict," *Wall Street Journal*, April 9, 2022.
38. Ibid.
39. David C. Gompert et al., *War with China: Thinking through the Unthinkable* (RAND Corporation, 2016), 29.
40. Quoted in Talmadge, "Would China Go Nuclear?," 56.
41. Ibid.
42. "Wartime perceptual dynamics are likely to exacerbate fearful Chinese assessments of the security of their nuclear arsenal under these circumstances as well. It is one thing to be confident about the deterrence provided by even small numbers of nuclear weapons in a world where conventional deterrence is also holding steady and the prospect of an adversary attempt at damage limitation is remote. It is more difficult to be confident in a world where those nuclear weapons already have failed to deter the onset and escalation of a massive conventional war on one's home territory, and many of the state's nuclear weapons have been disabled or destroyed." Ibid., 70.
43. Stacie L. Pettyjohn and Becca Wasser, "A Fight over Taiwan Could Go Nuclear," *Foreign Affairs*, May 20, 2022.

Index

For the benefit of digital users, indexed terms that span two pages (e.g., 52–53) may, on occasion, appear on only one of those pages.

Tables and figures are indicated by an italic *t* and *f* following the paragraph number.